The English Novel

By the same author

Sweet Violence: The Idea of the Tragic

The Idea of Culture

Scholars and Rebels: In Nineteenth-Century Ireland

The Illusions of Postmodernism

Literary Theory: An Introduction
Second edition

Marxist Literary Theory: A Reader
Co-edited with Drew Milne

The Ideology of the Aesthetic

William Shakespeare

The English Novel
An Introduction

Terry Eagleton

Blackwell
Publishing

BLACKWELL PUBLISHING
350 Main Street, Malden, MA 02148-5020, USA
9600 Garsington Road, Oxford OX4 2DQ,UK
550 Swanston Street, Carlton, Victoria 3053, Australia

First published 2005 by Blackwell Publishing Ltd

11   2013

Library of Congress Cataloging-in-Publication Data

Eagleton, Terry, 1943–
   The English novel : an introduction / Terry Eagleton.
      p. cm.
   Includes bibliographical references and index.
   ISBN 978-1-4051-1706-0 (alk. paper) – ISBN 978-1-4051-1707-4 (pbk. : alk. paper)
   1. English fiction–History and criticism.   I. Title.
   PR821.E15 2005
   823.009–dc22

                                                        2003026893

A catalogue record for this title is available from the British Library.

Set in 10.5 / 13pt Dante
by Graphicraft Limited, Hong Kong

The publisher's policy is to use permanent paper from mills that operate a sustainable
forestry policy, and which has been manufactured from pulp processed using acid-free
and elementary chlorine-free practices. Furthermore, the publisher ensures that the
text paper and cover board used have met acceptable environmental accreditation
standards.

For further information on
Blackwell Publishing, visit our website:
www.blackwellpublishing.com

For
Franco Moretti

CONTENTS

PREFACE

This book is intended as an introduction to the English novel for students, but also for any general readers who might find the subject interesting. Though it occasionally considers particular novels in some detail, it is designed largely to offer ideas about a writer's work as a whole, which a reader may then bring to bear on individual texts. I have tried to tread a precarious line between bamboozling readers and talking down to them; and though some parts of it may be more intelligible to a beginner than others, I hope that what difficulties there may be belong, so to speak, to the subject matter rather than to the presentation.

I must apologize for confining myself so high-mindedly to the literary canon, but this was determined by the need to discuss authors whom students are at present most likely to encounter in their work. It should not, needless to say, be taken to imply that only those English novelists presented between these covers are worth reading.

T.E.

WHAT IS A NOVEL?

A novel is a piece of prose fiction of a reasonable length. Even a definition as toothless as this, however, is still too restricted. Not all novels are writtten in prose. There are novels in verse, like Pushkin's *Eugene Onegin* or Vikram Seth's *The Golden Gate*. As for fiction, the distinction between fiction and fact is not always clear. And what counts as a reasonable length? At what point does a novella or long short story become a novel? André Gide's *The Immoralist* is usually described as a novel, and Anton Chekhov's 'The Duel' as a short story, but they are both about the same length.

The truth is that the novel is a genre which resists exact definition. This in itself is not particularly striking, since many things – 'game', for example, or 'hairy' – resist exact definition. It is hard to say how ape-like you have to be in order to qualify as hairy. The point about the novel, however, is not just that it eludes definitions, but that it actively undermines them. It is less a genre than an anti-genre. It cannibalizes other literary modes and mixes the bits and pieces promiscuously together. You can find poetry and dramatic dialogue in the novel, along with epic, pastoral, satire, history, elegy, tragedy and any number of other literary modes. Virginia Woolf described it as 'this most pliable of all forms'. The novel quotes, parodies and transforms other genres, converting its literary ancestors into mere components of itself in a kind of Oedipal vengeance on them. It is the queen of literary genres in a rather less elevated sense of the word than one might hear around Buckingham Palace.

The novel is a mighty melting pot, a mongrel among literary thoroughbreds. There seems to be nothing it cannot do. It can investigate a single human consciousness for eight hundred pages. Or it can recount the

1

adventures of an onion, chart the history of a family over six generations, or recreate the Napoleonic wars. If it is a form particularly associated with the middle class, it is partly because the ideology of that class centres on a dream of total freedom from restraint. In a world in which God is dead, everything, so Dostoevsky remarked, is permitted; and the same goes for a world in which the old autocratic order is dead and the middle class reigns triumphant. The novel is an anarchic genre, since its rule is not to have rules. An anarchist is not just someone who breaks rules, but someone who breaks rules as a rule, and this is what the novel does too. Myths are cyclical and repetitive, while the novel appears excitingly unpredictable. In fact, the novel has a finite repertoire of forms and motifs. But it is an extraordinarily capacious one even so.

Because it is hard to say what a novel is, it is hard to say when the form first arose. Several authors have been proposed as plausible candidates for the first novelist, among them Miguel de Cervantes and Daniel Defoe; but the game of identifying origins is always a dangerous one. If a lecturer proclaims that the paper-clip was invented in 1905, someone at the back of the hall will always rise to announce that one has just been unearthed from an ancient Etruscan burial site. The Russian cultural theorist Mikhail Bakhtin traces the novel back to imperial Rome and ancient Hellenistic romance, while Margaret Anne Doody in *The True Story of the Novel* likewise locates its birthplace in the cultures of the ancient Mediterranean.[1] It is true that if your definition of an automobile is fuzzy enough, it is not hard to trace the BMW back to the ancient Roman chariot. (This may also help to explain why so many premature obituary notices of the novel have been issued. What they usually indicate is that one *kind* of novel has died, while another has come into existence.) Even so, something like the novel can indeed be found in ancient times. In the modern era, as we have seen, it has been linked with the emergence of the middle class, but when exactly was that? Some historians would locate it as early as the twelfth or thirteenth centuries.

Most commentators agree that the novel has its roots in the literary form we know as romance. Indeed, these are roots that it has never entirely cut. Novels are romances – but romances which have to negotiate the prosaic world of modern civilization. They retain their romantic heroes and villains, wish-fulfilments and fairy-tale endings, but now these things have to be worked out in terms of sex and property, money and marriage, social mobility and the nuclear family. Sex and property, one might claim, are the themes of the modern novel from start to finish. So the English novel from Defoe to Woolf is still a kind of romance. In fact, nothing less than the magical

devices of romance will do if, like the Victorian novelist, you are going to conjure a happy ending from the refractory problems of the modern world. In the Brontës, George Eliot, Hardy and Henry James, you can find vestiges of 'premodern' forms such as myth, fable, folk-tale and romance, mixed in with 'modern' ones like realism, reportage, psychological investigation and the like. If the novel is a romance, however, it is a disenchanted one, which has nothing to learn about baffled desires and recalcitrant realities.

Romance is full of marvels, whereas the modern novel is nothing if not mundane. It portrays a secular, empirical world rather than a mythical or metaphysical one. Its focus is on culture, not Nature or the supernatural. It is wary of the abstract and eternal, and believes in what it can touch, taste and handle. It may still retain some religious beliefs, but it is as nervous of religious debate as a pub landlord. The novel presents us with a changing, concrete, open-ended history rather than a closed symbolic universe. Time and narrative are of its essence. In the modern era, fewer and fewer things are immutable, and every phenomenon, including the self, seems historical to its roots. The novel is the form in which history goes all the way down.

All this is very different from romance, as Cervantes' *Don Quixote* makes clear. *Don Quixote*, sometimes mistakenly called the first novel, is in fact less the origin of the genre than a novel *about* the origin of the novel. It is thus a peculiarly narcissistic piece of writing, a fact which becomes comically obvious when Quixote and Sancho Panza run across characters who have actually read about them. Cervantes' great work shows us how the novel comes about when romantic idealism, here in the form of Quixote's chivalric fantasies, collides with the real world. Cervantes was not the first author to challenge romance in this way: the picaresque novel, with its downbeat, streetwise anti-heroism, had done that, at least implicitly, before he came to write. But *Don Quixote* is a work which actually takes this clash between romance and realism as its subject-matter, thus turning a formal issue into a thematic one.

If there is one place where romantic idealism and disenchanted realism meet, it is war. Few phenomena have provoked so much high-flown rhetoric along with so much bitter disgust. But Cervantes' novel runs war a close second. Quixote, who has been driven insane by reading too many romances, models his life on books, whereas realism models books on life. He lives, as they say, in a book, and talks like one too; but since he *is* a character in a book, this fantasy is also reality. The novel, then, starts life as among other things a satire of romance, and thus as a kind of anti-literature. It sends up rhetoric and fantasy from a hard-headed realist standpoint. But since a novel *is* rhetoric and fantasy, this is comically self-contradictory. Cervantes backs the world against the book, but he does so in a book. For a novelist to mock the language of literature is a classic case of the pot calling the kettle black. The kind of novel which speaks up for 'life' against 'literature' has all the bad faith of a count who speaks with a Cockney accent.

Cervantes assures us that he will give us this history 'neat and naked', without the usual paraphernalia of literature. But a naked and neat style is just as much a *style* as any other. It is a mistake to think that some kinds of language are literally closer to the real world than others. 'Nutter' is no closer to the real world than 'neophyte'. It might be closer to common speech, but that is different. The relationship between language and reality is not a spatial one. It is not that some words are free-floating, whereas others are jammed tight against material objects. Anyway, one writer's neat and naked may be another's ornamental. In a similar way, some realist fiction seems to believe that, say, hair-dryers are more real than hermeneutical phenomenology. They may be more useful, but the difference between them is not one of degrees of reality.

One of the first great novels, then, warns us off novels. Reading fiction can drive you mad. In fact, it is not fiction which leads to madness, but forgetting the fictionality of fiction. The problem arises from confusing it with reality, as Quixote does. A fiction which knows itself to be fiction is perfectly sane. In that sense, irony is what saves us. Cervantes, unlike Quixote, does not expect his inventions to be taken literally, not least the invention known as Don Quixote. He is not trying to fool us. Novelists do not lie, because they do not imagine that we take them to be telling the truth. They do not lie in the same sense that the advertising slogan 'Refreshes the parts that other beers can't reach' is not a lie, even though it is not true either.

The innkeeper in part 1 of *Don Quixote* remarks that it is fine for romances to be printed, since nobody could be ignorant enough to take them for true histories. Indeed, there is plenty of romance in *Don Quixote* itself. Yet romance is not as innocuous as the innkeeper suggests. It is really a kind of dangerous narcissism, in which (as Quixote comments at one point) you can believe that a woman is chaste and beautiful just because you want to. It does not need to take account of the way things are. Romantic idealism sounds edifying enough, but it is really a form of egoism in which the world becomes clay in your hands for you to mould as you wish. Fantasy, which sounds alluring enough, is at root a wayward individualism which insists on carving up the world as it pleases. It refuses to acknowledge what realism insists upon most: the recalcitrance of reality to our desires, the sheer stubborn

inertia with which it baffles our designs upon it. Anti-realists are those who cannot get outside their own heads. It is a sort of moral astigmatism. It is just that Quixote's own errant individualism, ironically enough, takes the form of a devotion to the collective rituals and loyalties of the feudal order.

There is something admirable about idealism – Quixote's own ideals include protecting the poor and dispossessed – but also something absurd. So it is not just a matter of being a cynic rather than an idealist, but of upholding and deflating ideals in the same breath. Those who cannot see the world aright are likely to wreak grotesque damage upon it. Literary, moral and epistemological realism are all subtly interlinked. In Quixote's case, fantasy is very definitely connected to social privilege. A man who can mistake an ordinary woman for a high-born maiden is also someone who assumes that the world owes him a living. Power is fantastic to the core. But fantasy is also commercial to the core – a 'saleable commodity', as the priest observes to the canon in part 1 of the novel. Marvels and the market are no stranger to each other. Fantasy manipulates reality for its own self-serving ends, and reality, in the shape of commercial publishing, manipulates fantasy for its own self-interest.

Realism, it would appear, is out of favour because the ordinary reader delights in the exotic and extravagant. The irony is that the novel as a form is wedded to the common life, whereas the common people themselves prefer the monstrous and miraculous. Quixote's chivalric illusions are a kind of upper-class version of popular superstition. The common people do not wish to see their own faces in the mirror of art. They have quite enough ordinary life in their working hours without wanting to contemplate it in their leisure time as well. Labourers are more likely to resort to fantasy than lawyers. Cervantes' priest recognizes that the labouring masses need circuses as well as bread, entertainment as much as work: they need to see plays, he believes, but the plays should be censored to strip them of their worst extravagances. It is really only the cultivated elite who prefer their art to be plausible and true to Nature. Cervantes thus wins himself serious literary status by insisting on the verisimilitude of his writing – on 'probability and imitation', as the canon puts it – while at the same time craftily serving up crowd-pulling fantasies by creating a hero who acts them out.

If the novel is the genre which affirms the common life, it is also the form in which values are at their most diverse and conflicting. The novel from Defoe to Woolf is a product of modernity, and modernity is the period in which we cannot agree even on fundamentals. Our values and beliefs are fragmented and discordant, and the novel reflects this condition. It is the most hybrid of literary forms, a space in which different voices, idioms and belief-systems continually collide. Because of this, no one of them can predominate without a struggle. The realist novel quite often throws its weight behind a particular way of seeing the world, but it is 'relativizing' in its very form. It shifts from one perspective to another, hands the narrative to various characters in turn, and wins our sympathy for cases and characters we find discomforting by bringing them so vividly alive. In fact, this is one reason why the form was originally greeted with such suspicion. Imaginative realism can make a convivial comrade of the devil himself.

For Mikhail Bakhtin, the novel tends to emerge and disappear again, like a river threading its way through a limestone landscape. You find it, he thinks, when a centralized literary, linguistic and political authority is beginning to crumble.[2] It is when the verbal and ideological centre can no longer hold, as in Hellenistic Greece, imperial Rome or the waning of the medieval Church, that Bakhtin finds the novel emerging. Monolithic political, linguistic and cultural forms are giving way to what Bakhtin calls 'heteroglossia' or linguistic diversity, and this is represented above all by the novel. In his view, then, the novel is inherently anti-normative. It is a maverick form, sceptical of all authoritarian claims to truth. No doubt this makes it sound too inherently subversive. There is not much of the maverick about *Mansfield Park*, or much linguistic diversity in *The Waves*. In any case, not all diversity is radical, or all authority oppressive. Yet Bakhtin is surely right to see the novel as emerging from the stream of culture dripping with the shards and fragments of other forms. It is parasitic on the scraps and leavings of 'higher' cultural life-forms; and this means that it has only a negative identity. In its mixing of languages and forms of life, it is a model of modern society, not simply a reflection on it.

Hegel saw the novel as the epic of a prosaic modern world. It has all the range and populousness of the epic, without, for the most part, its supernatural dimension. The novel resembles the classical epic in its consuming interest in narrative, dramatic action and the material world. It differs from it, however, in being a discourse of the present rather than of the past. For the novel is above all a *contemporary* form, as its very name suggests. To this extent, it has more in common with *The Times* than with Homer. When it turns to the past, it is often to treat it as the prehistory of the present. Even the historical novel is generally a coded reflection on the present. The novel is the mythology of a civilization fascinated by its own everyday existence. It is neither behind or ahead of its times, but abreast of them. It reflects them without morbid nostalgia or delusory hope. In this sense, literary realism is

also moral realism. This refusal of both nostalgia and utopia means that the realist novel, politically speaking, is for the most part neither reactionary nor revolutionary. Instead, it is typically reformist in spirit. It is committed to the present, but to a present which is always in the process of change. It is a this-worldly rather than an other-worldly phenomenon; but since change is part of this-worldliness, it is not a backward-looking one either.

If the novel is a distinctively modern form, whatever its ancient pedigree, it is partly because it refuses to be bound by the past. To be 'modern' means to relegate to the past everything that happened up to 10 minutes ago. Modernity is the only epoch which actually defines itself, vacuously enough, by its up-to-dateness. Like a rebellious adolescent, the modern is defined by a definitive rupture with its parentage. If this is a liberating experience, it can also be a traumatic one. It is the form which breaks with traditional models. It can no longer rely on the paradigms offered by custom, mythology, Nature, antiquity, religion or community. And this is closely related to the rise of a new kind of individualism, which finds all such collective paradigms too constricting. Whereas the epic bears the signature of no one author, the novel bears the fingerprints of an individual writer, known as style. Its impatience with traditional models is also related to the rise of pluralism, as values become too diverse to be unified. The more values there are, the more of a problem value itself becomes.

The novel was born at the same time as modern science, and shares its sober, secular, hard-headed, investigative spirit, along with its suspicion of classical authority. But this means that, lacking authority outside itself, it must find it in itself. Having shed all traditional sources of authority, it must become self-authorizing. Authority now means not conforming yourself to an origin, but becoming the origin yourself.

This has the glamour of originality, as the word 'novel' would suggest. But it also means that the novel's authority is ungrounded in anything outside itself, which is what renders it precarious. In this sense, the novel is a sign of the modern human subject. It, too, is 'original', in the sense that modern men and women are supposed to be the authors of their own existence. Who you are is no longer determined by kinship, tradition or social status; instead, it is something you determine for yourself. Modern subjects, like the heroes of modern novels, make themselves up as they go along. They are self-grounding and self-determining, and in this lies the meaning of their freedom. It is, however, a fragile, negative kind of freedom, which lacks any warranty beyond itself. There is nothing in the actual world to back it up. Absolute value has evaporated from the world in the modern age, which is what makes for unlimited freedom. But it is also what renders that freedom so empty. If everything is permitted, it is only because nothing is intrinsically more valuable than anything else.

We have seen that the novel and the epic differ in their attitudes to the past. But there is another key distinction between them. The epic deals with a world of nobles and military heroes, whereas the novel deals with the common life. It is the great *popular* genre, the one mainstream literary mode which speaks the language of the people. The novel is the great vernacular literary art, which draws upon the resources of ordinary speech rather than some specialized literary language. It is not the first literary form in which the common people stage an appearance. But is the first to treat them with unwavering seriousness. Our contemporary version of this is no doubt the soap opera, which we enjoy not so much for the occasional dramatic turn of plot but because we find the familiar and everyday a strange source of fascination in itself. The modern equivalent of *Moll Flanders* is *EastEnders*. The staggering popularity of Reality TV programmes which consist simply in someone pottering mindlessly around his kitchen for hours on end suggests one interesting truth: that many of us find the pleasures of the routine and repetitive even more seductive than we do the stimulus of adventure.

The value of everyday life is the theme of one of the greatest works of literary scholarship ever published, Eric Auerbach's *Mimesis*.[3] For Auerbach, realism is the literary form which finds the workaday life of men and women supremely valuable in itself. One of the earliest examples of this in English writing can be found in Wordsworth and Coleridge's *Lyrical Ballads*, which, in however idealizing a form, speaks up for the common life as a source of creativity. The novel for Auerbach is an incipiently democratic kind of art, hostile to what he sees as the static, hierarchical, dehistoricized, socially exclusive art of classical antiquity. To adopt Walter Benjamin's terms, it is an art form which destroys the 'aura' of distance and majesty which clings to such classical artefacts, bringing life closer to us rather than raising it beyond our reach. Authors in *Mimesis* score high marks for being vulgar, vigorous, earthy, dynamic, demotic, grotesque and historically minded, and are rapped smartly over the knuckles for being stylized, elitist, idealized, stereotyped and non-developmental.

There is, so Auerbach argues, no serious treatment of the common people in the culture of classical antiquity. Contrast this with a text like the New Testament, which grants a humble fisherman like Peter potentially tragic status. According to the philosopher Charles Taylor, it was Christianity which first introduced the revolutionary notion that everyday life could

be precious in itself.[4] As Auerbach argues, it is the Christian gospel, with its image of God as incarnate in the poor and destitute, its carnivalesque reversals of high and low, which provides the source of realism's elevation of the commonplace. For Christianity, salvation is a humdrum matter of whether you feed the hungry and visit the sick, not of some esoteric cult. Jesus is a kind of sick joke of a Messiah, a parody of regal pomp as he rides a donkey towards his squalid death as a political criminal.

With the advent of realism, then, the common people make their collective entry into the literary arena, long before they make an appearance on the political stage. It is one of the momentous events of human history, which we now take casually for granted. It is hard for us to think ourselves back into a culture for which, say, relations between parents and children, or everyday economic life, was of little artistic merit. Auerbach, a Jewish refugee from Hitler, was writing about the novel while in exile in Istanbul at the same time as Bakhtin was writing about it as a dissident in Stalinist Russia; and both men saw in it a populist strike against autocratic power. In Bakhtin's view, plebeian culture nourishes forms of realism in the classical, medieval and modern epochs; and these finally burst through into the mainstream of 'high' literature in the shape of the novel.

There are problems with these claims. For one thing, realism and the novel are not the same thing. Not all realism is novelistic, as Auerbach is aware, and not all novels are realist. Nor do all novels smack of a plebeian vigour. There is not much earth beneath the fingernails of Mr Knightley or Mrs Dalloway. In any case, earthiness is by no means always subversive. A work of art is not radical simply because it portrays the experience of ordinary people. It is sometimes felt that the kind of realism which takes the lid off poverty and squalor, revealing the horrors of the social underworld to a sheltered middle class, is necessarily disruptive. But this assumes that people are insensitive to social deprivation only because they are unaware of it, which is far too charitable a view of them. Realism in the sense of verisimilitude – truth to life – is not necessarily revolutionary. As Bertolt Brecht remarked, putting a factory on stage will tell you nothing about capitalism.

If realism means showing the world as it really is, rather than how some ancient Egyptian priest or medieval knight conceived of it, then we are instantly in trouble, since how the world is is a subject of fierce contention. Suppose some future civilization were to discover a copy of Samuel Beckett's play *Endgame*, in which two elderly characters spend their time sitting in dustbins. They would not be able to tell whether the play was realist or

non-realist simply by looking at it. They would need to know, for example, whether stashing old people away in dustbins was standard geriatric practice in mid-twentieth-century Europe.

To call something 'realist' is to confess that it is not the real thing. False teeth can be realistic, but not the Foreign Office. Postmodern culture could be said to be realistic, in the sense of being faithful to a surreal world of surfaces, schizoid subjects and random sensations. Realist art is as much an artifice as any other kind of art. A writer who wants to sound realist might include phrases such as 'A florid-faced cyclist laboured unsteadily past them', when she could just as easily have written 'A carrot-haired boy crawled from under the garden fence, whistling tunelessly'. Such details can be perfectly gratuitous from the viewpoint of plot: they are there simply to signal 'This is realism'. They have, as Henry James remarked, the 'air of reality'. In this sense, realism is calculated contingency. It is the form which seeks to merge itself so thoroughly with the world that its status as art is suppressed. It is as though its representations have become so transparent that we stare straight through them to reality itself. The ultimate representation, so it seems, would be one which was identical with what it represented. But then, ironically, it would no longer be a representation at all. A poet whose words somehow 'become' apples and plums would not be a poet but a greengrocer.

For some commentators, realism in art is actually more realistic than reality itself, because it can show how the world typically is, shorn of its blunders and contingencies. Reality, being a messy, imperfect affair, quite often fails to live up to our expectations of it, as when it allowed Robert Maxwell to sink into the ocean rather than stand in the dock. Jane Austen or Charles Dickens would never have tolerated such a botched conclusion. In an unaccountable bit of bungling, history allowed Henry Kissinger to be awarded the Nobel Peace Prize, an event so outrageously surreal that no self-respecting realist novelist would have thought it up, other perhaps than as a piece of black humour.

It is dangerous, then, to talk about realism as representing 'life as it really is', or 'the experience of the common people'. Both notions are too controversial to be used so lightly. Realism is a matter of representation; and you cannot compare representations with 'reality' to check how realistic they are, since what we mean by 'reality' itself involves questions of representation. Anyway, what is so impressive about 'realist' representations? Why are we so struck by an image of a pork chop that looks exactly like a pork chop? Partly, no doubt, because we admire the skill which goes into forging the

resemblance. But perhaps also because of a fascination with mirroring and doubling which lurks deep in the human psyche, and which lies at the roots of magic. In that sense, realism, which Auerbach sees as the most mature of forms, may also be the most regressive. What was intended as an alternative to magic and mystery may itself be a prime example of them.

Not all novels are realist, but realism is the dominant style of the modern English novel. It is also the yardstick of so many critical judgements. Literary characters who are not 'realistic', in the sense of being credible, animated, well-rounded and psychologically complex, are generally awarded low marks by the critical establishment. It is not clear where this leaves Sophocles's Teiresias, the *Macbeth* witches, Milton's God, Swift's Gulliver, Dickens's Fagin or Beckett's Pozzo. Realism is a kind of art congenial to an ascendant middle class, with its relish for the material world; its impatience with the formal, ceremonial and metaphysical; its insatiable curiosity about the individual self; its robust faith in historical progress. In his classic study *The Rise of the Novel*,[5] Ian Watt regards all of these as reasons why the modern English novel emerged in the eighteenth century. He also adduces the middle-class interest in individual psychology, its secular and empiricist view of the world, and its devotion to the concrete and specific. As far as the ceremonial is concerned, it is also worth noting that the novel is not an 'occasional' form, like those masques, odes or elegies written – perhaps for an aristocratic patron – for special occasions. This, too, is a mark of its routine rather than patrician status.

For many eighteenth-century commentators, the answer to the question 'What is a novel?' would be: 'A trashy piece of fiction fit only for servants and females'. On this definition, Jackie Collins writes novels but William Golding does not. For these early observers, the novel was less like the *The Times* than the *News of the World*. It was also like a newspaper because it was a commodity you usually bought and read only once, as opposed to the more traditional practice of possessing a small clutch of edifying works which you perused over and over again. The novel belonged to a new world of speed, ephemerality and disposability, playing something like the role of e-mail to handwritten correspondence. 'Novel' meant sensationalist fantasy, which is one reason why writers like Henry Fielding and Samuel Richardson called their works 'histories' instead.

Eighteenth-century gentlemen did not by and large rate novelty very highly, believing as they did that the few truths necessary to a well-ordered human life had long since been apparent. The new was thus bound to be either bogus or trivial. Whatever was valid was also venerable. The novel

was not 'literature', and certainly not 'art'. To pretend that your narrative was a real-life one – that you had stumbled across it in a pile of mouldy letters or manuscripts – was a way of indicating that it was not romantic garbage. Even if your claim was not taken seriously, simply making it was a way of being taken seriously.

In the end, the English novel would wreak its vengeance on those who dismissed it as fit only for females by producing some magnificent portrayals of women, from Clarissa Harlowe and Emma Woodhouse to Molly Bloom and Mrs Ramsay. It also produced some distinguished female exponents of the craft. As a form, it would grow in importance as poetry became increasingly privatized. As poetry gradually ceases to be a public genre somewhere between Shelley and Swinburne, its moral and social functions pass to the novel, in a new division of literary labour. By the mid-nineteenth century, the word 'poetry' has become more or less synonymous with the interior, the personal, the spiritual or psychological, in ways which would no doubt have come as a mighty surprise to Dante, Milton and Pope. The poetic has now been redefined as the opposite of the social, discursive, doctrinal and conceptual, all of which has been relegated to prose fiction. The novel takes care of the outer world, while poetry copes with the inner one. It is not a distinction which Henry Fielding, let alone Ben Jonson, would have found all that intelligible. The very distance between the two modes reflects a growing alienation between the public and the private.

The problem for poetry is that it seems increasingly remote from 'life' as an industrial capitalist society is coming to define it. There is no obvious place for the lyric in a world of insurance companies and mass-produced meat pies. The phrase 'poetic justice' really means the kind of justice we would not expect to see done in real life. There is, however, an equal problem with the novel's very closeness to social existence. If the novel is a 'slice of life', how can it teach us more general truths? This is a particular problem for devoutly Protestant eighteenth-century authors like Samuel Richardson, for whom the artifice of fiction is only really justified if it conveys a moral truth. Otherwise it is idle, even sinful, fantasy.

The dilemma is that the more graphic you make your realism, the more this drives the moral truth home; but the more it simultaneously undermines it, since the reader becomes more attentive to the realist detail than to the universal truth it is meant to exemplify. There is a related problem here. You cannot, as a novelist, argue that the world should be changed in certain respects unless you dramatize what is wrong with it as compellingly as possible. But the more effectively you do this, the less changeable

the world may come to seem. Dickens's later novels portray a society so false, warped and stiflingly oppressive that it is hard to see how it could be repaired.

Richardson knew that in reading the realist novel, we believed and disbelieved in its discourse at one and the same time. We surrender ourselves imaginatively to the narrative, at the same time as another part of our minds appreciates that this is simply make-believe. Richardson speaks in his private correspondence of 'that kind of historical faith, which fiction itself is generally read (with), even tho' we know it to be fiction'. It is as though the part of our mind that is not taken in by the story is free to reflect on it and draw a moral lesson from it. In this way, realism can be preserved, but it can also serve a broader, deeper function. Writing of his novel *Clarissa*, Richardson comments that he wants nothing in its Preface which would *prove* that the work was fiction, but that he does not want it to be *thought* genuine either. This captures the realist quandary exactly. The reader must not be told that the book is fiction, since this might undermine its power. But if readers genuinely take it to be real, this in turn might diminish its exemplary force. *Clarissa* then becomes like a newspaper report of an actual rape, rather than a reflection on virtue, vice and sexual power in general.

It is not just moralistically minded authors like Richardson who confront this dilemma. Part of what we mean by a work of fiction is one which invites the reader to draw some general reflections from its story. This is why the sign 'No Exit' is not a work of fiction, though you could turn it into one easily enough by reading it, say, as a comment on the solitary confinement of the self. As far as drawing general implications goes, a real-life story will do perfectly well. So 'fiction' does not exactly mean 'not true'. It means something like 'a story (either true or false) treated in such a way as to make it clear that it has a significance beyond itself'. This may not be the snappiest of definitions, but it makes an important point all the same. This may help to explain why fiction often (though by no means always) uses language which calls attention to its own 'literary' status. It is as though such language is signalling by its very self-consciousness: 'Don't take this literally'. To say that outright, however, would be to risk blunting the impact of the story. It also helps to explain how fiction may be a potent source of ideology, since one function of ideology is to present a specific situation as though it were a universal truth. If a particular bunch of schoolboys collapse into internecine warfare when washed up without prefects and cricket bats on a desert island, this goes to demonstrate that all human beings are savages beneath the skin.

Realism and the exemplary would thus seem hard to reconcile. If Oliver Twist is just Oliver Twist, we feel the full force of his character. Yet this character does not seem to have any deeper symbolic dimension. We know him in the same way we know the serial killer next door – a man who like all serial killers looks utterly normal and nondescript, keeps himself to himself, but always has a polite word for you when you meet. Yet if Oliver is a signifier of heartlessness and oppression, then this deepens his significance only at the risk of thinning out his particularity. Pressed to an extreme, it would turn him into a mere allegory. Exemplariness without realism is empty, whereas realism without exemplariness is blind.

What we call fiction is the place where the two are supposed to converge. If you set out to paint a portrait of, say, the workings of the legal system, then fiction is probably the most effective way of doing so, since it allows you to edit, select, transpose and rearrange, in a way which most fully highlights the typical features of the institution. Real-life accounts of trials, juries and the like would probably contain too much that was trivial, irrelevant, repetitive or incidental to your purpose. It is in this sense that fiction is sometimes claimed to be more real than reality. If you are to outline the chief aspects of an event or individual in as cogent and economical way as possible, you may well find yourself veering spontaneously into fiction. You may find yourself inventing situations in which those aspects are most illuminated.

In his classic study of the novel *The Great Tradition*,[6] the critic F. R. Leavis defines a truly great novel in two chief ways: it must display what he calls 'a reverent openness before life', and it must reveal an organic form. The trouble is that these two requirements are not easily compatible with each other. Or rather, they would only be truly compatible if 'life' itself were to reveal an organic form. The novel could then be 'reverently open' to it without going baggy. It could be both representational and formally unified. The history of the novel, however, is bedevilled by the problem of being both at the same time. In the modern era in particular – the period of the novel's finest flourishing – human life seems less and less to have an inherent design to it; so how are the designs imposed upon it by novels not to be implausibly artificial? How are they not to falsify the novel's realist or representational functions? How is the very phenomenon of the novel not to be a monstrous self-contradiction? Novels present us with what look like objective images of the world, yet we know for a fact that these images are subjectively shaped. In this sense, the novel is an ironic, self-undoing genre. Its form seems at odds with its content. Its reflection of a contingent,

14

haphazard world continually threatens to undercut its coherence as a piece of fiction.

The English novel is to be found struggling with this difficulty as soon as it emerges. Authors like Defoe and Richardson tackle the problem by sacrificing form to representation. Defoe scarcely even tries to shape his fiction into a significant whole; instead, the formlessness of the narration reflects the dishevelledness of its subject-matter. The gap between form and content is closed by effectively ditching the former. Richardson takes a similar path in his celebrated 'writing to the moment', a technique which involves his characters recording their experiences as they happen. A Richardson character who was giving birth would most certainly have a pen and notebook in her hand. Here, once again, 'content' is what gives shape to 'form'. Richardson's novels are by no means as loose and baggy as Defoe's, but they must be scrupulous about not falsifying lived experience by foisting too obtrusive an artistic shape upon it. The pious puritan is naturally suspicious of all such artifices. He is also suspicious of any set of forms or conventions which might interpose themselves between him and his inner life. His inner life is where he finds signs of his salvation, and so must be accessible to him in all its raw immediacy.

Henry Fielding takes the opposite way out, cheerfully acknowledging the rhetorical artifice of his novels, and drawing ironic attention to the gap between form and content rather than seeking to conceal it. With commendable respect for his reader's gentlemanly good sense, Fielding does not allow us to forget that we are in a novel, or attempt to pull some cheap contrick on his customers. He is aware, for example, that while the requirements of formal design requires that his villains meet a sticky end and his heroes are granted happiness, this form is comically at odds with the actual state of the world. In an unjust society, you cannot represent things as they are and achieve a harmonious design at the same time. Human viciousness, in other words, is one reason why this gap between form and content cannot be resolved.

Or rather, you can resolve it, as Fielding and his successors often do; but you must make the reader aware that this reconciling of form and content can only come about because you are in a novel. It is not to be mistaken for everyday existence, which is why the novel is an ironic form. In reflecting everyday life, it also signals its essential distance from it. In the actual world, Fanny, Joseph and Parson Adams would probably have ended up in a ditch with their throats slit. All the same, the fact that we have a glimpse of such reconciliation, even if it is purely fictional, represents a kind of utopian hope.

The novel is a utopian image – not in what it represents, which can be gruesome enough, but in the very act of representation – an act which at its most effective shapes the world into meaning with no detriment to its reality. In this sense, to narrate is itself a moral act.[7]

Laurence Sterne spots the impossibility of reconciling form and realism, and plucks from the discrepancy one of the greatest anti-novels of all time, *Tristram Shandy*. Tristram, the narrator, cannot give a true account of his chaotic life-history and at the same time fashion a shapely narrative. His story thus falls apart at the seams, to make the point that realism is a self-deconstructing enterprise. As Roland Barthes comments:

> The real is not representable, and it is because men ceaselessly try to represent it by words that there is a history of literature . . . literature is categorically realist, in that it never has anything but the real as its object of desire; and I shall say now, without contradicting myself . . . that literature is quite as stubbornly unrealistic: it considers sane its desire for the impossible.[8]

If the novel is the modern epic, it is, in Georg Lukács's famous phrase, 'the epic of a world abandoned by God'.[9] It must strive for sense and unity in an age when things no longer seem to harbour any inherent meaning or value. Meaning is no longer written into empirical experience. 'Lucky the man who can say "when", "before" and "after"', Robert Musil observes in volume two of *The Man Without Qualities*. As soon as such a man is capable of recounting events in chronological order, Musil goes on, he feels content even if a moment ago he was writhing in agony. In their relationship to their own lives, Musil considers, most people behave like narrators: they like an orderly sequence of events because it has a look of necessity about it. The only problem is that the modern world 'has now become non-narrative'.

One way in which the novel seeks to overcome this difficulty is by the idea of character. 'Character' gathers into unity a varied range of events or experiences. What holds these diverse experiences together is the fact that they all happen to you. Another way is through the act of narrating itself, which involves pattern and continuity but also change and difference. Narrative implies a kind of necessity, as cause and effect, action and reaction, are linked logically to each other. Narrative orders the world into a shape which seems to emerge spontaneously from it.

Yet every narrative implies that one could always have told the story differently; so that despite its air of necessity, every narrative is contingent. Reality will accommodate a whole number of tales about itself, and will not

pipe up itself to sort the true from the false. There could never be just one story, rather as there could never be just one word or number. For many modern artists, there is no longer one big narrative embedded in the world itself, which we simply need the skill to decipher. And as this becomes clearer, plot becomes steadily less important to the novel. The fact that so many novels centre on a search, quest or voyage suggests that meaning is no longer given in advance. By the time of Leopold Bloom's pointless per-ambulations in *Ulysses*, there is no longer even a search for anything. Motion is now pretty much for its own sake. Narrative gathers fragments of the world together, as in biography, which is a way of shaping the individual life into a significant whole. History writing does the same at a more collective level. Yet history and biography also represent a constant struggle against time, which defers and disperses meaning. Time is history or narrative struck empty of significance, as one event follows on the heels of another with no real connection between them. Defoe's novels are a case in point.

The novel is a sign of our freedom. In the modern world, the only rules which are binding are those which we invent for ourselves. Politically speak-ing, this is known as democracy. We are set free from being mere functions of the grammar of God. It is we who give form and meaning to reality, and the novel is a model of this creative act. As the novelist conjures a new world into existence, in a profane parody of God's creation, so each indi-vidual shapes his or her inimitable life-history. For some commentators, in fact, this is where the novel is most truly realistic. What it reflects most importantly is not the world, but the way in which the world comes into being only by our bestowing form and value upon it. The novel on this view is most deeply realistic not because we can almost hear the sausages sizzling in Fagin's den, but because it reveals the truth that all objectivity is at root an interpretation.

This is not unqualified good news. If the only world we know is one which we have created ourselves, does not all knowledge become a point-less tautology? Aren't we simply knowing ourselves, rather than a reality independent of ourselves? Don't we only get back what we put in? Anyway, if form is what *we* impose, how can it have authority? The fact that I help to bring the world into existence makes it more precious; but it is also what threatens to undermine its objective value. We will see something of this irony at work in the fiction of Virginia Woolf.

If value and meaning reside deep inside individuals, then there is a sense in which these things are not really 'in' the world at all. This leaves value arbitrary and subjective. It also reduces reality to a realm of objects which

have been drained of meaning. But if the world is drained of meaning, then human beings have no place in which they can act purposefully, and so cannot realize their value in practice. And the less they can do this, the more they begin to disintegrate from the inside. As reality is bleached of value, so the human psyche begins to implode. What we are left with is a human being who is valuable but unreal, in a world which is solid but valueless. Meaning and value are driven from the public world, which is now just a soulless expanse of neutral facts, and thrust deep into the interior of the human subject, where they all but vanish. The world is thus divided down the middle between fact and value, public and private, object and meaning. This, for Georg Lukács in *Theory of the Novel*, is the alienated condition of the modern age, which the novel reflects in its inmost form.

How can you tell a story in such a situation? It seems less and less possible to pluck a narrative from a world of lifeless, disconnected objects. So the novelist can turn instead to the inner life. But this life has been driven in upon itself, beating a retreat from a soulless world; and it has become so subtle and densely textured in the process that it resists anything as straitjacketing and steamrollering as narrative. We shall see this in the sentences of the later Henry James, which try to say everything at once without simply logjamming. So the external world is becoming too poor for narrative, and the internal one too rich. Narratives of the inner world are a problem because the human psyche no longer seems a linear affair, as it did when what mattered was who your ancestors were and whether you would transmit their beliefs intact to your own children. Instead, it is a place where past, present and future interlock, with no clear frontiers between them. Nor will the inner life provide you with any sure way of distinguishing between what is significant and what is not, since what both have in common is that they happen to *you*. The interior monologues of Leopold and Molly Bloom in Joyce's *Ulysses* are a case in point. This deepens the general crisis of value, as all experiences seem to be mixed promiscuously together.

For Lukács, then, the novel is the product of an alienated world. Yet it is also a utopian response to it. Alienation is the condition in which men and women fail to recognize the objective world as their own subjective creation. Yet the very act of writing a novel offers an alternative to this condition, since a novel's 'objective' vision of the world is one rooted in the subjectivity of its author. The act of writing crosses the border between subjective and objective. The novel is one of the few objects in a reified society which manifests in its every objective detail the subjective freedom

in which it was born. In this sense, its very existence can be seen as an imaginary solution to the social problems which it poses.

The situation which Lukács depicts in *Theory of the Novel* is truer of the twentieth-century modernist novel than of the nineteenth-century realist one. The great works of nineteenth-century realism, from *Pride and Prejudice* to *Middlemarch*, are still able to relate fact and value, objective and subjective, inner and outer, individual and society, however much these relations may be under strain. As such, they spring from a buoyant, dynamic episode of middle-class history. It is this history which Lukács's later work on literary realism is concerned to investigate. It is only when middle-class civilization enters upon a major crisis, one which is at its height from the close of the nineteenth century to the end of the First World War, that literary modernism arises, and the novel shifts from being a primarily comic to a predominantly tragic form.

Then, indeed, the early Lukács's description of the novel form becomes more and more apt. It is an art which can no longer shape the contradictions which plague it into a coherent whole. Instead, as we shall see in the case of authors like Henry James and Joseph Conrad, those conflicts are now beginning to infiltrate the very form of the novel itself. They reflect themselves in the break-up of language, the collapse of narrative, the unreliability of reports, the clash of subjective standpoints, the fragility of value, the elusiveness of overall meaning. 'Organic form' is now so unattainable, or so flagrantly arbitrary, that it is either thrown to the winds or, as with a work like James Joyce's *Ulysses*, grotesquely parodied. The modern world is too fragmentary for the novel to mould it into a totality; but it is also because there is simply too much of it, too many specialist jargons and domains of knowledge, that this is no longer feasible. What the modernist novel tends to give us instead is a kind of empty signifier of a totality which is no longer possible: the silver of Conrad's *Nostromo*, Stevie's scribbled circles in *The Secret Agent*, E. M. Forster's Marabar caves, Virginia Woolf's lighthouse.

The realist novel represents one of the great revolutionary cultural forms of human history. In the domain of culture, it has something like the importance of steam-power or electricity in the material realm, or of democracy in the political sphere. For art to depict the world in its everyday, unregenerate state is now so familiar that it is impossible to recapture its shattering originality when it first emerged. In doing so, art finally returned the world to the common people who had created it through their labour, and who could now contemplate their own faces in it for the first time. A form of fiction had been born in which one could be proficient without specialist

erudition or an expensive classical education. As such, it was especially available to groups like women, who had been cheated of such an education and shut out from such expertise.

Women also bulked large among novel writers because the novel was supposed to be as realistic about the inner life as it was about the outer one. Women, stereotypically viewed as custodians of the feelings or technicians of the heart, were thus obvious candidates for producing it. This was not, however, simply a matter of stereotyping. Like all social groups under the unlovely sway of authority, women needed to be adept in finely detailed observation, vigilant in their reading of a potentially hostile world. They were spontaneous semioticians, who needed for their own sake to be skilled in deciphering signs of power, symptoms of dissent, and fruitful or dangerous areas of ambiguity. All this lent itself to the writing of fiction, even if the same set of talents lends itself to being a successful tyrant.

In this sense, the novel fostered a resistance to authority at the very time that it was becoming a resourceful medium of middle-class cultural power. If it served middle-class society so superbly, it was not in the first place because it championed the cause of mill-owners or fashioned demeaning stereotypes of striking workers. It was because it became the supreme arbitrator, in the sphere of cultural representations, of what was to count as real in the first place. And this version of reality involved an enormous amount of editing and exclusiveness. It also involved a certain organized violence wreaked on language. Part of the novel's appeal was that it seemed able to accommodate every jargon, argot and idiom, yet spoke no specialist language of its own. Instead, it conformed its discourse to what counted as the common language of its specific place and time. And this represented a genuine democratic advance. Rather than simply reflecting everyday speech, however, the novel also helped to draw up the rules for what was linguistically acceptable; and like all such rules, this involved a good deal of prejudice and coerciveness.

In some sectors of the novel, it also involved a certain hard-nosed, macho dismissal of 'literariness' – one still much in evidence in the kind of US creative writing courses which nurture sub-Hemingwayesque sentences like 'And he was still howling and blubbering and writhing on the slimy unforgiving wreck of the car hood and his teeth were all smeary with his own blood and I took a slug of the brandy and it felt like the sirocco blasting hot and dry and gritty right down into my heaving guts'. What is striking about this kind of language is its prissiness – its puritanical horror of the effete and extravagant, its suspicion that the 'literary' is somehow unmanly. Realism

20

has been responsible for a massive impoverishment of language as much as for an enrichment of it, as the average novel published nowadays in the USA or UK bears dismally uneloquent witness. The use of language as a pick and shovel is one of the least endearing aspects of contemporary realism.

The tradition recorded in this book is rather different. In some ways, the story of the English novel from the see-through style of Defoe to the lushly metaphorical Woolf is the story of a form of writing which becomes progressively more rich in texture. As reality grows more complex and fragmented, the means of representing it become more problematic as well; and this forces language and narrative into a more elaborate self-consciousness. There is an immense distance between the bluff assurance of Henry Fielding and the fastidious obliquity of Henry James. Even so, the finest English novels manage to combine a convincing representation of the world with a verbal virtuosity which is neither too sparse nor too self-regarding.

This is the outcome of a struggle which every novelist – indeed, every writer – knows, as he or she toils from sentence to sentence. How is this to be both accurate and artistically accomplished? How am I to avoid sacrificing truth to form, without for a moment forgetting that this is indeed a novel, and that everything that happens in a novel, however raw or pungent, harrowing or unspeakably pitiful, happens sheerly and exclusively in terms of language? We have seen that 'form' and 'content', design and representation, are hard to reconcile in narrative as a whole. But perhaps they may converge instead in what we know as style. And if this is so, then style provides a kind of compensation at the micro level for the larger problems which the novel finds itself confronting – problems which grow more severe the further we move into the modern era. Which is no doubt another reason why, as we pass from the Enlightenment clarity of an Austen to the modernist opacity of a Joyce, style becomes more and more eye-catching and important.

DANIEL DEFOE
AND
JONATHAN SWIFT

L ike the novelist and ex-convict Jeffrey Archer, Daniel Defoe's career spanned both debt and high politics, authorship and imprisonment. Chronologically speaking, art followed life in Defoe's career, since he began writing most of his works as an activist. In another sense, however, his life imitated his art, since it was a career quite sensationalist enough for one of his own novels. He was at various times a hosiery, wine and tobacco merchant, brick factory owner, political turncoat, underground political informant, secret government agent and spin doctor or state propagandist. He took part in an armed rebellion against James II, travelled extensively in Europe, and played a key role in the historic negotiations by which the kingdoms of England and Scotland were politically united.

Defoe was bankrupted more than once, imprisoned for debt, and sentenced to stand in the pillory on a charge of sedition for publishing a satirical pamphlet. He later wrote a 'Hymn to the Pillory', as well as publishing a 'Hymn to the Mob' in which, scandalously, he praised the mob for its soundness of judgement. It is hard to imagine any other major English author doing the same. He also produced *A Political History of the Devil*, a study of ghosts, an account of the Great Plague of London, and a work in fulsome praise of matrimony entitled *Conjugal Lewdness; or Matrimonial Whoredom. A Treatise Concerning the Use and Abuse of the Marriage Bed*. He was not a 'novelist' (that category, as a serious critical term, comes later), though he did attack 'Romances', meaning stories which entertained rather than informed. Works like *Moll Flanders* and *Robinson Crusoe* become 'novels' only in retrospect. Defoe simply wrote whatever he thought would sell, churning out works of all kinds for the rapidly growing mass market of his day. The printing press did not discriminate between different kinds of writing, and neither did Defoe.

Writing for Defoe, then, was a commodity, just as the world presented by his writings is commodified from top to bottom. He was not a 'literary' man: on the contrary, his writing is rushed, weightless and transparent, a 'degree zero' style of supposedly factual reportage which effaces its own status as writing. It is what he himself described as a 'mean style', one which seems to lack all consciousness of its own artifice. In Defoe's laconic, home-spun, rough-and-ready language we hear, almost for the first time in litera-ture, the idiom of the people. It is a language stripped of texture and density, so that we can gaze right through the words to the things themselves. 'The knowledge of things, not words, makes a scholar', he commented in *The Compleat English Gentleman*. A profusion of incident and adventure has to compensate for this lack of texture. The sheer fertility of his invention is astonishing. Defoe is not interested in the feel of things, any more than a grocer spends his days lovingly fondling his cheeses. He is interested in the practical use and exchange-value of objects, not their sensuous qualities. There is sensuality in Defoe, not least in *Moll Flanders* and *Roxana*, but not sensuousness. Defoe's realism is a realism of things, whereas Richardson's is one of persons and feelings.

After a lifetime as a mercurial jack-of-all-trades and professional survivor, Defoe died while in hiding from his creditors, determined perhaps to perish in the manner to which he was accustomed. He had been a Dissenter at a time when this reviled group were denied most civil rights. Like a good many major English novelists, as we shall see later, he was lower middle class or *petty bourgeois* in status, in tune with the common people yet more educated, aspiring and politically articulate. In his *Journal of the Plague Year* he scoffs at some popular superstitions but gives credence to others. Like many of those who sprang from this most politically nonconformist of social classes (one thinks of William Blake), he was a political maverick who affirmed the radical equality of men and women, maintaining that it was pure social convention which held women back. Sexual inequalities were cultural, not natural. The qualities which make characters like Roxana and Moll Flanders rogues and whores (either high-class or low-class) also mean that they are no man's permanent property. In this world, in fact, no relationship is permanent.

These women are efficient entrepreneurs of their own sexuality, as much in control of this profitable commodity as Crusoe is in control of the products of his labour. The prostitute utilizes her own body as the peasant ploughs his own land. Moll's beauty and quick wits are raw materials to be exploited, rather like the materials which Crusoe salvages from the shipwreck To reduce sex to a commodity in this way may degrade it, but it also demystifies it. It strips it of its chivalric trappings and feudal pieties. Instead, sexuality in patriarchal society is seen to be about power, gratification, possession and exploitation. To see it in this light may not be exactly sexual emancipation, but it is arguably an essential step towards it. When Moll Flanders breezily remarks that she was glad to be rid of her children, all right-minded readers are both scandalized and deeply sympathetic. Roxana is a 'she-merchant' who refuses to marry even a nobleman because it would be the ruin of her financial independence. To be a wife in her view is to be a slave. The puritan of Defoe's age prized both domestic bliss and economic individualism; the only problem was that they were fundamentally incompatible. This was obviously true for women, who were mostly excluded from the economic sphere in any case; but it was also the case for men, since in practice economic individualism meant trampling on the values of tenderness, affection, loyalty and companionship supposedly symbolized by the family.

To complete his progressive credentials, Defoe also championed the absolute sovereignty of the people, who could never, he thought, surrender their right to rebel against an unjust sovereignty. He defended the Quakers, and spoke up for the merits of an ethnically mixed society. Foreigners, he claimed, were a precious benefit to the nation. He scoffed at chauvinistic mythologies of England in his poem 'The True-Born Englishman', which insists loudly on the ethnically mongrelized nature of the English people, scorns the aristocratic notion of purity of blood, and ridicules the very idea of a true-born Englishman as an irony, fiction and contradiction. It is not entirely irrelevant to this polemic that William III, for whose government Defoe worked, was Dutch.

Though no social leveller, Defoe maintained that there was precious little difference between 'the counter and the coronet'. Trade, he claimed provocatively, was 'the most noble, instructive and improving of any way of life'. In a sense, his religious faith led him to a kind of social reformism, since if human nature was radically corrupt, one had to rely more on nurture than nature. 'What will all the natural capacities of a child amount to without teaching?' he inquires in *The Compleat English Gentleman*. It is upper-class Tories like Henry Fielding who stress the importance of natural characteristics, and Defoe was not slow to spot the politics behind this doctrine. It could be used to downplay the importance of education and social reform, and to justify innate, unalterable differences of rank.

Defoe did not entirely endorse the view that men and women were born like clean slates to be inscribed by social influences, but he certainly held that 'Nature produces nothing till she is married to Learning and got with child by Science'. Crusoe's island is a kind of blank slate or *tabula rasa*, waiting for Man to impress himself upon it. Defoe wanted to see the word 'gentleman' used more as a moral than a social term, though even he could not bring himself to concede that the word could be used of a tradesman. It could, however, be used of his cultivated son. He denounced the well-heeled aldermen of London in biblical style as men 'among whom are crimes black as the robes they wear; whose feasts are debauches and excesses . . . their mouths full of cursing and blasphemy'. He was also a doughty apologist for the poor, and took a boldly deterministic line about their situation: they were, he thought, forced into crime through no fault of their own. As he scathingly inquires in his periodical, the *Review*: 'How many honest gentlemen have we in England now of good estates and noble circumstances that would be highwaymen and come to the gallows if they were poor?' A rich man, unlike a destitute one, has no occasion to be a knave: 'The man is not rich because he is honest, but he is honest because he is rich'.

This is a scandalously materialist doctrine, more typical of Bertolt Brecht than an ardent eighteenth-century Christian. Moral values are simply the reflexes of material conditions. The rich are just those fortunate enough not to have to steal. Morality is for those who can afford it. Ideals are all very well for those who have plenty to eat. Defoe accordingly demanded laws which acknowledged the condition of the poor, rather than a system which first drove them to poverty and then hanged them for it. He believed, in his street-wise bluntly realistic fashion, that no moral or rational reflection could temper the formidable force of biological self-preservation, which he dubs Necessity:

> Poverty makes thieves . . . In poverty, the best of you will rob, nay, even *eat*, your neighbour . . . Necessity is the parent of crime . . . Ask the worst highwayman in the nation, ask the lewdest strumpet in the town, if they would not willingly leave off the trade if they could live handsomely without it. And I dare say, not one but will acknowledge it.

It is an early instance of what one might call the social-worker theory of morality. The conservative Henry Fielding, by contrast, argues in his essay on *The Increase of Robbers* that crime comes about by the poor imitating the luxury of the rich.

It is worth noting how Defoe's attitude denigrates the poor – they are mere victims of circumstance, without will or agency of their own – at the same time as it elicits our compassion for them. This is a risky move, since we tend not to feel sympathy for what we consider worthless. All the same, the claim strikes a devastating blow at the notion of the autonomous self, that ideological lodestar of Defoe's kind of civilization. Indeed, it lays bare an embarrassing contradiction at the very heart of that order. If middle-class society holds the autonomous self so dear in theory, how come that it violates it so often in practice? Does it really desire independence for its servants, wage-slaves and colonial peoples? Wouldn't you secretly prefer to have absolute freedom of action yourself, while denying it to your competitors in the marketplace? Middle-class society believes in the self-government of the people; but it is also a place where men and women seem to be little more than playthings of impersonal economic forces. Defoe's protagonists – Moll Flanders, Robinson Crusoe, Roxana, Colonel Jack – are all caught up in this contradiction. If they are in one sense creators of their own destiny, they are also the hapless victims of Providence, the marketplace and their own appetites.

Defoe, to be sure, was no critic of capitalist society. On the contrary, he was one of its most articulate spokesmen. His writing is flushed with the buoyancy and boundless vitality of capitalism in its pristine stage. In an essay entitled 'The Divinity of Trade', he sees Nature itself as a kind of capitalist, who in its unfathomable bourgeois wisdom has made bodies able to float so that we can build ships in which to trade; has hung out stars by which merchants can navigate; and has carved out rivers which lead straight to the eminently plunderable resources of other countries. Animals have been made meekly submissive so that we may exploit them as instruments or raw materials; jagged coastlines are thoughtfully adapted to the construction of sheltered harbours; while raw materials have been distributed with wonderful convenience throughout the globe so that each nation has something to sell and something to buy. Short of manufacturing the oceans out of Coca-Cola or implanting in us a biological need for Nike footwear, Nature has scarcely missed a trick.

As an enlightened radical (though one who believed in witchcraft), Defoe saw capitalism as an internationalist, socially emancipated form of life, one to be celebrated rather than castigated. For him, it was an exhilaratingly progressive affair. The merchant was the new principle of universal harmony and solidarity: 'He sits in his counting house and converses with all nations'. Trade and market dealings were steadily undercutting privilege, deference, hierarchy and mindless custom. Merit and hard work were beginning to bulk larger than blood and birth. Defoe was critical not of this bustling, dynamic form of life, but of some of the ideological cant which still clustered around it. There was a glaring discrepancy between what it actually did, and what it said it did – between its facts and its values. There was a rift, for example, between the moral assumption that men and women were free, and the plain material fact that they were not.

There was also a troubling contradiction between the way this social order elevated the individual to supreme status, and the way that in practice it treated individuals as indifferently interchangeable. Business, sexual or marital partners in Defoe's novels come and go, sometimes with about as much individuality as rabbits. But the main conflict lay between the amoral practices of a culture in which what really matters is money and self-interest, and the high-sounding moral ideals to which it laid claim. In Defoe's novels, this becomes a tension between the story, which is told because roguery and wickedness are inherently fascinating, and the moral, which claims that the story is told to warn you against imitating such vice.

It is the double-think of the tabloid press: 'You may find this tale of erotic romps in the council chamber shocking, but we feel it is our public duty to expose local authority sleaze'. The eighteenth-century writer John Dunton, who knew Defoe slightly, ran a monthly paper devoted to exposing prostitution called *The Night Walker: or, Evening Rambles in Search after Lewd Women*. It was not, as one might suspect, a wholly high-minded project. The naturalistic novel in the late nineteenth century did something similar, taking the lid off steamy sex and squalid social underworlds in a spirit of scientific inquiry. It is not, however, Defoe who is being hypocritical here, so much as society itself. The double-think, so to speak, is built into the situation he is depicting.

Like middle-class society itself, what a Defoe novel shows, and what it says, move at quite different levels. There is a blank at the heart of these works, where a relation between God and your bank balance, prayer and the purchase of slaves, ought to be. This is because a form of society is emerging in England which is moving beyond the religious and metaphysical in practice, but which still needs to appeal to such principles in theory. Unless it did, it would be hard put to justify its existence. In practice, the world is just one random material situation after another, without overall point or pattern. In theory, it all adds up to some beneficent Providence. In theory, things have God-given values; in practice, their value lies in what you can get for them on the market. In theory, moral values are absolute; in practice, nothing in this mobile, ceaselessly mutating society is absolute at all. The family, for a devout puritan like Defoe, is a sacred domain, as his work *The Family Instructor* suggests; it is just that ties of kinship are to be severed when they get in the way of your material advancement, as happens often enough in the novels. Family relations are sacrosanct bonds of blood; it is just that in practice they are to be broken, ignored or treated as purely instrumental.

The extraordinarily radical achievement of Defoe's novels is to tell the stark, unvarnished truth about this world, without posture or pretension. The result is a kind of sensationalism which rarely seems conscious of itself as such. The sensation, so to speak, lies in the subject-matter itself, rather than in the way it is presented. In fact, the tone in which it is presented is level, colourless and scrupulously neutral. In its English way, it does not go in for emotional histrionics. In *Crusoe*, it is as though the tone belongs to the cool-headed colonialist and the exotic subject-matter to his colonial subjects. These remorselessly unadorned narratives do not so much strip the veils of ideological decorum from early eighteenth-century England, as simply stare through them. They are not polemical, simply candid. They do not probe much into feelings, since feelings cannot be quantified, and in this society only what is quantifiable is real. In their unabashed amoralism, they are subversively faithful to what social existence is actually like, not to what it is meant to be like. In this situation, simply exposing the facts of the matter is explosive in itself. Realism itself becomes a kind of politics.

Defoe's novels, to be sure, have much to say about the importance of moral values; but there are times when they say it so perfunctorily that the gap between these values, and the facts presented by the fiction, is almost laughably apparent. Moll Flanders finishes her story by telling us how prosperous she has grown after her life of crime, remembering hastily to add as a dutiful afterthought that she sincerely repents of it. The moral of the story – crime doesn't pay – is blatantly contradicted by the outcome. The gap is so glaring, indeed, that some critics have wondered whether Defoe is not at times being deliberately ironic. When the shipwrecked Crusoe denounces the uselessness of the ship's gold to him on his island, but decides to keep it all the same, is this meant to poke ironic fun at his expense? When Crusoe, seeing Friday fleeing for his life from his fellow cannibals, reflects that he could do with a servant, and at the same moment hears Providence calling upon him to save Friday from death, is this coincidence of self-interest and spiritual revelation meant to raise a readerly smile? Is Defoe sending up

Roxana when she declares that she must keep her own money separate from her husband's so as not to mingle her own ill-gotten gains with his honestly acquired fortune?

The answer, perhaps, is that it doesn't really matter. What matters is not so much whether Defoe's intentions are ironic (how can we know anyway?), but what one might call the objective irony of the situation. In this social order, values and facts, the material and the moral, are acutely at odds with each other, whether Defoe is sardonically rubbing our noses in the fact or not. Moral values are mostly quite ineffectual: generally speaking, they are to be turned to in the face of a crisis or catastrophe, of a storm or a bout of sickness, or when you are affluent enough to put a life of crime behind you. As we have seen Defoe argue already, such values are mere reflexes of material situations.

Yet if this is what Defoe the literary realist and radical materialist believes, it can hardly be the credo of the devout religious Dissenter. Defoe the Christian naturally claims that moral and religious values are a reality in their own right. The problem with this claim is that they do not seem to mesh very tightly with the material world. They exist in a realm of their own, which may be real enough but which has little impact on one's actual conduct. Moll Flanders feels sorry for one of her victims even in the act of robbing him, but the sorrow in no way interferes with the proper business of relieving him of his goods. Like Colonel Jack, you can be a skilled pick-pocket yet still feel pangs of conscience. In the eighteenth century, tender sentiment and hard-nosed self-interest were no strangers to each other. So either moral values lack force because they are too closely bound up with the material world, or they lack force because they are too remote from it. Defoe himself acknowledged the latter condition when he wrote that 'Prayers and tears no revolution make, Pull down no tyrant, will no bondage break'.

Morality in Defoe is generally retrospective. Once you have made your pile, you can afford to be penitent. In any case, it is only in hindsight, not least in the act of writing, that you can make sense of your life as a whole. You live forward, but understand backward. While you are actually living your life, you are too busy trying to keep your head above water to engage in reflection, let alone remorse. You must keep on the move or go under, run very fast to stay just where you are. It is hard to brood upon metaphysical mysteries while you are trying to keep one step ahead of your creditors or work out how to dispose of your latest husband. The narrative tumbles forward at such a hectic pace that one event constantly fades beneath the next, and that of another. Not one of the hordes of characters in *Moll*

Flanders has more than fleeting contact with the heroine – a typically urban situation which would be unthinkable in the settled rural communities of Jane Austen or George Eliot. These figures come and go in Moll's life like passers-by on Piccadilly. The most pressing question as the reader follows this endless metonymic process is: what comes next? Meaning and living are not really compatible.

Just as some dim-witted people are said to be unable to chew gum and walk at the same time, so Defoe's characters can act or reflect, but find it hard to do both together. Morally informed action is rare; moral reflection is what generally comes afterwards. This is one reason why two quite different literary forms rub shoulders somewhat incongruously within the covers of *Robinson Crusoe*: the adventure story and the spiritual autobiography. Of all Defoe's characters, Crusoe is the most successful in combining rational action and moral reflection. But this is partly because of his exceptional circumstances: he is, after all, on an uninhabited island, where there is work to be done but also plenty of time to meditate.

Defoe's novels display a kind of pure narrativity, in which events are not so much savoured for their own sake as registered for their 'exchange-value'. We are interested in what they leash momentarily together – in what caused them and what they lead to. Because life is pressingly material but also fast-moving, events seem both vivid and insubstantial. These novels are fascinated by process itself, not just by its end-product. There is no logical end to a Defoe narrative, no natural closure. You simply go on accumulating narrative, rather as you never stop accumulating capital. One piece of story, like one capital investment, leads to another. Crusoe is no sooner home from his island than he is off on his travels again, piling up yet more adventures which he promises to write about in the future. The desire to narrate is insatiable. Like amassing capital, it seems to have a point yet is secretly done for its own sake, with no particular end in view. There is no definitive settlement in Defoe, as there is in Fielding. All endings are arbitrary, and all of them are potential beginnings. You settle down only to take off again.

Because of this pure narrativity, few events in Defoe's world are experienced deeply enough to leave a permanent memory or impression. Characters like Moll or Roxana live off the top of their heads, by the skin of their teeth and (sometimes literally) by the seat of their pants. Coping with a random, shifting world means that the self has to be constantly adaptive. And this, in turn, means that there is no immutable core of selfhood which might draw morals and store up memories. Instead, identity is improvised, tactical, calculating. It is a set of reactions to one's environment. Human drives – greed, self-interest, self-preservation – are fixed and unchangeable, but to gratify them you have to be pliable and protean. The wit, prudence and canniness you need to cope with the plague in *A Journal of the Plague Year* are simply exaggerated versions of the qualities you need to deal with everyday life.

Selfhood implies some kind of interiority; but though one can find this in a character like Crusoe, at least in his occasional breaks from labour, there is precious little of it in some of Defoe's other protagonists. The self is not constituted by its relations with others. On the contrary, its dealings with other selves are external to it, and are purely instrumental in nature. Others are essentially tools of one's own purposes, or at best one's partners in crime. There is little sense of relationship as a value in itself; all relationships are contractual, not least sexual ones. Colonel Jack marries four times, despite the fact that he can do without women, and breaks up with one of his wives because she is overspending. In Hobbesian vein, self-interest is far more fundamental than reason or altruism. Only hunting for food is stronger than hunting for profit. Defoe was a rationalist in some respects, but he also had a typically puritan sense of the depravity of human nature, and the consequent fragility of reason.

The sole abiding reality is the isolated individual self; and the autobiographical form, which views the whole world from this lonely standpoint, is a suitable medium for this solipsism. Crusoe complains strikingly little about his solitude on the island, and for most of the time scarcely seems to notice it. It is the presence of other people, not their absence, which he finds most fearful, as when cannibals set foot on the beach. Defoe would not have been unduly impressed by Henry Fielding's remark that those who are anti-social live in constant opposition to their own nature, and 'are no less monsters than the most wanton abortions or extravagant births' (*Essay on Conversation*). The Nonconformist Protestant, as opposed to a liberal Anglican like Fielding, suspects that other people are likely to get between him and God. In this view, you can be moral even when you are by yourself – perhaps especially when you are by yourself. This is a notion which classical ethics would find as puzzling as the claim that you can be tenderly affectionate or uproariously amusing on your own. Crusoe's isolation is God's punishment for his irreligiousness, but it also plants the seeds of his salvation, since he now has time to contemplate his eternal destiny.

The self may be brooding and solitary, but in practice it is a function of its circumstances. It cannot rise sufficiently above its material environment to be an autonomous entity. The *narrating* self, to be sure, does exactly that: it delivers its tale with a cool, unruffled air which suggests a detachment from the experiences it records. The *narrated* self, by contrast – the one whose adventures the story describes – can attain no such equipoise. This involves a tension between past and present, since the narrator belongs to present time and the events he or she records belong to the past. The self is thus divided in the very act of autobiography – an act in which it tries to gather itself into a coherent whole. We shall see more of this when we come to look at Laurence Sterne.

It is convenient in a way that moralizing involves a backward glance, since it means that morality is unlikely to interfere with your actual behaviour in the present. On this view, religion and morality are rather like alcohol: it is when they begin to interfere with your everyday life that it is time to give them up. Once on his island, Crusoe thinks that he can see how this frightful fate lends retrospective meaning to his life: it is Providence's way of punishing him for his faithless youth. Things lack a meaning at the time, but they acquire one later on by being incorporated after the event into a kind of grand narrative. What was empirical at the time becomes allegorical in hindsight.

Defoe is intensely serious about Crusoe's burgeoning spiritual life. The fact that spirituality is hard to square with practicality is no argument against it. Yet though God is by no means dead, he would seem for the good Protestant to have withdrawn his presence from the world. This is one reason why Defoe's speculations on Providence ring fairly unconvincingly. Nothing can happen to you, he remarks in *The True-Born Englishman*, 'but what comes from Providence, and consists with the interest of the universe'. Taken literally, this suggests that rape, murder and human sacrifice play their role in maintaining cosmic harmony. He writes piously in the preface to *Crusoe* of how we should honour the wisdom of Providence and its works, 'let them happen as they will'; but far from letting things happen as they will, the frenetically active Crusoe is forever trying to shape them to his own purposes. He testifies to the wisdom of Providence by claiming that the heavens are chastising him for having lived 'a dreadful life'; but little we see in his career before the shipwreck would justify such a self-accusation. It is true, however, that his youthful neglect of his religious duties would weigh a lot more heavily in Defoe's eyes than in some modern ones.

If Crusoe is indeed to be punished, it should not be for skipping his prayers, but for such acts as selling his servant Xury into slavery and running a slave plantation. He is actually leading an illegal expedition to buy slaves when he is shipwrecked. But neither he nor his author would regard these actions as especially immoral, even though Crusoe waxes indignant absout Spanish imperialism in the Americas. As with the narrator of Conrad's *Heart of Darkness*, other people's imperialisms are usually more reprehensible than one's own. Colonel Jack advocates beating slaves, and there is no indication that his author demurs. Freedom is for Englishmen, not Africans. As a zealous puritan, Defoe believed that 'savages' were condemned to bestiality on earth and eternal torment thereafter. His radicalism had its limits.

Crusoe actually reprimands himself for *not* remaining on his plantation, where he was settled and contented, and suspects that it was his sinful restlessness in abandoning the place which has brought him to ruin. Divine Providence would clearly have preferred him to live off slave labour, and is chastising him for not doing so. There is, he reflects further, always some good to be extracted from evil: he may be cast away, but at least he is still alive. It is not in fact true that evil always yields some good, and even if it were true, it does not necessarily justify it. Auschwitz yielded some good in the form of mutual help and self-sacrifice, but nobody proposes this as a justification for it. Crusoe even persuades himself that God has punished him less than his iniquity deserves, a peculiarly self-lacerating view. He reminds himself lugubriously that even the most miserable of conditions could always be worse; praises Providence, perversely, for the considerate way in which it conceals from us the terrors which surround us; and consoles himself with the thought that only by being deprived of what we enjoy can we come truly to appreciate it. In the end, he abandons these cack-handed attempts to rationalize his situation altogether, accepting instead that Providence's ways are inscrutable and not to be questioned.

All this tortuous sophistry indicates just how hard it has now become to discern a purposeful pattern in reality. Nature is no longer an open book, but an obscure text to be deciphered with difficulty. The Protestant gropes anxiously in darkness for ambiguous signs of his or her salvation. Yet the whole point of a secularized universe would seem to be its contingency – the fact that nothing in it is actually 'meant'. An author like Henry Fielding uses the formal design of the novel itself to imply a pattern in events; but the result, as we have seen, is an ironic gap between the events and the pattern. All one now seems to be left with is secular experience – whatever one can taste, feel and weigh; yet it is in this unpromising domain that one must search for symptoms of salvation.

You must look for the divine in the very sphere which seems to deny it, since this is all you really have. In the literary realm, this poring over material fragments and psychological nuances, scanning them for their concealed significance, is known as realism. In the non-literary realm, it is known as Protestantism. Is the world a matter of accident or design? Or is God somehow present in the very contingencies of his universe? Could it be, paradoxically, that the more worldly one becomes – the more one accumulates wealth, climbs the social hierarchy and gains the respect of one's fellows – the more all this can itself be seen as a sign of God's favour?

This, in a word, is the famous Protestant work ethic; and like much about middle-class society it is anxious and self-assured at the same time. There is anxiety because you can never be quite certain of your salvation, given the obscurity of the divine plan. Signs, in this world as in some modernist literary text, are always bound to be ambiguous. This is one reason why you can never stop working, since even if you have no assurance of salvation right now, your future labours might always issue in one. Tropical islands are generally associated with indolence, but not in Crusoe's case. He is forever improving and extending his labours ('I really wanted to build my barns bigger') – so much so, indeed, that the obvious question poses itself: 'What for?' Crusoe is not a capitalist – it is an odd kind of capitalist who has no wage-labourers, markets, commodities, competitors or division of labour; but though he has no competitors, he behaves as though he does. Who would have thought that a fable of one man alone on an island could be so action-packed?

What all this unwittingly goes to show is just how futile and irrational the whole process of labour is, however rational it may be in its local details. Crusoe works a lot of the time for the sake of working, as capitalists accumulate for the sake of accumulation. Success in work may be a sign of salvation, but it is also a welcome distraction from the whole vexed business of heaven and hell. Crusoe's labour is among other things a kind of displacement activity. It saves him from having to think about his salvation. This compulsively labouring hero is like a man *en route* to execution who pauses to fasten his shoelaces and meticulously checks the knots. Defoe's protagonists concentrate on the means of life rather than inquiring about its end. In fact, as in capitalist society in general, the means of life rapidly become the end. This is partly because there are now no 'natural' ends to life, just as there are none to narrative.

Yet it is hard, even so, to ignore the fact that you are helplessly dependent on a Providence which lies beyond the reach of reason. This experience has a worldly parallel: it corresponds to the sense of being alone and adrift in a hostile world of predators and competitors, having to pick your way through nameless threats and terrors. To this extent, Crusoe's island is less an alternative to middle-class society than an aggravated version of it. His loneliness is a magnified version of the solitude of all men and women in an individualist society. If you are helplessly dependent in one sense, however, you can still be self-determining in another. How resourceful and energetic you are in your shaping your own fortunes may reveal whether you are among the small band of the saved. You can resolve the apparent conflict between being the plaything of Providence on the one hand, and working for your own advancement on the other, by claiming in good puritan style that success in the latter is a sign of having found favour in the eyes of God.

Defoe's heroes and heroines are great self-fashioners, men and women who seek to master their own circumstances and forge their own destinies. The bad news is that the world is an inhospitable place; the good news is that this mobilizes a set of admirable human resources. If middle-class England is a place of perpetual insecurity, it is also a place of opportunity. Just because there now seems no design in the world, you are free to create your own. It is just that in doing so, you attribute your success to a greater pattern called Providence, even if it is the very absence of such a pattern which allows you to make your own way in the world.

Robinson Crusoe can be seen as progressing, by and large, from anxiety to assurance. He starts off on the island as a frightened victim of its unknown terrors, and then turns to God in his sickness. Prayer and misfortune are a not unfamiliar conjuncture of events. What impels Crusoe to seek divine grace suggests that his conversion may be no more than a reflex of his material plight. From this point on, he grows in spiritual awareness, as well as in his confident mastery of the island – so that if the latter can be seen as a form of symbolic imperialism, as the presence of Friday would suggest, the implicit lesson is that religion and imperialism go hand in hand. Crusoe becomes a kind of colonial conquistador on his island – an efficient, self-disciplined leader who by creating law and order ends up as a kind of one-man political state.

The suggestion, then, is that given enough self-mastery you can evolve from a fearful state of nature to a state of civilization. In fact, however, these states are less sequential than synchronous. In colonialism, 'savagery' and civilization exist cheek by jowl, and what is plundered from the former goes to sustain the latter. At the same time, colonialist regimes are themselves divided between self-confidence and chronic insecurity, as the ups and downs of political and economic life pose a perpetual threat to their mastery. Something of this can be seen in what one might call the play of tenses in Defoe. The narrative is all about a kind of present-tense precariousness, in which your fortunes are unsettled and your future alarmingly uncertain; but all this is recounted with the authoritative detachment of the past tense, by a narrator who must have survived simply to be able to tell the story. Anxiety and assurance are thus combined in the writing itself.

Crusoe sees his urge to travel as a perverse form of self-destruction. 'I was born to be my own destroyer', he gloomily remarks. It is impious not to stay serenely at home, but he is powerless to resist the impulse to break away. This is fortunate in one sense, since had he done so there would have been no novel. For the narrative to get off the ground, the hero has to break with the normality of his petty-bourgeois background – though there is a sense in which Crusoe never really does so, since he behaves like an impeccable petty bourgeois even on his island. We half expect him to open a corner shop. His compulsion to travel, however, is clearly a kind of deviancy. Restlessness, or perpetual desire, is now the natural condition of humanity, and narrative is its literary expression.

Like life in general, narrative appears to have a goal, but in fact it does not. It is secretly indulged in for its own sake – even though, for a puritan like Defoe, this is as morally indefensible as self-pleasuring sex as opposed to the reproductive variety. Like everything else in a utilitarian world, including copulation, narrative is supposed to have a point. It should illustrate a moral truth. In reality, however, it is a form of guilty transgression – not only because stories work by continually overriding boundaries, but because story-telling as such is a kind of luxury or superfluity, and thus morally inadmissable. The only problem is that it is also a kind of necessity – even, perhaps, a neurosis, as may well be the case with the compulsively scribbling Samuel Richardson.

This is why Defoe has to insist that the story exists for the sake of the moral, even though it is farcically obvious that it does not. Realism, in the sense of an attention to the material world for its own sake, is still not wholly permissible, even though it is increasingly in demand in a society which believes in what it can smell, touch and taste. Realism must not take precedence over morality: Samuel Johnson insisted that the fact that a character or event in fiction was true to nature was no excuse for including it. In theory, this clash between the moral and the story can be resolved by arguing, tabloid-wise, that the more graphic and gripping you make the story, the more thoroughly you drive home the moral. As Defoe writes in his preface to *Roxana*: 'If there are any parts of her story which, being obliged to relate a wicked action, seem to describe it too plainly, all imaginable care has been taken to keep clear of indecencies . . .'. This has something like the effect of a solemn sex-and-violence warning on a video, one craftily guaranteed to augment its viewing audience.

Realism, then, is permissible if it serves a moral end; and this is strangely parallel to the way in which Defoe's characters are allowed to commit crimes if forced to do so by necessity, but not just for the hell of it. Colonel Jack's criminal activity as a boy is excused by his ignorance and need to survive. He is simply following the law of nature – self-interest – in grabbing from society what he needs to stay alive. Moll is originally driven to crime by necessity, which helps to make her more sympathetic and perhaps smooths the way to her later repentance; but there is no necessity for the series of illegal exploits she indulges in later, partly for the sheer delight of exercising her wits. Just as the inherent fascination of realism takes over from Defoe's supposed moral lesson, so Moll's crimes are perpetrated partly for their own sake – or rather, so to speak, for ours. She carries on thieving even when she is wealthy enough to retire. Roxana is likewise forced into an illicit sexual relationship by her fear of starving, but this is not enough to justify forcing her maid into bed with her as well. You are forgiven for being needy, but not kinky. Roxana becomes a whore from necessity, which for Defoe is quite enough to excuse her, but it is greed and vanity which compel her to remain in the trade.

The realist novel, as we have seen, emerges at a point where everyday experience begins to seem enthralling in its own right. This blending of the ordinary and the exotic is marked in Defoe's work. Part of the pleasure of reading it comes from the sheer excitement it can squeeze from the utterly mundane. There are reasons for this mixture of high drama and routine existence. Defoe lived in turbulent, unstable political times, and as a political adventurer found himself in the thick of them. In revolutionary epochs like his own, theatrics is part of the stuff of everyday life. He also had several careers as a small businessman, which meant that the drama of debt, bankruptcy, imprisonment and foreign expeditions was part of his daily existence.

Above all, the colourful and the commonplace came together in this period in the form of colonial adventure, which brought the chuckleheaded Englishman face to face with what struck him as outlandish and bizarre. Part of the pleasure of reading *Robinson Crusoe*, not least perhaps for its contemporary audiences, is to observe a familiar kind of rationality successfully at work in highly unfamiliar circumstances. Crusoe, who is both average and exceptional, potters about his island rather as though he were somewhere in the Home Counties, which constitutes something of a compliment to Western reason. Drop it in a jungle or a desert far from home, rather like the paratroopers, and watch how efficiently it copes. We enjoy seeing Crusoe's sturdy English practicality made to look less prosaic and more heroic, just as we enjoy watching a tropical island being gradually made to look a little more like Dorking. It is ironic in this light that the stoutly empiricist Crusoe, who would not have recognized an archetype had one fallen into his lap, should have become one of the great modern myths.

We moderns, however, are also likely to find this process rather funny, as when Crusoe rigs himself up with a very English umbrella. There is something both admirable and ludicrous about such cultural egoism, rather as there is about the colonial official in *Heart of Darkness* who shaves meticulously every morning in the middle of an impenetrable jungle. It is at once arrogant and innocent. James Joyce, who rather oddly numbered Defoe among his favourite authors, wrote of Crusoe as incarnating 'the whole Anglo-Saxon spirit . . . the manly independence; the unconscious cruelty; the persistence; the slow yet efficient intelligence; the sexual apathy; the practical, well-balanced religiousness; the calculating taciturnity'.[1] This, so to speak, is Crusoe as seen by Friday: Joyce is writing as a colonial subject of the British crown, and had no doubt run into the odd British soldier in Dublin who answered to this description. One or two of them turn up in *Ulysses*. The passage, which Joyce wrote while in Italian exile, also has something of the genially even-handed assessment of the imperial character of one who is now at a safe distance from it. Perhaps Joyce, as a fellow materialist, relished Defoe's intense physicality. He once described himself as having a mind like a grocer, and Defoe distils the true spirit of a nation of shopkeepers.

Seeing a very English rationality triumphing over alien circumstances allows Defoe's readers to remind themselves of the universality of their own ways of doing things. In fact, if their way of life really were as universal as they think it, Crusoe might have been saved the trouble of having to teach Friday about the Christian God, since Friday might well have been granted innate knowledge of him. In any case, Crusoe himself is afflicted by the odd twinge of cultural relativism. Who is he, he asks himself in the breast-beating style of the devout liberal or postmodernist, to interfere with a practice like cannibalism? Even so, the fact that so much of the novel is concerned with practical know-how lends a curious kind of support to the universalist case. Practical rationality, in the sense of knowing when to take shelter or how not to fall off a cliff, is more plausibly universal than any other kind of reason. This is why Friday can assist Crusoe in his labours before he can speak English properly, since the logic of the material world is common to all cultures. Stones fall if they are dropped in Haiti as well as Huddersfield, and four hands are better than two in both places for shifting heavy weights. Someone can throw you a rope if you are drowning even if what water symbolizes in their cultural system is quite different from what it signifies in yours. Practical rationality is in one sense the epitome of Englishness: if the English ever get to heaven, they will instantly measure the place up for double-glazing. Yet it is also what is most convincingly universal.

Exploring the criminal underworld is another way in which Defoe blends the bizarre and the commonplace. The underworld is in one sense an exotic aberration from everyday society; but it is also a microcosm of it, since the criminal is the nearest thing there is to the businessman. Both types need much the same qualities to prosper: quick wits, ruthlessness, resourcefulness, adaptability, a thick skin and a smooth tongue, a keen sense of self-interest and so on. Moll is thoroughly middle-class in her aspirations, and transports these talents into her career as a thief. She despises most criminals despite being in that category herself, is obsessed with gentility and keeping up appearances, and in general presents herself as a respectable middle-class puritan who just happens to be a hardened thief as well.

There is a venerable literary tradition of the businessman-as-criminal and vice versa, all the way from the rogues of John Gay's *The Beggar's Opera* to Balzac's Vautrin and Dickens's Mr Merdle. As Bertolt Brecht remarked: 'What's robbing a bank compared to founding one?' The thieves' kitchen is the business corporation without the veils of ideological respectability. Colonel Jack starts out as a petty thief and ends up as a successful capitalist in Virginia, without his talents having undergone any notable transformation. Henry Fielding's master-criminal Jonathan Wild is a satirical portrait of the politician Robert Walpole, bringing together the world of high politics and the world of high misdemeanours.

The idea of stumbling across virgin soil and building a civilization on it is one of the ultimate middle-class fantasies. No doubt this is one reason why the myth of Crusoe has proved so potent. Demolishing what has come before you may be necessary to make progress, and virgin soil saves you the trouble. You are also saved the moral unpleasantness of having to exterminate the natives. Defoe spoke for a capitalist and commercial class which was growing increasingly impatient with tradition. In challenging the sway of the gentry and nobility, it needed to discredit the power of antiquity in the process. Defoe is suitably sardonic about the aristocratic obsession with blood and breeding: why, he asks in *The Compleat English Gentleman*, do the gentry allow their children to be suckled by plebeian wet-nurses, thus imbibing what he ironically calls 'degenerate' blood? In *The True-Born Englishman* he declares the whole business of ancestry to be an irrelevance. It is an agreeable fantasy, then, to imagine that you could undo all this history and go back to the origin, starting the whole process again but this time with the middle classes in charge.

This is one of the wish-fulfilments lurking within *Robinson Crusoe*. Crusoe's island is empty except for a convenient manservant. Another such wish-fulfilment in the book is the desire to trace processes of production – of food, clothing, furniture and the like – all the way through from the raw materials to the finished product, in a society where these processes have become too complex and opaque for anyone to grasp as a whole. Since Crusoe builds his own world from the bottom up, the novel grants us this overall view. Its hero regresses to a time before the division of labour – the condition in which work tasks are shared amongst a whole army of specialists – and becomes a model of self-sufficiency. The middle-class dream of the purely self-determining human subject can thus be realized – but only when nobody else is around. There is an artisanal nostalgia in the book – a puritanical, lower-middle-class longing for a more decent, more transparent world of labour and consumption, a society of use rather than luxury. Because Defoe speaks up for small capitalism as against big, there is a critical edge to his enthusiasm for money, trade and markets. In his *Review* he laments the elevation of property over persons, whatever he may do in his fiction.

The desire to wipe the historical slate clean and start over again, however, turns out to be doomed to defeat. What defeats it in *Robinson Crusoe*, in one of the great uncanny moments of world literature, is a single footprint on the sand. There is, after all, no virgin territory. Someone has always been there before you. There is a threat to your absolute sovereignty known as the Aboriginal. In a similar way, Crusoe has to admit that he would not have flourished on his island without the tools and resources he managed to salvage from the shipwreck. There is no absolute origin, no pure creation from nothing. You forge your own destiny on the basis of a history handed down to you, which can never be entirely eradicated. It is in this sense that history knows no absolute breaks. Even so, Robinson Crusoe spends long years on his island without being disturbed; Jonathan Swift's Gulliver is not so fortunate.

Gulliver's Travels is a savage spoof of the kind of travel-writing represented by *Robinson Crusoe*. Many of its contemporary readers took the book as genuine, though one of them threw it angrily aside, loudly declaring that he didn't believe a word of it. One aspect of the work which makes it sound like the kind of thing Defoe might write is its style. Like Defoe, Swift writes a practical, transparent, thing-centred prose, without much texture or resonance. It has, as one critic has pointed out, no secret recesses or tentacular roots.[2] There is a striking lack of metaphor. It is a style of the surface, without much depth or interiority.

Swift is suspicious of depth, as he is suspicious of metaphysics and abstruse speculations. This indifference to metaphysical truths says something about the eighteenth-century clergy, of whom Swift was one. It is rather like a bank robber being indifferent to money. Tory gentlemen like Swift were amateurs, not specialists: they believed in a few commonsensical truths which the light of reason had made accessible to everyone. Swift would not have understood the idea of a specialized literary prose style. *Gulliver's Travels* is not, in the later sense of the word, a 'literary' work, and would not have been thought of as a novel. Swift's language, like Defoe's, effaces itself before the objects it presents, allowing them to shine straight through it. The ideal language would be one so transparent that it abolished itself. This happens in the book with those Laputian sages who, rather than speaking to each other, carry around with them a sack of all the objects they might need in the course of a conversation, and hold them up mutely to each other. In fact, language is a sort of bottomless sack, a way of carrying the world around with us without any weight at all. The Houyhnhnms avoid verbal elaborateness and maintain a perfect correspondence between word and thing – so much so, indeed, that they are incapable of lying. Flawless as they are in their representations of the world, they would make superb realist novelists.

Eighteenth-century travel-writing is supposed to be in some ways a 'progressive' form, eager to investigate, exploit new technologies, acquire fresh knowledge and experience, and seize new opportunities for wealth. It centres on enterprise, optimism and self-sufficiency – all Whig-like, middle-class, commercialist values. It also allows you to draw some satisfying contrasts between your own civilized condition and the benighted state of the peoples you come across in your wanderings. *Gulliver's Travels*, by contrast, is an 'anti-progressive' work in which the amnesiac protagonist learns little or nothing, since he seems to start out on each of his travels as a blank slate. The book, significantly, is not one seamless narrative like Defoe's novels, but a series of disconnected episodes. And Gulliver's memory seems to disappear down the cracks between them. In a parody of the travel book's customary optimism, he ends up out of his mind.

There is no conception here of a developing self, indeed precious little notion of selfhood at all. The Tory Swift, unlike the Whiggish Defoe, is not especially interested in individuals. He is concerned instead with universal truths, which Gulliver and the other figures are simply there to illustrate. Gulliver is merely a convenient narrative device, not a 'character' with whom we are invited to identify. We are not invited to share his experience, as Defoe invites us to share Crusoe's. Instead, we are asked to observe and judge it. Like Henry Fielding's Joseph Andrews and Parson Adams, Gulliver is sometimes used as a mouthpiece for his author, and sometimes as an object of satire himself.

Far from confirming his superiority to the creatures he encounters, Gulliver's travels reveal that they are pretty much the same as he is, if not somewhat better. The irony of the book is that however outlandish the beings you come across, human nature – if creatures like the Laputians and Lilliputians can be thought of for the moment as human – turns out to be much the same everywhere. Which is to say, not very admirable. The Lilliputians are cruel, scheming and sectarian, like pocket-sized replicas of Westminster politicians. This belief that human nature is both corrupt and unchangeable belongs with Swift's Anglican conservatism. He scorns the idea that there can be any dramatic progress or revolutionary change, or that we could unearth through our travels or researches any truths which are not plain enough already. God has given us all we need to know for our salvation, and sailing off to gawp at giants or disport oneself with midgets is just a fashionable distraction from that vital business.

Such travels simply flatter humanity, suggesting that its powers of knowledge and exploration are unlimited; whereas Swift is concerned to cut Man brutally down to size, reminding him with sadistic relish of how feeble and foolish an animal he is. He is typical of Anglo-Irish writing in his concern to debunk and deflate. Gulliver's various adventures are meant to reflect back on us humans, usually by placing us in an embarrassing light, not to bring revelations of enthralling new possibilities. For the conservative Swift, new possibilities are not in the least enthralling. He is right in a sense that other creatures we might encounter could not be all that different from ourselves, since if they were it is hard to know how we could know we were encountering them at all. To define something or someone as different implies some kind of shared standard. We know that the Lilliputians are different from us because they are much smaller than we are, which implies that we share the concept of size. We can tell that tarantulas are different from us because we have a language in which we can describe and identify them. If they were utterly alien, this would not be so. You cannot speak of difference unless you can also speak of comparability. The really different beings are those who are squatting invisibly in our lap right at this moment.

Travel-writing, then, is a morally dubious genre from a Tory-Anglican viewpoint. It is dazzled by the prospect of innovation, which is always an alarming prospect to a conservative. Defoe wrote an early *Essay upon Projects* which expressed just such enthusiasm for technical and scientific reform. Like Crusoe, travel literature is full of transgressive desire, forever yearning to break away from home, and is thus an implicit rejection of the Tory values of land, home, crown and country. It is seen by such Tories as the pornography of progress. It is full of monstrous fantasies, which are both indecorous and likely to cloud our commonsensical judgement. It encourages idle fancies and extravagant emotions, which are not good for law and order. It also tends to breed cultural relativism, which is just as politically unhealthy. It can be dangerously utopian and sentimentalist, claiming to have stumbled across primitive peoples who live in happiness and harmony. Since this denies original sin, and might inspire us to hatch various dewy-eyed utopian schemes of our own, it is to be resisted. It also reflects less than creditably on our own less-than-utopian society, and thus can be an indirect form of political critique. The fourth book of *Gulliver's Travels* sends up this utopian vision in the shape of the Houyhnhnms, who are certainly harmonious creatures but who also happen to be horses.

It would be a mistake, even so, to exaggerate the difference between 'progressives' like Defoe and 'conservatives' like Swift. Much eighteenth-century public debate concerns hammering out a political consensus after the sectarian ravages of the preceding century, and the novel plays a vital role in this mediating of political extremes. Swift referred to Defoe with patrician sniffiness as 'the fellow that was pilloryed. I have forgot his name', but there were occasions when Swift spoke up for commerce just as ardently as Defoe did, not least for its role in reviving a poverty-stricken Irish economy. He could also be intensely scathing about noble blood, freely confessing how little of it ran in his own bourgeois veins. Swift may have been a Tory, but he was a Tory radical, that oxymoronic animal who has contributed so richly to English culture from William Cobbett to John Ruskin.

In eighteenth-century England, then, the social and ideological battlelines were notably blurred. It was not a Whig merchant, but the classical conservative humanist Henry Fielding, who wrote in his *Voyage to Lisbon* that 'There is nothing so useful and beneficial to man in general than trade'. Defoe may be a progressive and Dissenter, but he outrageously hyped up his own ancestry and snobbishly altered his name from plain Foe to the more aristocratic-sounding De Foe. Men like Swift and Pope saw English society as being in the process of dismissing innate merit and selling out to power and money, both of which were odiously epitomized for them in the figure of the Whig prime minister Robert Walpole. But Defoe could also be stingingly critical of a money-obsessed civilization.

One can see the same crossing of political wires between Henry Fielding and Samuel Richardson. Richardson was the son of a Derbyshire joiner, had only a year or so of secondary education and became a printer, while Fielding was an Etonian with aristocratic connections. Richardson was an aggressive champion of the middle classes, declaring in coat-trailing fashion that tradesmen 'are infinitely of more consequence, and deserve more to be encouraged, than any other degree or rank of people'. Yet Richardson was appalled by the number of low-life characters in Fielding's novels, and claimed maliciously that had he not known who Fielding was, he would have thought that he was an ostler. In turn, Fielding criticized Richardson's *Pamela* for encouraging young gentlemen to marry their mothers' chambermaids, and would never have contemplated such a come-down himself. Instead, he married his first wife's maid.

The social situation, then, was remarkably fluid, and something of this ambiguity is captured by *Gulliver's Travels*. Gulliver is well-named, since his gullibility can be his downfall. He can be pathetically eager to identify with the peoples he finds himself among. In Lilliput he is foolishly proud of his title of Nardac, throws himself vigorously into the role of military leader, and hotly rebuts the charge that he has committed fornication with a Lilliputian female. The physical difficulty of copulating with a woman only a few inches high does not seem to occur to him, and he fails to raise this issue in his own defence. By the end of the novel he thinks that he is a Houyhnhnm and is living with horses. Despite the impediment of being English, he is able to pick up foreign languages with remarkable speed, though this is more a plot requirement than a genuine talent. Yet if one side of Gulliver is obsequiously keen to conform to foreign customs, the other side of him is a boneheaded English chauvinist who is complacently blind to his own cultural prejudices. His self-preening account of life back home shocks the horrified king of Brobdingnag into condemning human beings as odious vermin, but Gulliver is too carried away by his own pompous rhetoric to care.

These two aspects of Gulliver are in fact related. The lack of critical reflection which leads him to identify too easily with his own kind also leads him to identify too quickly with midgets and horses. He is either incapable of seeing his own prejudices from the outside, or too fawningly eager to throw them off and take on someone else's. He is either an imperialist or a cultural relativist, and the novel shows up the secret affinity between the two. There is not much difference between uncritically supporting the British crown and uncritically defending the sovereign power of Lilliput. If we should seek to empathize with other cultures, why not seek to do so with our own? If we are to excuse cannibals, why not corporate polluters as well?

If all cultures are in perfectly good working order, then there is nothing to choose between any of them, and no reason to suppose that, say, the Brobdingnagians are in any way superior to the British. In Swift's view, however, they undoubtedly are, as a rural, traditionalist, well-ordered civilization which is concerned more with the practical uses of things than with material luxury or abstract doctrines. In any case, the empathy of someone like Gulliver, who throws himself with such uncritical alacrity into shady set-ups like Lilliput, is hardly worth having. He is an upwardly mobile sycophant, a mercenary and hanger-on who is on hire to flatter any prince on whose realm he is washed ashore, which in turn suggests how little he is anchored in a nourishing tradition and civilization of his own.

Gulliver, then, is always either in over his head or too far out, and behind this lies a real dilemma. In Swift's view, human beings must be able to see themselves from the outside if they are to avoid the sins of vanity and pride. They must be able to objectify their own norms and values, see themselves as others see them, gaze upon their own form of life through the estranging eyes of others. Truth is a matter of proportion and comparison. And this is part of what is under way in *Gulliver's Travels*. The familiar must be made to look alien and monstrous, so that we can see it for what it is; and who better to perform this service for us than aliens and monsters who are nevertheless oddly familiar? The traffic, in fact, is two-way: the Brobdingnagians are appalled to see some of their own qualities mimicked by the diminutive Gulliver. If this is possible, they reflect, then their own nature must be contemptible indeed.

Once they can step outside themselves, men and women will be recalled to the chastening truth that nothing human is absolute. They will experience afresh their own frailty and finitude, the imperfection of their judgement, and the passions which cloud their reasoning. They will recognize how trivial most of their puffed-up projects are in the great scheme of things. Only by acting in this therapeutic awareness can they behave justly and charitably. Swift had good reason to know about prejudice: he was a slanderous, vituperative satirist, a polemicist who could be airily indifferent to the truth, and who defended religious and political intolerance. If Fielding's satire is genial, Swift's can be semi-pathological. He was a misogynist, an authoritarian, a reviler of the common people, a magnificent satirist and a courageous champion of Ireland as colonial underdog.

The problem with cultural prejudice is how you can get outside yourself without losing touch with humanity altogether and falling into madness, misanthropy and despair, as Gulliver ends up by doing. If you press contrasts and comparisons too far, you finish up by tumbling into the abyss of cultural relativism. Trying to see yourself from the outside, through the bemused or aghast eyes of others, is one way of puncturing pride; but it can lead simply to a different variety of it, as Gulliver, convinced that he is a Houyhnhnm, flees from the stink of the human and regards his own wife as a loathsome Yahoo. The other side of treating the alien as familiar is treating the familiar as monstrous.

If you are truly to get outside your own cultural skin you must find a way of doing it, somehow, from the inside. As Bertolt Brecht remarked, only someone inside a situation can judge it, and he's the last person who can judge. You must appreciate that all human cultures are partial, without keeling over into nihilism. Men and women need their ideals, like the placid, rationalist virtues of the Houyhnhnms, if they are to be more than just material beings; but they must not let these ideals terrorize or bedazzle them to the point where they lose touch with their material being altogether, and come to regard themselves with disgust. You must not rest in the body, but you must not repress it either.

The relations between body and spirit are a metaphor for Swift of the relations between being inside a situation and transcending it. The curious point about human beings is that they are bodies but also more than bodies, inside and outside themselves simultaneously. They are animals, but animals capable of reasoning, and so able to stand to some extent outside themselves and their material contexts and reflect critically upon them. Body and spirit are related, but they are not the same thing. When crazed utopianists, crackpot experimenters, obscurantist scholars and zealous Dissenters puff themselves up with windy rhetoric, Swift brutally deflates them to mere bags of skin and bone.

Yet though he clings to the material body as something concrete and certain, Swift is also notoriously disgusted by it. So those who really do see human beings as no more than bodies – mechanical materialists of various stripes – are equally the targets of his satire. We can observe this ambiguous relationship between body and spirit in the first two books of *Gulliver's Travels*, in which the hero encounters first the tiny Lilliputians and then the gigantic Brobdingnagians. With the Lilliputians, who turn out to be as mean and petty in moral character as they are in physical size, the physical and moral are reflections of each other. So we approach the Brobdingnagians expecting a similar sort of matching, only to discover that they are on the whole gentle creatures despite their awesome bulk. In this case, the material is no sure guide to the spiritual. Swift is continually setting such traps for the reader, setting up expectations which he then proceeds to frustrate. As one critic remarks, his relationship with the reader is 'intimate but unfriendly'.[3]

It is not a matter of finding some judicious middle way between body and spirit, but of leashing these contradictions together as best one can. There is no grand theoretical resolution to this dilemma; it can be tackled only in the living. The last thing one could accuse Swift of is balance. Human beings are not just a third term between Yahoo and Houyhnhnm. They are closer to the Yahoos, if only because they are not horses; but 'Yahoo' is also a Houyhnhnm-like way of *seeing* humans. No view of men and women which does not feel the force of this way of seeing can be valid, but this is not to say that it is the whole truth. Equally, the Houyhnhnms represent a largely admirable way of life: they are economic (though not social) egalitarians who run the sort of conservative social order Swift admires. They have no money, which is a point in their favour, lack the desire for power and riches, and hold that virtue is its own reward.

The Houyhnhnms are not particularly passionless, as some have claimed, simply decorously restrained in their passions. If it were not that they had four legs and a tail, they would not be entirely out of place in a Jane Austen drawing-room, taking tea along with Mr. Knightley. But that is the point. The Houyhnhnms are less a human possibility than, as one critic has put it, an insulting impossibility.[4] These equine idealists are really a device for embarrassing us. Ideals simply serve to show us how short we are bound to fall of them. It is in the nature of humanity to be pitched between extremities. Our norm is to be caught between opposed aberrations.

Gulliver's Travels is cunningly constructed to make the reader feel this instability, and to emerge from the book as dizzy and disorientated as its protagonist. Gulliver ends up believing that humans are Yahoos and that he himself is a Houyhnhnm; the Houyhnhnms see Gulliver as a Yahoo; readers smile at Gulliver's delusions, detaching themselves from the hero as he detaches himself from the Yahoos. Readers smile at the preternaturally placid Houyhnhnms as well, but in the uneasy awareness that they, too, are Yahoos from a Houyhnhnm viewpoint. To cap it all, the Yahoos are in some ways actually superior to human beings. They are physically stronger, for instance. And they are natural in the way non-human animals are, whereas we are unnatural to our own nature.

And where, in all this, is the Yahoo known as Swift? He would certainly seem to have dissociated himself from his crazed protagonist, but what does *he* make of the Houyhnhnms? It is not easy to say who is fooling who. With Swift, it is sometimes hard to say exactly who or what is being mocked. The book offers us no consistent perspective. It is in the very nature of a perspective that there should always be another one. At one point, Gulliver wonders whether there may be a race somewhere in the universe who would appear as tiny to the Lilliputians as the Lilliputians do to him. What is the 'correct' size to be, or the 'right' vantage-point to take up? The question of which perspective is the true one is hard to answer in an age which witnessed the invention of the microscope. How far back from or close up to the world do you need to be standing to see it aright? Is what we see down a microscope the truth, or a distortion of the truth?

The fact that sizes and vantage-points are constantly shifting in the book is an implicit critique of a naive belief in objectivity. The eighteenth-century novelists, having established their distance from the world of romance, are for the most part aware that a belief in raw fact is just as much a myth as romance itself. The novel, being the kind of literary form that it is, cannot help reflecting on the vexed relations between report and reality – on the way, for example, that your report or narrative does not merely reflect the real world, but plays an important part in defining it. Gulliver himself is a naive empiricist or believer in brute fact, a viewpoint that goes hand in hand with his 'progressive' interest in technical and mechanical matters. He is a 'new man': hard-headed, pragmatic, smug in his faith in progress, fascinated by chimerical schemes and projects, eager to festoon his text with maps and documents to guarantee its strict veracity.

All this, as we have seen, cries out for a degree of 'decentring'. You must not take your world complacently for granted in this way. Gulliver's uncritical cult of fact goes hand in hand with his political chauvinism. Instead, you must be able to step outside yourself if you are to be properly yourself. Being more or other than you are at any given moment is actually part of what you are. The subject has to be able to objectify itself in order to be truly a subject. But the risk is one of decentring yourself to the point of disorientation, becoming dangerously eccentric to yourself. And this is how Gulliver ends up. Swift does not hand us a solution to this dilemma. Instead, he disappears from sight and allows his readers to cope with these contradictions as best they can. It is in the nature of his satire not to propose a positive solution – partly because English gentlemen do not need to engage in anything as vulgarly petty-bourgeois as spelling out the truth in laborious detail, partly because this would simply offer yet another partial perspective.

In practice, truth becomes a question of irony, since this is what humanity is as well. It can only emerge negatively, obliquely, from a constant play and mutual cancellation of positions. Swift believed steadfastly in Truth and Reason; but they were not, alas, for us. For he also lived in an increasingly pragmatic age where all you really had to go on was the evidence of your senses. And this meant that Truth and Reason were not really within our power. 'Reason itself is true and just', he wrote in a sermon on the Trinity, 'but the reason of every particular man is weak and wavering, perpetually swayed and turned by his interests, passions and vices'. Like Defoe, then, he believed in a realm of absolute values which intersected less and less with the real world. The Houyhnhnms, perhaps, are an example of this. Even if they are right, they are irrelevant. Both Swift and Defoe are writing in a society which believes in truth, reason and justice in theory, but whose routine conduct has become so false, unjust and irrational that it can no longer credit them in practice.

There is an interesting ambiguity in Swift's presentation of the bestial, shit-smeared Yahoos. Are they meant to be an image of humanity in general, or of 'primitive' peoples in particular? There is evidence, for example, to suggest that the Anglo-Irish Swift saw the colonized people of Ireland as Yahoos. The Yahoos reflect among other things an Anglo-Irish fear and hatred of those they oppress. 'Yahoo', then, may mean all people or just some people, just as it may signify a human condition but also a way of perceiving that condition. And this leads to some interesting political ambiguities. If 'primitive' peoples like the Irish or South Sea islanders really are Yahoos, then this would seem to justify a smack of firm colonial government. But if Yahoos are humanity at large, then the colonial governors are (metaphorically speaking) bestial and shit-smeared too, which undercuts their right to rule. Colonialism then becomes a matter of a bunch of hypocritical savages lording it over a bunch of non-hypocritical ones. On this theory, the masters are as worthless as the natives – an opinion which, as in Conrad's *Heart of Darkness*, undermines colonialism (what right have they then to rule?) but also confirms some of its prejudices (the natives really are worthless).

This ambiguity reflects something of Swift's own double-edged relations to colonialism. As a member of the Anglo-Irish Ascendancy, he was, so to speak, colonized and colonialist at the same time. He was in the ironic position of belonging to a sidelined governing class – a body of Anglo-Irishmen who ruled over the common people of Ireland, but who felt shabbily treated by the British on whose behalf they governed. Swift played a key role in the British colonial state: at one stage he was the Tories' chief propagandist, and helped to draft the monarch's speeches to parliament. But there were also certain questions on which he spoke up eloquently for the Irish people against their British overlords. He was caught between the coffee houses of Westminster and the starving weavers on his Dublin door-step, rather as Gulliver is caught between Houyhnhnms and Yahoos. If he did not consider himself an Irishman / Yahoo, the British / Houyhnhnms sometimes did.

Swift the Yahoo can be heard loud and clear at the end of *Gulliver's Travels*, ventriloquized in Gulliver's magnificent tirade against imperialism:

> The colonial adventurers go on shore to rob and plunder; they see an harmless people, are entertained with kindness, they give the country a new name, they take formal possession of it for the king, they set up a rotten plank or a stone for a memorial, they murder two or three dozen of the natives, bring away a couple more by force for a sample, return home, and get their pardon. Here commences a new dominion acquired with a title by *divine right*. Ships are sent with the first opportunity; the natives driven out or destroyed, their princes tortured to discover their gold; a free licence given to all acts of inhumanity and lust; the earth reeking with the blood of its inhabitants: and this execrable crew of butchers employed in so pious an expedition, is a *modern colony* sent to convert and civilize an idolatrous and barbarous people.

If such a passage were to crop up in Defoe, indeed in many an English author, one might anticipate an immediate disclaimer: the British don't do that kind of thing. We are speaking of the Belgians, Spanish, French or Portuguese. Swift does indeed instantly append such a disclaimer, but it is wholly ironic: 'But this description, I confess, doth by no means affect the *British* nation, who may be an example to the whole world for their wisdom, care, and justice in planting colonies; their liberal endowments for the advancement of religion and learning . . .'. It is because Swift is Irish, conscious of the muddle, prejudice, nepotism, brutality and crass inefficiency of the British administration at Dublin Castle, that he is saved from the customary double-think.

Gulliver ends up unhinged by his hatred for his own species, a dreadful warning to his embittered creator of what he himself might turn into. Those who have lost touch with common humanity in their hubris, stepping out-side their situations altogether, end up in lunacy. This, however, is not at all good news for the common people. For in Swift's view this lunacy includes those radical reformers who seek to view their situation as though from the outside in order to change it for the better. These, too, are crazed experi-menters, intoxicated like the scientists of Laputa by their own hare-brained intellectual antics. The condition of the common people can be at best patched up somewhat; to imagine that it could be fundamentally trans-formed is a folly akin to using a quadrant and pair of compasses to measure someone up for clothes, as the Laputian tailor does with Gulliver.

The truly compassionate, in Swift's opinion, are pragmatists like himself who refuse to raise the hopes of the people with some insane idealism or rationalist utopia, since the result will only be to dash their hopes. The world is so wretched and corrupt that it is crying out for redemption, but to attempt to redeem it is simply to compound the problem. If you see people as Yahoos, you will lose all sympathy for them, acknowledge the futility of trying to help them, and retreat in disgust. If you do not see them as Yahoos, you will fly to their aid with some fancy project based on a trust in the innate goodness of humankind, which will probably make their condi-tion worse. Neither case is tolerable; Swift does not offer us any third way.

This, in fact, is part of the point of writing off the Houyhnhnms. The Houyhnhnms may represent an unreachable ideal, and one which may be in some respects flawed. They are hardly anyone's idea of a lively set of drink-ing companions, quite apart from the fact that they would have nowhere to put their beer money. But they also hold to the kind of rational, benevolent, egalitarian politics which for all its limits might well make some difference to a colonial situation. It is possible, however, that the supremely concrete, practically minded Swift finds these stoical rationalists dangerously abstract in their preference for the species over the individual. In his philistine Eng-lish way, the creator of Gulliver detests theories and abstractions; it is much to the credit of the Brobdingnagians that they are incapable of absorbing abstract ideas.

For a stout Tory like Swift, it is not conducive to order and authority for people to think too hard about basic principles. Yet one could always claim that if men had shown rather more of a Houyhnhnm-like care for their species as a whole, there might well have been less warfare and injustice. Abstractions can indeed be a form of violence, as the Laputians show well enough: these self-absorbed scholars may be loftily remote from the real world, but they are quick enough to crush political rebellion. If scholars can be damagingly dissociated from the body, so can militarists. What Swift and his fellow Tories could not grant is that abstractions can also be positive. For women, for example, to be able to conceive of themselves as a group rather than simply as individuals is a necessary step to their emancipation. For Swift, to stand back that far from concrete particulars is to court a kind of madness.

Swift's satirical technique is quite often to play off a powerless ideal against an intolerable reality. The ideal is so distant from reality that it allows us to take the measure of just how desperate things are. But it is also a contrast with its own perfection which helps to make our world look so dire. We need our visions to remind us of how imperfect our actuality is; but if we did not entertain such exacting ideals, we might not find our actuality as insufferable as we do. The ideal is remote enough to show up the gravity of our situation, but for just the same reason it is incapable of repairing it. To avoid being gulled by ideals, we need to cut them satirically down to size. The grandiose dreams of Reason, as we have seen, need to be confronted with the blunt fact of the body, with its unlovely habits and appetites. But this may leave us with such a fearfully hacked-down image of the human that we will need instantly to appeal to Reason to amplify it. Perhaps this constant dialectical see-saw, trimming our sails one way and now another, is the closest we can now come to a life of virtue.

This, in effect, is the trap which *Gulliver's Travels* springs. As with *A Modest Proposal*, the pamphlet in which Swift calmly advocates roasting and eating babies as a solution to Ireland's economic woes, there is no way out of this lethal logic as long as one accepts the terms which it sets up. Perhaps it is only by rejecting the very terms which the work offers us that we can break out of its closed ideological circuit; and perhaps this is part of what Swift's writing is encouraging us to do.

We must acknowledge, against the dewy-eyed utopianists and sentimentalists, that there is a good deal of the Yahoo in the human, and that these are the rocks on which any radical agenda is in danger of coming to grief. But we must also recognize that this is also how the human looks from an impossible Olympian viewpoint, whose final effect will be to plunge us into terror and despair. In the end, what horses think of us is neither here nor there – except, perhaps, for the Anglo-Irish Ascendancy, who sometimes seemed to love a horse more than they loved one other, and certainly more than they loved the common people.

HENRY FIELDING
AND SAMUEL
RICHARDSON

Whenever a new literary form appears on the scene, there are two main ways in which it can try to legitimate itself. Either it can point to its very newness as the source of its value, or it can appeal to tradition. It can claim excitedly that the world has not seen the likes of it before; or it can define what it is doing as a variation on already well-established procedures, thus hijacking some of the authority of the past for its own purposes. In the case of the novel, the very name of the genre suggests that it is its newness which is its most striking feature. Samuel Richardson is proudly conscious that he has invented a new species of writing – one which, as he remarks in his preface to *Clarissa*, is 'to the moment', recording experience as it actually happens like a news photographer's camera.

In Book 2 of *Tom Jones*, Henry Fielding likewise describes himself as 'the founder of a new province of writing', and goes on to point out with mock self-satisfaction what freedom this confers on him: 'so I am at liberty to make what laws I please therein'. The image is a political one, resonant of Crusoe on his island. Fielding is the governor of a newly established domain, and as a kind of absolutist monarch can make up the rules as he goes along. He is, to be sure, a benevolent sort of dictator: he will, so he promises us in *Tom Jones*, mercifully spare his subjects / readers the more tedious bits of his narrative by the elementary device of missing them out. Those readers who skip the boring bits of novels will get on famously with Fielding, since he saves them the trouble by doing it for them. Yet though he is paternally concerned about the welfare of his subject-readers, frequently arresting the narrative of his novels to check out how they are doing, he remains firmly, if good-humouredly, in control.

There is a cavalier touch about this. A gentleman is not to be confined by his own narrative, to which he should adopt something of the lordly air he assumes with police officers and land surveyors. Nor should he feel hampered by the bureaucratic regulations of others. If he obeys the laws, it is because he makes them himself. As a magistrate, indeed as the effective co-founder of the Metropolitan police force, Fielding was a dispenser of the law rather than a subject of it. Even so, it is not really true that he is at liberty as a writer to make up whatever laws please him, since unlike Samuel Richardson he is a Tory gentleman with traditionalist values and aristocratic connections. And this means that he is suspicious of individual innovation and experiment. What matters to him is tradition, classical precedent, and the collective, workaday wisdom of humankind.

It is these which are the true authors of human artefacts, whether they are laws, novels or political constitutions. For conservative Christian humanists like Fielding, Pope, Swift and Samuel Johnson, it stands to reason that what countless individuals have seen fit to believe and practise down the ages has more authority than an idea which some bright spark has dreamt up overnight. The modern must be a variation on the past, not a rupture with it. What we do is warranted in so far as it is, roughly speaking, in line with what our ancestors did. Change must only occur when it is unavoidable. In itself, as Samuel Johnson remarked, change is a great evil.

So it is that when Fielding comes to describe what he is up to in writing a work such as *Joseph Andrews*, he reaches almost instinctively for the categories of classical literature – though he then has to juggle with them a little awkwardly to capture the sense of what he is about. His novel, he announces in a famously overpacked phrase in its preface, is a comic romance – which is to say, 'a comic epic poem in prose'. All of which sounds like too much definition rather than too little, not to speak of sounding rather like a series of contradictions. It is clear that however this novel is to be described, it is certainly not as a novel.

Such a piece of writing, Fielding comments, differs from 'serious romance' in introducing 'persons of inferior rank, and consequently of inferior manners'. Literary categories, as often, are caught up with social ones. The novel, as we have seen, is in general more rooted in the life of the common people than more venerable genres; but it is interesting that Fielding should appeal to those classical genres to legitimate his introduction of low-life figures. The low social tone of the novel must be seen as in line with tradition, not as a transgression of it. It harks back to ancient comedy, which deals in the ridiculous and socially inferior.

There are several ways in which Fielding's classical leanings conspire with his view of the modern world. He calls *Joseph Andrews* an epic, which is the most public of literary forms. The epic is concerned with the world of action, rather than with individual psychology or personal relationships. Its focus is external rather than internal, objective rather than subjective. It does not attend to a single human figure but to a whole array of them, all set in a richly specified social context. And it judges them by and large by what they do, not by what they feel or believe. Fielding is likewise not much interested in complexities of feeling, and his characters are not meant to disclose a convincing inner life. Instead, they speak often enough in florid literary cliches or set-pieces. The emotional artifice of his prose is very striking. As such, the epic, indeed classical writing in general, acts for writers like Fielding as a valuable antidote to the subjectivism and individualism of the age. It treats individual character as a function of the overall plot, not as an entity in itself. Character, as for Aristotle, is only important as a way of promoting the plot; it is not a value in itself. Aristotle even considered that you could do without it altogether.

The epic does not centre the whole world on a single isolated consciousness, as Richardson's fiction tends to do. This, in Fielding's view, is as indecorous and morally offensive as trying to centre the conversation on yourself. People with a sense of propriety do not pick over their private feelings in public. They leave that to ranting Methodists and luridly confessional maidservants. The conservative will tend to see particular men and women as deriving their merit and identity from a larger pattern, and subordinating character to plot is a metaphor for this. Focusing on a single character also prevents you from uncovering the truth, since truth for Fielding is a result of rational, objective, comparative judgement. It is a public affair, not a question of private sentiment. It is out in the open, not secreted in the depths of the human subject. If the truth is obscured by sentimentalism or errant subjectivism – if there are as many truths as there are individuals – then there is no firm basis for right conduct, and the political state is accordingly in danger.

The novel as a form, as we have seen, was associated at the time with just such subjectivism and sentimentalism. It was full of fervid fantasies and indecently unconstrained passions. Morally speaking, it mixed together good and bad, with scant regard for the absolute distinction between them. What made all this worse was that the novel was also a *popular* form, avidly consumed by the lower orders. It was the kind of thing your valet or chambermaid was likely to read. These men and women, lacking the benefit of a classical education, were therefore thought to lack the benefit of restraint and judiciousness, and thus to be more susceptible to trashy sensationalism. A classical education was also a moral one, fit for building character and producing the administrators of empire. These men had studied the classics at school and university, and thus were deemed well-equipped for, say, bloodily suppressing those in India or the Caribbean who posed a threat to British imperial interests. Classics made a man out of you, whereas the novel had a distressing knack of turning men into old women.

Besides, a classical education gave you a sound grasp of the few central, enduring truths of human nature, an entity which was considered to be unchanging from Catullus to Clive of India, and which it required no specialized learning to understand. Hence the long-standing English antipathy to psychology, sociology, political science and the like, none of which was really necessary for a gentleman who had read his Aeschylus. Hence, too, the ingrained English cult of amateurism. All of this is reflected in the popularity of the novel in England – for the novel is itself a kind of 'amateur' human wisdom, which requires no technical knowledge on the part of either author or reader. Its moral insights are the fruit of shrewdness, sensitivity and worldly experience, not of an intensive course of psychoanalysis or a degree in the social sciences.

What Henry Fielding meant by 'nature' was exactly this sense of the few vital, unchanging elements which all men and women shared in common. It was this which it was the business of the novel to represent. Non-classical, non-conservative writers like Defoe and Richardson would by no means have entirely demurred; but they were also gripped by the uniqueness and complexity of the individual life, which interested authors like Fielding, Swift, Pope and Johnson fairly little. As post-Romantics ourselves, the products (whether we are aware of it or not) of a rich heritage of individualist thought, it is hard for us to recreate the mind-set of men like Fielding and Johnson, for whom what people had in common was a matter of intense fascination, while their individual differences were fairly trifling and not worthy of sustained attention.

On the whole, then, the neo-classical imagination is fired by the universal and damped down by difference. It is about as far from the postmodern imagination as one could imagine. The distinction between classical and non-classical is in no sense absolute: Tom Jones, for instance, is a credible, indeed all too credible human being, and Samuel Richardson had a steady eye on the exemplary status of women like Clarissa and men like Sir Charles Grandison. In general, however, the Tory traditionalists are enthused by what men and women have in common, whereas the Whiggish progressives are excited by the feel of a specific human personality. They are drawn to particular detail, whereas Fielding has in his sights a general type. This is one reason why he can skip bits of the narrative with no great loss, since realism in his view is not a matter of naturalistic detail. Those flat-footed narrators who insist on cramming their accounts with minute details even when nothing very remarkable is happening are compared in *Tom Jones* to stagecoaches which are obliged to complete their journey whether they are empty or full.

For modern taste, it is naturalistic detail which is 'realist' and typicality which is not. But this is not how it seemed to Henry Fielding. Realism for him meant being true to what was typical about human beings, not to what was peculiar about them. 'I describe', he writes, 'not men but manners, not an individual but a species'. When he assures the reader of *Joseph Andrews* that 'every thing is copied from the Book of Nature', he means that his story is realistic precisely because it conveys general truths about men and women, which are more weighty and enduring than local ones. What matters, for example, is the fact that someone is a thrifty innkeeper, not that he is a thrifty innkeeper with a squint. Too consuming an interest in such peculiarities is idle and perverse, even though an author may well include them to liven up the text. Fielding does not in fact simply provide us with types: he sometimes makes them splendidly particular as well. Only untutored people, however, are enthralled by marvels and prodigies, by the aberrant and outlandish. It is this which distinguishes Fielding's kind of sensibility from a modern or postmodern one. Virginia Woolf, one suspects, would be fascinated by the squint but only moderately by the profession of its proprietor. Dickens would be interested in both.

The fact that Fielding is interested in the typical does not mean that he is concerned with 'pure essences'. The typical is not necessarily pure. In fact, what is typical of human behaviour for Fielding is its mixture of good and bad. Moral absolutes rarely appear in human form, which in Fielding's eyes is no argument against them. It is just that there is a gap between the sacred and the profane, or the ideal and the actual, which shows up among other things in the morally hybrid nature of most people. If the novel is to be true to Nature, it must capture this composite state; but how then can it not implicitly call into question absolute distinctions between good and evil? How is realism itself not to be immoral? An author who believes in moral absolutes, but who is also a realist, may find the form of his or her writing undercutting its moral values.

The very tones of realism – shrewd, worldly wise, wryly tolerant – are at odds with the high tone of moral absolutism. Fielding is renowned for his broad-mindedness: he can joke about sex as Richardson cannot, and has the kind of 'relish for wholesome bawdy', as Ian Watt puts it, that one associates with the better class of gentlemen's clubs. You cannot be a gentleman and be shocked by sexual banter, since this would suggest that you were unworldly and unsophisticated. But it does not necessarily mean that you keep a string of mistresses either. Fielding did not make the puritan mistake of equating bawdiness with dissoluteness. There is, then, a dilemma: realism as a form can powerfully drive home a moral point, but it can just as easily undo it. How is realism not to sabotage its own moral message? Both Samuel Richardson and Samuel Johnson deeply disliked Fielding's mixing of moral qualities – though Richardson's insufferably upright Sir Charles Grandison is a dreadful warning of the priggishness which results when you fail to do this. As, indeed, is Fielding's own improbably saintly Amelia.

Knowing what is typical of a thing includes a knowledge of how it would typically behave, and this is vital to the question of realism. For realism is a matter of probability, which is another word for typical behaviour. The 'type' or 'essence' of a thing can be thought of as its characteristic range of possibilities, the forms of behaviour which, being the sort of thing it is, we can confidently expect of it. It is not typical of psychopaths to display a burningly sincere regard for other people's feelings, so that to portray one in fiction as doing so would be untypical and hence unrealistic. To know what is typical of things allows you to regulate and predict them, and is thus of value to conservatives preoccupied with law and order. You can reduce the quirky complexities of the world to a diagram of stable identities. Since these identities are fairly static, this, too, goes to confirm a conservative vision. People and things develop, but within fairly strict limits – the limits of their 'type'. Nobody is likely to astonish you by transforming themselves out of all recognition overnight.

This is one source of conservative pessimism, since it means that your capacity for moral improvement is fairly restricted. Some critics believe that Tom Jones gets better as the novel progresses, but the development, if that is what it is, is hardly dramatic. He is still pretty much the same Tom at the end as he was at the beginning, which cannot be claimed quite so confidently of Dickens's Pip or David Copperfield, or George Eliot's Dorothea Brooke. Character in Fielding, as in Jane Austen, is not a process and unfolding. It is a set of fairly predictable dispositions. A Tory like Fielding does not believe that men and women are really fashioners of their own destinies.

What is more important about them is their allotted places in family and society.

What fashions Tom Jones's destiny is not so much Tom himself, as the plot in which he finds himself caught up. And the point of the plot is not so much to land you in a better position than the one you started out in, which is true of some of Defoe's narratives, as to return you to where you properly belong. Your ending is implicit in your beginning. It is true that returning Tom to where he belongs by birthright, which allows him to marry Sophia Western, has the effect of uniting the two greatest landed estates in Somerset. By inventing a genteel pedigree for Tom, the plot manages to unite the two lovers without undermining the social structure, reconciling order and desire. Worldly advancement is not to be despised. But the point is to find where you fit in, not to make a tight-lipped cult of trying to improve yourself.

Fielding's plots are impressively shapely and symmetrical, which is another way in which his classical training interlocks with his conservative standpoint. He believes strongly in the idea of a providential pattern in the world, and plot in the novel is a metaphor for this benign destiny. It is plot which finally brings the virtuous round to a good end and the vicious to a sticky one, ensuring that the innocent get their reward and the guilty their comeuppance. In fact, it has to be the plot which accomplishes these things, since the vicious characters are unlikely to reduce themselves to misery, and it would be unseemly for the virtuous characters to work for their own advancement. How could they do so and still remain virtuous? One of the several aspects of Richardson's fiction which Fielding finds distasteful, and which he sends up in *Shamela*, his hilarious spoof of Richardon's *Pamela*, is the fact that a supposed innocent like Pamela is fairly obviously working for her own elevation, even if only unconsciously. Chastity for Pamela simply means that she will only trade in her virginity to the highest bidder.

Fielding rejects what he sees as the middle-class utilitarian view that virtue will bring you worldly success.[1] Goodness should not be just another form of self-interest. It should be entirely for its own sake. The idea that virtue is the certain road to happiness, he writes in a delightful sentence in *Tom Jones*, is 'a very wholesome and comfortable doctrine, and to which we have but one objection, namely that it is not true'. Virtue, then, has to be its own reward, since it is unlikely to win any other in a society as shabby as this. If *Tom Jones* were real life, Tom would no doubt have ended up hanged and Blifil might have become prime minister. He is certainly unsavoury enough for the job. It is only because they are in a novel that these characters can obtain their just deserts.

One reason why Fielding keeps reminding us that we are reading a novel is to enforce this ironic contrast between what should ideally happen to his characters and what is likely to have happened to them in real life. All the same, if one thinks of realism as a matter of typicality rather than real-life probability, it is more 'realistic' that Tom should end up marrying Sophia than that he should not. For 'typical' here includes a sense of what is *ideally* appropriate – of what is fitting from the viewpoint of providence, not just from the viewpoint of empirical events. What is ultimately real is not those events but a kind of moral paradigm which underlies them; and it is the privilege of the realist novel to show us this paradigm. In the happy ending, the empirical and the paradigmatic, everyday life and an ideal design, come harmoniously together. For once, what ought to happen does happen.

We must not, then, confuse fiction and reality, as novelists like Defoe and Richardson sometimes encourage us to do. This is among other things because they want their accounts to appear realistic, so that they will not be dismissed as the usual novelistic garbage; and since by 'realistic' they mean something like 'true to the minute detail of everyday life', they are concerned to close the gap between life and literature. Fielding, however, is not much interested in this version of realism, and therefore takes fewer pains to make us forget that his stories are invented. He is not, so he tells us in *Tom Jones*, concerned with that which is 'trite, common, or vulgar: such as may happen in every street, or in every house . . .'. To scoff at such realism (or naturalism, as we might more accurately call it), is a social as well as a literary judgement. It is all right for a gentleman to present low-life characters, but an unpardonable sin for a seasoned *raconteur* like Fielding, or indeed for any gentleman around the fire at the club, to bore his audience by not editing his narrative for maximum effect.

By drawing attention to the fictionality of his narratives, Fielding highlights the fact that the real world is a lot less just than the conclusion of his novels would suggest. Yet it is not just a matter of smiling at the ironic discrepancy between the two. For the plot also represents the way things ought to be. Realism, as we have just seen, has an ideal component to it. Plot is a kind of providential redemption of the bunglings and injustices of everyday life. And this ideal is important, since without it we would have no standard against which to assess the shortcomings of that life. Without some sense of justice, we can have no conception of injustice – though the gloomiest situation of all would no doubt be one in which examples of justice could *only* be found in novels. So we cannot abandon our ideals; but for them to be more than romantic day-dreaming or idle utopianism we need to keep a wry eye on the gap between them and the way things actually are. Otherwise, Don Quixote-wise, we shall try to translate our ideals directly into reality, with potentially catastrophic consequences.

There is, then, a tension between the actual events of a Fielding novel, which suggest that the world is a fairly grim place, and the formal organization of those events, which suggests symmetry, poetic justice and harmonious resolution. Fielding is enough of a traditionalist to believe devoutly in these values; but he is also enough of a realist to recognize how widely they are flouted in reality. In this sense, the tension in his work between form and content corresponds to one between the ideal and the actual. This is not so with a writer like Defoe, who does not really shape the content of his work at all. Events just flow haphazardly forward, with no attempt to elicit a design from them. As we have seen, Defoe believes deeply in the existence of such a providential design, but this is more a matter of what he says than what he shows. Whereas in a Fielding novel, something of that design is actually present in the tight economy of the plot.

Fielding's novels are funny, whereas funniness in Defoe is largely unintentional, and in Richardson fairly rare. Once more, Fielding appeals to classical authority for this kind of writing: Homer supposedly wrote a comic epic, now lost, which is sufficient guarantee for Fielding to indulge in a spot of knockabout humour and bedroom farce. Yet comedy is also a matter of his view of contemporary society, not just of his classical tastes. It belongs to his patrician outlook to be genial, amused, a touch laid-back. As a gentleman in real life and an ironically detached narrator in his fiction, he is sufficiently above the fray not to feel ruffled by it. He is presenting a spectacle for our enjoyment and instruction, not a world like Richardson's into which we are emotionally drawn. There is a very English contrast between the sometimes dark or turbulent content and the jocose, equable tone through which it is filtered. Like a lord in his shirt sleeves, Fielding is so much in control that he can afford to relax. The narrator is expansive, unbuttoned and worldly wise, conducting a civilized conversation with the reader about questions of morality, problems of judgement and qualities of manners. That judgement is a difficult affair, worthy of such extended debate, is well illustrated by Squire Allworthy in *Tom Jones*, who for all his grave mien of authority is harsh in his judgements of Tom, Partridge and Black George, blind to the hideousness of Blifil and far too soft on Square and Thwackum.

Because the treatment is for the most part kept external, we are unlikely to feel anguish, horror or deep indignation. We can recognize how morally squalid some people are without losing our cool. Since we are not allowed to forget that we are in a novel, this pushes the action off to the point where we can make reasoned judgements on it, rather than clamber on stage and pitch in. We are detached from viciousness by the playful artistic form, so that it comes to seem less reprehensible. Too close a scrutiny of certain events might undermine the comedy. Even Booth, the blackhearted adulterer of *Amelia*, is finally rescued by the plot. Besides, to view characters from the outside is to see how ridiculously vain and affected they are, and a sense of the ridiculous is not easily reconciled with a sense of moral outrage. Fielding believed that defects such as vanity and affectation were the most common of all human defects – an optimistic view, since they are scarcely the most repugnant of faults, and can respond to the scourge of satirical comedy.

In this concern with common judgement, the novel plays a crucial part in what has been called the eighteenth-century public sphere, in which gentlemen meet on equal terms to carry on an unconstrained dialogue about the public affairs of the day. The aim of this dialogue is impartial judgement; and the way in which Fielding deliberately distances us from the action is meant to serve this end. The reader is the author's interlocutor rather than his consumer. If this public conversation is to be fruitful, there can no pretence that author and reader are not actually there. This is another way in which Fielding's novels call attention to their own fictionality, in contrast to a later realism in which the distinctive voice of the narrator disappears into the work, and the reader is simply ignored. Since reality itself does not have an author or a reader, literary works which suppress these figures seem the most realist. For either figure to appear within the frame of realism is to break its magical spell. It is not until the modernist era that the novel will once again put its own artifice on show, if for rather different reasons from Fielding's.

Fielding's good-naturedness, however, is not only a matter of tone. It is also a whole moral vision, one which reflects a certain genteel way of seeing. Fielding admires the kind of good nature which seems to come spontaneously, as a self-delighting overflow of high spirits. For one thing, this puts some daylight between his own moral viewpoint and that of the middleclass Dissenters, for whom virtue is a matter of hard labour and austere self-discipline. A gentleman, by contrast, does not have to work for his good qualities. Fielding believes in self-discipline, a quality notably lacking in the impetuous Tom Jones; but it should conceal the labour which went into its making, appearing as easy and natural as art. He is enough of a spiritual Cavalier to reject the Roundhead notion that virtue is a grim, strenuous, self-repressive affair. He also finds almost aesthetically distasteful the idea of anxiously monitoring your inner depths for the faintest flicker of depravity. It smacks too much of self-righteousness, puritan cant and tight-lipped authoritarian zeal. He would not have prospered in some regions of the contemporary United States.

Fielding maintains instead that true virtue is something to be relished, rather like a glass of fine port or an excellent roast chicken. It is a matter of benevolent fellow-feeling, and thus has something of the ambience of the gentleman's club. It is part of the patrician ethic to believe that social sympathies are natural to us. You do not inquire why you should act in this benign way, any more than you inquire why you should enjoy a glass of port. Virtue is a matter of warm-heartedness, not of some cerebral duty, though like Tom it needs correcting by prudence and reflection if it is not to be led astray by its own reckless high spirits. Fielding is wryly aware that good-heartedness can get you into trouble just as much as lechery or ambition. Being carried away by your good-heartedness is a generous kind of error, however, and one more easily rectified than doing the right thing in a coldly legalistic spirit. When we behave with true virtue, we act from some impulse deep in our natures. There is a sense in which to live like this is to be most fully ourselves. In such moments we yield to the generous promptings of the heart, rather than dutifully following some ethical rule-book.

'Good-nature', Fielding writes in his *Essay on the Characters of Men*, 'is that benevolent and amiable state of mind which disposes us to feel the misfortunes and enjoy the happiness of others', and this with no self-seeking or functional motive in mind, not from any abstract contemplation of duty, virtue or even religion. This kind of virtue is 'without the allurements or terrors of religion', which would simply involve another kind of self-interest. Instead, benevolence is a sheer disinterested pleasure: 'What can give greater happiness to a good mind', Fielding inquires in his *Covent Garden Journal*, 'than the reflection of having relieved the misery or contributed to the well being of his fellow-creature?'

On this view, we have an innate moral sense which is quite close to the aesthetic one. Virtue, for example, involves imaginative sympathy with others, and so is close to the kind of capacity which distinguishes a novelist. It is also a kind of instinctive tact or feeling for what is right, the equivalent in the ethical realm of 'taste' in the aesthetic one. Like taste, it must be informed and educated: natural vitality is not enough, as coarse rural rednecks like Squire Western and Squire Trulliber well demonstrate. There is a callous, appetitive version of nature, as well as a beneficent one. In the end,

63

however, there is really no substitute for a built-in moral sense. Either you have it or you don't. Tom does and Blifil doesn't.

Yet Fielding does not seem to believe that most, or even many, men and women are good-natured in this fundamental sense. This would be just the kind of sentimentalism he would associate disapprovingly with pulp fiction. From a Christian viewpoint it would also be heretical, since it denies the doctrine of the Fall. 'Natural' would not seem to mean common or average. The normative is not exactly normal. If Fielding is not a Thwackum, the brutal Evangelical of *Tom Jones* who preaches the depravity of human nature, neither is he a Square, the rationalist who smugly overlooks human frailty. On the contrary, he is a hard-headed, worldly wise moralist with no mawkish illusions about humanity. He was, for example, a notably tough magistrate, who believed that all murderers should be hanged and did not consider that hardened criminals were worthy of compassion. To desire to save these 'wolves', he observed, was 'the benevolence of a child or a fool'. In his *Covent Garden Journal* he describes adultery as an 'execrable vice', however lenient his novels may be about sexual misdemeanours. The noble Lord in *Amelia* comes fairly close to being evil. Fielding comments in *Tom Jones* that he has scarcely ever discovered 'liberality of spirit' in the low-born, though the claim is countered in *Joseph Andrews* by the scene in which only the humble postillion boy comes to Joseph's aid when he is assaulted.

The problem is that it is hard for the poor to be virtuous because they are too needy, and it is hard for the rich to be virtuous because they have too many opportunities for vice. Allworthy in *Tom Jones* is unusual in combining goodness with power, a rare enough combination. On the other hand, Fielding remarks in his novel *Jonathan Wild* that while few people have the potential to be perfectly honest, not one in a thousand is capable of being a complete rogue. In the novel itself, most characters act out of self-interest, but none is so utterly ruthless as Wild himself. All men and women are capable of goodness, which rebuts the Calvinistic case that they are all sunk hopelessly in corruption.

It is true that there are genetically villainous types like Blifil who are born plain nasty, and whom no amount of education or social influence will redeem. Tom and Blifil are brought up in exactly the same environment, yet turn out morally speaking to be polar opposites. This is a smack in the face for the progressives who champion nurture over nature. Yet though education can have no effect on the thoroughly vicious, neither can it corrupt the truly righteous. As for those in the middle, it can certainly do some good. Fielding remarks in his novel *Amelia* that 'true goodness is rarely found among men', but this may in part be the effect of evil influences rather than innate qualities. Dr Harrison, a character in the novel, voices this opinion when he observes that 'The nature of man is far from being in itself evil; it abounds with benevolence, charity and pity . . . bad education, bad habits and bad customs debauch our nature, and drive it headlong as it were into vice'.

Reason, Fielding considered, could help hold our passions in check – a view directly opposed to the radical Protestant line that reason is powerless in the face of human depravity, which only divine grace can repair. It is also a view directed against those frigid rationalists who do not have enough passion to need controlling. Fielding does not want to give too much comfort to the progressives by pressing the environmentalist case about human conduct too hard, but he also needs to answer an embarrassing question: if virtue is in some sense natural, how come there are so many rogues around? The idea of corrupting influences can go some way towards an answer; but where do *they* come from? If the answer is 'human nature', then the argument seems to have undermined itself.

That the world is well populated with scoundrels presents a problem for the virtuous. There is a long tradition in the novel of the innocent abroad, the grandfather of them all being Don Quixote. One thinks of Gulliver, Joseph Andrews and Parson Adams, Laurence Sterne's Yorick and Uncle Toby, Samuel Johnson's Rasselas, Richardson's Pamela and Clarissa, Goldsmith's Dr Primrose, Jane Austen's Catherine Morland and Fanny Price, Jane Eyre, Oliver Twist, Dorothea Brooke, Catherine Sloper, Isabel Archer, Milly Theale and Tess Durbeyfield. Some of these, to be sure, are more innocent than others, and other fictional protagonists like Tom Jones are a combination of innocent and *picaro* (the picaresque rogue, like Thackeray's Becky Sharp). Because rogues can be lovable, the line between them and innocents is not always clear.

The problem with the virtue of innocents is that it is actually funny. Even the word 'virtue' itself has a faintly ludicrous Victorian ring to it. Fielding's Shamela speaks of her 'vartue', as though it were some kind of spiritual handbag to which she clings. The innocent are admirable, but there is something callow and credulous about them as well. Fielding's Amelia is shocked by Mrs Atkinson's machinations to win a commission for her husband, but Mrs Atkinson simply calls her a prude. Rogues may be reprehensible, but they are more fun than the god-fearing. The devil, as usual, has all the best tunes. Tom Jones is not exactly a rogue, but we relish his lusty animal spirits and forgive him his imperfections. Even Richardson's rapist Lovelace has his genuinely appealing aspects, and Clarissa cannot help but feel them. A whiff of danger can be an aphrodisiac. There is something mildly unreal about goodness, as well as something distastefully high-minded about the solemn rhetoric in which it is generally wreathed. Virtue gives rise to verbiage, and the understated English do not usually go in for such effusions. The upright are meek, passive, tediously well-behaved creatures. They have the pathos of victims rather than the spiritedness of heroes.

'Wherever virtue is found in any eminent degree', Cervantes writes in *Don Quixote*, 'it is always persecuted'. We feel sorry for the persecuted, of course, but they are not riotously good company. They may have all the merit, but it is rascals who have all the life. It is true that we are more likely to believe this of fictional rascals rather than real-life ones, since the former can do us no harm. You do not find yourself chuckling indulgently over those who have just cleaned out your bank account or broken your nose. Yet it is still a fact that virtue is hard to dramatize in ways that make it attractive. This, no doubt, is a comment less on virtue itself than on a particular modern version of it. A middle-class society which sees virtue in terms of prudence, thrift, chastity, abstinence and self-discipline is clearly going to find something secretly glamorous about sin. Samuel Richardson was alarmed to discover that his villain Lovelace had turned into a kind of Freddy Krueger, with a devoted cult following.

The trouble with holy innocents like Don Quixote, or Parson Adams of *Joseph Andrews*, is that it is not always easy to distinguish their moral innocence from simple ignorance, which is of no particular credit to them. As Quixote shows, a goodness which is simply blind to the world can wreak havoc in it. Goodness is necessarily out of line with a wicked world; but to be too far out of line with the way things are is a kind of madness. True virtue, as Milton maintained, must surely do battle with the world, which requires having knowledge of it. Yet how is innocence to have dealings with a corrupt world and still be innocent? Goodness can only survive in a predatory society if it calculates and looks sharp for itself; but how can it do this and still be spontaneous? It must be slow to impute malign motives to others, yet it is precisely this which lays it open to their nefarious schemes.

The more you are forced to defend your good nature, the less of it you would seem to have. If, like Fielding, you see virtue both as spontaneous and as in fairly short supply in the world, this means that the good will find themselves under constant siege without being furnished with the cunning and vigilance they need to cope with these onslaughts. If true goodness is in short supply, then those who practise it are to be all the more commended;

but for the same reason they cannot help appearing eccentric. Adhering to principles in a culture where most people violate them makes you as disruptive as a motorist who maintains the lowest possible speed on the motorway for hours on end.

Fielding advances his Christian ideals of charity, chastity and non-violence in deadly earnest, but he is bound to be aware that in this sort of society there is something absurd about them as well. Virtue is true in theory but false in practice, since it is generally ineffectual. And this, for anti-theoretical Englishmen like Fielding, Defoe, Swift and Johnson who put great store by practicality, is something of a problem. It is society's fault, not virtue's, that it should seem so ridiculous, but this does not stop you smiling at it. Those who find your virtue amusing are at once disreputable and right. Like the theoretical knowledge which the eighteenth-century novelists for the most part satirized, the claim that you should practise good nature is at once true and pointless. It has the hollowness of statements to which everyone perfunctorily assents, such as the proposition that death comes to us all or that you never know what's round the next corner. In a vicious society, sanctity is bound to appear sanctimonious.

This is why, in a comic double-focusing, Fielding uses morally righteous characters like Joseph, Fanny and Adams to expose the degeneracy of the world, while at the same time sending them up. The ideal and the actual put each other constantly into question. Innocent characters can act as transparent windows on to social life because, being colourless and unworldly, they do not obtrude their egos between the reader and how it is with the world. Like Gulliver, they have a kind of blankness about them, which is as admirable as it is annoying. The good nature of Heartfree in *Jonathan Wild* is ironically described as a weakness, but the irony is double, since in a sense it is. It certainly makes him alarmingly vulnerable to Wild's depredations. Joseph Andrews is ridiculous because chastity in a man seems comic; but the fact that he *is* a man also means that he can be active and powerful in a way that is harder for a woman of the period, and this allows us a rare glimpse of a kind of goodness which is not simply passive and victimized. Neither is Joseph scheming for his own self-advancement, which means that he is the right kind of Pamela.

Much the same is true of Parson Adams, who is in one sense yet another example of the idly theoretical nature of goodness, but who fails impressively to practise the stoical detachment he preaches. As a man who advocates moral indifference yet cannot help getting passionately involved, Adams demonstrates that there can be a constructive as well as hypocritical conflict between what you say and what you do. He is a sententious moralist of the kind Fielding distrusts, but he is also an example of how moral idealism can be a practical, worldly affair. There can, in short, be a worldly kind of unworldliness. You can be worldly in a positive sense, just as you can be unworldly in a negative one, like the misanthropic Man of the Hill.

As with *Tom Jones*, however, it will take the plot to bring the long-suffering trio of Adams, Joseph and Fanny round to a felicitous conclusion. If this is an inspiring image of Providence, it is also testimony to how feeble goodness actually is in this world. Richardson will allow no such consolations at the end of *Clarissa*; in his view, it would not be true to Nature to allow his novel a happy ending. If Fielding's novels show individuals adapting to the social order, *Clarissa* shows one being crucified by it.

The relation between innate goodness and social influences is one aspect of the relation between Nature and nurture. Another is the relation between desire and social class. Fielding recognizes that desire is no respecter of social class, and is thus inherently subversive. When Lady Booby makes erotic advances to Joseph, we are meant to disapprove of this impropriety – a lady should not sexually proposition her servant – but also to smile at it, since it reveals how human nature, class notwithstanding, is everywhere the same. By transgressing social rank so shockingly, Lady Booby reminds us of its importance, but also of its artifice. The incident satirizes and upholds the class system at the same time. We are invited to admire Joseph's refusal of her advances on both moral and social grounds: it goes to confirm his moral worth, at the same time as it underlines his respect for his superiors. Yet we, like the narrator, are also amused by his scandalized reaction to his mistress's flirtations, since knowing more of the world than he does we are aware of how 'natural' this 'unnatural' flouting of social hierarchy actually is. If Lady Booby is satirized, so is Joseph, in a typical piece of Fieldingesque double-focusing.

This ambiguity about the value of social standing is common in the eighteenth-century novel. In his *Essay on Conversation*, Fielding admits that social differences of this kind 'have in a philosophical sense no meaning, yet are perhaps politically essential, and must be preserved by good-breeding'. It is servile to worship riches, and contempt for others on account of rank is vile and base: 'that the fortuitous accident of birth, the acquisition of wealth . . . should inspire men with an insolence that is capable of treating the rest of mankind with disdain is so preposterous that nothing less than daily experience could give it credit'. This is scarcely revolutionary stuff: it belongs to true gentility to despise those who make a fuss of wealth or status. The lowest class morally speaking, Fielding adds, is the beau and fine lady. Even so, 'respect and deference . . . may be paid to the rich and liberal from the necessitous'. He would not wish to withdraw from those with titles 'that deference which the policy of government has assigned it'.

So rank means little or nothing in itself, but is nevertheless to be defended as an 'unavoidable imperfection'. Historically speaking, we have reached the point at which a belief in a common human nature is threatening to undermine the whole basis of social hierarchy. As a result, that system must now be defended less in traditionalist terms, as a divinely ordained order, than in the more pragmatic language of social custom, stability and convenience. It is the kind of objectively dishonest argument which Fielding himself would doubtless have been quick to satirize had the subject not been so close to the bone. By the end of the eighteenth century, the Enlightenment idea of a common human nature, nowadays derided by all devout postmodernists, will wreak havoc with social hierarchy and issue in political revolution. Class is a fiction, which one needs to be suitably ironic about, as Fielding is about his novels. Like the novel, however, it is a necessary fiction, and one's irony should not be allowed to keel over into iconoclasm.

Fielding's fiction, as we have seen, is more about judgement and observation than experience. It does not invite us to identify with its characters, rejoice in their triumphs or suffer alongside them. To use Bertolt Brecht's blunt words to his actors, Fielding is not performing 'for the scum who want the cockles of their hearts warmed'. Samuel Richardson, on the other hand, is much concerned to warm the cockles of our heart, provoke our tears, stir our sympathies and rouse our antagonisms. The reader must be allowed to share the experience of the characters; and this means developing a form of writing so immediate and transparent that it gives us access to that experience as it is actually happening. In *Pamela*, the heroine is scribbling away even as the debauched Mr B. is scrambling after her virginity, a situation wickedly parodied in Fielding's *Shamela*: 'Mrs Jervis and I are just in bed, and the door unlocked; if my master should come – Ods-bobs! I hear him just coming in at the door. You see I write in the present tense, as Parson Williams says. Well, he is in bed between us . . .'.

This is one sense in which realism, pushed to an extreme, capsizes into non-realism. 'On one knee, kneeling with the other, I write!', Lovelace tells us. 'My feet benumbed with midnight wanderings through the heaviest dews that ever fell: my wig and my linen dripping with the hoar frost dissolving on them!' It does not seem to occur to him to stop writing and change his shirt. One suspects that some of Richardson's characters would still be scribbling away as the firing squad raised its rifles. Such immediacy is as much an artifice as those TV stations who announce that they are bringing us the news 'as it happens', but angle and edit it even so. For the neo-classical Fielding, to pivot everything on the present moment in this way is a moral as well as literary mistake. It is to sacrifice context, tradition and comparison to a bogus immediacy, one which abolishes the distance essential for true judgement.

This, then, is Richardson's celebrated writing 'to the moment'; but it might better perhaps be described as a kind of anti-writing. Language must give way to experience itself. Words must have no material texture or density of their own, which might distract us from what they portray. The signifier must melt into one with the signified. There must be no troubling gap between experience and expression, content and form. Fielding's writing, as we have seen, thrives on just such a gap: we are made constantly aware of the ironic discrepancy between the shapeless stuff which is being represented, and how it is shaped by the author's art into significant design.

Richardson, by contrast, wants a kind of pure or 'degree zero' kind of writing, one which will be the medium of unambiguous truth. Language must not interpose its ungainly bulk between the reader and the experience. Yet he is glumly aware that this is an impossible ideal, one which writing itself undoes at every step. For one thing, it is naive to imagine that language simply 'reflects' experience, as Richardson's Lovelace is well aware. What do words like 'maybe' or 'prestigiously' reflect? Language helps to constitute human experience, not just to reflect it. For another thing, writing is bound to be somewhat slippery simply because it has to be interpreted; and this means that for every signifier, there is a whole range of possible signifieds. Nothing could in principle just mean one thing. The reader is not just a passive receptacle of the author's meaning, but an active co-creator of it. And this makes room for all kinds of ambiguities.

Richardson, as a devout puritan who believes in absolute moral values, is forever struggling to control his texts so as to ensure the correct reading of them. He is forever sanitizing and overhauling his works, 'policing' them for the least stain of social infelicity or potential indelicacy. 'Low' terms and mistakes of manners are ruthlessly expunged in the interest of 'polite' letters. This master printer is out to master print, wrenching it into the service of a single meaning. Yet his writing is constantly in danger of exceeding his intentions and generating 'illicit' interpretations which he hastens to disown.

Writing is needed to convey truth and reality to a reader; but it is also a sprawling mesh of dangerously open-ended signs, which threatens to undermine the very truth it conveys. The fact that the villainous Lovelace attracted a sizeable fan club among the novel's readers, while some readers found Clarissa's saintliness unbearably priggish, is a case in point. Alarmed at such perverse misreadings, Richardson adds more writing to what he has written already, in order to insulate his work from all conceivable misconceptions. But the more writing he adds, the more material there is to be misinterpreted.

The problem is exacerbated by Richardson's epistolary form – the fact that his novels are made up in large part of letters from one character to another. This achieves the immediacy he is after, as the letter – that most spontaneous, up-to-the-moment, self-confessional of forms – gives us access to the inner truth of his characters. But to write the novel in this way means abandoning an authorial voice-over – which means that there is no 'meta-narrative' to guide our reading of the mini-narratives of the letters. Much of the time, there is no Fieldingesque narrator to argue, advise, apologize or explain. What we have instead is an incessant circulation of material signs, in which letters come to take on a strange, fetishistic life of their own. These bits of matter seem to be imbued with the living presence of persons, and exert an uncanny power over men and women. In a sense, it is they which are the protagonists of the drama. They are pursued, protected, hidden, kissed, buried, wept over, physically assailed. Richardson is not so much writing texts about a drama, as writing about a drama of texts.

Words, in a sense, are stand-ins for things; and to that extent they can act as fetishes, as the letters in the novel do, since for Freud the fetish is a kind of stand-in which plugs an intolerable lack. Letters substitute themselves for physical presence, plug gaps in physical intercourse, and at times become almost a metaphor for sexual congress. The true fetish of *Clarissa*, however, is the body of Clarissa herself, which represents for Lovelace the unattainable fullness and perfection which might fill in his own terrible lack of being. The two thousand pages of *Clarissa* revolve around an act – the rape – which is never represented there. Lovelace's climax is also the novel's great anti-climax.

Signs, despite Richardson's intentions, do not succeed in nailing down reality. Language is a kind of supplement or addition to reality; yet with the 'non-event' of the rape, it is almost as though the physical is merely a kind of supplement to writing. After being raped, Clarissa more than once refers to her own body as 'nothing'; and though this may well register guilt and self-loathing, it must be taken together with her assertion 'I am nobody's', which rebuffs all patriarchal claims over her person. The violated body of Clarissa slips through the net of writing. The rape, so to speak, is the Real which resists representation. Indeed, one mildly fanciful critic has questioned whether it ever happened at all.[2]

On the one hand, letters are intimate revelations of the private self, torn from the individual's inner depths still dripping with emotion. Letters in Richardson are residues of the body: they come damp with tears, blotted with sweat or creased in haste or rage. Yet they also mark the point at which that private sphere borders on a public regime of power, property and patriarchy. In the letter, intimacy and political intrigue merge into one. It is thus not surprising that letters should become a kind of metaphor of sexuality itself, even if the actual body is necessarily absent from them. Pamela wears her text around her waist, and Mr B. threatens to strip her to discover it; and the libertine Lovelace is a literary *voyeur* who swears that 'I shall never rest until I have discovered where the dear creature puts her letters'. In fact, he will never discover 'where the dear creature puts her letters', never lay bare the sources of her subjectivity.

Letters in Richardson are forged, waylaid, stolen, lost, copied, censored, parodied, misread, submitted to mocking commentary, woven into other texts which alter their meaning, exploited for ends unforeseen by their authors. Writing and reading are always at some level illicit intercourse, since there can always be a fatal slip between intention and interpretation, production and reception. Letters are what lay the private, unprotected self open to the manipulations of a hostile world. Which is to say, by and large, the private domain of women to the public realm of men.

Ironically, however, Clarissa's kind of writing might today be seen as 'masculine', while it is Lovelace's which is stereotypically 'feminine'. Lovelace's language is playful, ambiguous and self-delighting, full of self-indulgent fiction and fantasy. For him, language is as compulsive and inexhaustible as desire: we are told that he 'has always a pen in his fingers when he retires', and the erotic *double entendre* is surely deliberate. This novel's unconscious is not coyly concealed but brazenly out in the open. For a man, Lovelace spends far too much time writing, rather as he might spend too much time shaving his legs. Like Laurence Sterne's Tristram Shandy, writing and living are for him almost synonymous. 'I must write on, and cannot help it', he observes. He is a kind of eighteenth-century post-structuralist, a Roland Barthes in knee-breeches who is obsessed with the act of writing, and who uses language strategically rather than truthfully.

Writing for Lovelace is a form of power as well as desire, a set of artful devices by which he hopes to ensnare Clarissa. He can unfix a sign as deftly as he can break a hymen.

Clarissa, by contrast, believes that language should be a transparent medium of the truth. The chaste woman rejects the promiscuous play of the signifier for a unity of signifier and signified, in which words say just what you mean them to say and no more. Behind the unified sign lies the unified self, one which must always be in control of its own meanings. Lovelace rejoices in the way his writing takes him over. His self is as protean and diffuse as his language. As a devout middle-class puritan, Clarissa believes in a sober, stable regime of sense, not in the licentiousness and instability of the wicked aristocrat. Even she, however, feels the lure of desire: she is forced at times to confess that writing for her, too, is obsessive and excessive. For Clarissa, language or writing are valid only as vessels of truth; they are not to be shamelessly indulged in for their own sake. We have encountered this already in Defoe: just as sexuality should be a form of reproduction rather than self-pleasuring, so writing should be a form of representation rather than a revelling in the signifier.

Yet this is a strange doctrine for a man who earns his living through spinning those baseless fantasies known as novels. Lovelace is no doubt among other things the product of Richardson's own writerly guilt. He represents the pleasurable self-indulgence which you are forced to sacrifice in the name of truth and justice; and these delights are made alluring in Lovelace in order to show that rejecting them really is a sacrifice. Richardson is that most virtuous of puritans, one who has a lively appreciation of vice. He could not have created Lovelace otherwise. Simply to be able to think Lovelace's thoughts, however censoriously, puts Richardson beyond the decorous limits of Clarissa, who could do no such thing.

Even so, it is testimony to the importance of truth and justice that one must write off the enticements of writerly pleasure, even if the result is an unavoidable sense of dullness. 'I laboured hard to rein in my invention', Richardson comments of *Pamela, Part II*, an odd remark for an imaginative writer. All one can add, reading this drearily moralistic work, is that he certainly succeeded. It is as though a chef were to boast that he had gone to heroic lengths to make his soup taste insipid. Yet how can a man who turns out *Clarissa*, a novel of almost one million words and by far the longest in English literature, be said to be moderate and judicious? Lovelace has been estimated to have written some 14,000 words in a single day, which would hardly have left him much time for erotic adventures. The very insistence and excess with which Richardson advocates the sober, temperate middle-class virtues threatens to undercut them.

Just as Lovelace's exuberant, mercurial language is a threat to Clarissa's integrity, so in a different way is her own devotion to truth. How is a woman to be true to her feelings without falling prey to exploitation? How can you tell the truth in a society as vicious as this without it being used to destroy you? For Richardson, as for Jane Austen later, it is a question of balancing candour and truthfulness with reticence and decorum. Reticence and decorum are natural to virtue, but they can always be travestied as haughtiness and prudery. Perhaps social life demands a certain amount of duplicity – but how is this to be distinguished from the frigid artifice of aristocratic culture?

There is also a problem of drawing a line between a lack of candour which is socially and morally necessary, and the artfulness of a Pamela. It is not true that Pamela is, in Mr B.'s words, a 'saucebox' and a 'hypocrite', but neither is it true that her thoughts are innocent. The fact that an unprotected maidservant needs to keep a wary eye on her virginity makes such innocence impossible. Pamela does indeed make a fetish of her chastity, but it is the culture of patriarchy which is ultimately responsible for this. She is forced to treat herself as a sexual object in order to avoid being treated as one by others. She is 'pert' and devious, with a quick strategic eye to her own interests; but her 'sauce' and impudence are among other things a spirited defiance of upper-class authority. We are allowed to see that Pamela may well be 'unconsciously scheming', as William Empson put it,[3] but that she also needs to look sharp for herself. Besides, in a striking innovation, the lively, racy language in which she expresses herself is the speech of the common people, placed here at the centre of 'polite letters' almost for the first time. We have heard something of this idiom in Defoe, but with much less spice and texture.

This, however, is only one of the languages of *Pamela*. The other is a colourless, sententious kind of discourse, which is hard to reconcile with the language of spontaneous feeling. Pamela is sometimes made to speak as no actual maidservant would, which is one indication that Richardson's writing is not full-blown realism. A polite, formal language is at work trying to 'normalize' and regulate the salty colloquialisms of common speech; but the two idioms do not yet sit comfortably together, as they will by the time of George Eliot. The racy, rebellious, Pamela-like side of Richardson is not quite at one with Richardson the middle-class moralist, any more than the speech of Lovelace is at one with that of Clarissa.

To write a novel, you need both Lovelace and Clarissa: both spirit and order, imagination and control. But they are not easy to reconcile, not least when your ideas of order and control are too rigorous. In both of Richardson's major novels, order and control win out over licence and excess; but the paradox of *Clarissa* is that they do so in ways which demand an extraordinary imaginative licence on the part of the novel itself. In *Pamela*, we are witnesses to the gradual incorporation of popular experience into the domain of high literature. But by the end of the novel, its strains of farce, festivity and sheer cheek have been more or less neutralized by polite society. Pamela herself is elevated into the gentry, to become a docile housewife mouthing moral platitudes, and her language sinks beneath Richardson's own. The lower middle classes have suppressed their social resentment and made their peace with their superiors.

There is another reason, however, why these novels are not like *Pride and Prejudice* or *Washington Square*. Realism in Richardson's work co-exists with fable, fairy tale, allegory, polemic, propaganda, moral homily, spiritual autobiography. Nobody capable of perpetrating *Pamela, Part II* can possibly have thought of his art along the realist lines of a Jane Austen. The fact that these various literary forms are not tightly unified is neither here nor there; the very idea of a tighly unified text belongs to a later phase of the novel. Richardson is not in the business of producing seamless works of art; on the contrary, his novels are best thought of as *kits*, great unwieldy containers crammed with spare parts and agreeable extras, which come complete with detachable appendices, addenda, 'restorations', revised passages and moralistic tables of contents. They are the work of a superb literary artist who would have found the whole concept of literary art strange and rather suspect.

Richardson is writing among other things as a champion of an aggressively emerging Protestant middle class; and this means that his writing is necessarily didactic. It cannot afford to conceal its moral values altogether beneath a cloak of realism. Those who disapprove of art which openly seeks to influence its audience – which is to say, almost all literary critics nowadays – are usually those whose own values have been widely accepted and need no noisy promoting. Such critics find 'preaching' distasteful, yet value the sermon as a literary form. As a good Protestant, Richardson saw nothing wrong with preaching. It was only when the middle-class values he promoted became more widespread that the novel was able to stop being explicitly moralistic, and could crystallize into its modern non-didactic form. Before then, however, there was a vital job to be done in campaigning for those militant middle-class values – and this meant challenging the profligate aristocracy, singing the praises of peace, sobriety, hard work and connubial love, and elevating the individual to highly privileged status. In these and other ways, Richardson was a true spiritual son of the greatest of all English literary puritans, John Milton.

All this might equally be described as a feminizing of values. The aristocracy's macho obsession with honour and military heroism was to give way to the meek, modest, pacific virtues. Dominance and arrogance would yield to civility and sensibility. Pity, pathos and benevolence were becoming more fashionable than the brawling and duelling of rough-neck noblemen. The middle classes, with the bloody sectarian conflict of the previous century still fresh in their memory, desired nothing more than a stable, peaceable environment in which to pursue their unheroic purpose of making as much money as they possibly could. Richardson's novels did not just reflect this ideological campaign; they were crucial weapons in it. His works helped to reform morals and manners, and to forge a cultural identity for the middle class.

To measure the astonishing social impact of these novels, we would have to compare them to the most popular films or TV soap operas of our time. The modern equivalent of Pamela or Clarissa would not be Mrs Dalloway but Harry Potter. Richardson's characters became public property and household names, swooned over, reviled, dramatized, pirated, turned into bawdy rhymes, quoted in the salons and solemnly commended from the pulpit. Like the Harry Potter phenomenon, they were multi-media affairs, converted into plays, operas, spoofs, waxworks, domestic commodities. Like all mythical figures, Pamela and Clarissa occupied some shadowy borderland between fiction and reality, at once more and less real than the world around them.

In fact, the mythical or fairy-tale qualities of these intricately realist novels are fairly obvious. *Pamela* is a Cinderella-like wish-fulfilment in which abduction and imprisonment turn out miraculously well, the rough beast becomes a Prince Charming, and the poor kitchen maid a beautiful princess. As in a cartoon there are horrendous dangers, but the heroine turns out to be gratifyingly unkillable. The novel ends up as a sickly celebration of male power, as its heroine is married off and brought to heel; but it has a utopian dimension as well, in the belief that the most inconspicuous serving maid can be as valuable as her superiors. Like Fielding, Richardson has to square the need for social hierarchy with what seems its pointless artifice. (His egalitarianism had its limits, however: the cast list of his novel *Sir Charles Grandison* is divided into 'Men, Women, and Italians').

Pamela, then, turns the ugly battles of class and gender into a comedy. In allowing Pamela her victory, the novel reflects the growing confidence of the socially aspiring groups who are dear to its author's heart. Richardson himself rose from being a lowly printer's apprentice to becoming a revered name in the ears of Goethe, Rousseau and Napoleon, and did so partly by writing about a domestic servant who becomes a fine lady. But scarcely had he concluded this pact with the rich and powerful than he tore it apart in *Clarissa*. Myth and folk-tale lurk within *Clarissa* too, as the story of a persecuted maiden; but it is also one of the rare English novels to be published before the end of the nineteenth century which is a full-blooded tragedy.

No less than one third of the work is devoted to Clarissa's death, a fact which prompted even the admiring Samuel Johnson to remark that the heroine was 'an unconscionable time a-dying'. But that is the point. In its unflinching realism, the novel spares us none of the torment of its violated, victimized protagonist – and, more to the point, spares her violators none of it either. Clarissa does not crawl away to die in a corner; instead, she *performs* her death, turning her body into a symbol and her dying into public theatre. If there is masochism and morbidity in this act, there is also a kind of martyrdom. If it is realist in its detail, it is superbly, defiantly implausible as a whole.

Clarissa represents an astonishing act of rebellion against the whole social system – patriarchy, upper-class licence, middle-class individualism – on the part of a solitary young woman whom that system has hounded to death. The critic Ian Watt comments that Clarissa 'dies rather than recognise the flesh',[4] but the truth is that she dies because she recognizes it only too well. What makes this act of absolute refusal even more potent is the fact that the woman who performs it is no revolutionary but a dutiful servant of the culture which destroys her. Deliberately withdrawing her body from circulation, Clarissa succeeds, Samson-like, in confounding her enemies, bringing them low by her own self-immolation. She is a forerunner of those Henry James heroines who vanquish by turning their faces to the wall. Closing his ears to the clamours of those readers who begged him to let his heroine live, Richardson knew that realism demanded that she die. Only in such a death could the truth of this exploitative social order be put on public view.

It is a truth which even goes beyond the opinions of the book's author. Richardson believed that 'men and women are brothers and sisters; they are not of different species'. Most of his closest critics and collaborators were women. He held that marriage should mean companionship rather than female slavery, and that women should be educated. On the other hand, he thought them good for nothing if they neglected their domestic duties, and denied that they should be independent of their husbands. As often happens with writers, the imaginative truth of his novel exceeded his own real-life beliefs. Many critics have responded to his heroine by defaming her. Clarissa has been pilloried as morbid, naive, narcissistic, self-pitying, self-deluded, masochistic and – from a woman critic – 'a ripe temptation to violence',[5] meaning that she deserves what she gets. Richardson himself has been just as roughly handled. 'His mind is so very vile a mind', wrote Coleridge, 'so oozy, so hypocritical, praise-mad, canting, envious, concupiscent'.

Clarissa is indeed a flawed character, prone to self-deception and moral self-admiration. 'So desirous to be considered an *example!*', as she herself mocks her own moral vanity. She can be irritatingly inflexible and exasperatingly perverse. Yet perhaps what some critics cannot really stomach is the fact that Richardson seems here to have pulled off the impossible, creating a character who is at once deeply virtuous and grippingly real. If she had understood herself better, and if Lovelace had not been so deeply in the grip of a false ideology, it is possible that they could have enjoyed a genuine relationship. Yet if the novel is a tragedy, it is because it is concerned not simply with the fate of a single couple, but with the nature of relationships in a false society. And that makes it more realist, not less.

LAURENCE STERNE

Samuel Richardson detested Laurence Sterne's novel *The Life and Opinions of Tristram Shandy, Gentleman*, complaining to a correspondent of its 'unaccountable wildness; whimsical digressions; comical incoherencies; uncommon indecencies . . .'. Here, as often, literary impropriety and moral dissoluteness go hand in hand. Bad literary manners mean dubious morals. To write in a certain way is to uphold or violate moral values – not just by what you say, but by how decorously or digressively, soberly or fantastically, you say it. Thomas Jefferson disagreed with Richardson, finding in Sterne's writings 'the best course of morality that ever was written'. The philosopher David Hume thought *Tristram Shandy* the best book written by an Englishman for the past 30 years, though he rather spoiled the compliment by adding 'bad as it is'.

One can see how the pious Richardson would not have been greatly charmed by a novel whose hero is almost castrated by a falling window in the act of urinating out of it. The fact that it is also the work of a clergyman would not have helped. But there was no doubt another reason for his discomfort. Sterne's *Tristram Shandy* can be seen as a monstrous parody of Richardon's 'writing to the moment' – a taste of the chaos and madness which result if you press that technique too far. Tristram, Sterne's (anti-) hero, is not exactly writing to the moment in the manner of Pamela or Clarissa. In their narratives, the time of writing, and the time written about, are identical; whereas one of Tristram's problems is to keep the time of his writing, the time written about, and the time of the reader, in some sort of equilibrium. Like Richardson, however, he is concerned (or pretends he is) that writing should be true to experience – that language should not be allowed to stand between the reader and the whole truth. For Tristram to write this autobiography, then, involves not cheating on the reader by leaving anything out. The result is that he starts his life-story not from birth, but from the moment of conception, and gives us so much detailed information that he never gets beyond being a small child.

There are, in other words, so many facts to be recorded and by-ways to be explored that the narrative can hardly stagger forward. Tristram is forever having to shift from one time-stream to another, double back to clarify a point, or hold up one part of the action while he gets on with another. Since characters experience the same events in different ways, each has his or her own psychological time-stream, and the narrator has to nip from one to the other as best he can. He must also keep an eye on his readers' time-streams, urging them on or slowing them down. The more he tries to forge a totality from his life, the more it comes apart in his hands. Indeed, at one point he helpfully provides us with a visual image of the (non)-progress of his story, in the form of a wiggly line. The book begins before the beginning and ends before the end. It ends six years after it was begun as far as the author's time-stream goes, but four years before the birth of its hero. In the end, we get neither Tristram's life nor his opinions.

Since everything in the world is complicatedly bound up with everything else, the narrator cannot say one thing without saying six others simultaneously, and so finds himself forever digressing. Digressing, however, is an odd word to use of his narrative, since there is really no norm or measure which he can digress from. The whole tale is one massive irrelevancy – a jest, a sport, a gratuitous act, a 'COCK and a BULL' story as Yorick comments in the novel's closing sentence. Knowing Sterne's addiction to ambiguity, we can be sure that the cock in question is not just a farm-yard animal. Because Tristram's own life is so closely meshed with the lives of those around him, we end up knowing a lot about them and very little about him. Since the human subject is an effect of the Other, Tristram must describe these others in order to get round to himself, which is why he never quite does. After two volumes of the book, he has still not got himself born. After nine volumes, we do not even know what he looks like. In writing forward into a future, he finds himself being dragged backwards into the past. The novel is about the attempt to get the novel started.

In order to tell your life-story fully, Tristram is gloomily aware, you would really have to stop living while you were writing it. Tristram lives faster than he can write, so he can never catch up with himself. Writing and living can never quite coincide. The more you write, the more you will have to write, since the more you will have lived in the meantime. You would also have to include the act of writing your life-history *in* your life-history – not least in Tristram's case, since writing is what he mostly does. Then you would need to include in your story the act of including the act of writing your story in your story. And so on *ad infinitum*. Sterne has realized that autobiography is an impossible form – and this, as we shall see later, for more reasons than one.

No sooner has the novel emerged in England, then, than it is deconstructed by this monstrous anti-novel. Sterne has spotted the fact that realism is ultimately impossible, because one representation leads to another, and that to another, until you are plunged into utter confusion. Every narrative must be selective – but then how can it be true to life? You cannot tell the truth, and shape the truth, at the same time. He has also spotted the fact there are really no rules to novel-writing. Echoing Henry Fielding, Tristram announces that 'I shall confine myself . . . to no man's rules that ever lived'. We are dealing with an inherently anarchic genre, in which – like living itself – you make it up as you go along. If Sterne's novel seems an astonishingly modernist work, it is partly because it comes at a time when the novel itself is still at a probationary stage, fluid and provisional in its procedures.

Tristram Shandy may seem like a comic aberration in the history of the novel, but what makes it aberrant – the fact that it flouts all the rules – is also what makes it so characteristic of the form as a whole. It is this which led a Russian critic to declare provocatively that it was the most typical novel of world literature.[1] In its very deviancy, it reveals the truth of the novel in general. It is the work which gives the game away, lets the cat out of the bag, unmasks the awful secret that the novelist is pretending to be faithful to the real world but can in fact do whatever takes his or her fancy.

Biography and autobiography might seem at first sight particularly resistant to set techniques. Since every human life is unique, how could there be established procedures for writing an account of one? In fact, there are set procedures in plenty. Biography and autobiography are among the most convention-governed of genres. And this is because no life is actually unique. Because we all belong to the same animal species, there are certain stages through which we all have to travel. Everyone has to have parents, be born, reared, educated, and launch out eventually on their own independent existence. The biographical form is highly predictable, simply because human biology is as well. It is biology which lies at the root of biography.

The fact that we get to know so little of Tristram as a person in five hundred-odd pages is indirect testimony to this truth. There is a hole at the centre of the text, and its name is Tristram Shandy. It is, in a sense, a work about nothing; indeed Sterne himself put in a good word for nothingness elsewhere in his writing – considering, he remarked, what worse things there were in the world. In a way, the protagonist is absent from himself, and this simply writes large how it is with all human subjects. This is not a novel centred like *Clarissa* on an all-privileged individual, but a satirical 'decentring' of the individual into the material forces which go into its making. It is a work about obstetrics and squashed noses, near-castration and wounds to the groin, a marred conception and a bungled birth.

All of this adds up to the trauma which we have to repress in order to become human subjects at all. There is an obscure wound or injury some-where at the very origin of the human subject – a kind of primordial Fall which we have to get over in order to become functioning individuals, but whose scars will continue to make their presence felt throughout our lives. For some, this is known as the unconscious; and Sterne in his own pre-Freudian way was mightily aware of it. We never get over our birth. There are no fully functioning individuals. The wound made by our being torn away from the bodies of others and liberated into individual consciousness will never entirely heal.

At one level, then, *Tristram Shandy* is an allegory of the coming into being of every human subject. It is just that its hero is more hilariously, devastatingly messed up than most of us. It does not help, for example, that he has a mad father. Walter Shandy is a crazed system-builder for whom nothing is ran-dom or accidental, and everything connects significantly with everything else. It is a condition to which we might today give the name paranoia. Determined to leave nothing in his son's upbringing to chance, he predrafts his development in his ridiculous *Tristrapaedia*. Inside this all-inclusive novel, there is another all-inclusive text fighting to get out.

Tristram, then, is 'written' before he can even speak; his body ends up literally mutilated by words. And this is simply a more literal version of the condition of us all, who – since we are not self-originating – are all 'written' or predrafted, in the sense that we must become human subjects on terms already laid down for us by others. Tristram struggles to be the source of his own narrative, but finds it constantly outrunning his control. Writing, so he hopes, is the way he will oust his heavy-handed father and become autono-mous, even self-generating. He can live his life through again, this time on his own terms. What he discovers is that nothing is less simple to master than script.

So there is, in fact, no origin; something or someone has always been there before us. If not, we could not be there ourselves. Tristram is preceded and preempted by his paranoid father, who symbolizes the Law which governs his being; and if Walter is mad, it is because the Law is mad too. It is mad because it believes that it should be obeyed simply because it is the law, rather than on any rational grounds. The novel itself, in all its chaotic muddle, represents Tristram's hopeless Oedipal revenge on his father. One text deconstructs another. Walter models his son's life on writing, requiring it to conform to the strict letter of the *Tristrapaedia*; but Tristram's own text will show how his life rebels against such orderly discourse. As the son of a rigidly deterministic father who does not believe in chance, Tristram's own existence is a chapter of horrendous accidents.

In the seventeenth and eighteenth-century war between the Ancients and the Moderns, Walter is a kind of mad Ancient – a crazed rationalist full of elaborately useless learning, for whom the real world must conform to the categories of the mind. He believes in rigorous chains of cause and effect in which nothing can happen by chance, but which can be manipulated by men like himself to ensure the best possible human outcomes. Tristram, by contrast, is a kind of mad Modern, determined to defeat his father's insanely well-ordered system by telling the story of a life (his own) which has no design or coherence at all. Walter simplifies complexities, while Tristram gets bogged down in them.

Walter believes that the sign constructs reality, which is why he is convinced that giving his son the right name will help to ensure a contented life for him. For him, mind and materiality are harmonious, while for Tristram the one constantly thwarts the other. He has been crushed – literally so – by his father's madcap schemes, and the novel is his way of struggling to get out from under them, or at least to expose them to public ridicule. In order to do this, however, he has to recount a tale of himself which is so digressive and all-inclusive that it becomes a kind of lunacy of its own. One form of madness is pitted against another.

Like any good Modern, Tristram is a materialist and empiricist who scorns abstract notions and trusts to what he can see and feel. Walter, by contrast, is an idealist for whom concepts are more real than things, and who lives at a lofty distance from the actual world. By manipulating concepts, he believes in his Enlightenment fashion that he can persuade the world to do his imperious bidding. Tristram, by contrast, has no such control over his environment; he is, rather, its bruised, battered victim. This is comic in one sense, since in an agreeable act of Oedipal aggression it discredits his father's fancy schemes and shows him up as impotent. The Law has feet of clay. In another sense, however, it is deeply disenchanting. Body and mind are as close as a sleeve and its lining, yet appear to have fallen apart at the seams. If Walter is all mind, Tristram is all body. Both characters are cut off from reality: Walter by his ideas, Tristram by his sense-impressions.

Sense-impressions are how you relate to the world; but they also block it out, since they are notoriously unreliable. If all we know is our sense-data, as it is for an empiricist like Tristram, then we can have no idea whether these truly correspond to the way the world is. Perhaps we would need another set of sense organs to find out. We are all locked in the cell of our private senses, since my impressions of the world may be radically different from yours. A tragicomic breakdown of communication would seem to be built into this world-view; there is now a flaw at the very heart of reason.

This becomes even clearer when we consider the question of language. Sense-impressions are private, whereas words are public; and communication on this model involves fitting the two together. But how do I know that what I call purple is what you call purple? What if you attach associations to the word which are at odds with my own? *Tristram Shandy* has great fun with this alleged gap between things and words. It exploits the rich possibilities of mutual misinterpretation in order to portray a world in which there can be no assurance of shared meaning. We are all solitary creatures signalling to each other across empty space. It is a notably bleak novel, as well as a carnivalesque one.

This is one reason why the novel goes in for non-verbal devices like squiggly lines and marbled pages, since these are supposedly less ambiguous conveyors of meaning than words. 'Supposedly', since marbled pages and squiggly lines need of course to be interpreted, which takes us back to language. You do not escape language by punching someone on the nose or kissing them on the lips. It is only in language that such actions have the meaning they do. The other way to repair the ravages of language is to communicate emotionally rather than verbally, as in the kind of word-less communion that Walter and Uncle Toby can occasionally achieve with one another. There can be common feeling, if not common sense. And since this happens at the level of the body rather than the mind, it is, like squiggly lines and square boxes, a material affair. For the eighteenth century, sympathy and sensibility hovered somewhere between the physical and the spiritual.

What is also ambiguous in this way is a book. For a book is a material object which is also a 'text' – and a text, being a matter of meaning, is not material. You can only have meaning if you have matter – which is just a way of saying that meaning needs a material medium such as print, paint or the voice. But meaning is not reducible to matter. The relation between the physical book, and the meanings it contains, is thus rather like the relationship between body and soul. The two are distinct, but they are not divorced. Sterne is fascinated by the material presence of a book, and his use of headings, diagrams, blank pages, typographical devices and the like keeps us constantly aware of the materiality of what we are reading.

The mystery of the book for Sterne could be summed up in a single question: how come that these little black marks on white paper can signify human meanings? How extraordinary that a whole complex human world can lie secreted in this stack of processed rags, waiting for a reader to catalyse into life! It is akin to the bemusement that an alien visitor to earth might feel on suddenly realising that there are certain peculiar lumps of matter which don't just lie around the place like rocks or razor-blades, but which are somehow *expressive*. And these peculiar lumps of matter are what we call humans.

Books are objects in space; but they are also processes in time, since the reader has to turn their pages one at a time in order to follow the storyline or the argument. Books therefore tend to impose a linear logic on their materials. They imbue them with a certain uniformity, as Walter Shandy's system does to human life. In *Tristram Shandy*, however, 'book' and 'text' are constantly at loggerheads, as the book seeks to organize the text into an orderly sequence, and the text fights hard to break free. The displaced Dedication and Preface are obvious examples of this, but so is the way that the text keeps jumping ahead, curving back on itself, or struggling to run several themes simultaneously. Tristram's history is 'digressive, and it is progressive too – and at the very same time'. If the novel is an impossible form, it is partly because it aims at a linear representation of a reality which is not in itself linear at all. It is therefore bound to falsify its own materials. There is something about narrative itself, or literary design, which is a lie. There is even something falsifying about language itself, since to say one thing means excluding another. Life and language are at odds with each other, despite the fact that the aim of the realist novel is to bind them tightly together.

Language in Sterne's novel is not just inadequate for capturing the external world, or for communicating with others. It is also inadequate for articulating the truth of the human subject, which is what autobiography tries to do. All it succeeds in doing is splitting the subject in the very act of trying to gather it into a whole. This is why autobiography is an ironic form. When you recount your life-history, the 'I' which is doing the recounting strives for an identity with the 'I' which is being portrayed. A novel like

Richardson's *Pamela* would persuade us that this is possible. The narrator is at once subject and object of the whole process, and the act of writing consists in showing how these apparently separate selves are really one.

It is this which Sterne's novel exposes for the artifice it is. For the two selves are divided in the first place by time, one occupying the present tense and the other the past. But they are also divided by the act of writing itself, as the writing 'I' interprets (rather than simply recalls or reflects) the self it writes about, and thus puts a distance between the two. Tristram is both a character in his own story and a 'character' in the whimsical way he tells it, but he is never a unified self. He can never coincide with himself, if only because the writing he undertakes in order to do so interposes itself between his present and past selves. His tale is coherent enough only to be able to show us how much in pieces he is.

Writing about your childhood as an adult, you have the advantage over the self you are describing of knowing what came later. But it is hard not to interpret the earlier events in terms of the later – partly because the meaning of the earlier event really is decided in part by what it led to. When William Wordsworth, writing of his childhood in 'Tintern Abbey', exclaims that he cannot paint what he was then, the point runs deeper than not having the words to depict the strength and strangeness of his boyhood passions. It is also a question of how you write about a condition which precedes writing. In the very act of writing about his childhood, Wordsworth provides us with the most eloquent possible testimony of how it now lies at an irrecoverable remove from him.

In composing his life-history, Tristram hopes to make whole an existence which has been crippled and fragmented. If the process of living has scattered him across time and space, the act of writing will gather him together again. This, however, turns out to be as doomed a hope as any other in the book. For the process of writing itself works only by difference and division. In order to describe, say, the Golden Gate Bridge, you have to invoke contexts, metaphors, comparisons, phrases which lead to other phrases, until the 'bridge itself' may well come to seem buried under the verbiage you have generated. There is no single sign which would magically capture the essence of the bridge, not to speak of capturing the essence of the self. Even if there were, that sign would make sense only in relation to another sign, and that in turn to another.

In this sense, language seems self-defeating; and it is this which is comically magnified by *Tristram Shandy*. In order to tell us who he is, sedulously tracing every minuscule detail of his life, Tristram has to release such a torrent of language that it ends up by sinking him almost entirely. You cannot avoid this swamping simply by attending to the key moments of your career, since who is to be judge of this? If every piece of reality is caught up with every other, so that trifles can have momentous consequences, nothing can be safely dismissed as trivial. A wrong choice of name for a child may blight his future. Besides, one of the premises of the autobiography is the immodest assumption than everything that ever happened to you is worth recording because it happened to *you*. You are the only yardstick of value – and this is one of the dangerously individualist doctrines which *Tristram Shandy* is out to satirize.

Editing and existing would thus seem to be incompatible. The more information the novel provides, the less it manages to communicate. The more it tries to insure against the slipperiness of the sign by explicating every possible shred of meaning, chasing up every association and forestalling every conceivable misreading, the more the narrative logjams, buckles and all but collapses. In this sense, *Tristram Shandy* is a comically self-deconstructing novel. But this simply serves to reveal the problematic nature of all language, which in piling up more and more sub-clauses in order to pinpoint the meaning of a thing turns out to create more and more possibilities of ambiguity and misinterpretation. What if there is, after all, no truth of the human subject? What if the truth of Tristram's identity is just the potentially endless process of hunting for it? The human subject can express itself in its movement from one sign to another; but there is no way in which it can wrap up this whole process in a single sign, or bring it to a close. There can be no 'last' sign, since that, too, would imply the existence of another sign, and that of another.

Nor can you capture the truth of the self by searching for its origin, rather than anticipating its end. Tristram takes us back to the moment of his conception, so that this is one of those rare stories which begins literally *ab ovo*, or from the egg. But what counts as a beginning? We are the result not just of our conception, but of the kind of people our parents were before we were conceived, the material situation we were born into and the like. And this, in turn, raises the issue of our parents' parents, siblings, friends and so on. We are plunged instantly into a 'text' – a potentially infinite weaving of strands which we can never fully unravel. There is no saying where a human being begins and ends. Just as words are always versions of other words, so human beings are recycled versions of other human beings. We are, so to speak, plagiarized beings. *Tristram Shandy* contains a passage denouncing plagiarism, one which is itself plagiarized.

All of this strikes a grave blow at the humanist injunction: 'know thyself'. The self is now an enigma to itself. It is not just others who are opaque to us, but our own existence. Alienness is as close to us as breathing. Sterne's sermons are concerned among other things with the difficulty of examining our own motives dispassionately. Yorick in *A Sentimental Journey* seems comically unaware of the unconscious eroticism of his own motives. He thinks he acts for benevolent reasons when he probably acts for libidinal ones. It is remarkable how easily he is moved to generosity by a pretty face.

Nor can we use language to get back behind language, as Tristram is trying to do in writing about his infancy. Or, to put it another way, use our subjectivity to get back behind it. For the fact is that we become human subjects only by repressing a great deal which went into our making. It is only by virtue of such repression that we become the talking, thinking animals we are. So there is something curiously self-defeating about trying to use our language, or subjectivity, to investigate what brought it into being in the first place. Language and subjectivity cannot get back behind the act of repression which brought them into being. It would be like trying to pick ourselves up by our bootstraps. As subjects, we cannot describe whatever it was that made our subjectivity possible in the first place. It is here that we bump our heads against the limits of representation. You can never break through language in order to discover what set it in motion, since you would need language to do so. Similarly, you can never leap out of the skin of your own subjectivity in order to find out where you came from, since you need to be a subject in order to do so.

This is why Tristram's search for the source of his wounding is futile. For this 'wound' is what makes him a subject in the first place, and as such forever evades the reach of language. His pursuit is as pointless as Uncle Toby's efforts to pinpoint the exact spot where he was injured in the groin by fashioning a model of the military campaign in which the injury was incurred. The model is, so to speak, Toby's version of the realist novel – a meticulously exact representation which nevertheless keeps running up against something it cannot capture. It is no accident, either, that Toby's wound is a sexual one. So, in a way, is Tristram's, who has been worsted in an Oedipal conflict with his father.

Both characters are in some sense impotent: there is something missing to them both, and both are involved in the tricky business of trying to represent an absence. If this cannot be done, it is partly because the act of representation is a way of compensating for that impotence, not of tracking it to its source. Tristram's writing is a form of symbolic self-assertion, a kind of substitute manhood to make up for his real-life humiliations. Uncle Toby's model-building is a form of displacement activity. Yet Tristram's narrative wilts and droops, failing to hit its target or sustain its thrust through to the finish. There is no climax, just a perpetual anti-climax.

The narrator of *Tristram Shandy* is ostentatiously reader-friendly. His tone is genial, wryly amused, gently satirical. Like Fielding, he is holding a civilized conversation with his readers rather than preaching to them or parading his omniscience as an author. There is a clubbish, archly self-conscious intimacy between narrator and reader. The narrator is too good-naturedly laid-back to organize anything as rigorous as a formal plot. He must not pull rank on the reader by editing or selecting, which would involve a kind of discourteous manipulation on his part. It would mean that he knew things which the reader did not, which would ruffle the equality between them. It might even amount to a sort of cheating. Yorick remarks in the novel that 'the very essence of gravity [is] design, and consequently deceit'. All plots are plots against the reader. Instead, the narrator claims that he intends to develop a friendship with the reader as his work progresses. Like a 1960s professor, Sterne asks us to look upon him as a mate rather than a mentor.

A shapely narrative, then, would demand from the narrator an impersonality and objectivity at odds with his comfortable *bonhomie*. It would interfere with his ambling, button-holing style, with its implication that a gentleman is not to be hurried. You do not seek to force the reader's response to your text, as you would not stand over him while he finished his glass of port. When it comes to drawing a portrait of Widow Wadman, the narrator courteously hands the pen to the readers and invites them to sketch their own image of the character. Yet what if this is less courtesy than a kind of insolent indifference? What if all this good-nature conceals a satiric malice?

There is something disturbingly monomaniacal about Sterne's laid-back ludic spirit, which suggests that it may have less than friendly designs on us. His mischief and perversity tread a thin line between an engaging playfulness and an alarming eccentricity. His elaborate effort to be reader-friendly throws up such a thick web of pauses, asides, digressions, mock-elaborate apologies and the like, that readers cannot help suspecting that they are being taken for a ride in the very act of being fondly cajoled. The novel is so sedulously attentive to its readers, so eager to take excessive pains on their behalf, that it ends up bamboozling and disorientating them altogether. Sterne professes to believe in his sentimentalist way that nothing is too trifling for his attention – a benevolence which results in his forcing the reader non-benevolently to trudge through an enormous morass of irrelevant detail.

Sterne is well aware that writing is a form of dominion, and tells the reader at one point that "'tis enough to have thee in my power'. If he is gentle with the reader, we cannot avoid the queasy feeling that he could always get tough with us if he decided to. There is a kind of smiling sadism about his excessively self-conscious benevolence. Benevolence is not simply a virtue which his novel recommends; the novel is itself an example of it. It is as though the cold anonymity of print must not be allowed to stand in the way of an intimate relationship between narrator and reader. Tristram, who has submitted in life to the impersonal edicts of his father, is making his bid for freedom in writing his life-history, and will not meekly submit to the rules imposed by the printer.

The novel is what we might now call a thoroughly 'logocentric' work, one in which all is staked on the living voice and the illusion of immediate presence. Yet here, once again, living 'text' is at loggerheads with impersonal 'book' – which is why the narrator, with his tongue firmly in his cheek, tries to wrench typography itself into a kind of expressive medium. It is as though he wants to convert the material apparatus of the book into a medium of pure presence between author and reader. From this viewpoint, the book is a self-destruct device: it could only fulfil its purpose if it were to abolish itself, leaving author and reader affectionately face-to-face. Sterne does not encourage his readers to think of ourselves as part of a vast, anonymous crowd; we must imagine instead that the narrator is button-holing us personally, with a tender solicitude for our well-being.

All this is a satire of eighteenth-century sentimentalism, but it is probably a genuine expression of it as well. Sterne portrays a world in which reason, identity and communication are gradually collapsing, as men and women retreat to their own solipsistic enclaves. Each of them has his or her 'hobby-horse' – Walter his dogmatic system, Uncle Toby his model-building, Tristram his never-ending autobiography – which is the index of their eccentricity. Everyone in this society seems wrecked, damaged, washed-up, monomaniacal. The hobbyhorse may also be a kind of fetish, which plugs the dreadful gap in being everywhere apparent in the book. Yet the novel's own response to this panorama of futility is a vast, amused tolerance. If there is no longer any hope of reforming human beings, there is at least the perpetual possibility of smiling with and at them, in what Sterne at one point calls 'a kingdom of hearty laughing subjects'. He is well aware in his letters that this spirit of 'Shandeism' is his own particular hobbyhorse, his own defence against what he calls the 'infirmities' of existence.

The spirit of Shandeism in *Tristram Shandy* is focused on the figure of Yorick, who is probably a self-portrait on Sterne's part. Yorick is one of life's victims, associated with death and decay through his very name; but he is also a wit and jester in love with merriment, quick in his human sympathies, and furnished with a keen sense of the ridiculous. As such, he symbolizes both death's victory over humanity, and humanity's own jesting victory over it. If he is an object of sentiment, he is also an agent of satire. He combines the resources of the man of feeling with the vision of the man of infinite jest. The Yorick of *A Sentimental Journey*, by contrast, is an agent of sentiment and an object of satire. Uncle Toby, by contrast, lacks this satirical strain. He is the very image of the eighteenth-century Man of Feeling, and we are supposed to weep with him; but we are meant to smile at him all the same. It is admirable to be inoffensive, but there is less virtue in it than one might imagine if, like Toby, you are too innocent to recognize with any certainty that you have been offended. If Toby is a mite too sentimental for the novel's taste, Tristram himself is a shade too sardonic.

Everything is big with jest, remarks Walter Shandy, as long as we can find it out. The judgement is surely dubious; but Walter's sense that value lies in seeing a grisly world in the redemptive light of the ridiculous is very close to his author's own vision. Sterne thought that cheerfulness was a moral virtue, and preached the benefits of benevolence and spontaneous fellow-feeling. On the whole, however, he was cheerful despite his view of the world, not because of it. If he is more sentimentalist than Fielding, he is also less convinced of the idea of a providential design in the world. Like Fielding, however, he pokes fun at the sentimentalist belief that everything is potentially as precious as everything else. If things are valuable because of the emotions you invest in them; and if, like the Yorick of *A Sentimental Journey*, you can feel as tender about a caged starling as you can about a person; then you are at risk of undermining any objective hierarchy of value. This matters, because while it is salutary to see that caged starlings can be as important in their way as politicians, it is also important to see that genocide is more important than either of them.

A community of feeling is an admirable thing; but we are also meant to see that it is pretty much all you are left with in the wake of a collapse of common sense and rational action. All we can do is put up with each other's foibles. Pity and pathos stand in for the more active virtues, which might repair the situation which inspires you to pity in the first place. Hardly anyone in Sterne's world is capable of taking decisive action. Virtue survives, but it is impotent. *Tristram Shandy* is a defeatist tale of the blighted and battered, of impotence and disfigurement, of lives of quiet desperation conducted far from the centres of power and prestige. The family, that traditional oasis of affection in a brutal world, is now an assemblage of freaks, madmen and emotional cripples. Life is one long set of petty errors, annoyances and frustrations, the ruin of all grand ideals. Knowledge is just a series of hypotheses, language is a way of not communicating, and causality a snare in which you come to grief.

There is a puzzle about Laurence Sterne. He was born in Tipperary of an Irish mother who was herself born in Flanders, and an English military father of Yorkshire stock. Much of his early childhood was spent with Irish relatives, though at the age of 10 he was sent to school in England and spent the rest of his adult life there as a clergyman. So Sterne could be described as Irish, since he was born in Ireland of an Irish mother and spent his childhood there. Yet few think of him as such, given that he left the country at so early an age, and that England was the scene of his entire adult life.

The puzzle is that a writer who was relatively little exposed to the influence of Irish culture, and that only as a child, should seem to have absorbed so much of it. For there is a great deal in Sterne's work which is strikingly typical of Anglo-Irish writing as a whole. The 'modernist' experimentalism, for example, can be found throughout Anglo-Irish literature, largely because Ireland was a culture less respectful of realism than England. A literature which produced *Gulliver's Travels*, *Castle Rackrent*, *The Wild Irish Girl*, *Melmoth the Wanderer*, *Uncle Silas*, *Dracula*, *The Picture of Dorian Gray*, *Ulysses*, *Finnegans Wake* and *At Swim-Two-Birds* was hardly much fussed about plausibility. Sterne reads like a 'modernist' author not because he writes in the wake of realism, as the European modernists do, but because he predates it. He is writing at a time when realism has yet to settle into an established mould, and can seize advantage of this fluidity to bend its rules.

But it is not just a question of anti-realism. The mock-learning, the carnivalesque comedy, the twisting of linear narrative, the satirical wit and black humour, even the mixture of the comic and the melancholic: all these are fairly typical of Irish writing in English. One might add to this list the debunkery of high-flown ideas, the literary self-consciousness, the verbal sportiveness, the obsession with the body and the preoccupation with death, not to speak of jesting as a way of defying the direness of one's situation. Even the eighteenth-century cult of benevolence and sentimentality was dominated by Irish and Scottish writers: Steele, Goldsmith, Hutcheson, Hume, Adam Smith, Edmund Burke and others. Most of these characteristics of course have their English equivalents; they are in no sense the monopoly of Irish authors. But it is curious that so many of them should converge in Sterne's work.

Shandy Hall is situated in Sterne's Yorkshire; yet this stagnant rural enclave, full of idle talkers and crippled fantasists who have been by-passed by progress and are searching for the historical cause of their ruin, is not entirely remote from the colonial Ireland of the author's childhood. It is hard to believe that mock-learning or the bending of linear narrative were simply in the Tipperary air, or that a debunking of high-flown ideas was present in Sterne's genes. Perhaps it is an illustration of the old saying that we are all Irish in the eyes of God.

WALTER SCOTT
AND JANE AUSTEN

N ot long ago, it was popular to read the development of the novel from the eighteenth century to Jane Austen and beyond as itself a kind of narrative. On this theory, the novel starts out as a rather crude kind of literary form, which can handle plot (Fielding) or psychology (Richardson), but not both at the same time. If, like Fielding, it is concerned with formal design, it has to sacrifice psychological realism to do so; whereas the novel of psychological realism finds it hard to launch a shapely narrative. By the time of Jane Austen, so the story goes, the novel form has finally come of age, and the fullest degree of social realism and psychological intricacy can co-exist with an exquisitely well-balanced form. It is this which Austen will bequeath to the great realist novel of the nineteenth century.

The story of the novel, in short, reads rather like a realist novel itself. First there is disunity, then integration. There is something in this case, but it is more misleading than illuminating. For one thing, it makes the eighteenth-century novel sound like a dummy run for Jane Austen and George Eliot, whom it could not have known about, rather than a phenomenon in its own right. For another thing, it tends to overlook just how many losses as well as gains were involved in this process. For realism to triumph, a great deal that was valuable had to be sidelined and suppressed.

The late eighteenth and early nineteenth centuries was one of the most fertile, diverse and adventurous periods of novel-writing in English history, as Gothic fiction, romance, regional and national tales, Jacobin and anti-Jacobin novels, novels of travel, sentiment, abolitionism and the condition of women, stories of foreign and domestic manners, and works derived from ballad, myth and folk lore, tumbled copiously from the presses. The literary situation was exceptionally fluid, and the realist novel as we know it crystallized only gradually in this crucible of ingredients. Once that novel was up and running, it did not simply suppress these competing forms; on the contrary, it incorporated them, as a glance at the Gothic or romantic elements in, say, the Brontës would suggest. But in the act of assimilating them, it also tended to defuse them. The English novel gained in 'civility' and sophistication, but lost out to some degree in vision, passion and fantasy.[1] Not until the modernist fiction of the twentieth century would some of this ground be made up, as the novel was once more set free from the constraints of what was considered 'plausible'.

That this period should have witnessed such an extraordinary burst of novelistic experiment is hardly surprising. It was, after all, an epoch of dramatic social and political upheaval: revolution in France and North America, the Napoleonic conquests, the massive expansion of empire, Britain's dominance of the seas, the prosperity reaped from the slave trade, the rise of the European nation-state, the increasing capitalist 'rationalization' of the countryside as common rights were uprooted by so-called enclosures. The period saw the beginnings of the industrial revolution, the consolidation of middle-class power, and the first stirrings of the organized, politically vocal working class. It was a time of radical movements and ideas, which found themselves confronting what in the heyday of Scott and Austen was effectively a British police state. The new experiments in fiction had some of their roots in this era of vision and anxiety, in new liberations of energy and new forms of repression.

They also had many of their roots in the Gaelic margins. Writers of Scottish or Irish origin bulk remarkably large in eighteenth-century 'English' literature, and for a while Dublin and Edinburgh were probably more vital literary centres than London. It was on the colonial peripheries that questions of history and cultural identity, tradition and modernity, the archaic and the enlightened, romance and realism, empire and anti-colonialism, community and individualism, were inevitably at their keenest. The father of the realist historical novel is often said to be Walter Scott; and it was certainly Scott, with his pop-idol-like fame throughout Europe and America, who played a major role in establishing the novel as a genuinely 'serious' literary genre. He won for the form a new prestige and authority, so that now, the critics could console themselves, it was no longer just a genre for fantasizing females. His novel *Waverley* attracted the kind of celebrity that even today's literary superstars would envy.

Yet behind *Waverley* – the work of an author who pokes fun at the excesses of Gothic, sentimental, chivalric and female fiction – lies an obscure novel by an Anglo-Irish Gothic author, Charles Maturin's *The Milesian Chief*. Behind it more generally lies a hinterland of women writers, so-called national tales, romances, folk material and nationalist antiquarian research from which the reputable Sir Walter derived rather more than he was always prepared to acknowledge. In this sense, the canonical had its roots in the non-canonical, as is often the case. Irish women like Sydney Owenson (Lady Morgan), Maria Edgeworth and others were intensively involved in fiction about national and cultural identity, and its complex relations to gender, in a way which gives the lie to the prejudice that while the expansively 'masculine' Sir Walter wrote novels about the public world, female writers were all as domestically restricted as a Jane Austen.

The novel, Sydney Owenson remarked, is 'the best history of nations'. Cultural nationalism at the time of Scott and Austen involved myth and fantasy, popular customs and sentiments, the exploration of identity as well as the struggle to tell your own story. It was thus the kind of politics which lent itself particularly well to the novel, which also trades in such matters. At the same time, however, partly because of this colonial turbulence, there was a need for the British state to consolidate its power; and the novel played an indirect role in this project as well. If it was a vehicle of radical, Gothic, colonial, abolitionist or feminist dissent, it was also a sturdy instrument of political authority. It could play an invaluable role in defining the true meaning of Englishness or Britishness, at just the moment when these notions was coming under fire from cultural nationalisms at home and political revolutions abroad.

Scott's novels pay full heed to the trauma and devastation of Scotland's colonial past; but they see the need, precisely because of this tragedy, to move all the more swiftly towards an 'enlightened', thoroughly 'modernized' Scottish nation. It is a nation which has thrust its tribal 'savagery' and futile Romantic dreams behind it, accepting that its future lies in a peaceable political and economic integration with the British parliament and the British crown. The anarchic past has a drama and energy which is admired; yet it is one which the realist novel must tame and 'normalize'.

In this sense, Scott is one of the first great spokesmen of modern British conservatism. Those with experience of civil war, military rebellion and political disunity, which a Scottish writer of the time was likely to have, are always the most persuasive in their championship of order, hierarchy, authority and tradition. Much the same is true of Scott's contemporary Edmund Burke, an Irishman who threw his formidable eloquence behind the need to uphold the British state. Burke had known enough civil unrest in his native

Ireland to warn the English of its horrors when it broke out in France. The renowned 'moderation' of the English spirit does not spring from a history of peace and civility; it is rather a reaction to a British history of bloodshed and sectarian strife. It is with such figures as Scott and Burke that modern English conservatism, with its belief in maintaining a middle way between the 'fanaticisms' of both left and right, was born. The values cherished by Scott – liberty, tolerance, moderation, progress and commercial enterprise, all within a firm framework of rank, deference, loyalty, tradition, imperial order and a strong military state – have set the tone, by and large, for the politics of the British establishment ever since.

It is this refusal of both reaction and revolution which is often praised as the English spirit of compromise. Yet this 'middle way', like the so-called Third Way in today's politics, is in reality no such thing. It is not a middle path between Toryism and radicalism, but one between a backward-looking, increasingly clapped-out form of Toryism and a more updated, enlightened version of the creed. It is the difference in Scott's eyes between the Romantic Jacobites who are still loyal to the House of Stuart, and those more modern, moderate, pragmatic Tories like himself who accept the so-called Glorious Revolution of the House of Hanover. From a radical view-point, this stout commitment to capitalism and monarchy is scarcely a matter of being middle-of-the-road.

It is true, of course, that most of us instinctively see ourselves as some-where in the middle, flanked on both sides by fanatical extremists. It is natural to see oneself as in the centre and others as on the peripheries. It has to do, among other things, with where Nature has seen fit to locate our eyes. The only problem is that most of the fanatical extremists, whose eyes are in much the same place as our own, see themselves as being in the middle too. Not many people regard themselves as frenzied zealots or rabid bigots. Zealots and bigots are always other people. Extremism is usually a matter of where you happen to be standing. Those today who believe they have the right to wreck international agreements, maintain millions in pov-erty, or flatten other nations who are not even proposing to attack them, would no doubt be stung to hear themselves described as fanatics.

Liberals are prone to the belief that the truth usually lies somewhere in the middle – from which it might follow, for example, that the truth lies somewhere between the extreme of racism on the one hand and the extreme of anti-racism on the other. Or between wife-beating patriarchs on the one hand, and those who run women's refuges on the other. Or between those impoverished peasants who can no longer support themselves because their land has been poisoned, and the giant corporations who have poisoned it for the sake of profit. It is therefore not hard to see why, for some radical commentators, the idea that the truth invariably lies in the middle is itself an 'extremist' position to take up.

As one from north of the English border, Scott was peculiarly well-placed to recreate the way in which history was supposedly evolving from a backward clan society to a modern nation-state. In Scotland, this process had happened recently enough to provide the British as a whole with a lively reminder of the importance of a 'civilized', modernized political state. Ireland was still too embroiled in revolutionary turmoil to provide any such object-lesson. Yet Scotland was also a graphic reminder of the terrible price which had to be paid for such 'civility' in bloodshed, rancour and the destruction of the old clan society. Such an unflinching recognition lent Scott's voice an authority beyond the more complacent champions of progress of this time, as well as underlining the urgent need for such evolution.

Officially, Scott subscribed to the Enlightenment notion that 'barbarism' is a stage *en route* to civilization. In fact, he knew that in Scotland these two conditions were more synchronous than sequential, in the co-existence of the Highlands with the Lowlands. The contrast could hardly have been sharper: Scotland had witnessed an unprecedented period of economic and intellectual progress in the Lowlands, while the more backward Highlands had been politically crushed and economically devastated. Scott, then, was able to see history almost literally before his eyes, with the persistence of the Highland past into the present, in a way that an English writer of the day might well have found more problematic.

The key period of England's own bloody transition from the old regime to the modern nation-state is the seventeenth century, which was hardly as fresh in the historical memory as the failed Jacobite uprising of 1745 or the so-called 'clearances' in which Highlanders were driven from their land to make way for more profitable capitalist farming. The finest historical fiction tends to spring from periods in which history is visibly in the making – in which you can feel the ground shifting under your feet, and are capable of making new sense of the past in the light of the rapidly changing present. To grasp your present, not just your past, as historical is the litmus test of the historical sense. And this is easier when the 'past', as in Highland society, is still alive and kicking on your doorstep.

This model of gradual evolution from one historical stage to another plays an important part in modern English ideology. It is reflected in the nineteenth-century realist novel, with its characteristic movement from a state of displacement and disarray to one of settlement and resolution. In the eighteenth-century novel, by contrast, the unfolding of the narrative is still criss-crossed often enough by digressions, diversions, pauses for reflection or documentation, parodies, sermons, authorial interventions, interpolated tales and literary set pieces. It is as though there is a plurality of forms within a novel, of which realist narrative is merely one. There is no particular sense of being in a hurry to wrap up the plot. By the time of Jane Austen, almost all that agreeable clutter has been pared away so that plot can unfurl in all its purity.

Increasingly, then, the realist novel describes a single arc, from a sedate past through a fragmented present to a felicitous future. It is at root an optimistic form, for which breakdown and suffering are simply conditions which you may have to pass through in order to arrive at self-knowledge and self-fulfilment. There are, to be sure, many problems in the world; but reality is not problematical in itself, as it will be for some modernist writing. The nineteenth-century English novel is not a tragic art form. Tragedy may overshadow its conclusion from time to time, as with *Wuthering Heights* or *The Mill on the Floss*, but this is not the full-dress tragedy of a *Clarissa* (a novel which predates fully fledged realism) or of countless novels which come after it, from *Jude the Obscure* to *Under the Volcano*. Up to about 1880, the novel is a predominantly comic form; only after then is it mostly a tragic one. You cannot have genuine tragedy if you nurse a deep-seated faith that you are in a 'middle march' of human affairs from the cave dwellers to Queen Victoria. The fact that Queen Victoria, or at least the social order she ruled, was unimaginably *more* violent than the cave dwellers can be laid quietly to one side.

What this smoothly evolving time-scheme sets its face against is political revolution. As Franco Moretti has argued in *The Way of the World*,[2] the great realist novel is basically a response to the French revolution. In its preoccupation with the solidity of the everyday world, its shyness of absolute crises or ruptures, its nervousness of the political, its fascination with the individual, its preference for the normative over the extreme, its concern for settlement and integration – in all these ways, the realist novel can be seen as a cultural solution to a political problem. In its thickness of social texture, it portrays a world so substantial – so richly, irresistibly *there* – that the idea that it could ever be radically altered becomes almost unthinkable. From Burke and Thomas Carlyle to Wordsworth, Tennyson and Dickens, the French Revolution cast its long, chilling shadow over most of the English nineteenth century; and if you wanted to point to a single phenomenon which signified an alternative set of values, and signified them, moreover, in persuasively flesh-and-blood form, you could do worse than point to the realist novel.

Some of the literary forms which that novel shouldered out of the way were not quite so sanguine in their view of historical progress. It was no particular consolation to the bards and scribes of cultural nationalism to hear that the destruction of their communities was an essential (if regrettable) price to pay for progress. They were more likely to see such change as springing from the violent irruption of historical forces into those communities, rather than as some inevitable evolution. Gothic novel, national tale, balladic writing, historical romance and other 'non-canonical' forms were more inclined than realism to the elegiac and melancholic – to visions of ruins, ghosts, lost hopes, baulked dreams and unappeased desires.

What these forms registered was a culture in fragments, an identity in permanent crisis, and a history marked by disruption and dispossession. Much of this found its way into the 'official' novel, if only as local colour. Once politically subjugated, the Celtic nations could be 'aestheticized' – turned into a source of misty sentiments, quaint customs and agreeable archaisms. Irish and Scottish fiction were all the rage among fashionable readers in early nineteenth-century England, as polite fiction came to ransack the Celtic fringes for cultural icons and exotica, 'primitive' passions and folksy sentiments. And just as the canonical novel plundered its poor relations, so those poor relations gathered a good deal from more orthodox ideas.

Yet the two types of writing, canonical and non-canonical, were nevertheless very different, not least in their views of time and place. Time for the realist novel tends to be linear and one-dimensional; whereas time for the Gothic or Gaelic text is often doubled, as the novel delves into the ancient past as a way of illuminating the present and future, or as that past lingers fearfully on within the present in the form of spectres, hauntings, past crimes clamouring for vengeance, corpses which won't lie down. With the advent of modernism, time in the novel will once again become doubled, complex, synchronic. As for place, this for the realist novel is what you move through, exchanging one spot for another in a steady temporal process. All places are now provisional and unstable. Arrivings and leavings, entrances and exits, provide the inner rhythm of realist fiction. Much the same goes for the picaresque novel of the eighteenth century. For those on the threatened colonial margins, by contrast, place is where you are rooted, part of your identity, a spot through which time or history flows. Jane

Austen, who has her own reasons to be suspicious of metropolitan mobility, shares this traditionalist attachment to the local.

If Walter Scott plays so immensely important a role in the symbolic business of nation-building, it is partly because of his sense of region, margin and locality, not in spite of it. Scott has a genuine emotional attachment to these besieged enclaves: he has no desire to see their cultural specificity steamrollered by an abstract, uniform, modern nation-state. His genius, from the viewpoint of modern British nationalism, is to recognize that local cultures must as far as possible be preserved within a greater whole. The nation is a harmony of differences, not an homogeneous entity. The United Kingdom itself is a medley of nations peaceably co-existing. Like a work of art – indeed, like a novel – the nation is polyphonic, internally differentiated, a chorus of many voices orchestrated into one.

The empire must be like this too, as Britain seeks to govern its colonial peoples, not despite their customs and beliefs, but through them. Just as the bard had once bound together his clan or tribe into symbolic unity, so the modern novelist now inherits this role, forging a whole out of contending national interests. Realist fiction, which cultivates a diversity of voices and viewpoints within its overarching unity, is in this sense a paradigm of the liberal state. The difference-in-identity of the one reflects the difference-in-identity of the other. A nation thus fortified is then all the better furnished for its imperial role in the wider world.

In fact, the novel and the nation have always been closely allied. Just as novels are both unified and diverse, so nations are made up of individuals who are both different and akin, both strangers and colleagues. Benedict Anderson in his *Imagined Communities* sees the daily newspaper as a sign of this, gathering into community at roughly the same moment millions of men and women who will never actually meet.[3] But the realist novel plays more or less the same role, as an account of the nation's life which the technology of printing places in exactly the same form into thousands of different pairs of hands. In a disturbingly atomistic society, in which each individual is becoming his or her own yardstick, this is a crucial political task. But it is economically vital as well. If you are going to profit from printing such labour-intensive objects as bulky novels, you will need a good many consumers who speak the same vernacular language and share a world of cultural assumptions; and this implies the form of life we call a nation. Each reader consumes the text alone, but can do so only because he or she shares a national language, along with a whole freight of conventions and understandings, with countless, faceless colleagues. The idea that you could

101

share the same experience with thousands or even millions of other people in this way would have been astonishing to anyone who lived before the age of print.

The novel depends on this community of meaning, but it also helps to consolidate it. It may help, for example, to standardize a national language, rather than just to reflect it. It is a vital way in which a nation speaks to itself, manufactures shared myths and symbols, fashions collective narratives and hammers out moral values. It is the mythology of the modern age. English villages joyfully ringing their church bells to celebrate the wedding of Samuel Richardson's character Pamela is simply a bizarrely literal version of this symbolic solidarity. In this secular world, which as time goes on will have fewer and fewer sacred truths or spiritual practices to hold it together, print and the novel play their part in creating a community of the anonymous. In its fullest reach, this community is what we know as the nation.

In this sense, the novel does for the modern nation what the epic did for ancient society. Yet there is a vital difference. The classical epic is a form largely confined to the warrior nobility of the ancient world, whereas the novel must reflect something of the mixed, hybrid, heterogeneous nature of modern civilization. It must embrace the language of the common people as well as that of the elite. With the novel, a conception of 'the people' enters into literature, just as it enters into the politics of nationalism. The novel mingles high and low, the central and the marginal, offering a composite picture of a social world which is increasingly fragmented and diverse.

As the anarchy of the marketplace grows in modern society, the need for unifying political and cultural forms is ever more keenly felt. The novel must provide a *lingua franca* for individuals who are growing increasingly solitary, and whose social relations with others are becoming more and more functional. Symbolic solidarity must cut across the social classes. Because the novel began life as a popular form, and because it belongs to its technological nature to be widely distributed, it can perform this task more effectively than poetry or drama, both of which are more minority pursuits involving social rank or classical learning.

Despite his Romantic leanings, Scott was averse to the exotic and outlandish, putting his faith instead in reason, good sense and the rule of law. He was a child of the Scottish Enlightenment, one who rejected dogma, fanaticism and social revolution in the name of temperateness and civility. His heroes, as Georg Lukács famously points out in *The Historical Novel*,[4] are distinctly unheroic, mediocre characters. As with Dickens, it is the minor figures who have all the life. This, however, is a device which allows his middle-of-the-road protagonists to mediate between extremes and bring a clash of opposing forces into focus. In *Waverley*, it is a contention between Jacobites and Hanoverians; in *Ivanhoe* one between Saxons and Normans; in *Rob Roy* a conflict between clans and Lowlands, and in *Old Mortality* a fight between the Stuart monarchy and seventeenth-century Scottish Calvinist dissenters. The colourless nature of Scott's heroes is also a realist reaction to the Romantic 'great man' vision of history. These much-mythologized figures are humanized by Scott's realism, cut down to size and rendered more credible.

Yet Scott is also aware of just how much precious Romantic aura is dispelled by the modern state, as well as by the realist novel. The ideal is thus to combine Romance and realism – rather as the English nation-state combines the necessary but drab world of politics and economics with the glamour of empire, heritage and monarchy. In this way, Scott can reap the artistic benefits of portraying bold Highland rebels, dashing Jacobites and bible-spouting Calvinists, while nevertheless ensuring that their political causes are quashed in his conclusions. In setting out to write what he called historical romances, he hoped to weave together the realistic or historical with the colourful and exotic. Or, to put it another way, to bring together the swashbuckling military, religious and political drama of the Scottish past with the rather less eye-catching politics of the Williamite present.

Romance trades in the marvellous, and realism in the mundane; so that by blending these two narrative forms into one, Scott hoped to forge a literary style true to both the revolutionary drama and the everyday experience of his age. Or, if one prefers, true to a noble but barbarous past, and true also to an unglamorous but civilized present. As such, his Romantic realism provids a kind of parallel to the nationalism of his day. For nationalism is a Romantic brand of politics, casting a nostalgic glance back to a noble past, at the same time as it is a thoroughly modern movement.

Nationalism is much taken by myths, heroes and lofty ideals; yet it is also popular, in the sense of being anchored in the life of the mass of the people. It is thus a kind of mixture of Romance and realism, and much the same is true of Scott's own fiction. We have seen already how the novel starts out from the conviction that everyday life can be grippingly dramatic. But this is easier to demonstrate if, like Scott, one is dealing with a past in which everyday experience *is* one of crisis, disruption and upheaval – of gallant deeds, heroic suffering and tragic disaster. The novel can then be true to this everyday world without fear of monotony or banality.

There is another aspect to this blending of Romance and realism. Scott's novels are thronged with larger-than-life, flamboyantly individualist figures; but rather than standing gloriously alone, as they would no doubt do in conventional romance, they usually have their roots in the popular life of the common people. And this lends them a realistic edge which they might otherwise lack. Outlaws, rebels, smugglers and deserters who in the hands of Defoe or Fielding might be no more than individual rogues belong here to a broader social and political life.

With Scott and his contemporaries, the idea of characters as representing social forces enters the major novel for the first time. We still encounter the noble figures typical of previous literary genres, but these knights, chieftains and high-born ladies are now integrated by Scott's realist techniques into the mainstream of everyday life. They are not just bits of costume drama, but part of a collective historical action which involves the common people as well. With Scott and the historical novelists who came before him, the novel has found a way of representing abstractions like nation and culture, church and state, sovereignty and rebellion – and it does so by 'embodying' these ideas in plausible, flesh-and-blood individual figures.

This is indeed an innovation, since the very idea of 'social forces' or significant historical currents, of the kind we will come across later in George Eliot or Joseph Conrad, was pretty well unknown to the eighteenth-century novelists. Fielding, Defoe and Richardson simply did not think in such collective historical terms. Scott, by contrast, who lived at a time when history was visibly changing, and in a place where this was particularly evident, cannot really avoid seeing the world in such terms. And this is certainly one of his most vital contributions to the evolution of the novel.

Realism, one might claim, at least had the virtue of showing life as it is, rather than escaping into a world of chivalrous knights and black-hearted villains. Yet it is not clear just what counts as showing life as it is. Take, for example, the Gothic novel which flourished at the time of Scott and Austen, which hardly seems a mirror of everyday existence. It is a world of fantasy and paranoia, shock and violation, power and oppression, spectacle and excess. It lingers on in the current language of youth: gross, weird, bizarre, scary, wicked, evil. There are times when it allows us to indulge our fantasies so shamelessly that we laugh at its very barefacedness.

As such, Gothic represents the shadowy underside of Enlightenment reason, exposing the family as a cockpit of murderous loathings, and society as a tainted legacy of guilt and crime through which the unquiet spectres of the past still stalk. There are murky inheritances, skeletons in cupboards, concealed savagery and unspeakable secrets. It is a world of kitsch and sensationalism, full of creaking plot machinery and outrageously improbable devices. Like the Gaelic antiquarianism which influenced it, it is obsessed with texts, documents, testimonies. In this sense, it, too, is a literary form which owes much to the colonial margins. It is also one of the first great imaginative ventures into what we might now call sexual politics – a kind of social unconscious in which the sedate text of our everyday lives is suddenly flipped over to reveal the appalling disfigurements which silently inform it.

Gothic is by no means always a politically radical form. But it is worth considering whether, for all its extravagances, it might not be in some sense a more faithful portrait of a society in crisis and turmoil than, say, *Pride and Prejudice*. It is significant that Jane Austen launches her writing career with a splendid spoof of the Gothic form, *Northanger Abbey*, a work which also famously contains an eloquent plea for the novel itself to be treated as a serious form of art:

> 'I am no novel reader – I seldom look into novels – Do not imagine that *I* often read novels – It is really very well for a novel'. Such is the common cant. 'And what are you reading, Miss –?' 'Oh! it is only a novel!' replies the young lady . . . or, in short, only some work in which the greatest powers of the mind are displayed, in which the most thorough knowledge of human nature, the happiest delineation of its varieties, the liveliest effusions of wit and humour, are conveyed to the world in the best chosen language.
>
> (*Northanger Abbey*, vol. 1, ch. 5)

'I never watch television' is perhaps the modern snob's equivalent of 'I seldom look into novels'. In today's terms, it is as though Austen is claiming that there can be an artistically reputable kind of soap opera. Those who pride themselves on their superiority to such trash, she implies, are simply ignorant of the precious potential of the form, thus betraying their philistinism in the act of appearing to rise above it.

Catherine Morland, the heroine of *Northanger Abbey*, is a gullible devotee of Gothic who, rather like Scott's Waverley, lives in a perilous domain of fantasy; and the novel, like several of Austen's works, will bring her to a sober but salutary disenchantment. To establish the novel as an estimable art form, then, Austen must begin with an act of exclusion. Catherine's fervid daydreams are rebuked as un-English: such Gothic horrors, Austen reflects in prototypically English 'We don't do that kind of thing here' vein, might be found in Italy or France, but surely not in 'the central part of England'. Fantasy is all very well for foreigners. Gothic, Jacobin, feminist, sentimentalist and other bogus breeds of fiction must be clearly demarcated from the genuine article. The novel now has vital moral tasks to perform, and must not be contaminated by these aberrations.

If realism is to be defended against these extravagances, it is because it is in Austen's eyes a moral as well as a literary stance to the world. As a classical moralist, Austen believes that the ethical life is primarily about action, not about feelings, intuitions, inner states or intentions. This belongs with her opposition to Romanticism, as well as her distaste for the subjectivism and individualism she observed around her. Woolf and Lawrence, for example, did not exactly see moral questions in this way. Instead, the modern age fell into the mistake of thinking that morality was mainly about inner states, intentions, sentiments and the like. Austen, quite rightly, adheres to a more traditional conception of morality as primarily a matter of what we do, not what we feel.

For Austen, the foundation of all right conduct is true judgement, which depends in turn on being able to see things for what they are; and she is far from underestimating the extreme difficulty of this achievement. In a world of secrecy, self-deception and manipulation, few projects could be more fraught. Realism in the literary sense is in Austen's eyes an expression of this deeper moral belief; and her fear is that to violate literary realism can then involve you in a more fundamental kind of trangression. For her, the true opposite of realism is not Gothic or fantasy but egoism. The characters she commends are those who are able to see beyond their own private fantasies, opening themselves to the reality of others and their situations. Those she condemns selfishly indulge their own feelings, or brutally pursue their own interests. To attend to others' needs is a matter of decorum; but like most matters of decorum in Austen it runs much deeper than manners.

Catherine Morland is reproached by the narrator for her dangerous disingenuousness, but gently so. The tone is one we recognize instantly as Austenite: shrewd, amused, controlled, oblique, ironic, understated, though capable of sharpening from time to time into a rather more devastating dig. It is an accent which belongs to the society it criticizes, but which also maintains a certain cool distance from it. Perhaps it needs this distance in order to preserve its very notable air of symmetry and equipoise. It is a quintessentially 'English' tone, of which we shall hear reverberations all the way from George Eliot and Henry James to E. M. Forster and Malcolm

Bradbury. It is the tone of those who are sufficiently worldly wise to be well-versed in human vice and folly, but also sufficiently worldly wise not to be naively scandalized by them. It chides and tolerates at the same time.

Austen's irony is both worldly and unworldly, finding nothing to be surprised at in human immorality, but nothing to be cynically indulged about it either. It suggests a fairly low view of humanity, as befits an author who is a conservative Christian moralist, but not a misanthropic one. It implies that moral improvement is better secured by good-humoured satire than moralistic hectoring. It also suggests an equipoise and self-assurance in the face of others' defects, which hints at the secure, well-founded nature of one's own principles. It is the tone of those who wish to appear less rattled by the loose behaviour of others than they probably are.

Irony of Austen's kind is clearly different from the scabrous, virulent satire of a Pope or Swift – though like them she is concerned to defend a traditional way of life against outside interlopers and inside subversives. Her tone is less bluff and breezy than Fielding's, her irony more subtle but also on the whole less genial. It is the tone of one who is criticizing from the inside, constrained by the proprieties of the very social set-up she is taking to task, but also by the fact that the targets of her satire are for the most part her own kind. Or rather she is, like so many of the novelists who came after her, inside and outside at the same time, and the nature of her irony, which is reproving but not abrasive, reflects this ambiguity.

Austen was the daughter of a clergyman of limited financial means, finished her formal education at the age of nine, and earned £1000 at most from her writing. Her family, however, had a number of connections with the wealthier gentry. She hailed, then, from a subaltern section of the gentry, one which identified strongly with that class's values and traditions but found itself exposed and insecure. She is no great admirer of the high aristocracy, as we can see from her portrait of the appalling Lady Catherine de Bourgh in *Pride and Prejudice*. Such *grandes dames* and their overprivileged menfolk bring out her rebellious middle-class instincts. Rather as later nineteenth-century novelists find themselves marooned between the upper-middle class and the common people, so Austen lives out a similar conflict a few social notches higher, caught between patrician magnates and the middle classes.

One can glimpse something of this divided consciousness in the character of Fanny Price in *Mansfield Park*, the impoverished outsider who champions the values of the aristocracy more fervently than they do themselves. There are several examples in the ranks of English novelists of outsiders who prove more loyal than the insiders themselves. Indeed, we have just witnessed something of this paradox in the case of Walter Scott, non-English apologist for English ideology. Like Fanny, Austen herself, as a semi-outsider, can see rather more than the insiders can.

One should not be misled by Austen's good-humoured irony into imagining that she is, in the modern sense of the word, a liberal. It is here that she differs from Eliot, James, Forster, Bradbury and a whole lineage of English authors. The realist novel, as we shall see in the case of George Eliot, is in some ways a liberal form. Austen, however, is much more of an absolutist in her unswerving tough-mindedness. The fact that the principles to which she clings are so universally flouted by her characters is in her view no argument against their eternal validity. She can be complex and circumspect in her judgements, but this does not prevent her from bluntly suggesting in *Persuasion* that the death of Dick Musgrove is no great loss to humanity. It is hard to imagine George Eliot taking so severe a line. Mr Elliot in the same novel is unequivocally a heartless scoundrel, and the same kind of sternly unqualified judgement is made on a whole set of characters in the novels, from the callously philandering Willoughby in *Sense and Sensibility* to the obnoxious Mrs Norris of *Mansfield Park*. These moral ruffians are by no means cardboard cut-outs, but we are not invited to make subtly shaded judgements on them, as we might be by Eliot or James.

Austen's moral thought occupies a kind of transitional point between the eighteenth-century Christian divines she looked to for inspiration, and the moral sense of a George Eliot or Henry James. On the one hand, there are absolute moral principles on which you sometimes have to take a stand regardless of circumstance. This, indeed, is what 'absolute' in this context means. There are duties and obligations which we become aware of not by consulting others, but by withdrawing to our rooms to consult our private consciences. There is, in other words, a distinctly Protestant dimension to Jane Austen. In her own period, this sense of the absolute nature of duty, regardless of context or consequence, is associated with the moral thought of Immanuel Kant. It is a case for which the moral is more or less the opposite of the pleasurable. This, in effect, is the position of Fanny Price, who in order to remain faithful to her principles is forced to disappoint her friends, irritate her beloved patron and incur charges of dullness, obstinacy and ingratitude.

Refusing to fall in with the desires of her friends, Fanny is made forcibly aware of the loneliness of virtue in a society which derides it. But this itself is an irony, since the virtues which Fanny advocates are social ones. They include deference, sociability and a respect for the wishes of others. Conversely, those who are most superficially sociable, like Mary Crawford, are frequently those who are also most self-seeking. Fanny is one of a long line of actual or metaphorical orphans who troop their way through the English novel, some of whom come to a sticky end (Roxana, Becky Sharp, Jude Fawley), but most of whom make good (Moll Flanders, Colonel Jack, Tom Jones, Jane Eyre, Oliver Twist, David Copperfield). Orphans are particularly vulnerable figures; indeed, they act as a focus for social anxieties as a whole; but their lack of history and freedom from family ties is also a kind of opportunity, which is one reason why such forlorn figures are especially adept at ending up happy and well-heeled. Fanny Price is far too diffident and passive to aspire, so that the plot has to step in, so to speak, and grant her the fulfilment which she is too submissive to seek for herself.

If morality in Austen involves lonely, uncompromising duty, it is also viewed in a rather different light as closely bound up with social conduct. Since it is about conduct, it can be turned into a code; but since it concerns the fine-grained quality of such behaviour, it requires the eye of the novelist more than that of the moral philosopher. It is a matter of tone and nuance, of the telling gesture and the revelatory detail. It concerns small yet critical matters like remembering to light a fire for someone in their room, failing to wait for a companion who has gone off to fetch you a key, dragging a man's furniture around in his absence, or making a sarcastic remark to a spinster. All of this would figure as no more than the merest smear on the broad canvases of Fielding and Smollett, where skulls can be casually split open or beds set on fire without the author or even the characters turning a hair.

On this view, the moral life, ideally at least, is an agreeable affair, not an austere one. As with the elder Bennet sisters of *Pride and Prejudice*, it is all about warmth and liveliness, quick sympathies and enjoyably intricate acts of intelligence. It is true that there are times when all this has to be sacrificed to duty, as Fanny Price discovers; but it is better if this is not necessary. Fanny is an object-lesson in the fact that you can be too demure, as well as too scatty. Perhaps it is not too fanciful to see in her surname an indication of the price she must pay in sheer Elizabeth Bennet-like *joie de vivre* for sticking to her moral guns. Situated as she is, Fanny is simply not able to cultivate such morally admirable qualities as a keen sense of the ridiculous, not least of male absurdities, and this is bound to be something of a drawback in the eyes of her mischievous creator. Emma Woodhouse could probably write a good novel, but Fanny could not; and while this is a limitation, we are also expected to understand why it is so. Like Catherine Morland, but unlike the mercurial Crawfords, Fanny is incapable of acting – of being anyone but herself. If this testifies to her moral integrity, it also illustrates how restricted she is.

Morally upright conduct is inseparable from respect, compassion and sensitivity, and thus from manners, civility or propriety in the true senses of those terms. Civility means not just not spitting in the sugar bowl, but not being boorish, arrogant, conceited, long-winded and insensitive. Propriety includes not just how to wield a fish knife, but, as the word suggests, a sense of what is proper to others and to oneself – of what is due, fit and proportionate, rather than mean, incongruous or grotesquely excessive. A more weighty word for what is fit, due and proper is 'just'. The idea of propriety is bound up with notions of prudence, considerateness and respect: it would be improper to leave a young woman alone with a young man in certain circumstances, since she might be vilely slandered as a result, and so might unjustly suffer. Fanny Price reflects on how the decorous, orderly nature of Mansfield Park means that 'everyone's feelings were consulted'. This is not actually true – Fanny, as usual, is idealizing her adopted home – but it is how life ought to be. In the best of all worlds, to behave with social grace should involve a dash of divine grace as well. The fact that this is relatively rare in Austen's world does not mean that it is to be abandoned as an ideal, for then there would be no regulatory principles to guide one's behaviour at all.

For the champions of duty and conscience, we have an innate moral sense – a kind of inner light which will instruct us in the difference between right and wrong conduct quite independently of the opinions of others. For a more sociable idea of morality, this is not enough: we must be educated into virtue by the good influence of others, and this requires a degree of self-discipline and self-transformation. It is no wonder that Austen wrote a novel, *Persuasion*, which investigates the question of whether it is right to allow oneself to be morally persuaded by another. It is a question which goes to the heart of the conflict between simply following one's own conscience, and allowing oneself to be shaped by social pressures; and the novel's answer to the question is suitably shaded and ambiguous.

The question also touches on the issue of how much of an autonomous person you are, or should be. In Austen's world, where there are so many corrupting influences abroad, it is vital to look to your own principles and take your own decisions. Yet there is sometimes only a thin line between being bravely independent and being, like Louisa Musgrove in *Persuasion*, too stubborn and headstrong. If you must avoid too docile a conformity to others' cajolements, you must also beware of a wayward individualism. One problem with Catherine Morland's naivety is that it forces her to depend on morally unsavoury women like Isabella Thorpe. She simply does not have enough knowledge of the world to make her own judgements; and judgments in Austen are in any case notoriously frail, as with Elizabeth Bennet's too-hasty condemnation of Mr Darcy. If you pride yourself on your soundness of judgement, as Elizabeth does, you are likely to judge too swiftly and thus fall into prejudice. If this is one irony, the fact that her judgement on Darcy is not wholly mistaken is another.

One reason why judgement is so difficult is politeness. This is a culture of reticence, which conceals at least as much as it reveals. It is indecorous to exhibit your inner life for all to see, in some brash, Marianne Dashwood-like cult of the expressive ego. You should not assume that something is valid or significant simply because it is you who feel it. At the same time it belongs to good manners not to be secretive, aloof and evasive. You must nurture an inner life, but not to the point of subjectivism or unsociability. Social forms and conventions are ways in which the self comes into its own, not just artificial restrictions on its freedom. They help to mould the self into a shape most useful and congenial to others. Yet if such conventions are not *just* restrictions, they are that as well: being useful and pleasant to others inevitably involves some sacrifice of one's own gratification.

If you have to be educated into virtue, then being good is hard work, in contrast to the Romantic or sentimentalist view that it is a matter of spontaneous impulse. One reason why it is hard to be good is that if you are, you will tend to attract predatory characters, as Fanny's integrity attracts the louche Henry Crawford. As far as the moral life goes, Austen seems to believe in both innate dispositions and the importance of education. Some people just are naturally vain and selfish; but a lot of immoral behaviour in the novels flows from weak or irresponsible parenting, not least on the part of fathers. She rejects the sentimentalist delusion that morality is simply a question of doing what comes naturally – though she also seems to consider that when you *have* successfuly disciplined and transformed yourself, you will find, like the two elder Bennet sisters, that you do what is proper without needing to think too much about it. This is the right kind of instinctiveness, rather than, like Romantic impulse, the wrong one.

You need, then, to develop a spontaneous sense of what is morally appropriate – though it will not, to be sure, be an infallible one. The ideal situation is to be, like Richardson's Clarissa, so governed by what is proper that you could not even think a vulgar or unworthy thought, let alone give voice to one. In a similar way, a well-bred manner is an easy, natural one, not a matter of some frigid formalism. It belongs to good breeding not to be constantly thinking about it, like the dreadful Mrs Elton. In fact, to keep thinking about it is a sign that you haven't got it, rather as reflecting on what a wonderfully modest person you are is an indication that you are not.

Too much feeling or fantasy, then, is improper because they get things out of proportion. For a novelist to be suspicious of fantasy is in one sense as odd as for a physician to faint at the sight of blood. Even so, fantasy is to be treated warily, despite one's professional investment in it. It makes impossible, for example, a just proportion between how much you think about yourself and how much you think about others. It is 'sense' or reason which is here on the side of human warmth and compassion, and 'sensibility' which for all its frissons of sympathy and sentiment is covertly self-regarding. Austen does not subscribe to the new-fangled bourgeois prejudice for which reason is bloodless and calculating. She sees that this is an impoverishment of the traditional depth and richness of the faculty. To be reasonable means not to ride roughshod over others' wishes, embark on a loveless marriage, or insult a defenceless woman simply for your own frivolous amusement, as Emma Woodhouse does on Box Hill.

Emma has an excess of imagination, which involves causing damage to others. If you are too rich and socially prominent you are likely to be idle, not least if you are a woman banned from having a profession; and idleness can lead to imaginative self-indulgence, which in turn can result in harm to others. There is thus an indirect route from being extremely well-heeled to being morally irresponsible, which is the opposite of the paternalist ethic of *noblesse oblige* – the doctrine that wealth and high rank bring with them responsibilities to others. Emma is at the summit of her society, but exactly because of this she is a kind of transgressor. Those in control of the conventions can always bend the rules. Endowed with an excess of high spirits, she works them off by fashioning imaginary scenarios for others, rather as the indolent occupants of Mansfield Park amuse themselves by staging a play. She is like a bungling novelist who keeps concocting narratives for her various characters only to find that she has overlooked some crucial subplot, mishandled a relationship or left some vital thread dangling in the air.

Because of her social privilege, Emma sees others as actors in her own private theatre, rather than as they really are. She cuts reality to the shape of her own fancies, just like a novelist, but she lacks her author's sense of the recalcitrance of the real world. It is Knightley who embodies that reality for her, and marrying this gravely moralizing figure is both her reward and her comeuppance. There is something both fitting and incongruous in the alliance. Knightley is of course a deeply honourable character, but he also has the exasperating quality of those who are always in the right. As superego to Emma's id, he is a man who talks like a sermon, and for whom the novel expects us to have more admiration than affection.

If Emma's authorial schemes are foiled, it is partly because other people's lives turn out to be not as legible as she thinks. Sexuality in particular is a field of misperceptions and misinterpretations. And Emma, who does not know that she is in love with Knightley, proves to be in some ways as opaque to herself as others are to her. She talks Harriet into being attracted to the snobbish and self-seeking Mr Elton, which is a version of art (or imagination) creating reality; but reality strikes back stealthily to thwart her plotting. Here as so often in the history of the novel, design and real life don't quite slot together. Emma has too much freedom to improvise gratuitous schemes and experiment whimsically with other people's lives, while Fanny Price has too little. Austen herself, unlike her heroine, is a very English empiricist for whom judgement and reflection must be founded upon facts, and must be constantly corrected in the light of them.

The question, as often in Austen, is how to reconcile vivacity of spirits with sobriety of judgement. Or, as Henry James might have put it, how to be both fine and good. You need sprightliness, but not levity. It is best if virtue is also stylish, but this is not always a realistic expectation. The good, like Catherine Morland and Fanny Price, are admirable creatures, but one would far rather pass an hour over a cappuccino with Emma than with Fanny. Fanny and Edmund will no doubt have a loving marriage, but one suspects that it will not be quite the kind of household in which guests are generously plied with the whisky bottle. The point, however, is that the novel is aware of this too. If Fanny's dullness and timidity are a kind of irony, it is because the novel recognizes that this is the price which virtue, not least that of a dependent woman without resources, has to pay in a predatory social order. It is hardly virtue's fault that it is forced on the defensive. Fanny would like to affirm rather than refuse, but the profligacy of others makes this impossible.

To those who understandably feel dissatisfied with such an anaemic protagonist, the novel contains an implicit caution that if we would have her more vivacious, we might make her more vulnerable as a result. *Mansfield Park* does not really work unless we feel the genuine liveliness of the morally brittle Mary Crawford, who for all her faults can be notably kind to Fanny, rather as *Emma* does not work unless we sympathize with the heroine's skittishness as well as seeing its defects. We are made to appreciate that some of Emma's faults arise from being too animated for her narrow social sphere, a fact for which she is scarcely to be blamed. Austen believes like Fanny in a placid, tranquil rural existence, if only because there are fewer chances for vice in such situations; but she is shrewd and self-assured enough to be able to subject her own values to ironic criticism, allowing this placidity to look sluggish in contrast with Mary Crawford's sophisticated zest. It is the same bland self-ironizing which inspires her to present Mr Knightley, who speaks up for her own values, as such a sententious old stick.

For all her aversion to fantasy, Austen is not a rationalist, in the sense of one who trusts in the supremacy of reason. For one thing, her Tory Christian pessimism, with its sense of the irreparably flawed condition of humanity, would hardly allow her to be so. It is this sense of human imperfection which fuels her hostility to Marianne Dashwood's cult of sensibility, since Romantics like Marianne and her mother tend to trust to the innate goodness of human nature. For another thing, Austen is well aware that there are human situations in which reason or good sense are not much use, and says as much in *Northanger Abbey*. She sends up rationalism in the person of Mary Bennet in *Pride and Prejudice*, who talks as pompously as she does only because she is almost entirely inexperienced. Unlike most characters in books, Mary talks like a book. Catherine Morland may start off as a credulous *ingénue* with a Marianne-like faith in human nature, but it is a faith she will finally come to shed along with her Gothic illusions. Men and women are exposed as more cynical, egoistic and self-gratifying than she thought them. And though General Tilney may not be a Gothic villain, he is unmasked as a callous domestic tyrant. As far as patriarchy goes, England is not, after all, free from some of the most typical forms of Gothic horror.

If morality matters so much to Jane Austen, it is partly because of an historical crisis. It is not a crisis which enters her novels directly; indeed, it is not one which Austen is aware of as such, though she was certainly conscious of its symptoms. Unlike Scott, she does not think in historical terms. It is a commonplace that her novels have few comments pass on the great social and political events of the day. Nobody asks where Louis Napoleon is in Dickens, but plenty of people seem to ask where Napoleon Bonaparte is in Austen. In fact, Austen does allude to public events of the day, and her unfinished novel *Sanditon* raises colonial issues. So does *Mansfield Park*, in which Sir Thomas Bertram's elegant country estate is funded by his slave plantation in Antigua. In any case, as Raymond Williams points out in *The*

Country and the City,[5] Austen's novels concern the social history of the landed gentry, and it is hard to find a topic more central to English history than that. Jane Austen did not write about the family rather than society; on the contrary, the family in her day *was* society, or at least the governing sector of it. In the eighteenth century, a few hundred families owned a quarter of the cultivated land of England.

Yet the class which these families composed was morally failing, and it is part of the business of Jane Austen's writing to recall it to its traditional sense of duty. Throughout the eighteenth century, the gentry had been a superbly self-confident class, one whose political dominance over English society as a whole went largely unquestioned. As Austen is writing, it is about to confront a formidable rival in the form of the urban middle class, which is being ushered over the historical horizon by the industrial revolution. But this is still largely in the future; and even when industrial capitalism has arrived on the scene, the landed gentry will come to strike an historic bargain with it. They will continue to exercise political and cultural power themselves, even if, as the nineteenth century wears on, they will find themselves governing increasingly in the name of their middle-class inferiors.

What concerns Austen is not so much these challenges from outside, but threats to the governing bloc of gentry and aristocracy from within. The English landed gentry was a capitalist class – in fact, it was the oldest capitalist class in the world. We are not dealing, then, with a case of 'traditional' versus 'modern'. On the contrary, it is precisely because the rural gentry had long been a 'modern' as well as a 'traditional' class, involved in rent, capital and property as well as in balls in Bath and ceremonies at court, that the moral rot had set in. Land had long been a commodity, and it is certainly that in Austen's fiction. She has a notably quick eye for the size and value of an estate, along with the likely social status of its proprietor. But she is not generally so entranced by an estate's physical and natural appearance, and we rarely see anyone working in its fields. 'Land' is more a monetary abstraction than an expanse of soil. It is seen as property, not as a working environment, as it is in Thomas Hardy. The English countryside had long since been reorganized by market forces. In Austen's own day it was living through a particularly devastating phase of that process, in the enclosure of land for the purpose of increased profits.

Yet the class of rural gentry to which Austen belonged – a class of which she is both an astringent critic and an ardent champion – did not quite see itself in these crudely economic terms. Even though it was investing more and more in overseas trade and the financial markets, it could still regard itself as a paternalist, traditionally minded squirearchy. Its privileges, so it maintained, brought with them responsibility for the welfare of the lower orders. Hence the regulation trips to poor tenants' cottages and dutiful tendings of low-life sick beds which figure in Austen's writing. The gentry was not just a group of entrepreneurs but the apex of a whole rural way of life, one which was thought to embody the finest values of English society. Culture in the sense of the cultivation of the land – agriculture – generated rents, which in turn gave birth to culture in the sense of elegance of manners and nobility of spirit. In some ways, then, these landed aristocrats and country gentlemen continued to cultivate a traditional rural lifestyle, even if this cultural self-image was increasingly at odds with their economic base. It is this kind of rural order which Austen admired and upheld.

Yet the business dealings of the gentry were in danger of corrupting their traditional values from within, as well as bringing them into closer contact with the tainting influences of commerce, finance and the city. And this, in Austen's eyes, was at risk of insidiously undermining their moral standing. She drew, then, on the cultivation which genteel society afforded her, in order to criticize something of the material base which made that cultivation possible. Social mobility, for example, was on the increase, which posed a threat to the rural tranquillity which Austen esteemed so highly. Urban wealth, restless social ambition, moral frivolity and metropolitan manners were infiltrating the countryside. They were doing so not least through the marriage market, as landed capital sought a new lease of life by assimilating through marriage the children of urban capitalists and financiers.

Daniel Defoe comments on this process in *The Compleat English Gentleman*, where he writes of ancient families not scrupling to form alliances through marriage with what he calls 'bred' gentlemen: 'the heirs (of ancient families) fly to the city as the last resort, where by marrying a daughter of some person meaner in dignity, but superior in money . . . estates mortgaged and in danger of being lost . . . are recovered, the fame and figure of the family restored'. Conversely, Defoe adds, the gentry can become merchants with no loss to their 'blood'. It is the traditional English alliance between urban and agrarian capital, one which was later to be pursued in so-called public schools where the sons of both classes were able to rub shoulders. It played its part in securing for England an enviably resilient ruling class, one fit for its role in running an enormous empire.

All this, however, seemed to more conservative gentry like Austen to be in dire danger of lowering the moral and cultural tone of English rural life.

It was not just upstarts, blow-ins and social climbers like Mr Elton in *Pride and Prejudice* who were causing the trouble; Fanny Price, after all, is a kind of outsider too. It was moral laxity, social irresponsibility and poor steward-ship in the rural ruling class itself which lay at the root of the problem. The governing order is not so much under siege as in danger of imploding. So much is clear from the Bertram ménage of *Mansfield Park*, with the emotion-ally cold Sir Thomas, the inert, obtuse Lady Bertram, the insufferable Mrs Norris, the dissolute Tom and his disreputable sisters. Somewhat lower down the social scale, there is the ironic detachment of Mr Bennet, the empty-headedness of his wife and the scattiness of his man-mad younger daughters.

Some of these social developments are obvious enough in the novels themselves, in which we can watch a two-way traffic between landed and urban capital. Sir Thomas Bertram, as we have seen, is a colonial proprietor as well as a rural magnate. The Crawfords of *Mansfield Park*, despite their fashionable metropolitan ways, have income from landed property, while the landowning Dashwoods of *Sense and Sensibility* are rural capitalists who are busy enclosing common land and buying up farms. Sir Walter Elliot of *Persuasion* is a landed aristocrat, but needs to regenerate his precarious in-come from non-landed sources. Darcy in *Pride and Prejudice* is a rich land-owner of a venerable family who has inherited his estate, whereas his friend Bingley is looking to purchase an estate since he will not inherit one. Sir William Lucas in the same novel has risen from trade to a knighthood, while Mr Bennet has some landed wealth but has married into the profes-sional middle classes. Catherine Morland of *Northanger Abbey* is a middle-class woman who marries into an ancient landowning family.

Jane Austen was by no means opposed in principle to trade or the profes-sions. On the contrary, it is greatly in Edmund's favour in *Mansfield Park* that he is a clergyman, and one who robustly defends the idea of a professional vocation to the sceptical Mary Crawford. Austen is not against mobility within the class system, as is plain when Catherine marries into Northanger Abbey and Fanny into Mansfield Park. Neither is there anything inherently shameful about urban or mercantile capitalism. The danger lies at the moral and cultural level, not at the material one. For it was on their culture, in the broad sense of values, standards, ideals and a fine quality of living, that the landowning classes had relied for so much of their authority. Their purpose had been to achieve hegemony – to win the loyalty and assent of their underlings by their moral example – rather than simply to rule them by force. And the English landed classes had been on the whole remarkably successful in this project. If this hegemony now started to crumble from within, in a society already shaken to its roots by riots, spy scares, agrarian discontent, economic depression, working-class militancy, the threat of revolution abroad and invasion at home, then the situation could scarcely be more serious.

'Manners', wrote Edmund Burke, 'are more important than laws'. This, in a word, is the creed of the kind of gentry whom Austen commends. It is by translating laws and codes into beguiling forms of behaviour that men and women come to appreciate their force. What secures the allegiance of the lower orders is not simply a set of abstract precepts from on high, but the graceful, well-ordered, socially responsible forms of a whole way of life. It is culture, nor coercion, which is the key to sound government. Indeed, what else is the realist novel but a way of translating abstractions into living characters and dramatic situations? As such, it is a small model of political hegemony in itself, winning our approval for its values not through abstract argument, but by transforming those values into lived experience. The common people may scarcely make a showing in Austen's novels, but they are bound to figure implicitly in any reflection on a decline in ruling-class standards. Not just the common people of England, either: if English upper-class 'character' is flawed and defective, how can one govern the empire?

Nothing could be more ominous, then, than a governing class which is plagued by moral misrule. The custodians of English culture have become infected by various forms of anarchy, from the disowning of parental authority to the giddy pursuit of fashion, from vulgar self-seeking to heartless economic calculation, from sexual flightiness to the worship of money. And Austen, as we have suggested, raises her voice to recall them to their true vocation. It is one of the limits of her vision, however, that she portrays the problem chiefly as a moral one, rather than grasping its historical and political roots. If this sounds too exacting a demand, as though one is asking Jane Austen to write like Karl Marx, we should recall that this was among the achievements of Walter Scott.

Whatever his political blind spots, Scott did not imagine that what had gone awry was simply a matter of morals and manners. He was therefore sceptical of the idea that it could be repaired simply by a change of individual heart. He was aware that powerful historical forces were at work in society, moulding the values and moral qualities of individual men and women. And he was able to see this because of the history to which he himself belonged, which was very different from Austen's. It is hardly surprising that a politically powerless woman sequestered from the public sphere should see matters primarily in moral and personal terms. Austen was in fact too hard-headed a realist to have any great faith in the likelihood of moral regeneration; but she could not conceive of a political dimension to questions of moral conduct, in the way that, say, Mary Wollstonecraft could.

Even so, this limited viewpoint captured a good deal of the truth, and did so because of its limitations rather than despite them. It is sometimes pointed out that the English have a deep-rooted tradition of moral thought, but not so well developed a heritage of political, sociological and philosophical ideas. Morality rather than sociology is the English forte, from Samuel Johnson to George Orwell. And this is one important reason why the novel has flourished so abundantly in England, since the novel (as we shall see when we come to look at George Eliot, Henry James and D. H. Lawrence) can be seen as a supremely moral form. In fact, the evolution of the nineteenth-century realist novel is bound up with a sea-change in the very idea of morality – roughly speaking, from morality as a matter of timeless codes and absolute principles, to morality as a concern with qualities of lived experience.

In English culture, then, the moral has acted in one sense to displace social and political thought. This is evident enough in the fiction of Jane Austen, whom we admire among other things for her extraordinary moral intelligence. Only Henry James is her equal here. On the whole, the English have preferred to preach rather than to analyse, to attend to sins and solecisms rather than social structures. Yet moral values, as we have argued, were indeed vital to the continuing authority of the English upper classes – so that this preoccupation with morals and manners was not simply a displacement of more fundamental questions. Morals and manners were part of high politics. And since they were primarily the concern of women, women being stereotypically supposed to be specialists in such matters, this meant that so-called women's issues lay very close to the heart of the public sphere, even if they were rarely acknowledged to do so.

If one way in which women can help regenerate the gentry is by writing about it, another is by marrying into it. Both Catherine Morland and Fanny Price bring precious resources to the upper classes by grafting their sound qualities on to it through marriage. Marriages in Austen do not need to involve material equality: a woman with a small marriage portion can marry a much grander man, as the elder Bennet sisters do. The affluent Henry Crawford courts the penniless Fanny Price. These, to be sure, are all transactions *within* the larger class of gentlemen and gentlewomen; you can marry outside your class, but not beyond the pale of polite society as a whole. It is wrong to disdain the lower orders, as the snobbish Emma does, but it is equally wrong to encourage them to aspire beyond their station, as Emma does too.

A title and a spectacular fortune are of no value to you if you do not love their possessor. Indeed, few things are more morally appalling in Austen's world than marrying for social or financial gain. All the same, the fact that you should not make a fetish of wealth and status does not mean that you should cavalierly ignore them. Some of Henry James's characters can forget about wealth, but this is because they have enough wealth to do so. You need love for marriage – but it must be a rational love, one based on a sound judgement of the material situation. Austen rightly rejects the Romantic prejudice that love and reason are incompatible. It would be unreasonable to marry on a pittance. You cannot enjoy a true harmony of minds with someone whose social background is simply too different from yours. Material goods, so the tough-minded Austen recognizes, will not make you happy in themselves, but properly handled they can be mightily conducive to it. As Virginia Woolf insisted in her materialist wisdom: nobody can love well unless they have dined well.

When Elizabeth Bennet remarks that she first became aware of her affection for Darcy when she set eyes on his elegantly laid-out estates, we suspect for a moment that her author is being ironic, as though Elizabeth were to confide that she fell in love with him when she first clapped eyes on his bank balance. But the comment is not of course intended as ironic, since the material or external can and should be an outward sign of the inner or moral. The taste, sound judgement, sense of proportion, and blending of tact and imagination which went into the fashioning of Darcy's estates testify to a morally estimable character. It is not surprising in this light that Jane Austen should have remarked that she could imagine marrying the poet George Crabbe even though she had never met him. Ideally, there is a correlation between the moral and the material, of which marriage is the consummation. In choosing a marriage partner, both the inward or spiritual (love) and the external or material (rank, property, family) must be given due weight. Marriage is the union of the subjective and objective. It is the place where social forms and moral values most vitally intersect. If you can overemphasize the material dimension of marriage, as Samuel Johnson did when he claimed to believe that the whole process should be nationalized and organized by the Lord Chancellor, you can also make the opposite mistake.

In reality, though, the moral and the material are far from harmoniously unified. It is possible, for example, to be both poor and generous-minded, like Miss Bates in *Emma*. Material impoverishment by no means entails moral impoverishment, just as social grandeur by no means entails moral magnificence. If it did, the word 'gentleman', which hovers ambiguously between a social and a moral sense, would be less of a fraught term in English social history than it is. The tenant farmer Robert Martin in *Emma* is a gentleman, and a man morally esteemed by Mr Knightley, but this does not mean that Knightley would invite him on a shoot or propose marriage to his sister. Aristocrats can be ill-bred, and some of those like Willoughby who have excellent manners have atrocious morals. The problem with manners is that they can run deep, but are nevertheless easily counterfeited.

It is appropriate to have such outward signs of inward grace, despite the naive Romantic assumption that forms and appearances do not matter. The drawback is that such essential outward signs can always be used to dissemble. Austen herself was a great believer in forms, even though she was aware that it was not always easy to mark off this creed from a vapid formalism. Like Roland Barthes, she knew that the way to avoid such formalism was not to fight shy of form altogether, but to take it with immense seriousness. She was also a deep believer in the materiality of social and moral values, in contrast to some high-minded denigration of the material world. Moral states should make their presence felt in material ones.

We are not yet at the historical stage where the moral and the material, or 'culture' and 'society', will be at daggers drawn, as they are for the later Coleridge, Matthew Arnold and John Ruskin. It is still possible for Austen to see links between these two spheres – between, for example, a courteous social manner and a generosity of spirit, or between high social rank and moral responsibility for others. But she also knew that it is sometimes hard to draw the line between a proper materiality and a self-interested materialism.

The English have traditionally admired balance, symmetry, moderation and sound judgement, and there is plenty of these qualities in Austen. They are present not only in the values she speaks up for, but in the very formal design of her fiction itself. Form in Austen is already a moral position. Yet she is not, any more than Walter Scott, a devotee of the middle way. Sense is more trustworthy than sensibility; objectivity more precious than subjective feeling; deference, hierarchy and tradition more to be prized than dissidence or individual freedom. Like Scott, she is a 'modern' conservative rather than a Romantic reactionary, believing as she does in the need for reform and improvement within the status quo. But this does not make her a middle-of-the-road liberal any more than it makes Scott one. At a time when the novel form was at its most fertile and innovatory, capable in principle of taking many different paths, the path that was, so to speak, 'selected' for it by literary history was that of a conservative realism. Of this, Scott and Austen were the major representatives.

It is true that some later writers in this tradition were to be far more liberal or radical in their vision than Austen and Scott themselves. Yet a certain tone, and certain definitive limits, had nevertheless been set. The English novel was *en route* to becoming a marvellously subtle medium of psychological truth and social investigation. Such achievements, however, rarely come without a price. A certain norm of what was possible, reasonable and desirable in fiction had now been established, which for the most part involved excluding the 'non-realist'. It was because this norm was to prove so powerful that it was hard even to raise the question of what exactly counted as 'realist', and what did not. Not to speak of who got to decide.

THE BRONTËS

There were four surviving Brontë children, not three. The sisters had a less celebrated brother, Branwell, whose scapegrace career might have sprung straight out of one of their own novels. Being the sibling of those sisters can't have been easy, but Branwell made a more spectacular hash of it than seemed strictly necessary. Hash, indeed, is the word. When he was not cadging gin money from his cronies, Branwell was busy poisoning himself with various shady chemical substances scrounged from the local pharmacy. Chronically unemployable, he spent much of his time carousing with raffish, down-at-heel artists in a Bradford hotel, and with characteristic ill luck took up portrait painting at just the point where the industry was being killed off by the invention of the daguerreotype. He had a strange passion for boxing, and a morose conviction of being eternally damned.

Flushed with dreams of literary grandeur, Branwell scribbled 30-odd literary works between the ages of 10 and 17, most of it second-rate melodrama. One of his characters, the dissolute, self-destructive Alexander Percy, anarchist, atheist and aristocrat, is clearly Branwell himself shorn of the dope and gin-tippling. Percy is in debt to the tune of £300,000, a suitably glamourized version of his author's slate at Haworth's Black Bull, and is egged on by his villainous comrades Naughty and Lawless to commit parricide to restore his fortunes. That Oedipal fantasies of father-killing should crop up in Branwell's writing will come as no surprise to anyone even mildly acquainted with the character of his tyrannical father. One of Percy's most trusty comrades is a lawyer who lives in 'Derrinane Abbey'. Derrynane, in County Kerry, was the seat of the barrister Daniel O'Connell, the Irish nationalist leader (indeed, so it has been claimed, the most popular politician

of nineteenth-century Europe), who was then conducting his mass political campaigns against British colonial rule in Ireland. We shall see the significance of this in a moment.

The tragicomic Branwell also amused himself by experimenting with exotic pseudonyms, and drawing pen portraits of himself hanged, stabbed and licked by hell fire. Despite his assurance of eternal damnation, he taught in the local Sunday school, savaging the cowed children of Haworth in befuddled vengeance for his misfortunes. His old-school father provided him with a Romantic education which completely unfitted him for industrial middleclass England. His imagination was prematurely arrested, obsessionally fixated on heroic, traditionalist, military figures like Wellington and Bonaparte. His sole bid for fame came when he visited London with the vague hope of becoming an art student. Overawed by the metropolis, conscious of his own shabby, provincial appearance among its sophisticated crowds, he wandered around the streets of the capital in a dream, kept his letters of introduction to famous artists firmly in his pocket, and drank away his money in an East End pub. He returned to the Haworth parsonage with an implausible tale of having been mugged. He ended up, bathetically, as a ticket clerk on a Yorkshire railway station, where he promptly embezzled the takings. In September 1848, he scrawled his final document – a begging note for gin – and expired soon after in his father's arms, wasted and bronchitic.

Branwell's first name was actually Patrick, after his Irish father, and he himself lived a flamboyant stage-Irish existence. Indeed, almost everything he did conformed to the English stereotype of the feckless Mick: idle, drunken, pugnacious, rebellious, imaginative, extravagant, improvident. None of this was lost on the good people of Haworth. On one occasion, Patrick Brontë Senior took to the hustings as a Tory candidate for parliament only to find himself howled down by the crowd. When Branwell intervened loyally on his behalf, the local populace demonstrated their displeasure by burning an effigy of him with a potato in one hand and a herring in the other. The Brontë family may have tried to conceal their Irish origins, but their canny Yorkshire neighbours evidently kept it well in mind. At about the time that they were adorning Branwell's effigy with a potato, that crop was failing catastrophically in the Great Irish Famine, leaving one million of the Brontës' compatriots dead and driving millions more into exile.

By 1847, around three hundred thousand of those Irish emigrants had washed up in the port of Liverpool. One London journal portrayed them, and their famished children in particular, as looking like starving scarecrows dressed in rags with an animal growth of black hair obscuring their features.

Two years earlier, Branwell Brontë had himself taken a trip to Liverpool, where he might well have witnessed such scenes. The Great Famine was yet to break out at the time of Branwell's visit, but there would no doubt have been a good many semi-destitute Irish hanging around the city, most of them Irish-speaking. A few months after Branwell returned from the port, his sister Emily began writing *Wuthering Heights* – a novel in which the male protagonist, Heathcliff, is picked up starving off the streets of Liverpool by old Earnshaw. He is described as 'a dirty, ragged, black-haired child' who speaks a kind of 'gibberish'. The novel will later portray him as savage, lunatic, violent, subversive and uncouth – all stereotypical nineteenth-century British images of the Irish.

Whether or not Heathcliff was originally Irish, the Brontë sisters certainly were. 'Brontë country' for the English means a stretch of Yorkshire, whereas for the Irish it still signifies a region of County Down, the birthplace of Patrick Brontë Senior. The Brontës's father Patrick was a classic example of the scholarship boy, the son of an impoverished Ulster family which had struggled its way from cabin to cottage to tenant farm. He himself had worked as a blacksmith, linen-weaver and schoolmaster, before blazing an ambitious trail to Cambridge University, holy orders, high Toryism and an Anglican parsonage on the Yorkshire moors. Somewhere in the process, the Irish family name Brunty was Frenchified to Brontë, and Patrick liked to boast of aristocratic friendships cultivated at Cambridge. Like Heathcliff, he transformed himself from humble outsider to English gentleman, though with rather more success than Emily's creation. You can take Heathcliff out of the Heights, but you can't take the Heights out of Heathcliff.

In converting himself into an autocratic right-wing English cleric, Patrick was proving his fidelity to two venerable Irish customs: getting out of the place as soon as you could, and becoming more English than the English in the process. From Richard Steele, Oliver Goldsmith, Richard Brinsley Sheridan and Edmund Burke to George Bernard Shaw, Oscar Wilde and Brendan Bracken (Winston Churchill's impeccable anglicized personal secretary), the aim of the Irish immigrant was to beat the British at their own social game, thus demonstrating that imitation is the sincerest form of mockery.

If the Brontë sisters were ethnically divided between Irish and English, they were equally divided as female authors. 'Author' suggests authority, a capacity to speak commandingly in one's own voice, which was for the most part denied to nineteenth-century women. Hence the sisters' custom of concealing their gender behind male pseudonyms, a ploy all the more necessary because of the 'indelicate', indecorous nature of their turbulent texts. For some Victorians, it was bad enough having to read about bigamy, social climbing, grotesque physical violence and interracial marriage without the additional outrage of knowing that a woman's delicate mind lay behind these scandalous subjects.

The Brontës were caught up in social and geographical contradictions as well. They were provincial novelists, writing from a rugged, far-flung rural fastness for the cultivated readership of the metropolis. This underlined their isolation, a condition which was already apparent in the educated consciousness which cut them off from the common people, and to which their restricted circumstances as women mightily contributed. As with Dickens, solitude in their fiction sometimes seems, ironically, the situation of all men and women in a brutally individualist society which abandons them to their own devices. The sisters very 'eccentricity' is resonant of a common condition. To be alive in this social order is to be an orphan. Charlotte's protagonists typically set out on their narratives bereft of all kinsfolk, with nothing but their own robust enterprise to sustain them. The self in these novels is naked, unhoused and therefore perilously vulnerable; but for the same reason it is conveniently set free from all constraint, able in classic middle-class style to write its own script and forge its own destiny.

The Brontës' environs were more those of Nature than culture – though if they wrote for people who might never have climbed a hill, they also addressed themselves to those who might never have seen a mill. Haworth may have been marooned in bleak moorland, but it was close enough to the Yorkshire mill towns for the sisters to have witnessed a good deal of near-destitution on their own doorstep, not least in the so-called Hungry Forties. The Brontës were caught between country and city, rather as D. H. Lawrence was later to be brought up in a twilight zone between the rural east Midlands and the Nottinghamshire coal field. Indeed, the years of the sisters' childhood were a time of ruination for thousands of hand-workers scattered in hill-cottages throughout the region – one aspect of that destruction of the handloom weavers which Karl Marx described in *Capital* as the most terrible tragedy of English history. The Brontës' later years coincided with strikes, Chartism, struggles against the Corn Laws and agitations for factory reform. Indeed, the West Riding of Yorkshire where they lived was perhaps the stoutest stronghold of Chartism and working-class radicalism in the north of England. One contemporary government official wrote that there was 'a ferocious civil war' boiling in the district; and the Brontës' own village of Haworth had several worsted mills and a more than century-old industry.

The sisters grew up near one of the sources of the Industrial Revolution, in an English county divided between large landed estates and intensive manufacturing; and far from being mysteriously sequestered from all this, living only in their own private imaginative world, their fiction is profoundly influenced by it. In fact, Charlotte's novel *Shirley* is explicitly set in a landscape of industrial manufacture, large-scale capitalist agriculture and working-class unrest. The Brontës were not, then, three weird sisters deposited upon the Yorkshire moors from some metaphysical outer space. On the contrary, their lives were shaped by some of the most typical conflicts of early Victorian England – conflicts between rural and urban, colony and metropolis, commercial south and industrial north, female 'sensibility' and male power.

In this sense, one can detect in the sisters' own individual crises of identity the 'identity crisis' of a whole social order, which with the early emergence of industrial capitalism is being shaken to its roots. The wretchedness, desire, repression, punitive discipline and spiritual hunger which mark the Brontës' fiction, intensely personal though they are, also speak of a whole society in traumatic transition. It is, as Raymond Williams puts it in consciously Blakeian terms, 'a world of desire and hunger, of rebellion and pallid convention'.[1] The so-called 'industrial novel' – the Brontës, Elizabeth Gaskell, Disraeli, Charles Kingsley and their colleagues – is not merely recording these cataclysmic upheavals: it is a forensic instrument in the attempt to interpret and assimilate them.

Religiously speaking, the Brontë family belonged to the Anglican establishment, and were in this sense socially respectable; but their father Patrick was 'Low church', and from him and their Calvinist Cornish aunt they inherited a Dissenting, Evangelical strain. Their mother was strongly Methodist. This tension between orthodoxy and dissent was then reflected in their social status. In common with most of the leading novelists of nineteenth-century England, the Brontës, as children of an educated. ambitious yet far-from-affluent parson with the inferior status of a 'perpetual curate', sprang from that unstable, ambiguous spot in the social hierarchy, the lower middle class. Dickens, son of a financially harassed clerk who had seen the inside of a debtors' prison, hailed from much the same precarious point, and never ceased to be fascinated in his fiction by the poignant, preposterous world of the shabby-genteel. Despite his fascination with London, his home town was in rural Kent, so that this street-wise Cockney was actually up from the country. George Eliot was the daughter of a Midlands farm bailiff,

and Thomas Hardy the son of a small-time West Country builder. Even Jane Austen, though hardly of the shop-keeping or pen-pushing classes, occupied a similarly ambivalent position towards the lower edge of the upper class.

The major nineteenth-century English novel, then, is for the most part the product of the provincial petty bourgeoisie, not of the metropolitan upper class. As we have seen already, the novel had always been regarded as something of an upstart, ill-bred form, and thus an appropriate literary mode for those who are socially aspiring, sidelined or displaced. Moreover, writers like Dickens and the Brontës, caught as they were between conflicting spheres and allegiances, were able to dramatize some of the definitive contradictions of a mobile, dislocated, rapidly altering social landscape, in a way less possible for those like Thackeray or Trollope more comfortably ensconced in a single social domain. Because of their equivocal position, they could look both up and down the social hierarchy, thus taking in a broader, richer, more complex range of experience.

The novelist who has a populist ear for the voice of the people, yet at the same time commands the resources of high culture, is likely in such circumstances to outflank all competitors. The lower middle class – 'contradiction incarnate', as Karl Marx caustically described it – is wedged painfully between a higher, more civilized realm to which it aspires, and a plebeian world into which it is in perpetual danger of being thrust down. Ursula Brangwen of D. H. Lawrence's *The Rainbow* feels as a child 'the grudging power of the mob lying in wait for her'. And this potentially tragic conflict between aspiration and self-undoing lies close to the heart of Victorian society.

It certainly lies close to the heart of the Brontës. All three of the sisters became governesses, a role which exactly captures the contrariness of their social condition. The most vivid account in their fiction of the social violence inflicted on the governess is Anne Brontë's *Agnes Grey*. The governess is a servant, to be hired and fired like a footman; but she is an 'upper' servant, one employed because of her learning and cultivation and entrusted with the children of the family. If she is the social inferior of the hard-headed Yorkshire manufacturers who hire her talents, she also feels herself their spiritual superior, throttling back a ferocious resentment at being treated like a housemaid, and inwardly indignant at having to care for their pampered brats. Her culture has become a commodity – the point at which an inner world of spiritual value and an outer world of economic necessity come incongruously together.

All this is reflected in the curious contradictions of what one might call the Brontë sensibility. On the one hand, there is a streak of dissent, blunt exasperation and turbulent rebellion, directed often enough at the privileged gentry. This more earthy aspect of the sisters admires in stereotypically north-of-England style whatever is plain, shrewd, hardy and cool-headed. It values energetic enterprise and individualism, the advancement of one's interests through canny calculation; but this self-promoting impulse can also take the form of radical protest and an egalitarian sympathy with the victims of the system. There is an angry, injured demand for recognition in the Brontës which is genuinely dissident. On the other hand, there is the side of the sisters which aspires to gentility, feels a conservative or Romantic reverence for rank, heroism, tradition and social achievement, and dutifully conforms to the established conventions. If the outsider feels irate at the social system, she or he is also the one most likely to value what status and security it has to offer. Besides, you do not kick away the ladder you are trying to climb. It is not hard to read in this fissured sensibility something of the actual situation of the Brontë sisters, wedged as they were between male and female, patrician and plebeian, Irish and English, metropolis and province, deference and rebellion. They are an extraordinary combination of gushing Romantic fantasy and astute rationality, quivering sensitivity and bluff common sense.

Of all three sisters, Anne Brontë's fiction is the least touched by these contradictions. Whereas Charlotte's heroines are both allured and repelled by worldly success, *Agnes Grey* and *The Tenant of Wildfell Hall* enforce a more simple contrast between love, truth and moral integrity on the one hand, and social achievement on the other. It is not a matter of reconciling true love with the upper-class marriage market, as it is in *Jane Eyre*, but of rejecting the latter for the former. The upper classes in Anne's fiction are for the most part vain, shallow and egoistic, and in both of her novels they are countered by morally righteous protagonists who feel nothing of the glamour of worldly status, the promptings of social ambition or the seductiveness of Romantic fantasies.

One can read Charlotte Brontë's novels, by contrast, as strategies for reconciling the conflicting sets of values we have outlined. Charlotte's heroines are typically divided selves – women who are outwardly demure yet inwardly passionate, full of an erotic and imaginative hungering which must be locked back upon itself in meekness, self-sacrifice and stoical endurance. This is as true of Lucy Snowe, heroine of *Villette*, as it is of Jane Eyre; indeed, it speaks eloquently of the situation of all women of intellect and

aspiration in a stiflingly patriarchal order. A woman must look out for herself in a predatory society; yet in Charlotte's novels, the sturdy self-reliance which this involves is at odds with the need to find true security by submitting to the protection of a more powerful male. The self's lonely integrity must be defended by silence, prudence and cunning, yet this involves a self-lacerating mutilation of one's spontaneous being.

The point, then, is to harness prudence to the ends of passion, reaching for your fulfilment only when such an act will not make you dangerously vulnerable. The strategy of Charlotte's novels revolves on allowing these solitary, self-tormenting figures their emotional and imaginative self-realization, but in a form which will satisfy the social conventions, and thus bring them status and security at the same time. To fulfil your desire outside such conventions, not least for an unprotected woman, is to be perilously exposed and defenceless. To fulfil it within the conventions means that the extravagant demands of romance can be met with no detriment to the sober requirements of realism.

One can see well enough how this strategy operates in *Jane Eyre*. Jane herself is both demure and dissenting, ambitious and self-effacing, submissive and self-assertive; and the narrative, by conveniently disposing of Rochester's mad wife Bertha, allows her to fulfil both her erotic desires and worldly aspirations without the social disgrace of committing bigamy. Jane refuses the temptation to transgress the social conventions, and will reap her reward for it, ironically, by winning herself a husband who is attractively unconventional. She also refuses the dreary life of moral duty offered to her by the austerely fanatical missionary St John Rivers, which would both deny her fulfilment and remove her from the social world altogether. What Rivers demands of her is self-sacrifice; but if this sounds disagreeable enough to us, it is by no means entirely so to Charlotte Brontë. On the contrary, for her characters to renounce self-sacrifice demands considerable self-sacrifice.

Why is this so? It is because Charlotte's fictions are as enthralled by the vision of relinquishing the self as they are by the prospect of affirming it. In this, as we shall see, she has something in common with George Eliot. In a potent blend of social conformity, Evangelical guilt and female submissiveness, the lure of self-abasement in Charlotte's fiction is especially strong. It is, paradoxically, one way in which the self can be most deeply gratified. Few passions are more seductive than the passion for self-immolation. There is a Romantic allure, for Jane Eyre as much as George Eliot's Maggie Tulliver or Dorothea Brooke, in the vision of a martyr-like surrender of the self to some loftier cause or superior power. Yet there is always a danger that one will abnegate the self without reaping any value in return; and it is this that Jane must learn to avoid. Her schoolfriend Helen Burns chooses this saintly, self-abnegating path, but Jane is determined not to follow her along it. 'I must keep in good health, and not die', she tells the odious Mr Brocklehurst with commendable impudence, and so indeed she does. She must find a form of self-effacement which will bring self-fulfilment in its wake. Submission is a virtue, but only up to a point.

This, seen perhaps a shade cynically, is what happens in her relationship with the devilishly Byronic Mr Rochester. Part of what wins Rochester's heart is exactly Jane's Quakerish, deferential mien, in contrast to the flashy egoism of a frigid beauty like Blanche Ingram. At the same time, however, the lower-middle-class rebel finds a resonance of her own nonconformist spirit in the cavalier licence of the gentry. Rochester would not find Jane attractive if she was simply dull, so the novel must ensure that she blends flashes of spirit and flirtatious self-assertion with her docility, without any suggestion that she is, in Lucy Snowe's revealing words about herself, 'bent on success'. Worldly success will spring from a proper unworldliness, rather as spiritual victory for St John Rivers will flow from martyrdom. It is just that what counts as martyrdom for Rivers would be spiritual suicide for Jane.

D. H. Lawrence once described the ending of *Jane Eyre* as 'pornographic', and one can see what it is about it which would scandalize a male chauvinist like him. In order to prepare the way for Jane and Rochester's union, it is not enough to topple mad Bertha in flames from the rooftop; it is also necessary to cut the wickedly beguiling Rochester down to size by maiming and blinding him. This achieves a number of ends simultaneously. For one thing, he is less likely to go off philandering if he can't see, which helps to secure Jane's power over him. In a gratifying reversal of the power relationship, it is now he who is humbly dependent upon her. But taming his anarchic energies also ensures a certain fulfilling equality between the two lovers, shrinking the social gulf between them; and Rochester is not so symbolically castrated as to cease to captivate Jane as her ruggedly handsome lord and master. In some ways, indeed, he is now even more of a seductive rough beast.

Crippling the object of Jane's affections is also the novel's way of wreaking vengeance on Rochester for threatening to lead its heroine astray, as well as a guilt-stricken self-punishment on Jane's part for her own illicit desires. The smouldering social and sexual resentment which Jane has prudently throttled back throughout the narrative is now, so to speak, released by the novel itself on her behalf in a lurid Gothic melodrama – and its target is the symbol of social order and sexual aspiration, the local squire Mr Rochester. He is the novel's sacrificial offering to social and moral orthodoxy – yet he is sacrificed in such a way as to allow Jane her deference and self-achievement along with her rebellion. She is also granted a deeply gratifying victory over horrors like the Reed family – in fact, over several of those who have rivalled her or done her down. This fantasy of wish-fulfilment is so blatant that, without the softening effect of Jane and the novel's more homely, down-to-earth dimension, it might well prove too distasteful for the reader. We are repelled by too-palpable fantasies of this kind in fiction as we are in our friends.

If the relationship between Jane and Rochester takes the form of a power struggle, so in fact do almost all human relationships in the Brontës' fiction. In fact, they have a distinctively sado-masochistic quality about them, which is part of what made the sisters' writing so scandalous to some of their contemporaries. It is not quite the kind of thing one finds in Mrs Gaskell. With Jane, Lucy Snowe and William Crimsworth, protagonist of Charlotte's novel *The Professor*, there is a delight in both domination and subjugation, one which reflects something of the complex class dynamics of the Brontës' world. The lower middle class is caught between deference and defiance, and it is as though sado-masochism is the 'political unconscious' of this ambivalence, the form it takes in the sphere of the erotic and interpersonal. Sexual ambiguity is both painful and pleasurable, which can also be true of both exercising power and submitting to it. Charlotte Brontë's fiction admires autocracy as much as it feels outraged by it.

The allure of self-sacrifice, in which the self reaps pleasure from the prospect of its own deathly dissolution, belongs with this sado-masochistic syndrome. In terms of sexual stereotypes, sado-masochism involves a crossing of masculine and feminine roles. William Crimsworth of *The Professor* is really a cross-dressed version of a Charlotte heroine, and the sisters themselves 'cross-dress' in order to become authors, taking on male pseudonyms. The heroine of *Shirley* is a mill-owner and landowner, and thus a woman with stereotypically masculine status and authority. Even the virile Rochester, who has an intriguing resemblance to his tall, black-visaged, emotionally tempestuous wife, disguises himself as a woman, symbolically divesting himself of his manhood in an egalitarian overture to a woman (Jane) who herself reveals many of the 'masculine' virtues of endurance, rugged self-reliance and self-enterprise.

William Crimsworth of *The Professor*, like Jane Eyre, is both spirited and cautiously conventional. Like Jane, too, though far more consciously, he learns how to turn his cool, protective self-possession to devastating advantage, in his turbulent power struggles with his female pupils. He is both man and woman, victim and master, exile and insider, rebel and conservative. Lucy Snowe of *Villette* is another of Charlotte's schizoid heroines, outwardly frigid yet inwardly fantasizing, who finds her fulfilment in the figure of the agreeably autocratic Paul Emmanuel.[2] Paul, who tenderly informs Lucy that 'you want so much checking, regulating, and keeping down', is himself both Romantic dissident and traditionalist Tory, defiantly individualist yet morally and socially orthodox; and it is just this combination which Charlotte's novels need to resolve their conflicts. To unite with such a figure is to have your own spiritual waywardness confirmed, but also enjoyably chastised.

Villette offers us an ambiguous, indeterminate conclusion, as it is not clear whether Paul is drowned at sea. It is as though the Romantic, wish-fulfilling impulse in the novel is too insistent to have Lucy's happiness snatched cruelly away, even as the book's more bitterly realist vision suggests that suffering, not least for women, is more probable in this sort of world than felicity. It is thus the only one of Charlotte's novels to sound a semi-tragic note – though the end of *Jane Eyre* is ominously overshadowed by an echo of the spiritual absolutism of St John Rivers, who is allowed the last word now that he no longer poses an actual threat. In the end, Charlotte's writing has the comedy of the picaresque, in which a solitary yet resourceful protagonist finally attains to social integration. Yet it also knows much about the torment and instability of identity in this kind of society – the perils and humiliations which must confront the exposed self on its trek to fulfilment, all of which threaten to strike its achievements hollow.

To turn from Charlotte to Emily is to shift from comedy to tragedy. What distinguishes *Wuthering Heights* is its refusal to compromise its desire, to strategically negotiate it, in the manner of Charlotte's fiction. The story of Catherine and Heathcliff is one of an absolute commitment and an absolute refusal. There is now an implacable conflict between passion and society, rebellion and moral orthodoxy – which is to say that Emily's great novel is that rare phenomenon, a tragic novel in the epoch of high realism.

Take, for example, Catherine's need to choose between Heathcliff and Edgar Linton. What she does, confronted with this dilemma, is try for a Charlotte-like compromise which tragically fails. Catherine rejects Heathcliff

as socially inferior and opts instead for the landowning Linton; but she hopes, even so, to maintain a Charlotte-like split between her inner and outer selves, the Romantic and the realist, by gracing the social sphere as Mrs Edgar Linton while holding fast to her love for Heathcliff in some more inward dimension. Desire and social convention may thus be managed together. Catherine's conviction that she *is* Heathcliff, that because their identities are at one she can never fundamentally betray him, unsurprisingly fails to impress Heathcliff himself, who would rather be a real-life lover than an ontological essence. He takes himself off in high dudgeon, and the tragic action is accordingly triggered. In this novel, so it would seem, there is a remorseless absolutism of desire which will brook no trade-offs or half-measures, and which finally drives both lovers to their death. Death is the outer limit of society, its natural or metaphysical Other, the only place where a ferociously destructive desire is finally appeased. And even that, so the novel's ending suggests, may be a touch optimistic.

This is not to take sides between Heathcliff and Linton, not least because the complex, decentred narrative structure deliberately complicates any such partisanship. As far as that option goes, there have been two broad schools of *Wuthering Heights* opinion: Heights critics and Grange critics, camps as intractably at odds as the fans of Celtic and Rangers. Heights critics are secretly in love with Heathcliff, finding in his dark, primitive, subversive existence a source of natural vitality far more fertile and fulfilling than the selfish, brittle, skin-deep civilization represented by the Lintons. This, one may note without excessive surprise, is a view largely endorsed by Heathcliff himself, for whom Linton is little more than an overbred fop. On this reading of the novel, the passionate, egalitarian relationship between Heathcliff and Catherine sketches a utopian possibility which, finding no place in a brutal, hierarchical society, must finally take up its residence in the realm of mythology.

For Grange critics, who seem to have included Charlotte Brontë among their ranks, such an account absurdly idealizes both Heathcliff and Catherine, as well as unjustly demeaning the Lintons. Heathcliff on this view is less some fertile life-force than a pitiless exploiter – a brutal, demonic, domineering property baron who treats Catherine violently and could never have developed a mature relationship with her. It is hard to imagine him drying the dishes or bathing the baby. From a Grange viewpoint, the couple's so-called relationship is an infantile, imaginary symbiosis which can survive only by shutting out the social world. Indeed, given that their liaison lacks any real sense of otherness or alterity, the very word 'relationship' is problematic.

There is something curiously impersonal at stake in their frenzied loving, which Grange critics might associate with its dehumanizing violence, and Heights critics with a domain of mythology deeper and richer than personal identity.

It is also a curiously sexless kind of desire, which can equally be seen both ways. For those to whom this is a regressive relationship, its sexless quality may be an unconscious defence against incest. Perhaps Heathcliff and Catherine are half-siblings, which might account for their profound, persistent sense of affinity. Or perhaps the relationship seems impersonal and unconventional for just the opposite reason – that in its sense of equality and unswerving mutual commitment, it prefigures a future world in which men and women might shuck off the crippling constraints of gender. Perhaps those whose perception is clouded by the existing power structures can only see such social possibilities in mythical or metaphysical terms, or as a state of Nature beyond the social altogether.

Are the two lovers, then, outside the social order in the way that revolutionaries are, or in the manner of a child who is allowed to run half-wild? Are they anti-social in a positive or negative sense, or are they both at the same time? It seems hard to speak of the Catherine–Heathcliff 'relationship' in conventional ethical terms such as compassion, affection, friendship, even love. But is this because, like infancy, it falls below the ethical realm, or because, like a revolutionary form of life, it goes beyond it? In the censorious eyes of the Grange, Catherine and Heathcliff are frozen in some mythological sphere, incapable of entering on the historical world. Linton may be insipid and effete, but he is a kindly, tender husband to Catherine, which Heathcliff is unlikely to have been. He may exist at the 'shallow' level of the social and the ethical, lacking the enigmatic depths and fierce animal energy of a Heathcliff, but the savage injuriousness of that energy could benefit from a touch of Edgar's pity and humanity.

Both Heights and Grange critical accounts have something to be said for them. But this is not to argue that the truth, as the good liberal instinctively imagines, lies somewhere in between. Lockwood is one of the good liberals of this book, and turns out to be a narrator at least as biased and befuddled as he is reliable and perceptive. *Wuthering Heights* is less a middle-of-the-road than a dialectical work, which allows us to see what partial justice there is on both sides without ceasing to insist on their tragic incompatibility, or fondly trusting that these two cases add up to some harmonious whole. The difference with Charlotte is instructive here. With Charlotte's novels, we are almost never in doubt what to think, since we have an authoritative

narrator to steer our responses and cue our judgements. It is true that this voice-over is sometimes disturbingly resonant with pride, spite, prejudice, petty malice, sly self-exculpation, eloquent omissions and special pleading; but it rarely leaves us in doubt about who is meant to be villainous and who virtuous.

By contrast, the complex, Chinese-boxes narrative structure of Emily's novel, in which one potentially unreliable narrative is embedded within another not entirely trustworthy one, and that perhaps within another, places any such assured assessment beyond our reach. It is clear enough, for example, that Nelly Dean has her knife into Heathcliff, which limits the value of her testimony. And we are only a few pages into the book before we realize that its first narrator, Lockwood, is hardly the brightest man in Europe. *Wuthering Heights* is a novel without a meta-narrative, and this formal quality is closely related to its complex seeing. It is not in a hurry to tell us whether Heathcliff is hero or demon, Nelly Dean shrewd or stupid, Catherine Earnshaw tragic heroine or spoilt brat.

Charlotte's novels give us direct access to a single, controlling consciousness; Emily's work interweaves its various mini-narratives in a way which makes this impossible. Malice, spite and pride are here emotions explored by the narrative, not, as occasionally with Charlotte, qualities of the narration itself. The book also makes matters more opaque by its garbled chronology. Charlotte's narratives tend to unfold in a straighforward linear way, reflecting the progress of the protagonist; *Wuthering Heights* reveals a more convoluted relation between past and present, progress and regression, the time-scheme of a narrator and the time-schemes of which he or she speaks.

We have seen that Charlotte's novels portray a conflict between genteel cultivation on the one hand and down-to-earth practicality on the other. What for her is a clash of values or lifestyles becomes in the more ambitious, cosmically framed *Wuthering Heights* a complex dialectic between Nature and Culture. During the Brontës' lifetime, England was in transition from being a largely rural to a predominantly industrial nation; and the sisters themselves, as we have seen, were geographically as well as historically cusped between both worlds. What was also in transition, as English history shifted from Wordsworth to Darwin, was the perception of Nature itself. If Nature in Emily's novel remains a source of vitality and transcendence, it is also creeping much closer to the vision of an evolutionary universe red in tooth and claw. Indeed, Emily writes in another place of how 'Nature is an inexplicable puzzle, life exists on a principle of destruction;

every creature must be the relentless instrument of death to the others, or himself cease to live'.[3]

In *Wuthering Heights*, this might well serve as much as a description of human society as of Nature. As the nineteenth century unfolds, there is a merging of Nature and culture in the minds of some thinkers, so that an evolutionary version of Nature as violent, predatory and pitiless is projected on to social relationships themselves. It is 'natural' for men and women to tear each other to pieces, even if, ironically, this conformity to Nature is from a civilized viewpoint 'unnatural'. At the same time, an early industrial-capitalist society which is itself a notably callous, exploitative place begins literally to shape Nature in its own image, which consequently becomes less and less a matter of Wordsworthian strangeness and solace.

Heathcliff the child may be 'natural' because he springs from outside the social community, and has his heart set on a fulfilment which goes beyond its limits; but as an adult he is also 'natural' in the sense of embodying the predatory, competitive, anti-social appetites of capitalist society itself. He is at once too much the outsider and too much the insider. What he is precisely not is a rough diamond – a man whose farouche exterior, rather like Rochester, conceals a compassionate heart. On the contrary, beneath that flinty exterior beats a heart of stone. It belongs with the novel's magnificent realism to refuse any such sentimentalist reading of its male protagonist – while at the same time insisting, against those like Nelly who would blacken him from the outset, that he is the heartless crook he is because of the monstrous treatment he received at the hands of the Earnshaws as a child. It was, the narrator observes, 'enough to make a fiend out of a saint'.

That his villainy has rational causes, however, does not mean that it is non-existent. On the contrary, the real condemnation of the social order which oppresses him lies in the fact that it is terrifyingly real. Once his entirely reasonable desire for Catherine is rebuffed, it becomes pathological and implacably destructive – a desire, in fact, for death, self-violence and negation rather than for any achievable relationship. Even so, we are meant to keep in mind that it is the society which refuses Heathcliff human recognition which drives him in the end to hijack its property and cultural capital, and outdo it in its own exploitative techniques. What forces him increasingly on to the inside of this world of cheating and property-dealing, ironically, is a desire which knows no earthly confine.

Some Victorian thinkers, like the Positivists and Social Darwinists, collapse Culture into Nature; others, like George Eliot and T. H. Huxley, recognize the need for human civilization to resist slipping back into some primordial slime. Thomas Hardy understands that human culture has its basis in Nature, but that it should not therefore make the complacent mistake of assuming that Nature is spontaneously on its side. But the problem with either cheering for Culture or championing Nature is that humanity seems to be straddled amphibiously between the two, made up of both worlds but fully at home in neither. Or – to put it another way – there can be no simple-minded affirmation of the Heights as a vital, natural community, any more than there can be some one-sided option for Thrushcross Grange as an oasis of civility in a cruel world. If crotchety old Joseph is hardly an image of utopia, neither are the overcivilized Lintons.

Instead, *Wuthering Heights* grasps the ambiguous relations between Nature and culture – the ways they are both related and mutually resistant. They are related, for example, in the fact of kinship, which is both a biological and a cultural reality, and which provides the novel with a vital organizing principle. They are also related in the reality of work, which consists in 'humanizing' the raw stuff of Nature. Humanity is a natural species, a random offshoot of evolution; yet what is distinctive about the human form of animality is its ability to transcend its own limitations and construct its own world. It is this constructed world that we know as culture, or perhaps as history. Culture, then, goes beyond Nature but also has its roots in it. Indeed, it is only because we are the peculiar sort of natural animals we are that we are able to rise above the natural world.

There is a less abstract way of putting the matter. The Lintons, who are the largest capitalist landowners in the district, literally draw their culture from Nature, in the sense of living by exploiting the land and those who labour on it. The fatal blindspot of this kind of culture, however, is that it refuses to acknowledge its dependency on Nature, and imagines itself instead to be an autonomous sphere. The cosy, well-appointed drawing-room of the Grange is the product of material labour, but at the same time shuts that labour out. The Heights, by contrast, is home to that peculiarly English class, the yeomanry, meaning those minor gentlemen who work their own land. It is thus closer to the realities of Nature and labour than Thrushcross Grange, as well as in general a more egalitarian, rough-and-ready place where you eat in the kitchen rather than the dining room, and where the lines between master and servant (is Hareton a servant or not?) are more blurred than among the Lintons.

Yet exactly because the Heights is the more 'natural' place, it is also more harsh, unmannerly and casually violent, 'uncivilized' in a negative sense as well as a positive one. The point about the English yeomanry is that the family is a working unit, so that personal relationships are cramped and moulded by economic constraints. There is little room in this tight, harshly functional community for the finer feelings, the enjoyment of relationships or spiritual values for their own sake, or indeed for non-family or non-working members. If Heathcliff is the former, Catherine is the latter. Heathcliff's intrusion into the Earnshaw family, as a creature seen ambiguously as both a gift from God and as dark as the devil, marks him out as what the ancient Greeks called a *pharmakos* – that double-edged being, at once sacred and polluted, who represents the dregs and refuse of humanity, and who poses a radical challenge to the community he confronts. If it can transcend its fear and accept this outsider thrust gratuitously upon it, a power for good will flow from this act; if it rejects him, it is cursed.

The Earnshaws, however, have no place for the sheer superfluity which Heathcliff signifies. The niggardly, mean-minded, brutally utilitarian spirit of an old Joseph would not recognize a spiritual value even if one leapt into in his lap. One of the novel's boldest achievements is thus to demystify the Victorian ideal of the family as a protected enclave of humane value in an inhuman social order. In the tight-fisted world of the peasantry and yeomanry, the family *is* a socio-economic order, warped and pressurized by those imperatives, and so much less easily romanticized. We shall see something similar in the later Dickens. The grotesque domestic violence in *Wuthering Heights* is scandalous even to the calloused modern reader, let alone to the high-minded Victorian one.

It is as though the Heights cannot afford to be humane, whereas the Grange can. To put the point cynically: if you enjoy enough of an economic surplus, then you have the leisure and resources to engage in personal, moral or spiritual issues for their own sake. And this is known as culture. Culture springs from having more material labour at your disposal, not less. As we have seen, it tends snobbishly to disown its down-at-heel parent, Nature; but in doing so it can cultivate the resources to indulge in friendship, art, the intellect and humanity as ends in themselves, free of the exigencies which disfigure human affections at the Heights.

It is true that culture involves violence just as Nature does. For one thing, it uses such force to defend its property: the Lintons set the dogs on the trespassing Catherine and Heathcliff, thinking they are after their rent money. For another thing, there is a kind of irascible oversensitivity which springs from having a neurotic excess of civility rather than a lack of it, as

the Lintons sometimes testify. In general, however, it would seem a choice between being compassionate but overprivileged, and down-to-earth but destructive. Culture is either damagingly intimate with Nature, or cripplingly remote from it. If Culture seems a mere reflex of Nature in the Heights, it is too clearly a refuge from it at the Grange. Part of the problem, too, is that what drives civilization to develop – human desire – has an excessive, implacable, uncompromising quality about it which resembles Nature more than it does civilization, and which threatens to scupper the very culture it is busy constructing.

Rather as *Villette* offers us both a happy and a tragic ending, so it belongs to *Wuthering Height*'s subtle power to suggest that the conflicts with which it deals both are, and are not, resolvable. On the one hand, there is no Charlotte-like wish-fulfilment: instead, we are offered a starkly tragic finale, as the love (or is it need?) of Heathcliff and Catherine for one another bursts through the social conventions to lash itself quiet in the unsocial domains of death, Nature and mythology. Perhaps it fails to find fulfilment even there. On the other hand, we are not invited to indulge some simple-minded Romantic opposition between passion and society. Desire has been revealed as a profoundly subversive force, indifferent to social distinctions; but the novel also shows that not all desire is creative and not all convention is hollow. This is why, in the final coming together of Hareton and young Catherine, there is a tentative, exploratory movement beyond the tragic deadlock of Catherine and Heathcliff – though one which lingers in its shadow, rather than disavowing it in some callow call to put the past behind you and turn a brave face to the future. The language of the scene in which young Catherine teaches Hareton to read is coy and saccharine, comfortably 'Victorian' in tone in a way that the novel as a whole is not. And it is, after all, the dead lovers themselves who are the subject of the work's last words.

What we have in the love of young Catherine and Hareton is a convergence of labour and gentility, as the crude natural energy which Hareton symbolizes can be tamed and gentrified without being emasculated. Nature and Culture, Heights and Grange, might thus finally meet in harmony. Yet if this cannot redeem the shades of Heathcliff and Catherine, neither does it have much of a material basis, at least in terms of the novel. The tale which *Wuthering Heights* has to tell, among other things, is that of the decline of the English yeomanry; by the end of the story, the Heights has been swallowed up by the Grange, as small agrarian capital is confiscated by a more powerful species of the same animal. And this reflects a real historical development in nineteenth-century English society.

At the level of actual history, then, there is nothing like the equipoise between 'natural' vigour and genteel cultivation which the novel strives to achieve at the level of values. In any case, if the more rugged, positive qualities of Heathcliff live on in Hareton, the fact remains that it is the scheming Heathcliff himself who was largely responsible for undermining the world of the Heights and indirectly ensuring the victory of the Grange. Heathcliff belongs economically with the Grange, but culturally with the Heights. As such, he is both a sign of the future, which belongs to large-scale rural capitalism, and a bittersweet memory of a past which was both more barbarous, and more rooted and resilient, than anything the future is likely to bring. It is characteristic of the novel's complex seeing that it refuses any simple judgement here.

In the story of Catherine and Heathcliff, what one might roughly call Romance and realism meet only to collide. Desire and social reality are tragically at odds. Yet if this is true of the novel's content, just the opposite could be claimed of its form. What makes this work almost unique in the annals of English fiction is its extraordinary fusion of realism and fantasy, imaginative extravagance and the everyday world. It is as though passion, far from obscuring that workaday world, lends its most casual details an almost hallucinatory clarity. There are times when it is hard to decide whether an incident represents high spiritual drama or domestic farce, or to draw the line between the passionate and the pettish. Raymond Williams speaks of the novel's 'exceptional fusion of intensity and control'.[4]

In Charlotte's writing, by contrast, these literary modes are far less unified. It is the uneven, heterogeneous nature of her fiction which catches the eye, the way it mixes Gothic, romance, fairy tale, picaresque, ghost story, melodrama and social realism. It is as though the romance or Gothic novel must now come to grips with new kinds of social experience at the heart of early industrial England, and must struggle to accommodate these bleak realities within its symbolic frames. Or – to put it the other way round – as though a new, arresting brand of social realism has still not entirely shaken itself loose from more traditional, less realist forms.

Indeed, it still finds these forms in some ways indispensable. When realism hits a genuine social problem, it can always resolve it by reaching back to these older forms and borrowing a magical device or two from them. If it is realistically unlikely that Jane will return to the now conveniently marriageable Rochester, a mysterious voice in her ear can always prompt her to do so. The ghostly intimation, the improbable coincidence, the lost and rediscovered relative, the opportune legacy, the timely death: all these

tricks of the literary trade are still accessible to a social realism which needs them to smooth its rough edges and resolve otherwise recalcitrant conflicts. Realism and romance thus meet in the form of the Brontës' fiction, as they do in its subject-matter. We shall see much the same accommodation in the case of Charles Dickens.

CHARLES DICKENS

Dickens has been hailed as the first great English novelist of the city, though he himself, ironically, grew up mostly in small-town Kent. The idea of the natural and 'organic' lurks behind a good deal of English fiction, from Fielding and George Eliot to Hardy and D. H. Lawrence; but the urban-centred Dickens is almost entirely untouched by it. The contrast between the city and the country is not just one between smoke and sheep. It is also a difference in the way men and women perceive the world around them, a matter of the tones, textures and rhythms of experience. As England shifted in the course of Dickens's own lifetime from being a mainly rural to a largely urban society, those who were brought up in the countryside but had migrated to the towns had to learn new temporal rhythms and bodily habits, different perceptual skills and styles of emotional response. In the early 1850s, only about one third of those living in London and the major English towns had actually been born there. As the urban population swelled, people would for the first time no longer know where their food and drink came from.

Dickens's London was a commercial rather than industrial metropolis, which is why the focus of his fictional attention is clerks, lawyers and bankers rather than industrial workers or manufacturers. His only 'industrial' novel, *Hard Times*, exposes him as pretty ignorant of industrialism; we never even get to know what is produced in Bounderby's factories, and the city of Coketown is portrayed in vaguely impressionistic terms, almost as though he was seeing it from a train. It is an external view of a supposedly external civilization. Dickens was remote from the world in which the average age at death of a Manchester worker in the 1840s was 17. But he was equally remote from the rural domain of a George Eliot. As an aspiring young writer in London, he liked to present himself as a man about town, a dandy or *flaneur* who prided himself on being streetwise and for a while adopted the *nom-de-plume* of Timothy Sparks. There is more than a touch of the Artful Dodger about the youthful Dickens.

The city speeds life up, but it also requires us to cope with a welter of fragmentary sensations, as disparate bits and pieces of reality surge at us from all angles only to burst like bubbles and give way to a new set of fleeting perceptions. The urban dweller needs to be vigilant, adaptive, able to cope with diversity and discontinuity. He or she grows a new body and evolves a new sensory apparatus. History, in the sense of a gradual evolution, gives way to a succession of disconnected moments. The city quickens our senses but also thins them out, so that the world seems at once vivid and two-dimensional, immediate yet unreal. The body has to learn to weave its way through masses of other bodies which are at once intimate and alien, feeling itself both vulnerable and self-protective. The space of the village is in some sense continuous, whereas the space of the city is shifting, carved up, parcelled out.

In these circumstances, we each grow a new 'mass' identity, a face for the crowd, which ironically serves to intensify our sense of solitary uniqueness. It is now less possible to answer the question of who we are by pointing, as people traditionally did, to kinship, community and genealogy, networks which the city has unravelled. Dickens is preoccupied in novels such as *Oliver Twist*, *Little Dorrit* and *Great Expectations* with the mysterious sources of human identity – with how we came to be who we are, whether we are who we think we are, whether we are really the authors of ourselves or spring from some murky ancestry or shady source of wealth of which we know nothing. The city highlights our dependence on one another, but it also reveals how individual lives are pitched arbitrarily together, randomly colliding rather than permanently interrelated. In modern urban society, we all exist in the interstices of each others' lives.

The bodily reflexes of the city dweller are sharpened and multiplied in some ways, blunted and stereotyped in others. We are both stimulated and disorientated, swept up in a frenetically energetic world which engulfs us at the same time as it appears to turn its back upon us. The typical relationship is now an anonymous two-minute encounter with a shopkeeper or newsvendor. For the first time, we now run into far more strangers than we do familiars. Because the public and domestic realms are rigorously divided, the people we know in the public sphere have private lives mysteriously closed to our scrutiny, so that we rarely get to see them in the round. It is as though each human body masks a whole impenetrable hinterland of experience. We can be intimate with others without having a clue where they live or what their children look like, a condition which a traditional country dweller would find deeply bizarre. Everything we touch is constructed, scored through with the traces of human labour and purpose, so that there seems to be no 'other' to society itself; yet this thoroughly humanized world can also appear as blankly indifferent to humanity as a tornado.

If Dickens is an urban novelist, it is not just because he writes about the city, but because he writes about it in an urban kind of way. His prose style is alive with the swarming energies of his surroundings, full of hyperbole, extravagant gestures, unpredictable connections, rapid thumbnail sketches, melodramatic exclamations, abrupt shifts of tone and theatrical display – rather than, like Jane Austen or George Eliot, given over to the painstaking unravelling of human complexities. If Austen's is an art of the cameo, Dickens's is one of the poster. He is thus a living refutation of the conventional view that the former is inherently superior to the latter. Characters emerge from the narrative only to evaporate again, rather as they do on Oxford Street. It is an art *of* the streets rather than simply about them: graphic, flamboyant, amplified, sometimes brash and shamelessly manipulative. Like a street performer, Dickens's effects need, so to speak, to be visible from the back of the crowd. His mode of characterization, as Raymond Williams astutely observes, belongs to the street as well, in the sense that the way he perceives men and women – vividly but externally, caught in a single posture or defined by one or two idiosyncratic features – is the way we take in passing strangers on busy street corners.[1] These figures are at once animated and enigmatic, expressive but hard to decipher. So if 'realist' means 'true to the situation', these two-dimensional figures are actually more realist than fully rounded ones.

We all no doubt seem a little threatening or eccentric to each other before we come to open our mouths and speak; and the modern city, unlike the small village, is the place where most of our encounters consist of seeing rather than speaking, glimpsing each other as objects rather than conversing as fellow subjects. We consume impressions of each other rather as we consume commodities, with no more knowledge of what went into the production of other people than we have of how a pork pie was assembled or how the sewers beneath our feet were built. We are aware that behind the appearance of each of these enigmatic creatures lies a subjective life much like our own; but because we cannot see this life as a whole, subjectivity itself comes to seem opaque and inaccessible, like a secret which each of us carries furtively concealed on our persons.

Being a human subject is a process in time; but this evolution is not something we can see, and in the city what is real is what you can perceive. Characters in Dickens therefore tend not to develop in the way that George Eliot's do. Character, Eliot observes in *Middlemarch*, is 'a process and an unfolding' – but this view of it may well be more rural than urban. In a small, close-knit rural community of the kind that Austen or Eliot depicts, our everyday familiarity with others means that we can see our way round them, imagine their lives as a whole, in a way that the city makes much less easy.

There is, then, a kind of alienation built into Dickens's very way of seeing, a fetishism of appearances by which characters come to be defined by their noses, waistcoats, boots, knees, fob-watches, tricks of speech or peculiar gait. This gives rise to a puzzle: do these appearances indeed conceal some cryptic identity, some hinterland of selfhood on which we can never gain a foothold; or is the self really nothing but the way it appears, and the idea of some persistent core of identity simply an illusory depth projected by these surfaces? If the latter is the case, this may explain why Dickens's characters so often appear like inanimate objects, since inanimate objects clearly have nothing to conceal, even though we might fantasize that they have. But the reverse can also be true, as objects or institutions in this world seem to be imbued with a sinister, jovial or manipulative life of their own.

We have entered a phase of social history in which all the real power seems to have been taken over by material things – money, institutions, commodities, power relations – while human beings themselves, falling under their tyrannical sway, are reduced to the level of coalbuckets and candlesticks. It is money which motivates Dickens's plots from start to finish. In *Our Mutual Friend*, Shares, suitably capitalized, becomes a character in its own right, rather like young Pip's Great Expectations. The frightening recognition has begun to dawn that this Frankenstein's monster of a social order, which so smugly celebrates the sovereignty and will-power of the individual, is in fact lurching wildly out of control, masterable by none of those who create it. It is as though society as a whole is an orphan whose progenitors can no longer be traced. 'Nobody's Fault' was one of Dickens's original titles for *Bleak House*.

In his classic study *The Fall of Public Man*, the sociologist Richard Sennett contrasts what he sees as an eighteenth-century notion of human nature with the burgeoning nineteenth-century cult of 'personality'.[2] Natural sympathies for the eighteenth-century, so Sennett argues, are what we share in common. They are not differentiating, so that to act naturally is not to stand out as unique. The family was such an arena of natural affections, a place where emotional demands were seen as essentially simple. And these natural affections, nurtured in the private world of the family, could act as a curb on the passions of the public sphere. There is, as we have seen, an embarrassing problem about how to square this communality of feeling with distinctions of social rank, which seem in one sense natural and in another sense lacking all foundation in Nature.

This, however, is rather less pressing a problem in the nineteenth century, since now the whole conception of shared natural sympathies is yielding ground to the idea of the inimitable personality. And Dickens is the great literary exponent of this notion. What we now have in common, paradoxically, is idiosyncrasy. Personality is all about difference, and so in a sense is anarchic. It is what is gloriously unpredictable about a person, the outward sign of their autonomy. The English love a lord, but they love a 'character' – meaning an amiable eccentric – even more. There can no longer be a typology of character, since everyone is irreducibly themselves; and if we can no longer categorize men and women one crucial source of knowledge and stability is denied us. As Nature comes to mean Darwinian strife rather than Wordsworthian harmony, it is less and less reliable as a moral norm. George Eliot was brought up in rural England, but is deeply suspicious of Nature in the sense of natural appetite. Dickens has an urbanite's lack of interest in the countryside, which he associates with death and regression. Sheep are simply too undynamic for his taste.

What is important about you is no longer the affinities you have with others of your kind, but the features that mark you off from them. When the characters of Fielding or Austen speak, they sound roughly similar, given some differences of class, gender and the like. Almost everyone in Dickens, by contrast, has his or her inimitable quick-fire delivery, churlish mumble, wheedling whine, verbose ramblings, pious cant or portentous rhetoric. In a rapidly fragmenting society, it is becoming harder to formulate common standards of the natural. The more culture comes to swamp Nature with the spread of urban industrialism, the more difficult it is to know what counts as natural in the first place. Dickens is severe on 'unnatural' behaviour like cruelty to a child, yet he portrays a world so thoroughly culturalized that it is hard to know by what 'natural' standards such 'unnatural' conduct can be judged.

The idea of a natural order involves a scepticism of appearances. It suggests that the truth about you is not immediately manifest, but is a matter of your place within a general scheme. For the cult of personality, by contrast, the truth of the self is disclosed in instantaneous impressions. In the sensorily intense world of the city, immediacy becomes an index of truth. What you seem to be is what you are. There are no hidden depths to the self any longer – which is not to say that the self is a superficial affair, since you can only speak of surfaces if you have depths to contrast them with. But now men and women seem to sport their identities like necklaces or cravats, so that what you see is what you get. The visual signifer becomes what it signifies. You can always tell a Dickensian villain by his louche demeanour, just as you can tell a virtuous woman by her modestly downcast eyes and remarkably trim figure. A bewitchingly handsome Fagin or a spotty, over-weight Little Dorrit would be inconceivable. In Dickens, you cannot be virtuous and have greasy skin.

There is, then, a continuum for Dickens between the moral and the physical. Or, indeed, between the personal and the social: Bounderby, the wicked capitalist of *Hard Times*, is, as his name suggests, a 'bounder' or low-life outsider, which conveniently facilitates our dislike of him. George Eliot would probably have forced us to make a complex judgement between his social role and his personal character, but Dickens has no such scruples. Eliot insists on the difference between outer appearance and inward reality, as when she remarks rather bitchily of the sexually alluring Hetty Sorel in *Adam Bede* that 'there is no direct correlation between eyelashes and morals'. There does, even so, appear to be a direct correlation between Adam's moral integrity and his rugged good looks.

Dickens's novels hover ambiguously between this view of the self as a set of shifting impressions, and a more traditional belief in identity as a stable continuity over time. Characters sometimes wear their souls on their sleeves, and sometimes demand as much laborious deciphering as an ancient manuscript. They are either flamboyantly self-dramatizing or disturbingly clandestine. People either improvise themselves on the spot, or persist mysteriously in their secret being like pieces of furniture. In one sense, everything on the streets is out in the open, instantly available; yet the social order which lies behind these streets is inscrutable, operating by some arcane logic of its own. This is partly because, rather like a modernist work of art, it seems to exist solely for its own sake. It reproduces its power and privilege with scant regard for the people it is supposed to serve. It has the enigmatic quality of a closed, self-reproducing system, whose logic has come unstuck from human reason and purpose.

The Jarndyce law suit of *Bleak House*, which is a mystery even to the lawyers involved in it, and which finally consumes itself (rather as Krook in the same novel spontaneously combusts), is perhaps Dickens's most memorable image of this condition. Who, if anyone, is actually running this system? Can social processes any longer be traced back to their human agents? Even those who are supposed to govern this order, like the bureaucrats of the Circumlocution Office in *Little Dorrit*, appear to be as mystifed by its workings as Jo the crossing sweeper of *Bleak House*. The illiterate Jo cannot even read the signs around him, let alone decode the social relations of which he is part. There is no way to make coherent sense of this ominously illegible world.

If there is continuity in Dickens between the moral and the physical, it is partly because the moral self is not something you can smell or taste, which is how the world of the city defines what is real. Urban experience seems hostile to abstraction, which makes it hard to dramatize something as evolving and intangible as the moral life. So translating it into physical terms makes the moral self more tangible. This, however, seems to work better with vice than it does with virtue. Dickens's crooks are fascinating, but his virtuous characters are generally insipid. Nobody would invite Little Nell to dinner if they could swing an acceptance from Quilp or Silas Wegg, just as nobody would chat up Oliver Twist if they could share a pipe with the Artful Dodger. Esther Summerson is admirable, but Uriah Heep is magnificent. One would not pass up a *tête-à-tête* with Miss Haversham for an evening with David Copperfield.

This is one reason why Dickens has sometimes won low marks from the critics. 'Character' in literature, so we are informed, should be complex, rich, developing and many-sided, whereas Dickens's bunch of grotesques, perverts, amiable idiots and moral monstrosities are none of these things. But this is because they are realistic, not because they are defectively drawn. As we have seen, they are true to a new kind of social experience. Dickens's grotesque realism is a stylistic distortion in the service of truth, a kind of astigmatism which allows us to see more accurately. The last thing he is is temperate, judicious and even-handed, in the manner of a great liberal like George Eliot. On the contrary, his imagination is inherently biased and partisan, seizing on a few salient features of a situation rather than giving us a rounded portrait. His very perceptions are skewed, incapable of neutrality or disinterestedness.

The life of the novels lies in their nooks and crevices – in sadistic dwarfs, drunken midwives and narcoleptic servants rather than in their relatively conventional story-lines. Dickens's imagination, with its extraordinary brio and exuberance, is wayward, lavish, perverse, unenthralled by the average or orthodox. It has a pathological, death-obsessed streak. It delights in material clutter and revels in the off-beat detail. It portrays a society in which, para-doxically, individualism is now the norm – in which it is hard even to speak of perversity or grotesquerie because it is difficult to define the standard from which it deviates. Part of what we mean by the Dickensian city is a place where men and women have never been simultaneously so intercon-nected and so isolated. In this world, being orphaned has become a general condition. Whereas kinship matters greatly in rural communities, it figures far less in the city. At the very moment when the city forces people to depend on each other most deeply, not least for simple material survival, every predictable obligation, traditional contract, bond of kinship, common language and stable frame of reference melts into air.

If the so-called natural sympathies have been weakened in force, how-ever, they have not entirely disappeared. Instead, they have been converted into that corrupt mode of feeling we know as sentimentality. Sentimental-ity, which Dickens notoriously dishes out in lavish doses, is the kind of specialized, self-conscious cult of feeling one would expect from a society where feeling no longer comes habitually. It is not surprising that hard-nosed politicians, not least in the United States, are given to shaking with sobs and bursting publicly into tears, since this theatricalized form of emo-tion is the only version of feeling which someone unused to the stuff would be likely to understand. In this sense, sentimentality is often the flipside of hard-headedness, though not, to be sure, in the case of Dickens. It is really a brand of narcissism – an emotional self-indulgence in which you revel in your own feelings rather than in what occasions them. Sentimentality is the feel-good factor of middle-class society. This is one reason why company executives who beat their wives or throw thousands out of work can be moved to tears by images of ageing donkeys or starving children.

There is a gap in Dickens between conventional moral norms and the graphic immediacy of experience one finds in the city streets. It is the gap between Mr Brownlow and Fagin in *Oliver Twist*, a novel which cannot make up its mind about whose world is more real. Is Fagin's criminal under-world simply a nightmarish interlude from which you awaken, sweating and terrified, in the arms of your prosperous middle-class relatives, or is it Brownlow and orthodox society which is two-dimensional and Fagin who is real? Fagin, a Jew with an Irish name, may be a perverted version of a paternalist, and his den of thieves a warped version of the family; but he is a father figure to Oliver even so, and those sausages he is frying on their first encounter count heavily in his favour, as food in Dickens generally does. Brownlow's bourgeois residence is comfortable and secure, but nothing

like so anarchically enjoyable. Dickens likes his environments a touch dishevelled, with the odd toddler lost under a moth-eaten sofa. By the time of the later novels, conventional society has become paper-thin, a set of shiny surfaces, empty speeches and ritual gestures. When the Artful Dodger protests to the Old Bailey magistrate that 'this ain't the shop for justice', his author is by no means wholly convinced that he is wrong.

This rift between the moral and the vivacious is to some extent a gender gap as well. Put crudely, the women in Dickens have the morality, whereas the men have the life. Like most generalizations, this one demands instant qualification: there are some remarkably complex, animated women in the fiction, along with some egregiously stuffy, cardboard cut-out men. Amy Dorrit is in no sense a female stereotype, to say nothing of the astonishing portrait in the same novel of the lesbian separatist Miss Wade. Rosa Dartle of *David Copperfield*, Estella of *Great Expectations*, Bella Wilfer of *Our Mutual Friend*: these are by no means studies in meekness and submission. Even so, Dickens's women characters tend by and large to divide between passive paragons of moral virtue like Agnes Wakefield of *David Copperfield* or Esther Summerson of *Bleak House*, and laughable eccentrics like Betsy Trotwood, Peggoty, Mrs Sparsit, Miss Flite and Miss Haversham. Self-assertiveness in Dickens's women is often a kind of irritating or amusing foible. It could be claimed that much the same is true of his male characters, who tend to divide between bloodless embodiments of middle-class moral integrity like Nicholas Nickleby, and quirky or rumbustious low-life figures like Wackford Squeers. But his virtuous male figures can be active and resourceful in a way that his virtuous woman are generally not. And as usual with the Victorians, women are morally idealized only at the price of being desexualized.

The gap between life and morality is also reflected in the way that moral values in Dickens appear to transcend material circumstance, having an absolute quality about them. If his good characters appear incorruptible, his bad ones seem irredeemable in their wickedness. Unlike George Eliot, his moral imagination is sharply dualistic, impatient with subtle gradations. This can have some curious consequences. Oliver Twist, through brought up in a workhouse and pitched among East End whores and pickpockets, has a preternatural goodness which nothing could apparently contaminate. Where he got this saintly innocence from is as much a mystery as the origin of his impeccable Standard English. But if people like Oliver really are incorruptible by society, then this unwittingly makes characters like Fagin seem less malevolent. If vice could never make a dent in Oliver's virtue, it poses less of a threat than the novel would like to claim. Conversely, if the wicked really are absolutely so, like Blandois in *Little Dorrit*, then goodness cannot affect them, and this shows up its limits.

Dickens's novels have to strike an uncertain compromise between their official moral values, and the freaks and eccentrics who grip their author's imagination. The point of a Dickens novel may lie in its formal narrative, but most of its life is to be found lurking in its margins and subtexts. In any case, morality implies choice, and a lot of Dickens's characters seem unable to be anything but themselves. They are trapped in their own identities as in a prison-house, or like second-rate actors forever landed with the same bit part. Other characters, by contrast, are too fluid and mobile to have anything like moral solidity, changing their identities like hair-styles. Things in Dickens in general are either bewilderingly capricious or oppressively inert. He is not a man for the middle way.

Several of the topics we have touched on converge in one of Dickens's favourite subjects: children. He is the first English novelist, indeed one of the first English writers of any kind, to place children at the centre of his fiction. In the eighteenth-century novel, children scarcely exist. In Dickens, they are symbols of natural feeling who easily evoke a sentimental response; in what one might call the 'unconscious' of his novels, they are often associated with Nature, death and a flight from the city. Yet from Oliver Twist and Paul Dombey to David Copperfield and Amy Dorrit, they are also the bruised victims of social oppression. The child thus spans Nature and society, uniquely combining the purity of the former with the brutality of the latter. There is something particularly scandalous about the centrepiece of natural sympathies being at the same time the focus of injustice and exploitation.

In the figure of the child, the claims of Nature can be brought critically to bear on the atrocities of culture. Dickens detests the Victorian Evangelical view that children are the wicked, and speaks up movingly on their behalf. From the Murdstones of *David Copperfield* to Mr Podsnap of *Our Mutual Friend*, he has an uncanny ear for Evangelical unctuousness and cant, and a quick eye for the sadistic violence it conceals. It would be hard even for Dickens to do better than the magnificently malign portrait of the smarmy Reverend Chadband of *Bleak House*. If he is particularly well placed to champion children, it is because he was for the most part an overgrown child himself. Freud, to be sure, would consider this true of us all, but like gardens some of us are more overgrown than others. Distinguished visitors to Dickens's home would smile indulgently to see the great man crouched on the carpet playing with his children, only to realize after a while that he was taking the game with disturbing seriousness and appeared notably reluctant to break off.

Children are the most harrowing symbols of oppression, being blameless and unprotected; but for the same reason they provide an uncertain place from which to launch a critique of society as a whole. For the child cannot grasp the inner logic of that order any more than the early Dickens can. Like him, it sees reality in fragments, and is incapable of abstracting from its own harshly immediate circumstances. Ironically, the one who suffers most poignantly can have no knowledge of the root causes of its suffering, or of how it might be remedied. Nor can it take such remedial action itself. All the child wants, understandably enough, is relief from its plight. If it is a mute indictment of the system which shackles it, it also unwittingly lets it off the hook. Asking for yet more inedible gruel is unlikely to remove the need for workhouses.

Dickens's fiction is thronged with prematurely aged children and childish adults. The Artful Dodger, Smike, Little Nell, Paul Dombey, Little Dorrit and Jenny Wren are examples of the former, while Mr Pickwick, the Cheeryble brothers, Mr Dick, Mr Micawber, Dora Copperfield, Harold Skimpole, Wemmick's Aged Parent, Jenny Wren's father, Maggy and Joe Gargery are instances of the latter. Some strange disturbance in the natural order of kinship has occurred, so that children who are thrust into premature maturity through hardship are forced to assume responsibility for profligate adults who disown their duties. The novels are full of false patriarchs as well as beaming paternalists, metaphorical as well as literal orphans, domestic ogres, surrogate parents, child wives, aged couples who act like Babes in the Wood, and waifs of indeterminate age. As far as child brides go, it is only with the most heroic self-restraint that the Dickens of *Bleak House* forgoes marrying off the twinkly-eyed middle-aged John Jarndyce to the attractive young Esther Summerson.

There is something perverse about this kind of desire, but then there is something perverse about Dickens's families in general. The Dickensian family, not least in the earlier writings, remains to some extent the kind of forum for natural affections which it was for the eighteenth century. Domestic life from the Cratchits of *A Christmas Carol* to the Wemmicks of *Great Expectations* is a haven in an unholy world, a refuge from a heartless social order. The family is carnivalesque, gloriously anarchic and emotionally spendthrift, and is generally to be found clustered clamorously around the dinner table. Food in Dickens's orally fixated sagas is always a sign of well-being. But even in the earlier fiction the family hearth can prove a morbid, manipulative place as well, and in some of the later novels it is more a microcosm of a possessive, power-hungry society than a humane alternative to it. Dickens understands that the family is a medium of social power as well as a form of resistance to it. From the Murdstones of *David Copperfield* to the Smallweeds of *Bleak House*, the Dickensian family is a scene of sadistic violence and emotional starvation as much as it is an oasis of cosy tranquillity. It is a kind of prison, and by the time of *Little Dorrit* the Dorrit family will literally live inside one, just as Dickens himself did for a time as a child. *Great Expectations* offers us a grisly parody of a family, in which Pip's sister is his mother, his brother-in-law Joe Gargery is both his father and his elder sibling, while the true begetter of his adult self is a convict.

The younger Dickens tends to indulge his shiftless adults, but Harold Skimpole of *Bleak House*, a down-at-heel dandy with a horde of neglected children, is treated with no such tolerance. His childlike innocence is just a thin rationale for squalid egoism. By the time of the later novels, mutual responsibility has become the keynote. The Romantic, sentimental Dickens is coming more and more to commend practical men like Alan Woodcourt, Inspector Bucket, Rouncewell, Doyce and Joe Gargery (respectively a physician, detective, manufacturer, inventor and blacksmith). It is these sturdy souls who are championed against the aesthetes, bohemians, aristocratic relics like the *Bleak House* Dedlocks, and the spiritually vacuous upper middle classes represented by the Veneerings of *Our Mutual Friend*.

This parasitic caste is not simply obnoxious but criminal. The hidden sources of its wealth lie in crime (Merdle of *Little Dorrit*, Magwitch of *Great Expectations*), sweated labour (the factories of *Hard Times*) and the dust heaps of *Our Mutual Friend*. Poverty, suffering and lawlessness lie at the roots of social identity – an understandable attitude, no doubt, on the part of one whose own father was locked up for debt. Orthodox society is not only oppressive but unreal: beneath its polished surfaces, overstuffed drawing rooms, bureaucratic paperwork and purely fictional stocks and shares lie the material realities of violence: the debtor's prison, the workhouse, the blacksmith's forge and the anonymous labour of the poor, all of which the Pecksniffs and Podsnaps of this world hypocritically disown. (Pecksniff, the oily humbug of *Martin Chuzzlewit*, became a word banned from usage in the Victorian parliament as an unacceptable insult.)

In the end, it is only by turning back and acknowledging the disreputable sources of one's wealth, status and identity that one can hope to build on firm foundations. The wellsprings of identity turn out to be contaminated, as in some version of original sin. In a rhythm of death, dissolution and

regeneration, one which informs both the river imagery of *Our Mutual Friend* and the plot of *A Tale of Two Cities*, you must lose your life, symbolically at least, in order to find it. But there are always those unregenerates, like the villainous Rogue Riderhood in *Our Mutual Friend*, who will fail to achieve this baptismal rebirth. Pip in *Great Expectations* must return to the forge – the scene of crime, violence, kinship, labour and sickness – in order to shuck off his false social persona. Having done so, he can relaunch himself as a gentleman and marry Estella, thus achieving the best of both worlds – though it is significant that Dickens originally conceived of no such happy ending. Little Dorrit, similarly, returns at last to the prison, the touchstone of reality in a society held together by the rotten parchment of shares, wills, credits and legal documents. It is a world in which the dead prey on the living, as the fortunes of the present are dependent on tangled, tainted inheritances from the past.

It has been pointed out that Dickens began his career in a Pickwickian age of stagecoaches and country inns, and ended it in a Victorian England of heavy industry, state bureaucracy, trade unions, large-scale banking, state education and a burgeoning railway system. He lived, in other words, through the transition from *laissez-faire* individualism to a more corporate, integrated kind of capitalist order; and the change is reflected in his writing. Early novels like *Nicholas Nickleby* and *Martin Chuzzlewit* are shapeless, anarchic and overpopulated – unwieldly, inorganic works which sprawl in all directions, pinned together by the flimsiest of plots and outrageously reliant on coincidence. If some modern authors shyly withdraw from their own works, Dickens bounds into his novels with all the zest of a brash self-publicist, didactic, moralizing and sentimental by turns. He is a showman with a canny eye to the big theatrical effect, painting in broad strokes and primary colours. His art has the aura of the theatre, marketplace or public meeting, preaching to its readers one moment and cajoling them the next. As producer of the show, he is not averse to seizing the microphone from one of his own characters and loudly proclaiming his opinions.

Dickens's works are full of anxiety and disorientation, yet also shot through with the comic exuberance of a still buoyant middle class, one which is in the process of transforming the face of the earth. There is sometimes a jocoseness, an arch geniality of tone, even in the portrayal of social horrors, as though the author does not really know what to feel about what he is presenting. Dotheboys Hall, the brutal school in *Nicholas Nickleby*, is both horrendous and highly entertaining, just as *Hard Times* is at once discomforting and fun to read. The novels remain buoyant, generous-spirited, even exuberant, in the teeth of the human catastrophes they record. It is this writerly exuberance, in the end, which provides a positive alternative to the grim world which the writing portrays. These books seem powered by an insatiable appetite for experience, revelling in their own high spirits and effervescent energy even when what they are showing us is appalling. Even appalling situations, however, can usually be resolved by wheeling on a so-called 'Christmas figure': Mr Brownlow in *Oliver Twist*, the reformed Scrooge, the Cheeryble brothers of *Nicholas Nickleby*, Mr Boffin in *Our Mutual Friend*. The Christmas figure is usually a bumbling paternalist with a smile on his lips, a tear in his eye and a purse in his proffered fist. He is a fairy-tale solution to the problems of a society in crisis.

The mood of the later novels is distinctly darker. It would not be ideologically acceptable for Dickens to end his novels on a tragic note, since the Victorians, like the governing classes today, regarded gloom as socially subversive. In works like *Little Dorrit* and *Great Expectations*, however, he is pushing these limits as far as he dares. By the time of *Bleak House*, the festive spirit has notable soured. John Jarndyce is a muted, blighted version of a Christmas figure who must stand helplessly by as his ward Richard Carstone is sucked into the vortex of the Chancery court. What is at stake now is a whole system, which an individual change of heart is powerless to affect. The social can no longer be crudely reduced to the personal: Merdle, the formidably powerful banker of *Little Dorrit*, is a timorous, nondescript little man who lives in terror of his own butler. The early Dickens would scarcely have been capable of such a subtle distinction between the social and the individual. *Dombey and Son* is a transitional novel in this respect. On the one hand, Dickens is still blaming individuals – not least the stereotypically cold-hearted capitalist Dombey – for social problems. Yet the novel, with its celebrated account of the coming of the railways, is also beginning to think in terms of networks and systems – of social forces which cannot be simple-mindedly reduced to individual vice or virtue.

Even so, *Dombey and Son* is significantly ambiguous in its attitude to the railways. If it is enthralled by their dynamism, it also sees them as death-dealing and destructive. The novel laments social change as much as it celebrates it. It is a typical Dickensian combination of exuberance and anxiety, which says a lot about the Victorian middle class's attitude to social progress. Dickens's heart is with places like Staggs Gardens, full of quaint charm and

lovable grotesques, even as his reformist Victorian head instructs him that these stagnant enclaves, by-passed by history, must yield to the iron march of progress. There is a good deal of the brisk modernizer about Dickens, with his impatience with red tape, his scorn for traditionalism and aristocratic privilege, his zeal for social reform, practical skills and industrial enterprise. If he were alive today he would carry an electronic organizer and could be separated from his mobile phone only by a crowbar. Scandalized though he was by so many aspects of his age, he considered the nineteenth century by far the most enlightened period in history. In fact, his attitude towards history in general (he wrote a rather slapdash, sectarian history of England for children) was as philistine as his attitude to art. He would have agreed with Henry Ford that history was largely bunk.

In all of these ways, Dickens was a fairly middle-of-the-road, progressively minded middle-class Victorian, a man who sent his sons to Eton and basked in the applause of the age. Championing the underdog is not necessarily a sign of radical sentiments. He was something of an English chauvinist, suspicious of that disorderly place known as Abroad, and (as we observe in the Mrs Jellyby scenes of *Bleak House*) scathing about what we would now call overseas aid. Though he lampoons the Utilitarian Gradgrind in *Hard Times*, he was himself quite close in some ways to that circle of thought, and numbered such hard-headed reformers among his friends. The fact that Gradgrind is an intellectual, in fact the only real intellectual Dickens ever portrays, might account in part for his contempt for him. Dickens himself is strikingly uninterested in ideas, in contrast with Eliot or Hardy. He is much closer in this respect to Thackeray and Trollope. He would be fascinated by a social scientist's moist, blubbery lips, not by what he was saying. Despite his animus against the gentry, he had a very English weakness for the English gentleman, and there is a lineage of charming cads in the novels from James Steerforth of *David Copperfield* to James Harthouse of *Hard Times* and Eugene Wrayburn of *Our Mutual Friend*.

These disreputable toffs appeal to the more raffish side of Dickens; it was the stuffy, pompous middle class he was allergic to. He has, however, a typical middle-class fear of the mob, which emerges in both *Barnaby Rudge* and *A Tale of Two Cities*. If he found chaos strangely alluring, he was also extremely frightened by it. Despite being a social upstart himself, or perhaps because of it, he is especially hard on *parvenus* like the creepy Uriah Heep of *David Copperfield*, who is trying to get his clammy fingers on the boss's daughter, or Bradley Headstone, the violently self-repressed schoolmaster of

Our Mutual Friend. Part of his snobbish objection to the *Hard Times* capitalist Josiah Bounderby is that he boasts in a prolier-than-thou way of a deprived childhood.

At the same time, there is a good deal of the Romantic humanist in Dickens, which sits rather uneasily with his tough-minded reformism. He is stern on Gradgrind's cold-hearted fetishism of facts; but this says more about Dickens's own Romantic impatience with rational argument than it does about the Utilitarians. His case against them is typically caricaturing and impressionistic. There was a good deal more than soulless number-crunching to the Utilitarians, who won a number of vital radical reforms from the Victorian system. In any case, no project of social reform can dispense with hard data. Facts can be far more explosive than Dickens seems to realize. It is naive to imagine that statistics cannot be subversive. This side of him, represented in *Hard Times* by Sissy Jupe and the circus performers, elevates impulse and intuition over cold-blooded analysis, and fantasy and imagination over reality.

The Romantic Dickens is not only critical of particular social institutions, but, like many a Romantic, suspicious of institutions as such, in contrast to personal relationships and the compassionate heart. In the nineteenth-century combat between Utilitarianism and Romanticism, the head and the heart, Dickens in a sense supported both parties, though his heart was with the heart. His Romantic humanism can sometimes be little more than cosy sentiment; but it is remarkable that an author who painted the evils of nineteenth-century society more graphically than any other could nevertheless preserve such an abiding faith in human goodness and generosity. If this is naively utopian, it is also clear-sightedly realistic. It represents the Romantic heritage at its most affirmative.

The less creditable aspect of Dickens's Romantic humanism is unwittingly exposed by *Hard Times* itself, a novel which recognizes that what is at stake is a whole industrial-capitalist system, yet which can find little to oppose to it but the anarchic spontaneity of a circus. With the enormously profitable culture industry before our eyes, we ourselves are perhaps better placed to appreciate that entertainment is part of the problem rather than the solution. In such conditions, 'culture' and fantasy are not an alternative to hard facts and hard labour, but simply the other face of them. The idea of culture as harmless entertainment is the philistine's view of it. Culture is reduced to the question of what to do with people when they aren't at work.

A circus performer in the novel complains that people can't always be working, not realizing that the captains of industry could not agree more. Mill-owners were not in general averse to music halls. Governing powers have always recognized that the common people need circuses along with bread. Laying on leisure allows men and women to recuperate from work so that they can return to it refreshed. Laying on organized fantasies, whether as circuses or television soap operas, provides those whose working lives are less than glamorous with substitute fulfilments, as well as providing a safety-valve for energies which might otherwise prove socially disruptive. Today, the organized fantasy known as sport plays just such a vital role.

There is, in fact, a powerful counter-system in *Hard Times*, but it is dismissed out of hand. This is the trade union movement, which is grossly caricatured in the unappetizing figure of Slackbridge and the persecution of Stephen Blackpool. Dickens's Romantic distaste for institutions thus extends to those intent on changing them. *Hard Times* contemptuously writes off one of the few organized forces in Victorian England which challenged the very injustices the novel itself protests against. Dickens's idiosyncratic, vividly particularizing imagination is restless with such necessarily impersonal matters. Instead, it focuses on the lone individual, Stephen Blackpool, whose deference, confusion and passivity are made to seem more commendable than a struggle for better wages.

Along with Blackpool, the novel seems to believe that any fight to promote one's own interests is bound to be selfish and sectarian. It is a prejudice which can only buttress the power of Blackpool's exploiters. On this view, women are simply being selfish in demanding an end to the drudgery of housework. The general impression left by Stephen's death is that he dies a martyr to working-class bigotry, which is not actually how he meets his end at all. One wonders how much of Blackpool's self-confessed 'muddle' is not in the mind of his author. Dickens modelled the strike in the novel on a real-life one in Lancashire, which he observed personally and reported on in his journal. But the journalistic report is far more positive about the event than the novel, commending the self-restraint of the strikers. The imagination, in short, is not always a creative affair.

Hard Times magnificently conveys the feel of a new kind of industrial order, with its disciplining of the body, stunting of the imagination and shrivelling of natural sympathies. In doing so, it makes connections between the organization of industrial labour, the habits of feeling which it breeds, sexual misery and bloodless theoretical doctrines. But at the same time it simplifies all this to a timeless battle between virtue and wickedness. It also reduces it to a fable of the poor princess Louisa escaping the clutches of the wicked ogre Bounderby, and the rough beast Gradgrind turning overnight, if not into a charming prince, then at least into a suitably repentant father.

It is not clear how Gradgrind's becoming a more caring father would affect the social system represented by Bounderby's factory. Because the prospect of radical change lies beyond the novel's scope, it must fall back instead, like so much Victorian fiction, on moralism, an individual change of heart and a fairy-tale resolution. And this is one reason why Dickens's realism, like that of the Brontës and much Victorian writing, is never 'pure', but comes to us interleaved with other, more traditional forms: Gothic, romance, moral fable, caricature, sermonizing, popular fiction and the like. Without the aid of these forms, the problems raised by the novel could never be resolved by it; and Dickens is writing in an age when, unlike today, readers demanded resolutions and felt cheated if they were not delivered.

As Victorian society becomes more integrated, Dickens's later novels draw on its corporate institutions to achieve some artistic unity for themselves. If there is industrial manufacture and the educational system in *Hard Times*, there is also the railways in *Dombey and Son*, the law in *Bleak House*, the prisons, finance capital and civil service bureaucracy in *Little Dorrit*, and the garbage system of *Our Mutual Friend*. All of these provide ways of unifying Dickens's otherwise rather ramshackle works. Whereas Jane Austen's social world is fairly homogeneous, Dickens's is made up of a whole set of mini-worlds, different galaxies between which there is often enough empty space. By using the great corporate systems of Victorian England, he can hope to pull these separate social spheres together. The law, bureaucracy and finance capital offer images of human interdependence in a society of solitary individuals; yet the irony is that they also play a powerful role in wedging people apart. What provide these later novels with their principle of unity, paradoxically, are systems of conflict and division.

It is as though positive relations between people are now so inconceivable that you can only picture the connections between them in negative terms. The fog in *Bleak House* engulfs everyone from the paupers of Tom-all-Alone's to the august figure of the Lord Chancellor; but this is just to say that what all sectors of this society have in common is an impenetrable obscurity. The fog permits us a panoramic view of London as a whole, but only by allowing us to see very little everywhere we look. The very name 'Tom-all-Alone's' suggests that solitude is what we share. Indeed, solitude is now so pervasive and intense that it borders on a kind of madness, not least

with the eccentric Miss Flite and the sinister Krook. The more materially interdependent characters become, the more they are locked into their solipsistic worlds, bereft of any common speech.

The disease which seeps from the impoverished East End of London to lay siege to the well-heeled West End is another of *Bleak House*'s images of negative interdependence. Viruses are radical democrats, disdainful of social distinction. It is in the name of common responsibility that the West End should tackle sanitation problems in the East End, but it is also in its own selfish interests. If they get infected, so might you. Common responsibility, then, is a challenge to the ruling order, but is also in some ways convenient for it. Thinking corporately benefits it as well as undermines it. Another powerful centripetal force in the book is the Jarndyce law suit, linking people and places which are apparently unconnected. Vholes, Miss Flite, the Dedlocks, Jo, Tulkinghorn and the rest may be bound into their solitary selfhoods like straitjackets, but they are also meshed together at some deeper level. In a sense, then, solitude is a fiction. The reality is that we are members of one another; the problem is that we are bound up with each other in a way which conceals the fact from our consciousness.

Which is to say all of these sealed-off worlds finally add up to a *plot*. There is indeed a grand narrative here, but it is buried beneath appearances as the truth in fiction generally is, and must be dredged laboriously to the surface. The novel thus employs a detective – Inspector Bucket – as a kind of surrogate of the novelist himself, plotting and piecing together, bringing submerged relationships to light, gradually disclosing a unifying sub-text beneath the book's diffuse domains. Artists, scientists and sleuths can all reveal forces invisible to the naked eye. Dickens's notoriously casual way with coincidence now takes on a deeper meaning, as we shall also see later with Thomas Hardy: events which seem disconnected really do have secret affinities. And this is as true morally as it is materially: as Esther Summerson observes, we are all responsible for each other. This is not the kind of sentiment which would have particularly struck the author of *Pickwick Papers*.

The critic F. R. Leavis, having first dismissed Dickens as a mere entertainer, finally concluded that he was a serious novelist.[3] What he failed to note was a third possibility: that Dickens is both a serious novelist and a great entertainer. Few major English writers have been so careless of the well-patrolled boundary between 'high' and 'low' art. He also succeeded in bursting through the literary barriers between adult and childen's fiction: in a poll of schoolchildren in the 1880s, he proved to be by far their most favoured author. Dickens has none of the intellectual resources of George

Eliot, and little of the psychological subtlety of Henry James. As we have seen, his psychological effects are the kind that can be seen from the back of the hall.

He was, rather, a writer of prodigious imaginative power and superb rhetorical mastery, who unlike Eliot or James remained in touch with caricature, lampoon, melodrama, sentimental ballad, oral legend, popular theatre, everyday culture. No other classic English novelist has been so wildly popular, and hardly any has been so uproariously funny. Dickens takes the popular arts of farce, caricature, sentiment and polemic, and harnesses them to complex aesthetic ends. The vivid flatness of his figures may reflect the art of the streets; but as we have seen, it also says a great deal *about* the streets, raising caricature, grotesquerie and broad-brush portraiture to a new kind of artistic perception. If people bounce off each other in popular farce, so they do in the new world of the city, so that these traditional ways of seeing become freshly realistic.

Dickens was no revolutionary, though he was an ardent, tireless reformer. He was never the kind of threat to Victorian society that Thomas Hardy was. His views on education were fuzzily libertarian, and he disliked both patrician *hauteur* and middle-class pomposity. Yet he also feared the kinds of social forces which might have helped to transform nineteenth-century England into the place of common responsibility he pleads for so eloquently in *Bleak House*. It is, even so, a familiar truth that an artist's imaginative vision may be more radical than his or her real-life opinions. Dickens wants to assist the poor and reform a self-serving state bureaucracy, improve sanitation and streamline the law. Yet the society he presents in his later fiction is so thoroughly false and dehumanized that it would require a good deal more than better medical facilities in Tom-all-Alone's to set it to rights.

GEORGE ELIOT

You can tell that George Eliot is a liberal by the shape of her sentences. Whereas Dickens's prose is declamatory and impressionistic, Eliot's sentences unroll like undulating hills, full of wry asides and scrupulously qualifying sub-clauses. There is an equipoise and authority about her prose style which is very far from the panache and hyperbole of a Dickens. Eliot's prose makes the kind of strenuous intellectual demands on the reader that Dickens's never does, yet it is also full of playful affection and good-humoured irony. Her writing is mellow yet incisive, marked by a well-tempered wisdom and a genially tolerant wit. If she suffers or rejoices along with her characters, she can also stand at a judicious distance from them and deliver dispassionate judgements on their behaviour. This is not an author who is likely to be impulsive or one-sided.

Given her supple, coolly rational prose style, we are not surprised to find that she rejects absolute moral judgements of the kind that Dickens goes in for. Nobody in Eliot's fiction is either transcendently good or wicked beyond redemption. The besetting sin of her characters is egoism, which is hardly the most heinous of offences. The worst that can happen to you in Eliot's world is not spontaneous combustion or being battered to death by your vicious burglar of a lover, but 'never to be liberated from a small shivering hungry self', as she remarks of Edward Casaubon in *Middlemarch*. Besides, egoism is a fault which can be repaired. What can repair it is the imagination, which allows us to rise above our own interests and feel our way sympathetically into the lives of others. And the supreme form of this imaginative sympathy is known as the novel.

The novelist, in other words, is now becoming a kind of moralist, in a tradition which will pass to Henry James and D. H. Lawrence. It is not just that Eliot shares her earnest moral sentiments with the reader. It is also that the very act of imagination involves projecting oneself beyond one's own ego into the lives of others. The artistic imagination is thus the paradigm of human compassion. The novel is a model of morality because it can feel its way sensitively into a whole galaxy of human lives, showing us how each of these men and women experiences the world from a different angle. If traditional morality works by universal principles, the novelist-as-moralist can go one further by bringing these principles to bear on uniquely particular situations, which for Eliot is the only true basis for moral judgement.

Besides, the novelist can penetrate to inward facts as well as recording outer ones, shifting from states of affairs to states of mind, and tracing the delicate interactions between them. The novels are both inside and outside the life they document, rather as Eliot herself as a writer was both inside and outside the rural community. If she writes affectionately of this provincial form of life, the fact that she *writes* about it already places her outside it. She knows the Poysers, Tullivers and Dodsons from the inside, but is now distant enough from their doings to pass some rather condescending judgements on them. We need to get at a distance from situations in order to judge them; but true judgement also involves delving behind the external appearances of other people, or the brute facts of the matter, to grasp something of their inner make-up. There must be some mid-point between ardent empathy and Olympian detachment – some vantage-point which is neither warped by prejudice nor tainted by indifference.

It is this double-focusing of 'inner' and 'outer' which the novel form is supremely well placed to accomplish. Casaubon in *Middlemarch* is a bloodless old pedant who speaks like a legal treatise and dies of a 'fatty degeneration of the heart', a phrase almost calculated to inspire the reader to place a large asterisk in the margin and write 'symbol' beside it. But just as we are about to write him off, the novelist steps in to remind us that Casaubon, too, has a palpitating inward life which should win our respect. This is a typically liberal gesture, and one very far from the world of a Dickens. Even egoists must be regarded non-egoistically, and tolerance shown even to the intolerant. Liberalism and the realist novel are spiritual twins. Arthur Donnithorne of *Adam Bede* may be a sexual predator, but he is no Alec D'Urberville; so to forestall the reader's too-easy response, the novel takes pains to insist that he has a loving nature.

In this sense, knowledge, imagination, feeling and morality go together, and the name of this unity is art. The more you understand the truth of

another's situation, the more you can grasp how the world seems from their standpoint; and the more you do this, the less likely you are to pass external, dogmatic judgements on them. For Eliot, this fellow-feeling is the very essence of morality. Novels can put things in context, and thus temper our impulse to judge them too absolutely. They can reveal buried histories, or hidden patterns of force and causality, which make the apparently vicious or selfish actions of men and women more intelligible. The role of art, Eliot writes in her essay 'The Natural History of German Life', is to deepen human sympathies, 'amplifying our experience and extending our contact with our fellow-men beyond the bounds of our personal lot'. Writing and reading, then, are implicitly political acts, breeding social solidarity. Fiction stirs men and women into 'that attention to what is apart from themselves . . . which may be called the raw material of moral sentiment'. The novel, in other words, is an antidote to egoism – not just in what it says but in what it does, in its form as much as its content. Another Victorian antidote to egoism is work, which in Adam Bede's opinion gives you a grip on things outside your own petty lot. In the case of a professional writer like Eliot, these two remedies come to much the same thing.

The idea that lack of sympathy springs from lack of knowledge – that to understand all is to forgive all – is a typically liberal mistake. It is one which Eliot shares with her fellow-novelist Elizabeth Gaskell. It is not the fact that we do not understand anti-Semitism which impels us to condemn it. The sadist has a quick sense of what his victim is feeling, which is exactly what makes the infliction of pain so pleasurable to him. You can feel what a beggar is feeling without being in the least moved to toss her a coin. Immorality is not just lack of imagination. Eliot does not really see, as the later Dickens does, that sympathy is not enough because human relationships may be distorted by social institutions. It is a matter of structures, not just of sympathies; and this is no doubt easier to see in the anonymous city than it is in what Raymond Williams has called the 'knowable community' of the country village.[1] It takes more than personal sympathy or the compassionate imagination to break down the social barriers between men and women, bosses and workers, or masters and servants. In this sense, ironically, it is the less realist Dickens who takes the more soberly realistic view. Eliot's doctrine rests on a rather optimistic view of humanity, one which is typical of her liberal humanism. It is at odds with the Romantic view that knowledge and feeling are polar opposites, as well as with the Victorian suspicion that scientific knowledge (the theory of evolution, for example) was eroding moral values altogether.

This is not the view of Adam Bede, who believes that 'feeling is a kind of knowledge'. Nor is it the opinion of his author, who was one of the most distinguished intellectuals of her day, a woman who was already a celebrated public figure before she came to pen her first line of fiction. Eliot was formidably well-versed in art, music, history, languages, theology, psychology, sociology and the natural sciences; and one of the momentous achievements of her art was to convert this body of knowledge into the stuff of imaginative creation. By the alchemy of her prose, scientific learning is transmuted into image, feeling, narrative, imaginative scenario. She is able, in a fine phrase of Shelley's, to imagine what we know.

Victorian England was awash with new ideas which had yet to be 'naturalized', absorbed into the bloodstream of the culture to become a kind of spontaneous wisdom. Knowledge was rapidly outstripping customary habits of feeling. Ideas were changing, but patterns of symbolization and emotional response were still caught in a previous age. Alarming new doctrines like those of Darwin were still to be fully assimilated into the sensibility of the age. You might acknowledge in an abstract sort of way that the universe was millions of years older than you had imagined, but you could not really be said to believe this until it had reorganized your body – your perceptions, habits of feeling and emotional reflexes – as well as your mind. A rationalist, increasingly secular society was in need of a new mythology, and it was Eliot's fiction above all which accomplished this task for her anxious contemporaries.

Modern society, in her view, should not simply leave myth behind (Eliot believes that very little should be left behind), but should raise this 'primitive philosophy', as she called it, to a 'higher' stage where it would be compatible with reason. Her name for this, taken from Continental thought, was the Religion of Humanity, a rationalist equivalent of religious belief. The scientific evidence which was shaking religious faith had to involve more than rejection and refutation; it had to give birth to its own affirmative brand of humanism, not least if science and atheism were not to prove socially subversive. New forms of knowledge had to transform feelings and values, not exist in perpetual conflict with them. Fact and feeling, the head and the heart, blend in the texture of Eliot's level-headed yet lively prose style, as well as in the subject-matter of her novels. She sees her own art as akin to scientific inquiry rather than the enemy of it. The more we investigate Nature, the more we come to revere its unfathomable mysteries, so that science lends support to a sense of religious awe rather than undermining it.

In general, the English novel is not remarkable for ideas. It has little to compare to a Robert Musil or Thomas Mann. Instead, a fair amount of English fiction from Jonathan Swift to Kingsley Amis is devoted to satirizing the intellect, showing how high-minded notions are likely to get bogged down in the messy contingencies of everyday life. By and large, the English novel is sceptical, earth-bound and empirical, preferring to be guided by good sense rather than by Goethe. Conrad, Joyce and Beckett take an interest in ideas, but they are not English. Henry James was commended by his compatriot T. S. Eliot for having a mind so fine that no idea could violate it. Though the French or Germans might regard this as a peculiarly backhanded compliment, Anglo-Saxons would not. Both James and Eliot were American converts to English culture who demonstrated their kosher Englishness by their scepticism of the intellect. The supposedly cerebral T. S. Eliot can find almost no role for the intellect in art. England is the home not of ideas but of customs and traditions – which means, roughly speaking, ideas which were once controversial, but which now feel so natural that we no longer need to argue about them. They seem more like instincts than rationally contestable theories. Radical republicans ask whether the royalty is a reasonable institution, whereas conservatives just know in their hearts that Britain could never survive without a monarch. It was another foreign blow-in trying to outdo the English at their own game, the Irishman Edmund Burke, who played a major role in bequeathing this notion of tradition to the nineteenth century.

George Eliot, exceptionally, is both a theorist and a traditionalist. She has a passionate engagement with ideas, but she is just as dedicated to the value of custom, feeling and habitual affections. Another way of putting the point is to say that she is a woman intellectual, for whom thinking and feeling are not as damagingly divorced from each other as they are for some male varieties of the species. Moral truths and scientific doctrines can thus be translated into each another. If tradition means that the dead are somehow borne along with the living, then Eliot can find evidence for this in the latest evolutionary hypotheses. If tradition insists that men and women conform to their environments, Eliot will use the new scientific theories to show that such adaptation is the surest way for the species to flourish. *Silas Marner* may be a charming folk legend, but it is also full of complex reflections on chance, providence, causality and the nature of historical evidence. Silas himself moves from religious faith to the cloistered egoism of a miserly existence, and from there to what Eliot called the 'truth of feeling', as he discovers the love of little Eppie and through her a whole human fellowship. If this is the simplest of moral fables, it is also an allegory of the historical progression from religious superstition to modern-day materialism, and from there to the Religion of Humanity of the future.

John Goode has spoken of *Adam Bede* as 'the first major exercise in programmatic literary realism in English literature', and the key word here is 'programmatic'.[2] It is with Eliot that realism in the English novel becomes theoretically self-conscious, not least in the famous chapter of *Adam Bede* 'In Which the Story Pauses a Little'. (This is ironic, since holding up your narrative to insert a brief treatise on realism is not exactly realist.) Realism for Eliot is the doctrine that truth and beauty are to be attained only 'by a humble and faithful study of nature' – and the word 'faithful' here means both accurate and loyal. It is a moral term as well as a factual one: you can only depict the world truthfully if you also portray it lovingly. As for 'humble', only by sympathetic self-forgetfulness can you lay yourself open to the world as it is. In this sense, the sheer act of writing involves the author herself in the kind of compassionate surrender of selfhood which so many of her characters strive for as well. The process of attaining knowledge is itself a moral act. Sympathy lays bare things as they are. Without imagination, you cannot see the world aright.

But the act of knowledge is also a political one, in two different senses. First, because you cannot be sure in advance what is worth knowing, which means that the lowliest manifestations of life are as worthy of attention as the highest. Indeed, if reality is a complex web of interconnections, the humblest and the highest are intimately related. The theory of evolution has blurred the distinction between man and mollusc. So there is something inherently democratic and liberal-minded about literary realism. It involves a loving fidelity to the value of the ordinary – to what Eliot in *The Mill on the Floss* calls the 'sweet monotony' of everyday life, and what one of her less appreciative Victorian reviewers called 'the people . . . with all their coarseness, ignorance, and prejudice – poor, paltry, stupid, wretched, well-nigh despicable'.[3] Both the liberal and the scientist in Eliot trust to the power of the prosaic. Her writing is a powerful blow on behalf of those whose lives have been thought too humdrum and obscure for epic or tragedy. Whereas the truth is that this obscurity, not least when it comes to the lot of women, is exactly what makes them fit subjects for tragedy. The fact that Eliot has to break off her narrative to engage in some special pleading on this subject indicates the contentiousness of the case, as does the fact that she promotes the literary rights of people like the Poysers with more than a touch of patronage. But it is clear, despite the apologetic ironies, that the middle-class

writer, with his or her ardent preoccupation with everyday life, is now in supreme command of the literary scene.

Realism of both the literary and the moral kind demands that you be selflessly open to things as they are, not as you would wish them to be; and this, too, also carries a political implication. It is a rebuke to abstract theory and idle utopianism. You must accept people as they are, in all their quirks and mediocrities. This is both generous-spirited and wryly pessimistic, since one reason why you should accept people as they are is that it is a fruitless task to try to change them. The point is to interpret the world rather than to change it – or at least change it substantially. Eliot speaks of 'quiet perceptions . . . undiseased by hypothesis', an obvious smack at radical thought. Like many an Anglo-Saxon intellectual, she is deeply suspicious of intellectuals. The phrase 'liberal intellectual' borders on the oxymoronic, since liberals are wary of doctrinal systems. For Eliot, those who 'pant after the ideal' are in one sense admirable; but they also risk a withering of human sympathies, even if, ironically, the ideal in question is one of love and compassion. Theories and ideals are necessary to raise us above an unreflective, animal-like routine, but in doing so they threaten to restrict the rich inclusiveness of life. There is a problem, then, in being a realist and a reformer at the same time: you need to take the world as you find it, but an excess of such tolerance may mean abandoning your vision of progress.

The novelist, then, is a kind of social scientist, exploring through the lens of her fiction the microscopic processes by which character and circumstance interact. The realist novel is a kind of imaginative sociology – one which can forage beneath external facts to lay bare the inner recesses of human consciousness. It is thus a diagnostic kind of social knowledge, rather than a merely descriptive one. As such, it fulfilled a vital function. As industrial-capitalist society ran its course, there were now whole reaches of social experience which seemed dangerously opaque to middle-class politicians and intellectuals – the life of small rural communities, for example, or of the urban working classes. Eliot speaks in her essay on German life of how little the 'natural history' of the working classes has been studied, as though they were some rare species of racoon. Since knowledge is power, the Victorians needed an account of these largely unmapped territories from the inside; and the realist novel could provide it more effectively than a whole army of earnest-minded researchers.

Sociology might reveal the general laws by which human societies evolved; but the novel, uniquely, was able to do this *and* show how these laws were fleshed out in human passion, psychology, lived experience. The novel could shift its focus back and forth from part to whole, which meant that it could yield something more than the merely fragmentary, but also something more than a purely abstract or theoretical picture of the whole. Few people were more strategically placed to bring this off than a female intellectual novelist of modest rural origins. If the intellectual is typically in pursuit of the whole picture, the woman is perhaps more likely to be responsive to the claims of feeling and local experience. If the intellectual is typically ambitious and wide-ranging, one from a modest rural background is likely to recognize the need for such high-flying notions to stay rooted in the habits of feeling of ordinary people. And if a novelist needs to be reasonably well-educated, with a few mildly original ideas about the world, he or she also needs a quick sense of the concrete and particular.

The nineteenth-century novel, needless to say, was more than a convenient instrument of middle-class knowledge. It was not just a set of coded despatches from darkest England, informing the ruling class of what the natives were getting up to. It could also challenge the very basis of that social order. There is much of this rebellious impulse in Eliot's own fiction, but it is tempered by a zealous belief in tradition and continuity. It is not hard to see in this conflict something of the running battle between George Eliot the enlightened middle-class metropolitan liberal, and the provincial farm bailiff's daughter Marian Evans (her real name), who preserved a life-long commitment to the rural, conservative, lower-middle-class community from which she sprang. It is the dilemma of the intellectual who is not far removed in origin from the common people. Thomas Hardy and D. H. Lawrence were both to grapple with it later.

In *Adam Bede*, for example, Eliot admires working-class Methodism as a cultural phenomenon, one which spiritualizes the common life and binds the self to a communal tradition. Yet the liberal intellectual in her regards most Methodist belief as crass superstition. Popular culture is commended more for its form than its content. The question, then, is how the life of the free spirit is to be reconciled with the duties and affections of everyday existence. Or, to put it another way, how the earlier phase of George Eliot's life is to be reconciled with her later career. Can the two somehow be combined, so that 'educated' consciousness can find a root in a more commonplace, collective existence without losing its largeness of mind? And can the traditional life of the countryside shed its bigotry and benightedness while preserving what is precious about itself?

The answer of *Adam Bede* to this question is largely affirmative. Impressively, the novel manages to combine complex realism with old-world rural

charm. Though its countryside is a thoroughly capitalist set-up, it still has a festive, semi-feudal aura about it, not least in the village games, dance and birthday party. There is a carefully stratified class structure, but the various social classes are more harmonious than in, say, *Middlemarch*, where the gentry and aristocracy tend not to hobnob with middle-class bankers and manufacturers, nor they with small tenants and artisans. All this, however, also helps to conceal a rather more grim social reality: Donnithorne the squire is a social exploiter; his son Arthur is a sexual one, with alarmingly reformist ideas about efficiency and land enclosure; and the Poysers belong to an economically precarious tenant class. In a magnificent scene late in the book, Mrs Posyer turns out to be a flaming class rebel, wrathfully driving the landlord off her property. This is scarcely the rural England of jocund ploughmen, spicy nut-brown ale, and idyllic shepherds making bashful love under the hawthorn bushes, to quote Eliot's own sardonic words in the journal she edited, the *Westminster Review*.

Adam Bede is backdated to the end of the eighteenth century, with Britain at war with revolutionary France and mill-hands labouring not far from rural Hayslope in the factories of Stoniton. Yet its static, intensely visual, Dutch-painting style of presentation helps to dehistoricize it. This is the age of the Methodist challenge to the church establishment, as we see with Seth Bede and Dinah Morris; yet this, the French wars and industrial labour touch only lightly on the rural community. The rural order is resilient enough to withstand historical change, rather as the community of *Middlemarch* is narrow-minded enough to do so. Eliot is interested among other things in *Adam Bede* in demonstrating certain supposed laws of nature and society, and stripping away a fair degree of history helps with this investigation in the same way that stripping off someone's clothes helps in discovering whether their blood is circulating efficiently.

Adam himself is an idealized figure, which is not to say an uncriticized one. He embodies what his author regards as traditional lower-middle-class rural values: honesty, hard work, practicality, social deference, moral integrity, loyalty to his roots, a pragmatic approach to life, a scepticism of fancy theories and utopian ideas. Interwoven with these virtues are a number of equally traditional rural vices: intolerance, inflexibility, moral self-righteousness, a reluctance to adapt, develop or forgive. Adam is a workaholic who enjoys drinking whey more than beer, breaks out into hymn-singing at embarrassingly unpredictable moments, and speaks like a second-rate anthology of thoughts-for-the-day. He is full of moral tags and sententious sayings, and though the novel takes the measure of his defects, it does not always seem

to appreciate quite what a prig he is. Eliot ensures that Adam is finally humanized by his suffering, forced to be less stiff-necked and unbending; but she also ensures that this ambitious artisan ends up with a timber yard and marries the right Poyser niece (Dinah) rather than the wrong one (Hetty Sorrel). As John Goode puts it, 'What Adam really has to learn is not to marry beneath him'.[4] He is a shining example of the Victorian gospel of self-help and robust individual enterprise. In this novel, however, such individualism is compatible with social integration, as it also is in *Silas Marner*. This will not be the case in *The Mill on the Floss*.

As a cross between simple craftsman and local sage, Adam is a kind of synthesis of Nature and culture. In him, the bonds and obligations of culture have become a kind of second nature. Culture raises natural instincts to a higher level, but it must remain rooted in them if it is to flourish. Adam is thus both idealized and ordinary, as the fact that he is a foreman – one of the people, but set in authority above them – indicates. Dinah Morris, similarly, is a working woman who is raised above the commonplace by her religious fervour. She says things like 'I trust you feel rested and strengthened again to bear the burthen and heat of the day', not quite the kind of language one might hear after several pints of cider in the local inn. Both Adam and Dinah maintain a balance between Nature and culture, unlike Arthur Donnithorne and Hetty Sorrel. Arthur is culturally divorced from Nature as a gentleman, but he is also a creature of his sexual instincts, so that he combines culture and Nature in all the wrong ways. Hetty is pure natural instinct – a kind of precultural, even prehuman creature who is seen by the novel as an animal, insect, flower or fruit. Her very surname suggests a horse or a plant.

Egoism for Eliot is our natural condition. 'We are all of us born in moral stupidity,' she comments in *Middlemarch*, 'taking the world as an udder to feed our supreme selves'. It is the rationalist's version of original sin. 'Decentring' the self, acknowledging that we are one among many and that the world is indifferent to us all, is the laborious achievement of culture, a wisdom to be painfully acquired. Hetty fails to make this transition from Nature to culture, egoism to altruism, the Imaginary to the Symbolic. She is stuck at a lowly point on the evolutionary scale, and is treated before her tragic catastrophe with a mixture of patronage and genial malice. If Dinah has too many morals, Hetty has too few. One would hesitate a long time before marrying either of them.

Hetty is Nature not as pastoral, but as destructive and Darwinian. She signifies pure natural appetite or desire, and her real crime is to disrupt the social bond between Adam and Arthur, or master and man. Desire is natural

in the sense that it is no respecter of social rank. Adam and Arthur, too, are reduced by their quarrel over this young woman to pure animal instinct, as they fight over their courtship of her. Human culture was wrested out of Nature by a lengthy, strenuous struggle, but it can always slide back again. Appetite is the enemy of civility. Once this female force of Nature has been sent packing, however, the bonds between master and man can be gradually reknit. As a convicted criminal, Hetty is, so to speak, transported out of the novel, leaving Hayslope little the worse in the long run. Though the tragic events of the book revolve on her, it is their implications for others which concern the novel most, so that she is both centred and sidelined.

In one sense, Hetty is elevated above the ordinary by her downfall. It is a courageous move on the novel's part to turn this frivolous young narcissist into a tragic protagonist. This is Eliot's democratic realism in action. Yet Hetty is more an object of our sympathy than a fellow subject, and we are not allowed access to her inner life in the way we are to Maggie Tulliver's. If this novel can restore social equilibrium rather more smoothly than *The Mill on the Floss*, it is partly because Hetty – the character who transgresses, refuses to adapt and resists being incorporated – is treated so superiorly and externally. What in Maggie Tulliver will take the form of a disruptive quest for personal self-fulfilment is here little more than the errings of sexual appetite.

Natural instinct acknowledges only the whims of the present, whereas moral culture is what binds you to tradition. It is culture which preserves the unity of the self by weaving your past, present and future into a coherent narrative, so that your present actions can be informed by a rich heritage of loyalties and affections. This is not some chuckleheaded conservatism: as a liberal, Eliot believes devoutly in what she calls in *Middlemarch* 'the growing good of the world', in the possibilities of progress and enlightenment. It is just that such progress must build on the past without breaking with it, which is how Eliot sees evolution in general as taking place. The process of human development, she writes in her essay on German life, must reach 'that perfect ripeness of the seed which carries with it a life independent of the root'. You must rise above your historical inheritance, if you are not to be the prisoner of it; but you must do so by drawing on the resources of that tradition, and thus in a way which keeps faith with it. 'I desire no future that will break with the ties of the past', cries Maggie Tulliver. Origins in Dickens are often obscure, while in Charlotte Brontë's fiction you are conveniently set free of kinship so as to make your own way in the world. For Eliot, by contrast, acknowledging where you come from, and remaining loyal to it, is the only sure way of moving beyond it.

The political upshot of this is reform rather than revolution. Indeed, Franco Moretti, as we have seen earlier, argues that the nineteenth-century realist novel, with its trust in tradition, continuity and gradual evolution, is an implicit riposte to the French Revolution.[5] If this sounds a touch fanciful, it is worth noting that Eliot herself writes in *Middlemarch* of the French Revolution as a warning to the English against unmitigated zeal. She began writing *Adam Bede* with the French revolution of 1848 still fresh in her memory, and there is a pointed contrast between the novel's gradualist, 'organic' view of human society and that disruptive political event. This may well be one reason why Eliot chose a rural setting, in which social relations seem more settled and natural than they did when viewed from the Parisian barricades.

Without an anchorage in tradition, the self is perilously wayward and anarchic. The same is true if you press the doctrine of sympathy too far, since then you simply melt into accord with every mind you encounter, with no stable centre of selfhood of your own. Will Ladislaw of *Middlemarch* is an instance of this emotional dilettantism to begin with, before he buckles down to higher things. It is a version of what John Keats calls 'negative capability'. Sympathy enriches the self, but it is also in danger of diffusing it. In any case, the impulse to give the self away is always a suspect one in Eliot's fiction. It is a familiar trap for women, who have been conned too often into believing that true freedom lies in servitude. But it is also suspect because there is a kind of altruism which is really just a devious form of egoism, as in Arthur Donnithorne's desire to be thought well of by his tenants, or the cult of martyrdom to which both Maggie Tulliver and Dorothea Brooke are dangerously attracted. Dramatically relinquishing the self may just be a perverse form of self-affirmation. There can be, as Ladislaw observes to Dorothea, a 'fanaticism of sympathy'.

On the other hand, too deep a root in a traditional way of life stunts your individuality, stifles your freedom, frustrates your legitimate ambitions and narrows your largeness of mind. All this is most obviously true of women, who must struggle for education and independence far more vigorously than men. But there is a fine line between being too deeply and too shallowly rooted – between having too much of a self and having too little of one. You can be too rigid like Adam, or too easy-going like the liberal-minded Mr Irwine. Adam can be softened up by the events of the novel with no detriment to his sturdy, oak-like nature, but the same cannot be said of Tom

Tulliver, Maggie's stiff-necked brother in *The Mill on the Floss*. What could still be just about contained within the framework of comedy and pastoral in *Adam Bede* threatens in the *Mill* to erupt into full-blown tragedy.

The pharisaical Tom is unrelenting almost to the end, and Maggie herself is no simpering Hetty Sorrel but a formidably complex figure. If Tom and the lower-middle-class Dodsons are premodern characters, living by unreflective custom, Maggie is a prototypically modern protagonist, rebellious, self-questioning, restless with restriction, and in passionate pursuit of her own fulfilment. The fact that she is a woman in a patriarchal rural community makes this emancipation all the more fraught. Tom and the Dodsons are admired rather in the way that Adam Bede is: they practise the stout petty-bourgeois virtues of thrift, honesty, loyalty, industriousness and obligations to kinsfolk. But they could never have written the novel, as one suspects Maggie could have done.

The crisis of the narrative turns on Maggie's need to choose between her fidelity to the rural society of St Oggs and her love for Stephen Guest. This is not a choice between duty and affection, head and heart, but between two kinds of affection. To opt for Stephen would be to allow the impulse of the moment to triumph over the claims of history, kinship and community. The line between self-fulfilment and self-indulgence is perilously thin. It is a question of communal loyalty versus selfish individualism. It is also a question of 'Nature' – a delicious yielding to desire, which dissolves the self to a kind of dreamy nothingness – versus the claims of culture, which in this context means the claims of others. (Though an excess of culture can also lead to selfishness, as with the pampered Rosamond Vincy of *Middlemarch*.) Culture, morality and altruism are aspects of a single reality.

Sympathy with others fulfils the self, but it may also mean abandoning one's own unique path to selfhood. This, in the view of emancipated liberals like Stephen Guest, is a profoundly unnatural act. From one viewpoint, Maggie is faced with a Hobson's choice between natural selfishness and unnatural self-sacrifice. For the liberal Guest, self-realization is an absolute imperative; and Eliot is close enough to this ethic herself to appreciate its force. For her, however, yielding to 'natural' desire means giving way not only to egoism but to a kind of determinism. As Maggie drifts down the river with Stephen, she disowns her own moral agency, luxuriantly helpless to shape her own destiny. Once again, self-surrender can be a subtle form of self-pleasure. Throughout the novel, Maggie has a hunger for the seductions of oblivion – which is to say with Freud that, like the rest of us but rather more so than some, she is in the grip of the death drive. Her austere cult of

self-renunciation is one instance of the perversity by which the self rejoices in its own dissolution.

It would be ironic for Maggie to make a liberal-individualist option for Stephen, since by whisking her off down the river he is depriving her of what the liberal cherishes above all: the right to choose for oneself. Maggie finally exercises that supremely individual choice – but what she chooses, ironically, is communal responsibility rather than individual happiness. If this is one irony, another is that the rural community to which she turns back to is a prejudiced, parochial backwater which gives her no credit for giving up the man she loves. In fact, it is not difficult to read Maggie's decision and its aftermath as splendidly perverse. In the end, she opts for death with a man who does not love her (her brother Tom) rather than life with a man who does.

In doing so, she sacrifices herself for her mulish bully of a brother, as well as for a neighbourhood which is not worth her loyalty. It is not hard to see this as yet another example of what Philip Wakem scathingly calls 'a narrow self-delusive fanaticism'. To stay faithful to the age-old sentiments of rural life is to opt for a stifling sectarianism. There may well be value in remaining faithful to one's past; but if this means keeping faith with a man as carping and self-righteous as Tom, it scarcely seems much of a moral achievement. Is maintaining a continuity of selfhood really so precious in itself, regardless of what it involves you in? Is Maggie just the self-deluded victim of a joyless Protestant morality for which the key to life is a 'sad patient loving strength'? Does she suspect in good puritanical fashion that if you are not in agony then you must have gone astray?

The novel allows for this harsh reading, at the same time as it counters it. For the fact is that if it kills off Maggie in a surge of guilt and expiation, it kills off Tom as well. The extraordinary ending of *The Mill on the Floss* allows Maggie to be reunited with her brother, and with the way of life he symbolizes, but to obliterate him at the same time. It is as though the full force of the novel's pent-up desire is unleashed, like the river Floss itself, threatening to sweep away the very world for which this dutiful young woman has laid down her personal happiness. And this is a sweet sort of vengeance, even if it means that Maggie herself will not be around to savour it. In the book's apocalyptic finale, Maggie is granted her Romantic self-fulfilment, along with her submission to the local pieties – but only in a way which rounds violently upon the whole stiff-necked social order which has done her down. If she is finally granted the pleasures of self-annihilation, it is in the form of a triumphant self-affirmation.

In a sense, then, Maggie achieves what Philip Wakem has accused her of seeking: 'a mode of renunciation that will be an escape from pain'. Like the water of the Floss itself, the event both generates and destroys. The judgement of society is both endorsed and rejected, just as Tom is both embraced and wiped out. Formally speaking, the conclusion of the novel reveals a smiliar blend of acceptance and refusal. If it strives to preserve realism, it also threatens to burst beyond it into a realm of fantasy and wish-fulfilment. Like Maggie, it is regressive and rebellious at the same time.

The novel is determined to grant its heroine her victory, even if it has to go to the death for it. This includes a triumph over Tom, who in his dying moments acknowledges his sister's moral superiority. Maggie thus crushes him and wins him over at the same time, establishing an equality with her brother which is also a kind of power. Most of Eliot's novels only just manage to fend off tragedy, and the ending of this one can be read as both tragic and anti-tragic. Or perhaps it is an example of the ambiguity of all authentic tragedy, in which the very act of submitting to your destiny reveals a courage which transcends it. There is a parallel, perhaps, with the conclusion of *Jane Eyre*, which allows Jane both deference and revenge, equality and dominion, expiation and redemption. It is as if she had died locked in an embrace with Rochester in his burning house. In this society, simple human recognition between a man and a woman seems to demand a flood, an inferno or, as with Catherine and Heathcliff in *Wuthering Heights*, death and destruction. Much the same, as we shall see, can be said of Jude Fawley and Sue Bridehead in Thomas Hardy's *Jude the Obscure*. In all of these cases, equality between men and women touches on something which presses against the confines of literary realism, and cannot really be articulated within them.

It may be that Maggie dies racked with false consciousness, immolating herself for a red-necked rural world which is worth no such renunciation. Like its heroine, *The Mill on the Floss* is homesick for a rural ideal which it recognizes scarcely exists. The true idyll is childhood, not the English countryside. The actual rural community is one of struggling tenant farmers and a bull-headed resistance to change. This is not a fable of the death of the old organic society at the hands of sharp commercial practitioners like Guest and Wakem. It is true that small-scale rural capital like old Tulliver's mill is now thoroughly ensnared with urban banking and agricultural industry, a collusion which is helping to bring it low. But there is nothing particularly new about the Guests and the Wakems, and the rural community's own defects play a vital role in its collapse.

If there are criticisms to be aimed at St Oggs and Dorlcote Mill, however, there is not much to be said for the world of urban capitalism either. It is not just a question of Maggie being rescued from her troglodytic relatives by town-bred liberals who respect the autonomy of the individual. Stephen's liberalism is real and admirable; but it is also a spiritual version of the rather less admirable individualism of his capitalist father. Rootless freedom is no answer to Tulliver intransigence. Maggie's refusal to break with her community must be set against the backdrop of a self-seeking Victorian society for which human relationships should not stand in the way of your self-advancement. Her fear of 'natural appetite' is not just a shyness of sexuality; it is also a repudiation of the so-called enlightened individualism which was the ruling orthodoxy of George Eliot's England. It is just that it is hard to know where legitimate desire ends and self-seeking appetite begins. In this respect, Maggie may well have miscalculated.

In this sense, Eliot's revisiting of her rural past is not a retreat from her contemporary world, but a way of engaging with it more deeply. In places like Hayslope and the region around Dorlcote Mill, one can find a 'corporate' way of life which may well be claustrophobic, but which at least has some regard for what contemporary capitalism scorns: custom, kinship, locality, tradition, work as a value in itself rather than a means of self-promotion. Yet there is an historical irony here. Industrial-capitalist society in Eliot's time was itself in transit from an early unbridled individualism to a more corporate, regulated version of itself. We have seen something of this transition in the later Dickens. Affirmations of individual freedom were now yielding ground to so-called scientific sociology, which exhorted men and women to promote the good of the whole over their own petty appetites.

The curbing of self-interest had always been necessary for human loyalties and affections; but it was now increasingly in demand from the industrial-capitalist system itself. Only in this way could class conflict be effectively quelled, and the common people be persuaded to identify their own interests with those of their masters. Eliot's career as a novelist falls largely in the period between the strife-ridden 1840s and the return of social unrest in the 1870s. It is a time of relative economic prosperity, when the political emphasis falls on unity, class harmony, corporate existence, the need to assimilate individuals into the social whole. One can trace the effects of this not only *in* Eliot's novels, but in the way in which she conceives of the novel form itself.

Individualism is no longer enough; instead, in an increasingly interdependent social order, one must come to think in more collective terms. A

late work by Eliot, *Impressions of Theophrastus Such*, speaks of the need for 'corporate existence' and 'the pride which identifies us with a great historic body'. It is, she writes, 'a humanising, elevating habit of mind, inspiring sacrifices of individual comfort, gain, or other selfish ambition, for the sake of that ideal whole'. Such corporate existence is endangered by mixing too much with foreigners: Eliot warns us of the dangers involved in undergoing 'a premature fusion with immigrants of alien blood'. The whole text is cast in the jingoist rhetoric of the age of imperialism, and this from the author of the Judaeocentric *Daniel Deronda*. The idea of sacrifice is now rapidly assuming Kiplingesque overtones.

To think in corporate terms means trying to conceptualize social life as a whole, as well as grasping the underlying dynamic by which it develops. Since these laws are intricate and invisible, what you need to dredge them to light is either a scientific sociology, or a kind of fiction which delves beneath the appearances of things to unravel their secret causes. And this is the realist novel. Only by understanding these laws, and submitting to their inevitable evolution, can the individual flourish. Or, as a German contemporary of Eliot's put it, freedom is the knowledge of necessity. We must lay bare the logic of Nature, acknowledging its sublime power over us, if we are to harness this logic to our own ends. In this sense, too, submission and affirmation come to much the same thing.

This is more or less the view expounded by Eliot's Felix Holt, who, so we are informed by his creator, is a political radical. In fact, the full title of the novel in which he appears – *Felix Holt, The Radical* – is about as accurate as *Genghis Khan, Man of Peace*, or *George Bush: Intellectual and Moral Sage*. Felix is an updated urban version of Adam Bede, the sort of man whom one would not wish to sit opposite on any but the briefest of train journeys. He believes in prudence, sobriety, hard work and self-discipline, and the extent of his political radicalism is to become accidentally embroiled in a mass riot and strive to head it off. This is rather like being branded a criminal for trying to avert a bank robbery. Eliot's sympathies may embrace the rural lower middle class, but they do not stretch quite as far as the urban working class. The proletariat is brutish and unruly, given to demagoguery and blind disorder.

In fact, far from running wild, the nineteenth-century working-class movement called for *more* social order, pressing for a state which would repair the damage wreaked by unruly market forces. Felix rejects political activism and trusts instead to a gradual process of popular education, which will bring men and women to appreciate 'the nature of things' and thus cool their political ardour. He is less a socialist than a Stoic. There is a sense in which the novel itself protests against this rather sanguine view of history, in the bleakness and social nostalgia of the finely wrought scenes centring upon Mrs Transome.

Eliot's advocacy of kindship, tradition, custom and community is typically Romantic. But Romanticism also believes in individual fulfilment – and in Eliot's work these two kinds of loyalty are often enough at loggerheads. One response to this dilemma is the realist novel itself, which is supposed to do justice to the individual life, but also to the whole context within which it exists. What, however, if the novel is now the only way of imagining that broader context? What if it is the only kind of 'totality' left to us? An anxiety of this kind haunts Eliot's finest work, *Middlemarch*, which is all about failed or false totalities. Casaubon is in pursuit of a spiritual or intellectual totality, the so-called key to all mythologies; Lydgate is searching for a materialist equivalent of this, in his scientific inquiries into the primitive tissue of all life; Dorothea Brooke is allured by the vision of some mighty project which would transform human life as a whole, while at the same time allowing her to achieve self-fulfilment. Even Bulstrode, the unsavoury Evangelical banker, refers his less than creditable everyday actions to some divine plan which will justify them.

All of these attempts at totality, whether Romantic, mythological, scientific or providential, finally come to grief. In some cases, this is because they are damagingly abstruse and theoretical, unlike a good realist novel. Or if may be, as with Lydgate's medical researches, that they are admirable in themselves but are undone by the ensnarements of everyday life, which in Lydgate's case means pretty faces and provincial politics. Total views of the world may be too remote from ordinary experience, as with Casaubon and Dorothea, or too entangled in it. Common life, in a typically Eliotic ambiguity, is both nourishing and narrowing. The only totality which really flourishes is the novel itself, a grand narrative deeply suspicious of grand narratives. What cannot be achieved in content can be attained by form. The book itself is a great web of interconnections which weaves together part and whole, idea and image, knowledge and experience. Its mesh of mini-narratives, along with its constant shifting of narrative viewpoint, reveals how different human egos or social worlds grasp the world in their own distinctive way, but also how they share a reality in common.

The image of society as a web, and the idea of one's history as a complex continuity, are spatial and temporal versions of the same way of seeing. If society is a web, however, then this has political consequences. To begin

with, it is an argument against radical change. There is no centre to a web, no focal point or fundamental principle which would allow us to alter it as a whole. Besides, if all the filaments of our lives are so delicately interlaced, pulling too impatiently on a single strand may unravel the whole fragile structure. This, then, is an argument for reform rather than revolution – but so is the fact that action taken at any one point in a web will spread along its strands to have an effect on the whole. The very interwovenness which means that evil spreads like typhoid also means that goodness can never just be local. Simply by doing good where we are, Dorothea holds, we are somehow widening the skirts of light against the powers of darkness. Will Ladislaw shares her opinion: there is no use in trying to take care of the world as a whole, since that will happen anyway if we delight in what is true or beautiful. 'Act locally, act globally' is the slogan of this doctrine.

Ladislaw, as a Bohemian dilettante averse to the idea of a profession, starts off with too little selfhood, and finally acquires some solid identity as an activist in the cause of political reform. But since he does this with no detriment to his liberated cosmopolitan spirit, he ends up by combining principled identity with a flexibility of selfhood, thus becoming an ideal candidate for a George Eliot heroine to marry. Mr Brooke describes him as a blend of Shelley and Burke, meaning perhaps that he unites Shelley's idealist ardour for liberty with a judicious appreciation of the complex, evolutionary nature of human affairs. He is both rebel and pragmatist, another reason why any self-respecting Eliot heroine should rush him to the altar. Dorothea Brooke moves in the opposite direction from her future husband, beginning with too-ardent, 'theoretic' demands which she will finally have to scale down.

Dorothea's genteel uncle, Mr Brooke, has too lax and shambolic a self; if his niece has too many ideas, he has too few. We are invited to see that his spirit of moderation, while valuable in itself, is also a form of moral and intellectual indolence, as well as suggesting one reason why he is an irresponsible landlord. Reform has to start at home. Brooke's woolly reformist ideals are grotesquely at odds with his discreditable practice, rather as Bulstrode's religious faith is at odds with his corrupt conduct. There is a notable gap between the latter's otherworldly zeal and his worldly self-interest. Theory and practice – another language for the whole and the part – are hard to combine in this novel. Medicine promises one way of doing so, since a physician like Lydgate is both a theorist and a practitioner, searching ambitiously for the basic tissue of all life while doing good in a more modest local way. The science of medicine is another example of how knowledge

and human compassion, fact and value, can reinforce rather than obstruct one other. Physicians bring their knowledge to bear on human needs, while the fact of human need acts as a stimulus to further research. But Lydgate, too, betrays a gap between his noble intellectual ideals and his morally commonplace character.

Middlemarch ends by putting a brave face on failure. Dorothea has no beloved brother to rescue in a flood, and as a 'foundress of nothing' is denied her St Teresa-like fulfilment. It is a realistic enough destiny for a Victorian woman. The good she does will be obscure rather than historic, and the novel rationalizes this compromise as brightly as it can. Perhaps we are persuaded that this settling for half is mature wisdom, in contrast to youthful naivety. Officially, history is in a middle march between ignorance and enlightenment, and the good of the world is steadily growing; but this profoundly disillusioned novel puts its author's own beliefs into question, as novels often do. The ambitiousness of its form contrasts with the cheerlessness of its content. The town of Middlemarch proves largely resistant to reform; Casaubon dies tormented by his own failure; Bulstrode is disgraced; Lydgate expires early and unfulfilled; and the Adam Bede-like values of hard work and moral integrity are confined to the marginal presence of Caleb Garth. Looking back on the great expectations of the first Reform Bill from the vantage-point of the second, it does not seem that history is on the side of the enlightened. From this point on, as radical hopes are baffled and the British economy moves into steep decline, there will be little talk of progress in the English novel.

Remarkably, however, Eliot does not give up. It is hard to see how one could rekindle social hope after this grimly disenchanted novel; but though the age of liberal enlightenment is drawing to a close, she comes up towards the end of her career with her most boldly utopian work of all, *Daniel Deronda*. The utopia in question is Zionism – a choice which may ring a little oddly in many ears today. But early Zionism is seen by the novel as a radical, anti-colonial movement, and the book's hero, Daniel, becomes caught up in it after discovering that he is a Jew. This, in Eliot's eyes, provides him at a stroke with the best of both worlds: a fulfilling Romantic identity, and integration into a rich historical culture. In Dickens, discovering who you really are often comes as an unpleasant surprise; but Deronda is provided on a plate with an enviable sense of selfhood. Like Will Ladislaw, he moves from an early, rather rootless liberalism to a mature self-realization – from 'a too reflective and diffuse sympathy' to 'the blending of a complete personal love in one current with a larger duty'. Or, as Matthew Arnold might have

put it, he moves from Hellenism to Hebraism – literally so, as far as the latter creed goes.

No Eliot character could ask for more than a blending of personal love and larger duty. If this synthesis had been on offer to Maggie Tulliver, she would not have needed to die. The best *Middlemarch* can do is to furnish Dorothea with the personal love and Will Ladislaw with the larger duty. The problem with larger duties in George Eliot is that they threaten to obliterate the self rather than fulfil it; but Deronda is able to realize his deepest sense of identity precisely by surrendering himself to such a cause. This, however, is because of the type of political destiny which the novel, with wondrous convenience, has selected for him. Zionism or nationalism are Romantic brands of politics, full of vision, poetry and rhetoric, and thus ideal vehicles for reconciling the public sphere with the personal one. What is conceivable in Jerusalem is out of the question in Westminster.

Daniel's ideal is that of 'a mind consciously, energetically moving with the larger march of human destinies, but not the less full of conscience and tender heart for the footsteps that tread near and need a leaning-place'. It is not clear how a mind can be full of a tender heart, how you can feel tender about footsteps, or how exactly footsteps can lean; the slackness of Eliot's writing here betrays the nebulousness of her thought. But it is gratifying to know that you can march hand-in-hand with history while being a liberal humanist as well, responsive to the personal and the local. The fine balance between the individual life and the corporate whole which *Middlemarch* aims for in its formal technique becomes for Deronda a real-life project. Or rather, a real-life project of a notably unreal kind.

It is not, however, a possible project for the Maggies or Dorotheas of this world. Not only because they are women, which means that they can neither become political activists nor discover that they are circumcised, but because Zionism is not an England-based enterprise, and so can figure as no more than an abstract solution to the problems of those stuck in St Oggs, Middlemarch or Silas Marner's Raveloe. In the end, you can achieve a unity of personal identity and corporate existence only by abandoning England altogether. The totality must be a displaced one, exported to the Middle East, where Deronda travels to discover his destiny. And this is a stinging criticism of conventional English society, which is represented in the novel by Gwendolen's repulsive husband Grandcourt. There is no way in which the values represented by Deronda and his Jewish heritage can be brought to bear on a spiritually arid English society. The novel accordingly splits down the middle, in a formal reflection of this ideological divide. A politically

barren England must be abandoned for the cultural or ethnic politics of Zionism, which can infuse spirit and passion into public life. Deronda breaks away – but he breaks away in order to sign up to a cultural tradition. Rebellion and integration can be reconciled here, as they cannot elsewhere in Eliot's fiction.

In leaving for the East, however, Deronda must leave the novel's downtrodden heroine, Gwendolen Harleth, marooned in a spiritually vacuous England. What is redemption for him is a kind of limbo for her. Like Mary Magdalen, Gwendolen glimpses her redeemer only to see him vanish again, though in this case to Palestine rather than Paradise. Gwendolen and Deronda are both at odds with orthodox society; but it is the man who can turn his back on it, not the woman. In doing so, he turns his back on her as well, leaving her with little more concrete to cling to than a vague ideal of goodness. One may contrast this with the situation of Romola, in Eliot's novel of that name, who is stirred by Savonarola to enter upon public life.

If Daniel's project is not English, neither is it exactly realist. One might stumble across a Bulstrode in real life, but hardly upon a Mordecai, Deronda's charismatic Jewish mentor. In this last novel, Eliot throws a good deal of the realist tradition to the winds, as Hardy will do in his own last work, *Jude the Obscure*. *Deronda* is an extraordinarily original, risk-taking work, a finale which is also an audacious new beginning, a sudden leap into what for most contemporary readers was a disturbingly unfamiliar world of ethnicity, arcane symbolism, cosmopolitan culture, mysticism, mythology and aesthetics. It is a book in which myth, romance, Gothic, theatre, allegory, fantasy and biblical allusion play as important a part as social realism, even though it is the only one of Eliot's novels to be set in her own time. As her fiction moves up to date, its forms move backwards to the prerealist past. It is as though her contemporary moment is so drained of value that only a return to these more traditional resources can renew it. The formal gulf between realism and romance is also a social chasm between Gwendolen, the injured woman trapped in a vapid social world, and Daniel, the enterprising man about to move off into a realm of exotic adventure which sounds as though it is straight out of a novel.

This, in fact, is a work of art which is very aware of art, just as *Jude the Obscure* is a text peculiarly self-conscious about writing. *Deronda* is a dense web of literary and cultural references, and reflects a good deal on art and music. Some of the 'real' events it records are also 'fictional', in the sense of being symbolic or allegorical of something else; so that this is a fiction which

is highly conscious of fictionality. Zionism itself is a fiction – a vision, a hypothesis – which will finally take on historical flesh. *Daniel Deronda* is, very deliberately, a meticulously plotted organic whole; and as such it offers a model of a certain idea of history. What if human history itself were to have the inner unity and purpose of a work of art? Or at least might be lent such unity and purpose?

Actual history seems to have come unstuck, as *Middlemarch* might testify, and reform seems to have been rebuffed. Yet perhaps there is a hidden spiritual history, of which Judaism is one mighty expression, in which everything is subtly interconnected with everything else, as in a great realist novel or an accomplished piece of music. There is a good deal of coincidence in this work, but also strange flashes of precognition, as dreams, desires and shadowy impulses prove to be harbingers of events to come. In one sense, this is simply the idea of tradition pressed to a semi-mystical extreme. If tradition means that the present teems with the burden of the past, then why cannot these organic affiliations work the other way too, and the present become pregnant with a future which is yet to be born? Perhaps we can read history backwards and forwards at the same time, rather as we can with the complex symbol web of a novel like this one.

The idea of precognition also presses to a logical limit Eliot's belief in the world-shaping power of ideas. Perhaps our hopes and beliefs, if felt fervently enough, help to bring about the situations they envisage. Perhaps the very fact that I have an impulse to become prime minister foreshadows the fact that I will eventually do so. In England, history appears to be headed nowhere in particular, and ideas seem to have lost their socially transformative force. The age of Will Ladislaw is over – indeed, was over quite some time before the appearance of the work in which he figures. Ladislaw is a hero of the first Reform Bill seen in the disenchanted backward glance of the second. *Daniel Deronda*, however, can compensate for this chilling lack of vision by turning to the alternative histories of Judaism and Zionism, which unlike late Victorian England are both telological – they have a goal – and form a spiritual whole. This makes these histories a kind of art, and indeed *Daniel Deronda* proposes some suggestive parallels between art and a political cause like Zionism. Art, too, liberates the individual self, yet subjects it to the chastening discipline of an order larger than itself. Like the most creative kind of politics, it involves renunciation and hard labour, but also love and personal fulfilment. In the case of *Middlemarch*, the art of the novel itself represents a purposive whole which seemed to be in the act of disappearing

from history itself. In *Daniel Deronda*, it is as though the tables have been turned, and history itself has become a work of art. But this is a very special history indeed, one far from both Hayslope and Grandcourt's upper-class world. In the end, Eliot's determination to keep the faith forces her writing beyond England, as well as beyond the limits of realism.

THOMAS HARDY

Not all that long ago, a standard account of Thomas Hardy might have run rather like this: Hardy was a self-educated author who struggled his way up from the ranks of the common people, and wrote gloomily fatalistic novels about an English peasant society whose traditional way of life was being undermined by external urban forces. Not a word of that account is in fact true, except perhaps for 'author', and to inquire why not might lead us to a more accurate understanding of the man and his fiction.

Hardy was not from the common people. Not everyone who lives outside London is a country bumpkin. He was the son of a rural builder who employed six or seven workmen, and after attending a reputable high school qualified as a professional architect. Far from being self-taught, he was considerably better educated than the great majority of men and women of his age. As Raymond Williams sardonically points out, the patronizing adjective 'autodidact', which has been used alike of Hardy, George Eliot and D. H. Lawrence, probably means simply that none of them went to boarding school or Oxbridge.[1] Any English writer who did not, yet can still pronounce 'monocephalous', must presumably have grubbed his or her knowledge from dusty second-hand tomes scanned by candlelight in a roofless cabin.

Nor did Hardy write of peasants, for the excellent reason that hardly any of them existed in rural England. Technically speaking, a peasant is a farmer who owns and works his own land – and the land enclosures of the late eighteenth century had driven most of this class from the English countryside, in contrast, say, to the situation in France. By Hardy's time, farming in

England had long been a capitalist, market-oriented enterprise based largely upon landowners, tenant farmers and landless labourers. There was thus no sharp social divide between country and city, since the social relations which prevailed in the latter were equally dominant in the former. There was also a rural lower middle class of dealers, craftsmen, shopkeepers, traders, artisans, schoolteachers, cottagers, small employers and the like, with whom Hardy, as an offspring of that class himself, especially identified. It was this class, not the 'peasantry', which he saw as preserving the cultural continuities of the countryside; and its steep social decline in his own day meant the catastrophic loss of that precious heritage.

As with most of the classic English nineteenth-century novelists, then, Hardy's allegiances lay neither with the governing classes nor with the plebeian masses. Instead, he draws many of his major protagonists from the mobile, unstable lower middle class – one trapped between aspiration and anxiety, and therefore typical of some of the central contradictions of the age. In this sense, Hardy could attend to the plight of this obscure social grouping without losing a grip on broader issues. Gabriel Oak of *Far From The Madding Crowd* starts off as a hired labourer before graduating to become an independent farmer and then a bailiff. Giles Winterborne of *The Woodlanders* is no simple-minded yokel but a merchant and dealer. Michael Henchard, later to become mayor of Casterbridge and a speculator in grain, begins his career as a hay-trusser, a skilled type of rural craftsman. Like many such craftsman, he is forced to become a kind of internal migrant in his own country, wandering the roads looking for work.

Tess Durbeyfield, daughter of a lifeholder and small dealer, has been reasonably well-educated by a London-trained teacher at a National School, and though she speaks the West Country dialect at home can speak Standard English well enough when she chooses. (In this sense, she is a precursor of Paul Morel of D. H. Lawrence's *Sons and Lovers*, who speaks Standard English but lapses into the Nottinghamshire dialect in moments of tenderness or intimacy.) Tempted though we are to read the story of Tess and Alec as a timeless fable of innocent peasant lass and wicked squire, Tess is in fact no more peasant lass than the *nouveau riche* Alec, with his purchased title, is genuinely a squire. Jude Fawley of *Jude the Obscure* is the ward of a struggling shopkeeper from an economically depressed village who becomes a baker's delivery boy and later a financially insecure stonemason with great expectations. These are not unskilled, illiterate rural labourers, though the threat of being forced down into that semi-destitute mass haunts several of them.

So also, however, does the hope of rising to higher things. If the mobility of this class is a sign of displacement in an economically ailing English countryside, it is also an index of aspiration. If Hardy's protagonists are so often tragic figures, or only narrowly avoid that fate, it is partly because they are caught between a vision of fulfilment and a frustrating reality. They are enterprising enough to aspire beyond the parochial communities in which they live, but lack the resources or good fortune to transcend those limits altogether. It is this, not naive Romanticism or sexual desire, which triggers the downfall of Eustacia Vye of *The Return of the Native*. What is at stake is not so much desire but its refusal. As with Hardy's great contemporary Henrik Ibsen, the drive to emancipation is too often deadlocked, betrayed, beaten back, turned against itself, stoically abandoned. As with Ibsen too, it also turns out often enough to be internally flawed, not just externally thwarted.

In Hardy's world, those too lowly to nurture such aspirations are usually immune to tragedy, as are most of those who have already achieved power and status. It is the internal migrants – the men and women caught painfully in the middle – who are most likely to come unstuck. The phrase 'returned native' captures this ambiguity exactly. Eustacia Vye is too cultivated and ambitious for the heath-dwellers around her, while Grace Melbury of *The Woodlanders* is also separated by education from her environment. She is, the novel observes, 'left as it were in mid-air between two storeys of society'. Clym Yeobright's fuzzily liberal-minded efforts to overcome this gap between native and exile by becoming an itinerant preacher to the people of Egdon Heath are not taken terribly seriously, either by the inhabitants of the Heath or by the novel.

There is nothing timeless about the rural order which these men and women inhabit. Hardy himself portrays Egdon Heath, in the poetic *tour de force* which opens *The Return of the Native*, as eternal and unchanging, but not long after his death it was planted from end to end by the Forestry Commission. It is the kind of irony he might well have relished. Rural England had been disruptively reorganized by the Enclosure Acts only a century or so before Hardy himself came to write, and during his own lifetime it was a place struggling with poverty, falling profits, unemployment, cut-throat foreign competition, trade union militancy, the impact of modernization, a steady haemorrhage of population from the countryside to the industrial towns, and the loss or decline of a range of traditional skills and customs.

All this was not just a question of external forces laying siege to a traditional way of life. Many of these developments came from within rural society itself, and had been in progress long before Hardy came to write. The triumph of Farfrae over Michael Henchard in *The Mayor of Casterbridge* is not the victory of the scheming capitalist over the traditional peasant: Henchard is himself a grasping profiteer, and Farfrae simply streamlines and extends his already thoroughly capitalist dealings. He is not some alien interloper disrupting a settled way of life, but a man who develops Henchard's own techniques, and in doing so contributes to the prosperity of the local community. If he starts off as an outsider in that community, so does Henchard himself. Hardy does not consider that the kind of modernization which Farfrae promotes is always to be lamented, any more than he believes that the traditional is always to be admired.

There was little 'pastoral' about this rapidly unravelling social fabric, and certainly nothing idyllic. If it has its attractive aspects, it is also a place of semi-destitution, sweated labour, economic instability and social isolation. *Far from the Madding Crowd* indulges in a kind of rural idealism from time to time, but it does not disguise the fact that its hero, Gabriel Oak, can lose his employment almost overnight. *The Mayor of Casterbridge* introduces us to a world of uncertain harvests and unstable prices. English agriculture is now having to compete with Continental rivals and the American mid-West, and from the mid-1870s the British economy lapses into a severe, prolonged recession. Like some of its fellow capitalist nations, Britain will look to its overseas empire to restore its fortunes, and will find itself embroiled not long afterwards in history's first global imperialist war.

Hardy, of course, is well aware that this is not quite how the countryside looks from the standpoint of Piccadilly or the Potteries. The aestheticised image of rural life as tranquil, traditionalist, organic and picturesque is largely an urban perception, just as the view that fat people are always jovial is largely held by thin people. *Under the Greenwood Tree* is a title craftily designed for metropolitan consumption, even if the novel is all about sexual competition, social snobbery and coquettish vanity. The fact that there are also a few cows dotted around the landscape cannot conceal this less than idyllic subject-matter. The pastoral image of rural life reflects the view of weekend trippers for whom Nature is a landscape to be gazed upon rather than a place to be worked in. Nature in this view is what you contemplate rather than where you live, stuff to swoon over rather than stuff to eat.

Hardy sometimes draws on the pastoral or Arcadian mode, not least in *The Woodlanders*, with its suggestions of harmony and fertility; but this is a curiously self-conscious, almost self-parodic version of pastoral, a highly literary instance of the form. It is as though the novel is fully aware of the literary mode within which it is working. And though the woods of *The Woodlanders* are outwardly calm, almost idyllic, viewed close-up they are a place of relentless evolutionary struggle. The novel plays off a Romantic view of nature against a Darwinian one, and this shuttling between conflicting standpoints is typical of Hardy's technique. His novels are concerned not just with a clash between Nature and culture, but with competing visions of Nature. The 'naturalness' of sexuality can be used to challenge repressive social conventions, but the 'natural' can also mean the brutally indifferent. In which case, it is more an image of society than an alternative to it. Nature is both the antagonist of culture, whether for good or ill, and a thoroughly cultural category.

Hardy, then, is not above cashing in on the pastoral ideology of the day-trippers from time to time, or indeed of treating it seriously, even if he also sees just how destructive it can be. Angel Clare's middle-class liberal idealizing of Tess Durbeyfield as an unspoilt child of nature is a case in point. Angel is that familiar, deeply untrustworthy figure in Hardy, the semi-emancipated middle-class liberal caught on the hop between his traditionalist upbringing and his enlightened ideals. Fitzpiers of *The Woodlanders*, and even Sue Bridehead of *Jude the Obscure*, are in some ways kindred spirits. But Hardy's writing also contains some lovingly detailed depictions of the natural world, and pastoral has its respected place. He remarks in *Far From the Madding Crowd* that 'the barn was natural to the shearers, and the shearers were in harmony with the barn', even though he also presents these harmonious peasants as a shiftless, drunken crew who haven't a clue how to treat a swollen sheep or put out a fire.

That Hardy's natural world is not idyllic does not mean that it is simply a site of capitalist exploitation. It is, to be sure, that as well: Mrs Charmond, the landowner of *The Woodlanders*, has Giles Winterbourne's house pulled down when his lease expires. Yet it tells in favour of Marty South and Giles Winterborne in *The Woodlanders* that they are intimate with the language of the woods, and heavily against Fitzpiers and Mrs Charmond (who actually owns the woods) that they dislike the place. It is just that Hardy is conscious that Nature, far from being the polar opposite of society, is always at some level socially defined. His judgement on Fitzpiers and Mrs Charmond is a straight class judgement: they are alienated from their natural surroundings by their social privileges. It is not the kind of thing one finds much of in Trollope. If Hardy offended some of his more conservative readers by such uncompromising class judgements, he also offended some of the more progressive among them by finally allowing the caddish Fitzpiers to marry

Grace. He does, however, hedge his bets here, as the marriage is unlikely to be happy.

Work is what transforms the raw stuff of Nature into meaning, gathering it into a human project. And in few English novelists is work as central an activity as in Hardy. When he looks at a landscape or a piece of Nature, he is usually preoccupied less by the thing itself than by the traces of history and humanity inscribed within it. In this respect, he is closer to Wordsworth than he is to Keats or Hopkins. In both the fiction and the poetry, objects and places are nexuses of memory and desire, hope or nostalgia; they are woven through with historical significances, sedimented with half-legible meanings. And these meanings can conflict, as what a bridge, an ancient stone or a tract of ploughland means for one person is not what it means for another. Objects are in this sense forms of irony, since they bring together divergent meanings. Hardy, in a word, is interested in Nature as a 'text' – which is not at all to suggest that he does not regard it as a material reality.

Because these traces of human meaning in things are typically faded or obscure, the material world for Hardy is a peculiarly enigmatic text – one which does not carry its significance on its face, but which needs to be skilfully deciphered by an observer. Nature and humanity have an affinity, in so far as the natural world is scored through with the traces of human actions and passions. But they are also at odds, since the material density of the world obstructs any clear reading of these signs. When Eustacia Vye stands motionless on the barrow in *The Return of the Native*, she seems like a natural extension of it; but then she moves, and we glimpse the discontinuity between Nature and the human.

For the Romantics, natural objects could be symbols, in the sense of things through which meaning flashed transparently. And that meaning often sprang from some transcendent realm. Neither of these things is true in the case of Hardy. Things in his world resonate with meaning, but often cryptically, ambiguously: Egdon Heath in *The Return of the Native* is both impassive and expressive, concealing and revealing meaning at the same time. 'To dwell on the heath without studying its meanings', the narrator comments, 'was like wedding a foreigner without learning his tongue'. Nature is a kind of language in which one needs to become fluent. Like human beings, it discloses itself only through a labour of interpretation. We can get Nature wrong, just as we can each other. Meanings are not folded into things by some transcendent power, but are bestowed upon them by human projects. And this implies that Nature has no meaning or value in itself. It is sheer indifferent, evolutionary stuff, which can be wrested into significance but which will always put up a struggle. A stonemason like Jude Fawley can feel this inertia at his fingertips. Since men and women try to wrest the world into meaning in conflicting ways, objects and landscapes are as much places of contestation as they are of consensus.

This is true above all of the human body. The body is the place where flesh and spirit, materiality and meaning, come together. So the body is itself a kind of signifier or symbol. Like Nature, it is a kind of language. But the flesh may either be an expressive sign of the spirit, or the two may run counter to one another. Thomasin of *Native* has a face which discloses 'an ingenuous, transparent life . . . as if the flow of her existence could be seen passing within her'. Tess Durbeyfield, on her first appearance, is similarly transparent: we see her at a dance, a ritual in which the body is at its most expressive, and her face is described as an open book in which one can read the various phases of her lifetime. After a spot of invigorating farm labour, even the cerebral Angel Clare begins to throw his limbs around: 'the muscles of his face had grown more expressive; his eyes looked as much information as his tongue spoke, and more'. Angels are not conventionally considered to have lithe physiques, but this Angel is gradually acquiring one.

Clym Yeobright's countenance, by contrast, is all too expressive, 'overlaid with legible meanings' and 'revealing a mutually destructive interdependence of flesh and spirit . . . the observer's eye was arrested, not by his face as a picture, but by his face as a page'. The novel goes on to compare Clym's features to written signs: they are unremarkable in themselves, but made meaningful by his facial expressions in much the same way that sounds which are meaningless in themselves become significant in speech. The face of his dying mother is like 'some strange old manuscript, the key to whose characters is indiscoverable'. In the bustling market place of *The Mayor of Casterbridge*, the body can literally become a form of communication, as farmers transact business through physical gesture: 'Here the face, the arms, the hat, the stick, the body throughout spoke equally with the tongue. To express satisfaction the Casterbridge man added to his utterance a broadening of the cheeks, a crevicing of the eyes, a throwing back of the shoulders, which was intelligible from the other end of the street . . .'. Farfrae learns to read 'the lines and folds of Henchard's strongly-traced face as if they were clear verbal inscriptions'. Even the bridges in Casterbridge frequented by social outcasts have 'speaking countenances'.

The face in Hardy, like the rest of the material world, is a kind of palimpsest in which you can detect the past dimly inscribed in the present. Like a cliff or a rockface, it is geologically layered. When Henchard looks at his daughter

Elizabeth asleep, 'there comes to the surface buried genealogical facts, ancestral curves, dead men's traits . . .'. The present is quite literally woven out of dead men and women, and the living make these corpses walk again simply by existing, secreting the past inside themselves like a ghost. Just as ancient Roman ruins underlie the town of Casterbridge, so past and present are somehow co-existent, strata of time stacked one on top of the other rather than laid out end to end. The present can never quite free itself from the past which went into its making, as Henchard learns to his cost when the wife and child he thought he had disposed of turn up again. If the present really could free itself from the past, then – since the past is what it is made out of – it would simply vanish from sight.

At its most positive, this notion of the body as language can become a utopian image of human fellowship. In *Native*, Clym Yeobright and his mother understand one another as completely as though 'their discourses were carried on between the right and left hand of the same body'. Jude Fawley and Sue Bridehead achieve 'that complete mutual understanding in which every glance and movement was as effectual as speech for conveying intelligence between them, [and] made them almost the two parts of a single whole'. But if flesh and spirit can be harmoniously blended, they can also be torn apart. If the body allows us to be expressive, it also allows us to be objectified. It is, so to speak, the 'outside' of ourselves which we can never fully command; or better, it is half-way between ourselves and others, neither fully outside us nor wholly within our mastery.

Several of Hardy's characters live out a conflict between the way they experience themselves as living subjects, and the way they appear in the objectifying gaze of others. It is one of his major ironies, and a potentially tragic one. It is, predictably, especially acute in the case of women. Tess Durbeyfield's awareness of her own 'pulsating life' is overshadowed by a sense of her blank externality for others. Her exterior, 'over which the eye might have roved as over a thing scarcely percipient, almost inorganic', conceals a subtle, passionate self, but nobody would know it at a glance. 'She was not an existence, an experience, a passion, a structure of sensations, to anybody but herself'. Nobody will take Tess as a whole person, as opposed to admiring her spirit alone, as the idealizing Angel does, or taking her body for sexual or economic profit. The pious Angel Clare and the profligate Alec D'Urberville are in this sense akin. Indeed, the novel itself oscillates between treating Tess as a object of erotic desire or 'scientific' investigation, and feeling genuine compassion for her. If she is a woman in her own right, she is also an object for the reader's consumption. Even so, as

Penny Boumelha argues in *Thomas Hardy and Women*,[2] it may well be that through the figures of Angel and Alec the story puts into question its own objectifying of its heroine, just as it may also call into question its own sublimated desire for her.

The self, then, includes a sense of its own alienated image. We see ourselves as others see others, and occasionally treat ourselves in that way too. In Hardy, this is a question of class as well as sexuality. Those who are likely to feel this tension most severely are the 'middling' characters whose desire exceeds their circumstances. But not exclusively so. When the farm labourers of *Tess of the D'Urbervilles* are at work in the field, the way they experience themselves as unique individuals is at odds with the view of 'an alien observer passing down the neighbouring lane [who] might well have been excused for massing them as "Hodge".' ('Hodge' was the patronizing term used at the time for farm labourers.) Jude Fawley, wandering through Christminster as a shabby, anonymous workman, begins to feel like a ghost. If enough passers-by stare through you, you feel absent from yourself. This is a society which uses your body, but which disembodies you in the process.

One desperate tactic for resolving this tension is to identify with the other's alienating view of you, turning yourself into a kind of object. A female field worker, Hardy remarks in *Tess*, 'is a portion of the field; she has somehow lost her own margin, imbibed the essence of her surroundings, and assimilated herself with it'. Clym Yeobright, caught between his ambition and his environment, takes the drastic step of deliberately closing down his consciousness, reducing himself to a kind of natural object on Egdon Heath. His failing eyesight is a mark of this shrinking subjectivity.

It is to this condition that several of Hardy's protagonists are finally brought, as casualties of what he will call in *Jude the Obscure* the 'deadly war waged between flesh and spirit'. It is a war which worsens as it develops, since the more barren your material circumstances ('flesh'), the more empty and inflated grows your ambition ('spirit'). If the flesh seems to obstruct the spirit – if social institutions thwart human desire, rather than acting as a medium of its fulfilment – you can always resort to the extreme strategy of severing the links between the two. Eustacia Vye in *Native* is a turbulent spirit, a young woman with dreams of fulfilment beyond her narrowly provincial environment. It is not hard to glimpse in her the sister of Jane Eyre, Maggie Tulliver and Dorothea Brooke. By the end of the novel, however, unable to free herself from these stagnant surroundings, she is forced to 'take a standing-point outside herself, observe herself as a disinterested spectator, and think what a sport for Heaven this woman Eustacia was'. It is a schizoid solution to the conflict, splitting yourself in two and contemplating yourself as though you were someone else. Maggie Tulliver tries on this tactic briefly in *The Mill on the Floss*, 'looking at her own life as an insignificant part of a divinely-guided whole'. In Eliot, however, as in Henry James later, self-diminishment may always be a subtle form of self-aggrandisement.

What Eustacia does, in fact, is try to turn herself into a late nineteenth-century naturalistic novelist. The naturalistic novel of Emile Zola and his colleagues aimed for a clinical, dispassionate view of human affairs. The novel became a kind of quasi-scientific experiment, placing men and women in specific circumstances and recording how their biological instincts induce them to react. There is a streak of this naturalism in Hardy, who from time to time likes to widen the narrative focus so as to gaze on human existence with the unperturbable eyes of the gods. With him, however, this is less a scientific doctrine than an imaginative hypothesis. It is one possible perspective among others. How would things look if you were to pull the camera all the way back? What would all this frenetic human striving look like from the lofty vantage-point of Mount Olympus? Or, indeed, from the viewpoint of the evolutionary process as a whole, which appears callously unconcerned with the fate of individual creatures or species? What would it feel like to view your own life in this fatalistic light, as though you were gazing on your own corpse?

To see other people as objects is, of course, a vital dimension of human existence. There could be no talk of relationship between creatures who lacked some form of objective material presence to each other. Objectification is part of what we are. It is just that the very conditions which make for such relationship also make for its potential undoing. We cannot talk or make love without bodies, but the fact that we are bodily beings means that we can exploit each other as well. Tess Durbeyfield spends much of the narrative resisting this reduction of herself to a thing. When Alec kisses her, for example, she makes herself 'dead', turning herself into an object in order to resist his attempts to do the same. When he seduces her, her spirit detaches itself dreamily from her body, leaving it a kind of corpse. Sue Bridehead in *Jude the Obscure* tries to get by with as little body as possible, as a protection against being possessed. In a materialistic society, dematerializing yourself may prove the only way to survive – which for a carnal being is ultimately no way at all. In any case, denying that you have a body may well play into the hands of those male idealists who see women as all spirit.

Several of Tess's most vulnerable moments involve this strategic withdrawal from her own body. It is remarkable how often she is to be found semi-conscious at times of crisis. By the end of the novel, Angel Clare is forced to acknowledge that 'his original Tess had spiritually ceased to recognize the body before him as hers – allowing it to drift, like a corpse upon the current, in a direction dissociated from its living will'. Tess will end up as a sacrificial victim at Stonehenge, while Jude Fawley speaks of giving his body up to be burned. The ultimate crime of this social order is to drive its subjects to sacrifice their own subjectivity, or to discard their bodies as sources of danger and corruption. Like most successfully repressive regimes, this is a society which does not need to wield a big stick; instead, it relies on its citizens scourging and dismembering themselves. And the citizens, with admirable public-spiritedness, do not disappoint it.

In the end, patriarchal England does not need to destroy Sue Bridehead: it can trust her to do it all by herself, through a guilty, self-lacerating submission to its law. Overwhelmed by the death of her children, Sue the pagan celebrant of life is glad that her children are dead, eager to flay her flesh and bring her body into corpse-like submission to a man she physically detests. By the time of this novel, inner and outer worlds have been ripped brutally apart. The 'flesh' of society, its conventions and institutions, cannot accommodate the spirit of the emancipated individual.

Michael Henchard of the *Mayor of Casterbridge* is a different kind of study in self-alienation. Henchard gets rid of his wife and daughter in order to be free, divesting himself more or less literally of his own flesh and blood, which then returns to plague him. As in some classical Greek tragedy, the mayor becomes the victim of his own free actions, which take on an alien life of their own and begin to determine his destiny. As with many an ancient Greek hero, freedom turns into dire necessity, as the ruler of Casterbridge overreaches himself and brings himself to nothing. Entranced by an illusion of freedom, one which means repudiating his fleshly ties to those closest to him, Henchard reduces himself to an object in his own narrative, and finally wants nothing more than to dispose of himself as an irrelevancy. He now sees himself simply an obstacle in the lives of others. The death which he comes to desire is the consummation of this reduction of himself to an object.

A similar pattern of self-undoing can be seen in his employment of Farfrae, the servant who finally outstrips his control and becomes his master. Once more, Henchard's own free action – in this case the hiring of a manager – ends up exerting an alien power over his existence. Like Oedipus, he will become an outcast once more, having governed his town but brought himself low. Like Oedipus, too, Henchard embraces his own destiny, turning

necessity into choice rather as his choice turned into necessity. In his deliberate self-dispossession, he becomes a sign of solidarity with the weak and
destitute, unmasking as hollow the success ethic of Farfrae and Elizabeth-
Jane. Like much classical tragedy, the story thus plucks value from failure, as
its protagonist moves from outcast to sovereign and then back to outcast,
but this time an outcast with the status of scapegoat. As a living image of
human breakdown and failure, the tragic scapegoat is intolerable to look
upon, and so must be thrust beyond the city walls. It is here, outside the
Casterbridge over which he ruled, that Henchard ends up.

If the split between flesh and spirit is especially marked in Hardy's women
characters, it is partly because patriarchal ideology insists that they be *seen*.
To feel sure of herself as a powerful subject, the woman must be conscious
of herself as an object of desire. Eustacia Vye, for example, has an almost
limitless desire to be desired. Sue Bridehead, so one critic comments, is
'exhibited' by *Jude the Obscure* in a series of visual images. A woman must
wear her visibility on her sleeve, so to speak. The point about patriarchy is
not that the woman cannot make something of herself, but that she can do
so only on the basis of what the gaze of the male makes of her. She must
negotiate her status as a subject from the state of being objectified. Hardy,
who is unusual among male English authors in placing female characters
right at the centre of his fiction, understands this very well, even if it is an
insight constantly at odds with his own stereotyping of women.

Bathsheba Everdene of *Far From the Madding Crowd*, for example, is a
strong, independent woman who resists becoming the property of a man,
and is in some ways commended for it by the novel; but Penny Boumelha is
surely right to detect an 'undercurrent of sexual antagonism towards her' on
the narrator's part.[3] Bathsheba must be 'tamed' if she is to make a suitable
spouse for Gabriel Oak, and is not averse to a spot of mild subjugation
herself. Hardy sometimes presents female sexuality as destructive, and
appears to share the sexist view of his age that women are in general closer
to Nature than men. The fact that he sometimes sees Nature as cruel, predatory and irrational ensures that this is not even a backhanded compliment.

The novels sometimes counterpoise Nature and culture, or instinct and
intellect, in a rather simplistic way, seeing woman as representative of the
former and men as typical of the latter. But Hardy's works are more than
just allegories of a clash between natural desire and social convention. Giles
Winterborne of *The Woodlanders* represents for Grace Melbury the claims of
Nature and instinct, as opposed to the overbreeding of Fitzpiers; yet it is an
excessive niceness about social convention which brings about his death. If

it is tempting to see Arabella of *Jude the Obscure* as symbolizing crude natural instinct in contrast to Sue Bridehead's intellectual cultivation, we should also remember her artificial hair, manufactured dimples, false pregnancy and sexual astuteness, hardly the stock-in-trade of a child of Nature.

It is not 'desire' which brings Jude Fawley and Sue Bridehead to grief, but the fact that their own conception of what a sexual relationship should be is at loggerheads with social orthodoxy. It is a conflict between versions of culture, not one between culture and Nature. What is at stake is not 'desire', but how desire is socially organized. This social organization is the 'flesh' with which the 'spirit' of emancipated human consciousness is at war. Jude and Sue are not persecuted mainly because they indulge their illicit desire, but because they have children outside of wedlock. The 'flesh' en-snares a woman not so much in the form of sexual desire as in the form of pregnancy, child-rearing, permanent sexual partnership and all that these involve.

We have seen that Hardy sometimes likes to pull the camera back and survey the scene from a God's-eye viewpoint. But his camera is more usu-ally angled so that a typical Hardy tale would begin: 'If you had been on this road at such-and-such a time, you would have seen . . .'. He is interested, in other words, in perspective or point of view; and this is relevant to what we have said already of subjects and objects, since perspective means the way an object is grasped from the standpoint of a particular subject. The object is given along with the place from which it is seen. This can involve a kind of irony, since irony is a clash of perspectives in which the same thing appears in different aspects. It is an irony of situation that crops up again and again in the novels, as the meaning of an event for one character is nothing like its meaning for another, or as the action someone takes to safeguard their own interests results unavoidably in the thwarting of someone else's. What is vital to one individual is marginal to another. There are times in Hardy when you cannot move without creating damage of one kind or another, and this is one of the classical preconditions of tragedy.

Irony, in other words, is not just a linguistic mode; it is a kind of kink or perversity built into the structure of a situation. Indeed, for a Darwinist age it is built into the structure of the world itself. In an evolutionary uni-verse, there is no single perspective from which things can be seen to add up. Instead, there are many different life-forms, each of which stands at the hub of its own universe; and all of these life-forms are at once intricately interrelated and in perpetual motion. You therefore cannot slice a cross-section down this world and pass absolute judgements on what is significant about it and what is not, since this would be to ignore time and change. You cannot predict right now what will flourish and what will perish, or what momentous effects some inconspicuous mutation may breed in the future. In Hardy's novels, a mislaid letter, unguarded gesture or missed appointment can trigger a full-blown human drama later on. Here, too, is one source of his notorious coincidences, as apparently unrelated bits of the world are shown to be subtly interconnected.

The present in Hardy may not only lead to an unpredictable future; it is also heavy with the burden of the past. If human society is a 'text', it is partly because its present is intricately interwoven with its past, to the point where it is sometimes hard to determine the break between the two. Indeed, attempts to break with the past may just end up repeating it. Michael Henchard makes one such desperate attempt at the beginning of *The Mayor of Casterbridge*, selling his wife to a stranger in order to begin his life afresh; but the past, as usual in Hardy, refuses to be repressed. Just as the free actions of others can stand in the way of your own fulfilment, so actions you yourself have taken in the past can confront you in the present as an implacable destiny. History is all we have to go on, yet it is in some ways a diseased legacy. It is not true that actions in Hardy are shaped by some iron determinism; but it is true that men and women can, so to speak, determine themselves. They can act so as to paint themselves into a corner from which there is no escape.

Destiny is among other things the failure to recognize our creations as our own. Like the splitting of body and spirit, it involves a kind of self-alienation. As George Eliot comments in *Adam Bede*, 'Our deeds carry their terrible consequences . . . consequences that are hardly ever confined to ourselves'. There is, she believes, 'a terrible coercion in our deeds', which determine us as much as we determine them. Human solidarity, then, is double-edged for Eliot, as it is for Dickens and Hardy. If it is a value to be cherished, it is also what allows human damage to spread beyond our control. As Mr Irwine observes in *Adam Bede*: 'Men's lives are as thoroughly blended with each other as the air they breathe: evil spreads as necessarily as disease'. And there is a sort of damage, as Adam Bede remarks, that cannot be made up for – one which is tragically irreparable. Once we have acted, our actions cannot be recalled. Simply by sealing an envelope, we have altered history for ever.

To see the world as structurally ironic is to see conflict as built into it, since human perspectives are bound to collide. This way of seeing may breed a certain gloom, but it also encourages a degree of modesty or self-irony, which is very characteristic of Hardy. Far from pinning his faith in metaphysical absolutes like the Immanent Will or the President of the Immortals, his way of looking tends to be piecemeal and provisional. The darkling thrush, in the Hardy poem of that title, seems incongruously joyful in its bleak surroundings; but this may always be because, perched high on its branch, it can see something which you cannot. You should be cautious about absolutizing your own perspective, seeing the world only from your own viewpoint; indeed, those in Hardy's fiction who do this quite often come to grief. To be stuck in your own standpoint is to become an evolutionary cul-de-sac, failing to adapt to a changing world. Instead, you must recognize that there may well be things going on in the middle distance which render your own vantage-point invalid or perilously partial. To survive and flourish, you have to think and act ironically.

This does not mean that you should try to contemplate things from the viewpoint of the whole, for in an evolutionary universe there is no such place. The world is 'textual' in the sense of being diffuse and decentred, with all of its component parts subtly interwoven. It has a plurality of centres rather than a single one, and you cannot pull one strand of it without bringing others with it. Hardy would have had little problem with the post-structuralist claim that 'there is nothing outside the text', and certainly would not have misinterpreted it to mean that the world consists only of language. It means, rather, that nothing in reality stands alone.

This is one reason why Hardy is not a Christian. It is because things are so diffuse and perspectival that he is the devout atheist that he is. 'God' would be the name for the world grasped as a totality, the Omega point at which all perspectives finally converge. But in Hardy's view there can be no such point in a world like ours. There can be no meta-narrative of divinity or totality, given the shapelessness of a random, evolutionary world. Even if God existed, he would be irrelevant to a universe of process, conflict and perspective. Little Father Time in *Jude the Obscure* seems to have the unnerving ability to see other people's lives in the round, as though from the viewpoint of eternity; but this spooky omniscience is linked with his fatalism and passivity.

Theology for Hardy is thus a subject without an object. In a curious sense, it is reality itself which is partial, unfinished and provisional, not just our views of it. It is as though perspective of a kind is actually built into the world. The only realist art, it follows, is one which reflects this open-ended condition, not one which, like that of the naturalists, seeks to round it off into a closed system. The naturalistic novelist is simply another surrogate for the Almighty. This means in turn that truth and partiality are closely related, which was hardly what the Victorian sage wanted to hear. For him, truth meant a disinterested view of the whole. He did not accept the proposition that truth might be one-sided. For Hardy, truth is not a question of the whole, as Hegel thought, since there was no whole.

Darwin, and the relativist way of conceiving of the world which he shares with philosophers like Friedrich Nietzsche, have thus put paid to divinity – but not in the boring, Alabama-high-school sense that the theory of evolution has shown us all to be monkeys in thin disguise. This atheism was part of what some of his contemporaries found outrageous about Hardy's work, as in G. K. Chesterton's lurid description of it as 'the village atheist brooding and blaspheming over the village idiot'. What is scandalous about Hardy, along with his social criticism and sexual outspokenness, is his churlish refusal to cheer his readers up. He was intolerably unafraid to be tragic, in an age which sought anxiously for spiritual solace and which looked to art to provide it. This was a relatively new direction for the realist novel, even if both Dickens and Eliot teeter on the brink of it. Novels are supposed to end with marriage, financial settlement, the miserable demise of villains and the prospect of rosy-cheeked grandchildren, not with an innocent woman being hanged or a man dying agonized and alone. To the Victorian mind, literature was meant to be edifying, not enervating. It was supposed to generate sweetness and light, not breed truculence and discontent. It is the conjunction of the atheist and the idiot, the critical intellectual and the lower orders, which most rattles the Roman Catholic Chesterton.

So Hardy is that rare figure, a tragic author of the Victorian age. He was a purveyor of what one critic has called 'the offensive truth',[4] and was pilloried for it by the critics. His first novel, *The Poor Man and the Lady*, was rejected for publication as too radical; Hardy himself described it as 'a socialistic, not to say revolutionary novel'. His last novel, *Jude the Obscure*, takes the three major ideological institutions of Victorian society – religion, education and sexuality – and censures them remorselessly. (One might add to that trio the institution of literature, as we shall see in a moment). Yet this sense of tragedy has little to do with some kind of cosmic fatalism. If the world is tragic in Hardy's eyes, it is not because things are implacably determined by some malevolent Will, but for just the opposite reason. In an evolutionary universe, it is the randomness of things – what he calls in *The Mayor of Casterbridge* 'the persistence of the unforeseen' – which is so destructive. In the great web of natural creation, everything is intricately bound up with everything else, so that action at one point in this tangled skein will create effects where they are least expected. You cannot be master over your actions, and the result of this may be the triggering of a process which nobody can control.

Such a process may have the feel of some metaphysical fate about it, but in reality it is nothing of the kind. There is certainly 'fate' in the sense of situations you can do nothing about: in the end, nothing can save Eustacia, Giles, Tess or Jude. Yet it is hard to believe that Hardy literally believed in the President of the Immortals, any more than he believed in the Archangel Gabriel. He described himself as a 'meliorist', meaning one who believes in the possibility of improvement; and though we should never automatically take an author at his or her word, neither should we dismiss what they say of their work out of hand. On this score, Hardy seems to be right: what sometimes looks like a predestined process in his novels rarely turns out to be one. It is usually possible to unravel the chain of cause and effect and see how things could have gone differently at any point.

Tess, for example, may announce theatrically that we live on a blighted star, but this is partly because she has been put in a thankless situation by her shiftless father, which leads to her crashing the family waggon and killing the horse. The reason for this, in turn, is that she fell asleep at the reins, and the reason why she fell asleep is that she had to rise early to make her journey because her father was in no condition to do so. The reason for this is that Mr Durbeyfield is fond of a drop of alcohol, and the reason for that is that he, rather like his daughter, tends to escape from a life of drudgery by seeking refuge in fantasy. As a result of all this, Tess is thrown into the arms of Alec D'Urberville, with ultimately tragic consequences.

It is not easy to say who was responsible for killing the horse, since Hardy is aware that no action is ever entirely one's own. It may be Tess herself, or the mail-cart driver she collided with, or her inept father, or those who profit by exploiting the Durbeyfield family's labour-power. Hardy is well aware that countless people are involved in the simplest action. The one suspect who can be safely exonerated is the President of the Immortals. Critics sometimes quote as evidence of its author's congenital pessimism the last sentence of *The Mayor of Casterbridge*, which speaks of happiness as being 'but the occasional episode in a general drama of pain', but in context it suggests just the opposite.

Much the same can be said of Hardy's treatment of Jude Fawley. *Jude the Obscure* does not suggest that Jude was kept out of Christminster by some malignant fate. It suggests that the university was not worth trying to break into in the first place; that Jude would have been better off sticking to his craft; and that his academic ambition, though an honourable thing in itself, is doomed to seek expression through institutions built to rebuff it. Even if Jude were to swing a place at Christminster, this would not alter the fact that the university exists among other reasons to keep people like Jude in their place.

The tragic contradiction of the novel is that the culture which represents a worthy aspiration for Jude is also one source of the deathly ideology which hounds him and his lover. The point, as Jude himself comes to recognize, is not so much individual improvement as collective advancement: 'All the little ones of our time', he remarks of Father Time in a memorable phrase, 'are collectively the children of us adults of the time, and entitled to our general care'. Jude puts in a word for human solidarity by taking a smack at that perversely distorted image of it, the nuclear family.

Jude's move to gain an education is not so much doomed as premature. By the close of the novel there is talk of poor scholars like himself being admitted to Christminster; in fact, Ruskin College – the trade unionist college in Oxford – was established not long after the book was published. Jude's tragedy may be absolute for him, but even he grasps something of its historical relativity. It is bitterly ironic that he spends his time reinforcing the very college walls which shut him out; but the novel goes out of its way to commend the bustling life of Christminster artisans over the spectral existence of its academics, and Jude would do well to attend to what his narrator says. The deadly war between flesh and spirit means among other things that a society obsessed with flesh, labour-power and material property is also one in love with spectres and ethereal ideals. It is at once grossly material and falsely idealistic. The more abstract and disembodied the spiritual life, the less it will provide a challenge to material interests. The scholars of Christminster ('a place of fetishists and ghost-seers') see spectres because they study the past, but also because they stare through low-born working men like Jude.

Sue Bridehead finally subscribes to an idea of fate, pleading with her partner to submit to 'the ancient wrath of the Power above us'. But these are the words of a woman whose children have just been slaughtered, which is hardly the time to make starry-eyed pronouncements about the cosmos. Besides, by living with Jude out of wedlock, Sue has had to endure the prejudice of a virulently self-righteous society. Jude's own response to their disastrous situation is political rather than metaphysical: 'It is only [a struggle] against man and senseless circumstance', he insists. Sue and Jude are a tragic couple not because they have been doomed by the gods, but because in a more enlightened society they might well have flourished. It is the fact that social conventions could have been different that makes their defeat so poignant. Their tragedy, like Tess's, is entirely avoidable, and this deepens rather than dilutes it. Jude has the rare ability to see himself historically, as most characters in fiction do not. 'When people of a later age look back upon the barbarous customs and superstitions of the times that we have the unhappiness to live in,' he observes, 'what *will* they say?'

Jude's appeal to circumstance will not prevail; but it is never wise in Hardy to resign oneself phlegmatically to one's fate. This is simply a way of bringing it on. Even if it is a dangerous delusion to believe that the world is spontaneously on your side, you can still make some difference to the course of events. There is, to be sure, no preestablished harmony between Nature and humanity; on the contrary, human consciousness is just an evolutionary accident, and is bound to be at loggerheads with the insensate world around it. For Hardy as for D. H. Lawrence, there is a kind of alienation implicit in the very fact of being conscious, which reminds us that we are not naturally at home in the world, and that the universe did not anticipate our coming. But none of this is to say that men and women are just the playthings of some Immanent Will.

It seems natural for us to assume that our meanings and values reflect more than just ourselves – that they are somehow rooted in the natural order of things. Hardy courageously rejects this consoling illusion, finding no basis for human values in Nature itself. Instead, we must come to terms with the unpalatable truth that there is nothing outside ourselves, either in the earth or the heavens, to legitimate our existence. As far as that goes, we must be our own guarantors. Hardy regards this as a realistic rather than nihilistic case; indeed, like many a classical moralist he regards clear-sighted realism as the foundation of all effective action. He is a realist in more than a literary sense. Those characters in his novels who are free of illusion and can see things for what they are are the ones most likely to thrive. But such moral realism is far from easy. Perhaps the most difficult achievement of all is to shake off our comforting idealism and acknowledge that the world simply is as it is, however we might like it to be.

This is not just dispiriting, however, since it means that if the world does not spontaneously speak the language of compassion or revolt, neither is it fluent in the language of reaction. If Nature assigns no very high status to human consciousness, neither does it ascribe any very high status to the consciousness of Bismarck or Queen Victoria. There is, to be sure, a touch of irony about a writer – one who prizes self-consciousness so dearly – seeing human consciousness as less than central to the world. The act of writing seems to assign the mind a centrality it no longer really has, in a Darwinian universe which evolves not by the power of ideas but by blind material forces.

The truth is that Nature speaks no language of its own. It has nothing to say about our projects. The universe has absolutely no opinions about us, and nihilists are simply those panic-stricken folk who imagine that this is a calamity rather than a simple fact. If a scrupulously neutral Nature does not reward our endeavours, however, it nevertheless leaves us free to pursue them. This is one reason why Hardy admires resourceful, adaptable, practically minded characters like Gabriel Oak, who refuse to yield to adversity. In contrast to this enterprise is the fatalism of a woman like Mrs Durbeyfield, who passively accepts her daughter's pregnancy as the work of Nature rather than the work of Alec D'Urberville.

A similar fatalism afflicts Sergeant Troy of *Far From The Madding Crowd*, who despairs when he sees the flowers on his lover's grave ruined by a waterspout. What he ought to have done, so the novel implies, is to have filled in the hole in the grave and replaced the flowers. There is no point in blaming your lack of initiative on the President of the Immortals. Giles Winterborne of *The Woodlanders* is criticized for taking Grace Melbury's rejection of him too stoically, doing nothing about it and simply fading out. If he had been vigilant about securing the lease to his property, some part of his tragedy might have been averted.

Hardy takes an interest in ancient Greek tragedy, which as we have seen echoes something of his own sense of the world. For the ancient Greeks as for Hardy, a certain kind of botching or 'missing the mark' is built into the world of human practice, as our freely chosen actions go astray, give birth to unintended results, become tragically or ironically deflected from their goals. This, incidentally, can make for comedy as well as for catastrophe. If it seems odd to allow Greek mythology and West Country hay-trussers to sit cheek by jowl in his work, this is partly because Hardy wants to show those reviewers who complained about the 'low social position' of his characters that these provincial men and women are quite as capable of tragedy as heroes and princes. There is, ironically, a democratizing bent to Hardy's use of mythology, since it lends value, dignity and universal significance to lives which might seem to the more hard-boiled of his metropolitan readers fit meat for bucolic farce. In this, he resembles the early George Eliot.

Hardy is not embarrassed by the incongruity of calling Eustacia Vye, the daughter of a down-at-heel bandmaster, 'Queen of the Night', or describing her with caught breath as 'the raw material of a divinity'. If this is ironic, it is not entirely so. Nor does he feel it out of the place to transform the dairy farmer Diggory Venn into the mysterious reddleman. Figures in Hardy are quite often framed in diverse ways, seen in contrasting lights, as Egdon Heath itself is an ambiguous blending of sky and earth, day and night. Is Alec D'Urberville pantomime devil, middle-class *arriviste*, melodramatic villain or symbol of diabolical evil? Does Tess spring from a ballad, a popular romance, a low-life rural novel, an early feminist essay or a classical tragedy? A host of literary, biblical, mythological and cultural allusions cluster around her, with scant coherence or consistency.

The novel in which Tess appears is marked by notable discontinuities of tone and narrative viewpoint, as though she is a hard woman to get into focus. She is, after all, a child of the degenerate aristocracy, a poverty-stricken farm worker and a reasonably well-educated lower middle-class woman all at the same time. Much the same narrative instability can be observed in *The Woodlanders*. Some of the key events of *Tess* (the seduction, for example) are reported only obliquely, or scarcely seen at all. Grace Melbury of *The Woodlanders*, so Penny Boumelha comments, 'migrates unsettlingly between pastoral survival, tragic protagonist, realist centre of consciousness, and melodramatic heroine'.[5] The self in Hardy, particularly the female self, quite often stands at the overlap of contending frames of reference. Eustacia Vye is seen both realistically and mythologically, and much the same is true of other Hardy's characters.

The critic John Bayley has remarked on Hardy's strange capacity to allow different elements in his fiction to lie side by side, as though unconscious of each other's presence.[6] In an age when the novel was becoming more unified and self-consciously 'artistic' – one thinks of Henry James, who spoke with odious condescension of 'the good little Thomas Hardy' – Hardy's own fictional forms are loose and mixed. He is not afraid to mix pastoral, satire, ballad, polemic, mythology, folk tale, farce, classical tragedy, rural comedy, mock-heroic, social commentary, melodrama, naturalism and philosophical musings with his literary realism, to create a literary cocktail which might make an aesthetic purist wince. He moves from the sublime to the ridiculous and back with enviable ease, and has a genial tolerance of coincidence and improbability. If there is sophisticated artistry, there is also a good deal of simple directness. Some of his forms cater to minority taste, while others have more a popular appeal. Like Dickens, his fiction draws on popular genres as well as 'literary' ones. He can swerve suddenly into allegory and out of it again, and behind his dense, complex realist plots one can sometimes still hear the resonance of some traditional ballad or folk tale.

All this seemed rustically quaint and clumsily provincial to some of Hardy's critics. On the other hand, he was not quite quaint and clumsy enough to be patronizingly categorized as a 'peasant' writer like John Clare. He was also rather too 'philosophical' for some critics' taste, too little concerned to assimilate his ideas to fictional form. Ideas and the English novel, as we have seen, have never formed the happiest of marriages. On the whole, that sort of thing could be left to the sinisterly cerebral French. Hardy was dismissed by some as a homespun, cracker-barrel kind of pseudo-philosopher, the kind of amateur sage who would probably bore you over dessert with a lengthy critique of Schopenhauer. His sense of the tragic could be rationalized as the temperamental melancholy of a man who had spent rather too long festering in the shadow of sheep pens and pig farms.

Hardy also violates the decorum of literary realism with his cinematic eye for what one critic calls the 'exuberant density' of the big scene. He is a dab hand at the carefully staged spectacular. He is not afraid to hold up the narrative for a while in order to insert some magnificent tableau or cameo, like the skilful descriptions of the Mellstock choir in *Under the Greenwood Tree*, the celebrated set-piece anatomy of Egdon Heath, the *tour de force* of a fencing scene in *Far From The Madding Crowd*, or the harrowing episode in the same novel in which the dying Fanny is half-dragged to the workhouse by a dog. One thinks also of the marvellous appearance of Giles Winterborne as a kind of fertility god or personification of autumn in chapter 28 of *The Woodlanders*, or of Grace Melbury's being caught in a crashingly symbolic man-trap. There is the hunting down of Tess at Stonehenge, and Jude's astonishing deathbed scene. Hardy's is an episodic fiction, and he does not always go out of his way to blend these full-dress occasions into some suitably organic whole. Yet this is not some rustic ineptitude. In typically pragmatic spirit, Hardy uses what serves his purpose, rather than allowing himself to be imprisoned by an ideology of literary realism. His novels are capacious, loose-jointed and generously inclusive, rather than studiedly 'artistic' or formally coherent.

Another complaint of some of Hardy's critics was that he could not write. This is rather a major drawback for a writer, akin to being a one-legged fashion model or a 17-stone jockey. Some critics have found his prose style laboured, maladroit and circumlocutory, crammed with clumsy Latinisms and creaking metaphors. It was left to Raymond Williams to point out that Hardy, like Tess, really works with two languages – what he takes to be an 'educated', 'literary' style, and his own more native, less formal idiom.[7] One can find instances of these different styles side by side on the same page. He is a provincial author writing with one uneasy eye on a metropolitan readership, and in seeing himself in this way through the eyes of others, he shares the self-alienation of some of his characters. In trying to approximate to what he takes to be 'literary' English, Hardy sometimes has his characters talk as though they have swallowed a geology textbook or a dictionary of classical quotations. When he describes a landscape, on the other hand, he can be far more direct, assured and sensuously specific. His writing dramatizes the tension in English class-society between a subtle but overabstract form of speech, and a concrete but constricted one. The divisions of that society, in other words, are inscribed in the very letter of Hardy's work.

By the time of *Jude the Obscure* – a novel whose epigraph is 'The letter killeth' – Hardy is beating a militant retreat from a realism he never entirely endorsed in the first place. The first sentence of the novel is 'The schoolmaster was leaving the village, and everybody seemed sorry'. This is scarcely a line of Jamesian subtlety or Conradian colourfulness. Instead, the prose is hard, graceless, ungenial. Hardy is not struggling to accommodate his readers any longer. The 'unliterary', in-your-face style of the novel contrasts tellingly with its self-conscious 'textuality', its brooding on writing, inscription, literacy, copying, citation and scripture. On the one hand, this is a raw, grossly materialist work, one which features pig-sticking, false pregnancy and the sheer wearisome logistics of getting from place to place; on the other hand it freights its narrative with a lot of highly un-English talk of theory and ideology. The novel is littered with ideologies – paganism, Tractarianism, medievalism and the like – which it ostentatiously refuses to 'naturalize' by dissolving them in the lived texture of its narrative. It is an almost aggressively theoretical work, of a deliberately rebarbative kind, at the same time as its focus is nothing if not prosaic and pragmatic. It is materialist, but not especially concerned to be realist.

How to be theoretical in the sense of nurturing life-giving ideas, while not denying the body in the process, is one of the problems which the book confronts. In refusing the 'literary' in its style, the novel keeps faith with the uneducated and verbally unskilled, while sharing its protagonist's consuming interest in texts. Yet writing, or Literature, is bound up with the cultural authority which keeps Jude out of Christminster. The letter – not least the letter of the marriage contract – is violent, so there is something curious about producing a novel which protests against this power. The letter of the Bible has been responsible for countless human deaths. The letter of the realist novel also risks killing, since, like other social institutions, it cramps and fixes the fluidity of experience in its representations. Literature, then, is among the key social institutions – the others, as we have seen, are sexuality, education and religion – on which the novel casts a relentlessly critical eye.

Jude the Obscure tackles this dilemma – the fact that it is literature protesting against literature – not only by its spare, functional, uncivil style, but by pressing as hard as it can against the boundaries of literary realism. What sort of verisimilitude is at stake in a book in which Sue Bridehead leaps from the bedroom window to escape the sexual advances of her Causabon-like husband, or Jude drunkenly recites the Nicene creed in a Christminster pub? Not to speak of the bizarre, science-fiction-like appearance of Father Time, who seems to have strayed into the novel from some Expressionist drama, and his grotesque hanging of the other children. Or the sound of Jude, 'literary' to the end, reciting the Book of Job on his death bed. There is not much attempt at an organic unity of narrative, just a dispirited shifting from place to place – an 'inorganic' structure which is highlighted by the topographical section headings.

Scarcely five minutes after they find the children dead, Jude is quoting from the *Agamemnon*. The book is stuffed with quotations, inscriptions, fragments of text, typographical devices. But this is also a novel which implicitly challenges novelistic representation, contrasting the mere imitation or reproduction of things with the creative energies of the act of production. (Hardy speaks of his own writings as 'productions of this pen'.) Reproduction in the literary sense is now uncomfortably close to conformism in the social one, or to the sexual sense of child-bearing. It is in the artisan's craft, shaping material stuff into expressive form, that *Jude the Obscure* finds an alternative to a society in which flesh and spirit, desire and the material world, meet only in deadlock. Such craft means bringing something new into the world, as Hardy does in writing his novel. The enemy of this production is *r*eproduction – the process by which the present is simply a pastiche of the past, one individual an obedient replica of another, and the beliefs of one generation a faithful facsimile of the beliefs of their ancestors. If literary realism is part of this reproductive logic, with its concern that the word should be a second-hand version of the thing, it is part of the problem rather than the solution, and Hardy's novel is unavoidably self-undoing.

If *Jude* is suspicious of reproduction, not least of the sexual variety, it is also because there is some opaque, impenetrable stuff at its centre which seems to elude such representation. One name for this impenetrable core is Sue Bridehead, whose first name inheres in the word 'obscure'. Sue is inscrutable partly because we see her as an object of the baffled masculine gaze, and partly because she dramatizes a kind of consciousness which cannot really be represented within conventional realist limits. She disturbs orthodox gender roles, as sexual rebel, sexless tomboy, epicene soul-mate of Jude, lover, mother and obedient servant of patriarchal law. Among other things, she shows us that sexuality in this misshapen social order has finally become impossible. In the contradictory figure of Sue – medievalist and New Woman, feminine and masculine, sexualized and gender-bending, rebel and timid conformist, unpossessable female and faithful comrade – the novel dramatizes a transitional form of consciousness, and does so all the more strikingly because it seems not quite to understand what it is up to. It is Sue, perhaps, who is the novel's real obscurity, and the book rarely allows us to see her straight. Most of what we see of its heroine is filtered through the consciousness of others, leaving her elusive in a way which both marks the limits of Hardy's own understanding, and which signifies the emergence of a style of consciousness which cannot yet be adequately encompassed.

If a fulfilling bodily relationship between men and women were compatible with full spiritual equality, then a truce might be called in the war between flesh and spirit. As it is, freedom for a woman like Sue may have to consist, ironically, in a refusal of sexuality – or at least a refusal to concede the death-dealing dogma that love, sexuality and marriage must always coincide. The novel sees that a purely negative freedom is at once vitally necessary and ultimately insufficient, compared to that corporate or collective freedom which Jude himself advocates, and which is the ethic of the emergent labour movement. In this sense, *Jude* explores the limits of liberalism. It exposes the lie of freedom of choice in an oppressive society, without abandoning what is precious in that creed. It also sees what is false about Jude's priggish scholarly dreams, while sympathizing with what is authentic in them. The tragedy is that in this social order, a legitimate desire for education and social advancement can be expressed only in forms which disfigure and betray it.

Jude and Sue achieve, preciously yet precariously, a certain comradely equality – an affinity which is underlined by the fact that they are cousins, as well as in some ways alter egos. The more men and women can establish friendship, however, the less gendered they become as well. Part of the tragedy of this society is that sexuality and friendship are forced into mutual antagonism. Equality between men and women is a rare condition in Hardy – not only because of masculine privilege, but because the man is typically the woman's social inferior. This 'poor man and the lady' motif stretches from Dick Dewy and Fancy Day to Gabriel Oak and Bathsheba Everdene, Giles Winterborne and Grace Melbury to Jude and Sue. It also crops up among other places in the minor novel *A Pair of Blue Eyes*.

This inverted mirror-imaging of social and sexual power, in which the dominant partner in the one case is the subservient one in the other, yields a remarkably powerful, complex picture. It acts as a counterweight to the more conventional image of upper-class exploiters in pursuit of lower-class women, as with Sergeant Troy and Fanny, or Alec and Tess. Just as the 'middling' character in Hardy is at once powerless yet ambitious, so the upper-class woman is empowered by her class but enfeebled by her gender. Hardy is the first of the major male English novelists to explore sexual politics with such a keen eye to the relations between gender and class. In the pantheon of eminent male authors, it was he above all who grasped the truth that sexuality is where the sickness and strife of a whole social order is most intensively focused. Sexual politics is the place where inner and outer lives both collude and collide. Sue Bridehead's challenge to marriage is an affront to existing social relations as a whole, a fact of which the novel in which she figures is fully aware. It is not simply a matter of 'linking' the sexual and the social, gender and class. On the contrary, to take sexuality with full seriousness as a topic in itself *is* to read it among other things as a neurotic symptom of a repressive society. *Jude the Obscure* ties labour and love, production and reproduction, into a knot which cannot be easily unravelled.

Hardy remarked grimly that the furore over *Jude the Obscure* (the Bishop of Wakefield, in a spontaneous burst of Christian tolerance, threw the book into the fire) had cured him of novel-writing for good. But it is doubtful that a novelist as distinguished as Hardy stops writing simply because he receives bad reviews. It was not, after all, the first time that he had done so. After the artistic extremism of *Jude*, Hardy would either have had to find a new literary form altogether, one which had moved beyond the bounds of realist representation, or stop writing. Like Jude and Sue, he needed to produce a new reality, rather than merely imitate an old one. The later Henrik Ibsen found himself in much the same situation, needing to break beyond the confines of dramatic naturalism but not quite able to surmount them. In the

event, Hardy compromised by turning to poetry. But the true inheritor of the major fiction is perhaps not quite the poetry. It is something like D. H. Lawrence's *Women in Love*, which has finally managed, on the other side of a global conflagration, to make the break into modernism.

HENRY JAMES

We have seen that the major English novelists of the nineteenth-century were mostly ambiguous figures, with one foot in and one foot out of conventional society. Whether as women or provincials, of non-English or socially modest background, from the countryside, the lower gentry or the lower middle class, they were hybrid, amphibious men and women – internal émigrés, so to speak, in the nation they inhabited. Towards the close of the nineteenth century, however, the metaphorical émigré gives way to the literal one. English writing is now dominated by expatriates from Ireland, Continental Europe and the United States. And of these, Henry James is the one who most persistently forges his art out of the condition of exile. He is interested, as he writes in *The Princess Casamassima*, in 'the disinherited . . . the expropriated'.

James himself had been a kind of internal émigré within the United States – not only because his New York family were outsiders in Boston, but because as leisured artists and intellectuals they felt disconnected from a society which was primarily devoted to commerce and industry. Yet is was from industry that their wealth sprang: James's Irish grandfather was a prosperous businessman. Ironically, the disinherited and expropriated who caught James's interest were those who were victims not because they were poor, but because they were exceedingly rich. It is the heiresses, artists and highly cultivated gentry who are the new outsiders in a world of increasingly massive corporations.

Hyacinth Robinson, the improbably named proletarian hero of *The Princess Casamassima*, is the son of a working-class woman, but also of a 'decadent' English aristocrat, so that in him the two kinds of dispossession – that of the underdog, and that of the displaced gentry – meet and acknowledge

214

one another. Hyacinth proves unable to balance these two aspects of his nature, and kills himself. James took instead to writing fiction, which he saw among other things as a kind of living death. Like many an émigré to England, he became more English than the natives: the droll, mannered, stylish, oblique, good-humoured prose of an exquisite work like *Washington Square* ('almost a pastiche of Jane Austen', as one critic has remarked), is testimony to this spiritual migration. The world portrayed by such a work is in fact a lot darker and more corrupt that the buoyant style would lead us to believe. By the time of the notoriously difficult later novels, James's obliquity had become a pathological inability to say anything straight.

The Europeans is one of several of James's works dealing with what has been called the 'international theme', meaning the relations between Americans and Europeans. James himself had migrated to Europe from the United States partly because he felt that the latter provided no fit home for art. Or, at least, for *his* kind of art. It offered, he thought, too thin, meagre a soil for great culture, too 'clear and colourless' an atmosphere. It lacked everything a distinguished art needed to flourish: a sense of history and custom, a complexity of types and manners, a climate of mystery, a set of antique social institutions, a capacity for relishing experience. Culturally speaking, it struck him as a kind of spacious void, marked by an absence of depth, an unlovely sense of duty and discipline, and a perpetual repudiation of the past.

Europe, by contrast, meant style, wit, irony, manners, tradition, depth, pleasure, obliquity, a wealth of sensations. It also meant evil, deception, treachery, corruption, oppressive power, stifling enclosure and sinister manipulation. In a further set of contrasts, Europe signifies artifice, plenitude, diversity and an anarchic flux of sensations, whereas America suggests Nature, mobility, spontaneity and limitless freedom – though freedom of a peculiarly vacant kind. The most negative qualities of Europe are not to be found in Eugenia and Felix, the European characters in *The Europeans*, since the book is a genial comedy whose more ominous undertones are significantly muted. It is not hard to imagine Eugenia growing into a Madame Merle, the wicked schemer of *The Portrait of a Lady*, but for all her brittle stylishness and lack of honesty she is an amiable woman. It is true that she is on the make, but more candidly so than Madame Merle.

There is, in fact, no simple opposition between Americans and Europeans in *The Europeans*, as there rarely is in James. For all their style and sophistication, Eugenia and Felix are actually Europeanized Americans, as indeed are Madame Merle and her ex-lover Gilbert Osmond in the *Portrait*. Gertrude

Wentworth, though actually American, is an eager recruit to European culture, a wild card or internal émigré within her excessively sedate family; while her brother Clifford is a drunk, hardly a shining example of American puritan morality. The American Robert Acton, who aspires to Eugenia's hand, is as devious, complex and charming as any European adventurer. And though the high-toned Wentworths may be austere, they are also refined.

In fact, though the novel pokes some gentle fun at the high-minded Mr Wentworth, it admires him and his family more than it censures them. They are mild, simple, dignified souls who believe in the need for strenuous moral judgements; and though there is enough of a Felix in James to find this amusingly solemn, he is, as we shall see, aware that we live in a rapacious society in which stern moral judgements, for all their aesthetic distastefulness, are sometimes unavoidable. Even so, the puritanical Wentworths seem simply unable to enjoy themselves, and strike the epicurean Felix as chronically unhappy. There is very little 'for the senses' in this morally bleak American world. Like Catherine Sloper of *Washington Square*, the Wentworths are incapable of artifice; and while this is commendable in its way, it is hardly an unqualified virtue in the eyes of a novelist for whom artifice is a professional pursuit.

Though the Wentworth's closedness to experience counts against them, however, it also involves a sense of duty and responsibility which the novel profoundly respects. If they take things too hard, Felix, a kind of latter-day Ladislaw, takes them too nonchalantly. He is one of James's idle aesthetic observers, an incurable aesthete for whom life is a delightfully entertaining spectacle rather than a deadly serious project; and though this is not allowed to weigh against him too heavily, it will do just this in the case of some later Jamesian voyeurs. Felix shows that there can be an innocuous sort of aesthete-adventurer, as opposed to a malign one like Gilbert Osmond of *The Portrait of a Lady*.

For James, the real affinity between the earnest Americans and the elegant Europeans lies in the fact that it takes the disciplined work of the former to produce the culture consumed by the latter. The origin of culture is labour – a fact which culture itself tends shyly to suppress. It is as though culture is ashamed of its own humble parentage, and cannot bring itself to mention it. Culture is the child of leisure, and leisure is the offspring of labour. The labour of others, needless to say. James's fiction is much preoccupied with voids, absences, hidden horrors, unspeakable secrets, metaphorical serpents curled beneath flowers, and one of the most ineffable secrets of all is the hard labour which makes all of this civilized elegance

possible in the first place. It is a world of which James is well aware, though he allows us no direct vision of it. Notoriously, we never get to know what the wealthy industrial Newsomes of *The Ambassadors* actually manufacture, though chamberpots have been suggested. In the Preface to *The Reverberator*, James confides that commerce has always been a mystery to him. He simply lived off it.

For this decorous civilization to survive, a less decorous truth must be repressed: the fact that it is parasitic on the sweated labour of anonymous millions of men and women, who are excluded from the very 'civility' they help to create. As Hyacinth Robinson of *The Princess Casamassima*, remarks, generations rot away and starve in the midst of luxury. James himself was a professional house-guest of the English upper classes for some 20 years, one of the most dutiful diners and assiduous weekenders of the age; but he privately considered that the genteel souls who issued the invitations were as rotten as the French aristocracy before the French Revolution. One assumes that he did not voice this sentiment over the dinner table.

What determines this society, then, must necessarily be absent from it, if the social order is not to collapse in a crisis of bad faith. Yet this absent reality, which cannot be symbolized directly, is present everywhere in its effects. In James's fiction, sex and work lie at the root of nearly everything, but they are, in the literal sense of the word, 'obscene' or off-stage, only obliquely mentionable, pervasive but usually invisible presences. Part of the fascination of *What Maisie Knew* is watching the child Maisie trying to make sense of a sexual imbroglio without knowing about sex. (Or does she? The situation, like much in James, is arguably more ambiguous than it appears). All Maisie has, so to speak, are the surface symptoms; the underlying reality, which determines most of what happens in the novel, eludes her awareness – as, for Freud, the roots of sexuality are in any case repressed from our consciousness. What Maisie knew is thus bound up with what she didn't know. Her blindness and insight are indissociable, and this for James is the condition of all our knowledge.

What is euphemistic in James's work, then, is not only his notorious later prose style, that cobwebby, fastidious, neurotically self-qualifying discourse which shies prudishly away from anything as vulgar as a bald proposition, but this deeper evasion – the way in which civilization is what it is only by disavowing its own material roots. In one sense, this mollifies its under-lying violence, as 'manners' come to muffle and deflect power-struggles and material interests. In another sense, however, it serves to intensify that vio-lence, since culture provides us with more diverse as well as more insidious

ways of dominating and manipulating. And the more culture there is, the more desires, objects of desire, and thus causes of conflict, spring into being. The problem with American society is that it has not yet arrived at the point where it can enjoy the fruits of its labours. Indeed, it probably never will, since the business of making money – the United States's supreme contribution to world civilization – demands a perpetual deferment of pleasure. The puritanical self-repression it involves prevents you from revelling in the end-product. The whole process is thus peculiarly self-defeating. Europe, by contrast, is not self-defeating but hypocritical. It understands that the point is to have so much money that you do not need to think about it, and so can turn your mind to higher, more spiritual ends. If you have an excess of material wealth, you can create a culture which seems autonomous of that wealth, averts its eyes disdainfully from it, and can be savoured as an end in itself.

You need, in short, to be extremely materialist in order to be a cultural idealist. It is money which allows you to fantasize – and money, indeed, is the most fantastic, mercurial phenomenon of all. Jane Austen and George Eliot would have thought this disavowal of wealth the height of vulgarity – as bad in its way as being too preoccupied with it. The culture of Europe, to use Freud's term, 'sublimates' its material life. The disinterestedness of art is a living denial of the material interests which allow it to happen. James never gave up on that disinterestedness, which he considered in a sense to be the height of virtue; but he knew the terrible price which had to be paid for it. The knowledge which culture displays is born of guilt and ignorance. There is a blind spot at the very heart of it. Moreover, the material abundance which allows a privileged minority to engage in fine living also involves a brutally competitive, acquisitive society which is the implacable enemy of such fineness, and which will crush you under its heel if it can. In this sense, the culture which seals you off from the material world also makes you more vulnerable to it, not least by fostering the illusion that you are insulated from it.

But it is, ironically, this blind spot at the heart of culture which allows it to work. Culture could not acknowledge its source in violence, scarcity and wretchedness and survive in the form it does. As James's secretary Theodora Bosanquet remarked of him, 'When he walked out of the refuge of his study and into the world and looked about him, he saw a place of torment, where creatures of prey perpetually thrust their claws into the quivering flesh of doomed, defenceless children of light'.[1] There are few more hard-headed, materialist writers than this author of urbane novels of

manners and devotee of summer tea-parties on the well-groomed lawns of English country houses.

There is, then, no simple contrast between Americans and Europeans, though a number of oppositions can be tried on: romance versus realism, innocence versus experience, the ascetic versus the aesthetic, even morality versus immorality. James's Europeans are connoisseurs of experience, collecting sensations as others might collect sea shells or acquaintances; but so in their different way are some Americans, not least those cultural tourists who come to Europe to get what they can out of it. Christopher Newman of *The American* is a kind of entrepreneur of experience, plundering what Europe has to offer in order to augment his cultural capital. Roderick Hudson, in the novel of that name, has a similar greed for such experience, and comes to a sticky end.

Chad Newsome of *The Ambassadors* is also a spiritual profiteer, an egoist who dips into Europe, acquires some skin-deep civility, and will return to America laden with a rich booty of perceptions and sensations with which to eke out the meagre supply back home. The tourist garners sensations indiscriminately, as indifferent to their inherent value as is the marketplace. Adam Verver of *The Golden Bowl* is the grandest of all James's power-hungry collectors, a cultural imperialist with such a gargantuan store of wealth that he is effectively in the process of buying up Europe for America, along with a couple of convenient spouses for himself and his daughter. But Adam is also one of James's supposed American innocents, who protects himself from life by means of art.

Since Europe suffocates under history, whereas America stifles for lack of it, it is easy to see the contrast between them as a matter of the dead versus the living. Europe is buried beneath a rubble of antique forms, rituals and monuments, while the United States has an infinite freedom but not enough material for it to go to work on. Yet the contrast is misleading as well as real, as Isabel Archer in *The Portrait of a Lady* reveals. Isabel has a typically American hunger for experience coupled with a puritanical fear of it, which means that her freedom remains abstract and unreal. She has a fear of invasion, possession, penetration and annihilation, and her tragic end might well suggest that this fear is perfectly well-founded. Yet if it turns out to be justified, it is also bound up with a false view of the self. And it is, of course, no way to live.

Isabel wants experience without commitment, since commitments limit your freedom. To settle is to wither, yet not to settle is to remain pure vacuous potential. So her freedom, like America's, is both vast and empty.

Any concrete content or involvement would only taint it, which is no doubt one reason why she rejects her suitors. In hankering after all experience, she can attach herself to none in particular, thus cancelling her liberty out. Perhaps it is this latent dread of the world which impels her to flee from it into the imprisoning embrace of Gilbert Osmond. This innocent, self-absorbed egoist allows herself to be framed, collected and appropriated like a work of art, thus escaping the complexities of actual existence. So American freedom, being negative, is really a kind of death, and thus ironically akin to Osmond's more European type of deathliness. The two continents are alike after all.

Even so, there are some subtle distinctions. Europeans live stylishly, devoted to forms and surfaces, but are conscious of an underlying corruption; Americans like the Wentworths live in a constant Protestant awareness of evil, yet are in fact unworldly innocents. As *The Europeans* astutely suggests, they have nothing to repent of yet are always repenting. Both parties are in different ways depthless: the Europeans because what is 'deep' for them is form, artifice and appearance, the Americans because in their candour, directness and spontaneity they seem to lack reticence and reserve, lights and shades, interior nooks and crannies. Their landscape, Eugenia complains, is all foreground. For them, there is no necessity for patiently deciphering the truth, as there is for James himself, because it is instantly available. Truth for them is simple, whereas for James it is slippery. As with contemporary America's cult of confessionalism, whatever is not instantly externalized is not real. 'I feel, therefore I must let it all out' is the American translation of Descartes's dictum.

Innocence in James is both dangerous and desirable. It is dangerous because, as in eighteenth-century fiction, it leaves you a prey to others in a malevolent world. The virtuous show up the viciousness which encircles them for what it is, but they also exacerbate it by providing it with an easy prey. In the short story 'Daisy Miller', innocence turns out to be bad for your health. But since it is also of course morally admirable, the problem becomes one of how to protect yourself with as little damage as possible to your generosity of heart and spontaneity of spirit. Innocence involves a degree of calculation, in which case it may simply negate itself. This is one reason why it is possible to read some of James's most apparently selfless heroines – Fleda Vetch of *The Spoils of Poynton*, Milly Theale of *The Wings of the Dove*, Maggie Verver of *The Golden Bowl* – as despicable schemers concealing their selfish ends behind a mask of saintly disinterestedness.

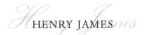

Everyone in this world seems to be playing some game; and to seem not to play a game, as the good-hearted, disinterested and self-sacrificing appear not to, might be the most devious game of all. Relinquishing power may be the supreme exercise of it, rather as not intervening in someone else's life can change it dramatically. Absence can alter the course of history. The present is largely made up of what failed to happen in the past. As with Richardson's Clarissa, self-immolation usually has an aggressive undertone. Is what looks like saintly altruism in James just an underhand way of hooking your man (Fleda), revenging yourself on a faithless lover (Milly), or bringing your husband to heel and destroying his mistress (Maggie)? Is the governess of 'The Turn of the Screw' selflessly devoted to protecting her pupils, or sinisterly manipulating them?

Even the most 'beautiful' act of self-immolation may have an exchange value on the sexual market. You may get what you want precisely by surrendering it so submissively. Even the virtuous Catherine Sloper hopes that she might get what she wants if she is sufficiently obedient to her father's prohibition of it. Maggie Verver entices back her wayward husband by the very saintly meekness and intelligence with which she endures his infidelity. Does this make her a martyr or a Machiavellian? Milly's decision to bequeath Merton Densher her fortune, even though she knows that he has deceived her, scuppers his relationship with Kate Croy. Was this Milly's intention or not?

If there is one game which transcends all these others, it is that of the artist himself. The name of his game is the novel, and this, like any art, is supposed to be a supreme example of disinterestedness. In fact, there is usually something in it for the artist himself: fame, power, the privilege of being paid for fantasizing so shamelessly in public. Here, too, disinterestedness can be in the service of interests. Is art supreme sacrifice or the last word in egoism? Or is the former just a cunning version of the latter? Besides, the leisure which allows you to write is dependent on the labour of others, so that art can never be entirely free of guilt. Your art may be beautiful, but what makes it possible is not. The aesthetic in James is by no means divorced from material interests, as is clear from the ruthless collecting instinct of Adam Verver, or of the proprietor of Poynton. In gathering your artistic swag, you reveal an acquisitiveness which is at odds with the supposedly dispassionate nature of art itself. Gilbert Osmond is both civilized aesthete and vulgar adventurer. The art industry brings together the precious and the predatory. Collecting artworks may not look like naked capitalism, since you do it simply for the delight of possessing these things, not necessarily for their value on the market. Yet exactly because there is no 'point' to acquiring these objects, they show up the passion for possession at its most pure. In the end, capitalism accumulates for its own sake.

Nothing in James's world can escape the infection of power, money, desire or deception. Yet art – the most elaborate deception of all – can strive to give them the slip, even though they provide it with its very subject-matter. Just as you can collect as an end in itself, so there is a sense in which an artist pursues his or her craft simply for the sake of it. There is no *point* to writing *The Ambassadors*, as there is a point to applying a band-aid to an injured finger. Like Strether at the end of *The Ambassadors*, the author gets nothing out of it for himself, other than the sheer unsaleable experience. You can only enter eternity empty-handed. Art is in this sense innocent: it cannot harm others in the way that action in James so often does.

It is not, to be sure, without its impact on real life. In 'The Author of "Beltraffio"' it actually kills a child, whose mother allows him to die rather than grow up to read his father's 'decadent' works. In 'The Middle Years', the ageing novelist Dencombe, who feels that life has passed him by, comes to see that living for his art has been worthwhile by the fact that an admirer is inspired to sacrifice a fortune for the sake of it. In general, however, James has no belief that art can be justified as a form of social intervention. Ironic detachment may be a less than reputable way of life, but it breaks fewer bones than zealous activism.

If art can do little harm, however, having no end in view and existing purely for its own sake, this is also testimony to its uselessness. If it is innocent, it is only because it is impotent. It is not the real thing, simply a fiction. The solitary novelist lives with his characters, who cannot be harmed because they have no real existence. But he is a crippled, deficient creature as well, since he avoids injuring others only by the drastic strategy of avoid-ing life itself. Instead, art *is* his life, a vicarious form of existence which demands the sacrificing of ordinary commitments and fulfilments (family, sexual relationships, public responsibilities) on the altar of *belles lettres*.

So art is also a kind of death, as well as a rich flourishing of life. James's story 'The Altar of the Dead' may well be a parable of this. And both art and death revolve on absence. Art is a failure or incapacity from which value flows, as in sacrifice. It is all about moral beauty and fine living, but what makes it possible is a self-abnegation which is not beautiful at all. Sacrifice, as we shall see, is a prominent subject in James's art, but the chief example of it is his art itself. Even this, however, can be a mask for self-interest:

St George, the successful novelist of 'The Lesson of the Master', urges the aspiring author Paul Overt to abandon all worldly preoccupations; but we cannot be sure that this is not just a cunning device to separate him from the woman he loves, who St George then proceeds to marry himself.

Art, then, is an example of morality in the American puritan sense: austere, dutiful, strenuous, self-repressive. But it is also a model of morality in the European sense, exquisitely sensitive to fine shades of experience, delighting in the fullness of human powers and perceptions. The novelist for James is someone on whom nothing is lost – a supremely intelligent observer who registers the nuances and unravels the implications of things, so that intelligence and moral insight are hard to distinguish. Indeed, there is probably no more sheerly intelligent English novelist than James. We may love Dickens or Hardy, but we do not find them notable for intelligence in the fine, inexhaustibly intricate Jamesian sense.

The convoluted later style, with its bafflingly intricate syntax and extraordinarily mannered mode of expression, is among other things an attempt to refine language to the point where not a particle of experience or wisp of implication can be lost to it. It is a way of trying to see an object from all angles simultaneously, weaving a linguistic web so close-knit and fine-grained that it allows no scintilla of meaning to escape. It is a style which tries to capture an idea or sensation in the very moment of its formation, registering it in all its irreducible density. James's prose presses the syntax of everyday experience to a point where it only just fails to come apart in his hands. It catches a unique consciousness in the act of its encounter with the world, so that perception and reflection are woven tightly together. Language is inescapably general, whereas experience is concrete and particular; so language must be packed with perceptions to the point of almost coming apart at the seams.

It is a style wickedly captured in Max Beerbohm's peerless parody 'The Mote in the Middle Distance':

It was with the sense of a, for him, very memorable something that he peered now into the immediate future, and tried, not without compunction, to take that period up where he had, prospectively, left it. But just where the deuce *had* he left it? The consciousness of dubiety was, for our friend, not, this morning, quite yet clean-cut enough to outline the figures on what she had called his 'horizon', between which and himself the twilight was indeed of a quality somewhat intimidating. He had run up, in the course of time, against a good number of 'teasers'; and the function of teasing them back – of, as it were, giving them, every now and then, 'what for' – was in him so much a

habit that he would have been at a loss had there been, on the face of it, nothing to lose . . .

(from *A Christmas Garland*, 1912)

In recording dialogue between characters, this style catches the unspoken vibrations of meaning between them, the subtexts of inference and insinuation, the verbal lunging and parrying which indicate a language saturated with power-struggle. No prose could be less 'American', less plain, direct and upfront. The later style, with its extravagant parody of the tentative, hesitant English, is part of James's revolt against his native land, with its cut-to-the-chase, tell-it-like-it-is fear of excess and elaboration. 'I am interminably supersubtle', he once declared in treasonably un-American fashion, while one of his compatriots complained that he was a man who chewed more than he could bite off. By packing his art so impossibly full, he pressed in his later work at the very limits of literary realism. Like *Tristram Shandy*, his writing strives to represent so much that it risks undercutting the act of representation itself. And this is a problem for a novelist who insists that the supreme virtue of the novel is 'the air of reality (solidity of specification)'.

James is writing at around the time when the very word 'moral' is undergoing a momentous shift of meaning. In an increasingly secular age, it is coming to mean less a matter of precepts and principles, than an intensity of what James himself called 'felt life', a capacity to live richly and deeply. And art is the paradigm of this. James rightly sees that morality is about happiness and self-fulfilment, not duty and prohibition. But he also recognizes that to secure such happiness may itself require a scaffolding of obligations and prohibitions, so that the more positive sense of morality does not simply cancel out the more negative one. Part of the problem of his fiction is that law and life, renunciation and self-realization, have to find some way of co-existing. From a traditional moral standpoint, the idea of morality as self-fulfilment may appear the very reverse of moral, since it seems to demand that, like a child, you are open to all experience indiscriminately. Art demands a susceptibility to sensation which is morally suspect. You must not sour your delight in the freshness of things by imposing rigid moral categories on them. If the artist is in one sense the new moralist, he or she is also the very type of the immoralist, one who regards all experience as grist to the mill and who deals even-handedly in squalor and saintliness.

If morality is about felt experience, then the very act of writing a novel, as with George Eliot, is itself a moral one. James would like to see the moral

and the aesthetic as at one: when he uses rather precious adjectives like 'splendid', 'fine' and 'beautiful' of a character's behaviour, both senses are blended together. As with Jane Austen, there is an ideal unity between manners and morals, divine grace and the social graces, style and substance. Yet James, like Austen, is well aware that this unity is rarely achieved in practice. There are moral horrors lurking beneath the surface of social existence which mere style is powerless to confront; and there are kinds of goodness, like that of the Wentworths, which are commendable but not in the least charming. In a society as predatory as the one James paints, virtue may involve sacrifices, denials and obligations which are hardly aesthetically appealing.

Besides, an Osmond-like obsession with form and style may actually blunt your compassion. Aesthetes are egoists who savour their own sensations, and treat others as objects of pleasure. They do not so much experience the world as consume, narcissistically, their own perceptions of it. Since one can reap just as much pleasurable sensation from things as from persons, this flawless sensibility conceals a callous indifference. There is a merciless, dehumanizing quality about art, just as there is about knowledge, which will bulldoze its way over men and women in pursuit of its ends. The aesthetic in James can mean either a spontaneous openness to fresh experience, or just the opposite: a world of mummified treasures and frigid formalism. If the former is more American, the latter is more European.

The artist needs to live, if only to gather materials for his or her art; but in James's eyes it is best not to overdo it. In embracing life in order to create, the artist threatens to distract himself from his creation. To live as little as possible – to be private, solitary and not to have a job, so as to devote your time to writing – requires having money, and thus leading a vicarious existence by living off other people's work and lack of leisure. As far as living goes, it is best to be inside and outside the game simultaneously, like one of the many artists, children, celibates, spiritual tourists, go-betweens and expatriates in James's work. The observer in one sense sees less, since participation is a form of knowledge; but in another sense sees more, being free of the partisan interests and self-delusions of those within the game. As an artist you become one of life's eternal observers, enjoying the kind of experience without engagement which Isabel Archer wished for but could not attain. If this is a privileged position, it is a privilege you have to pay for in terms of guilt and impotence. Nothing in James comes free.

Since fiction is in a sense unreal, as a discourse about things that never happened and people who never existed, it represents a kind of void or

absence despite its richness and plenitude. It signifies a paucity of life as well
as a wealth of it; and this is one of James's abiding themes. Much of his work
turns on absences, eloquent silences, missed opportunities, acts of refusal
and abnegation. A fine example is 'The Beast in the Jungle', in which Marcher
has dreaded all his life that some catastrophe will befall him, and confides
this to a woman friend, May Bartram. So obsessed is the protagonist by this
vision of impending doom that he fails to notice, rampant egoist that he is,
that May is in love with him. He loses her, and this is the catastrophe that
was waiting to happen. He realizes now, too late, that his frightful fate has
been for nothing to happen to him.

An 'aesthetic' view of morality is not content with codes and abstract
principles, but is intent on bringing them home to lived experience. James
believes steadfastly in this, but he also sees how it can collapse into an
amoral sensationalism. It can lead to subjectivism, too, as moral values come
to mean whatever seems right to you, without objective standards of judgement. An 'experiential' morality, of the kind James admires, must also take
care not to 'aestheticize' goodness, making it merely a matter of how fine
and 'splendid' an action appears. You must avoid the simplistic polarities of
the puritans, while recognizing that rigorous moral distinctions are nevertheless necessary.

Perhaps there is a way of writing which makes this distinction from the
inside of one's experience, so to speak, rather than foisting them artificially
upon it. Perhaps one can analyse, experience and evaluate all at the same
time, given a devious enough prose style. James's later style struggles to
weld together a rich diversity of experience, and so to preserve some sense
of a coherent self. All the same, this self is constantly on the point of drowning in its warm bath of sensations, and only James's prose can keep its
head above water. The European self is deliquescent, fuzzy at the edges,
saturated in history and cultural context; and while this is enriching, it is also
a threat to the moral or American conception of the self, for which identity
is much more substantial and sharply defined. Madame Merle tells Isabel
Archer that the self melts naturally into its environs and possessions; but this
'aesthetic' view of it clashes with Isabel's American conviction that identity
is a thing in itself, naked and unhoused, prior to its various social contexts.
The American fear is that if the self simply *is* its varied experiences, how can
it ever have enough unity to act as a moral agent? Experience for James may
be the homeland of morality, but it is also in danger of being its graveyard.

Plato believed that Truth, Goodness and Beauty were ultimately one,
while Aristotle saw virtue and intelligence as closely allied. The modern age,

by contrast, has been more struck by the tragic discrepancies between these things. We have seen already that for James beauty and goodness are not always reconcilable. In the world of his novels there are the fine, and there are also the good; but they do not always coincide. It is the good who matter in the end, but it is the fine who make life worth living in the meanwhile. We respect Mr Wentworth, but we take pleasure in Felix. Certain extraordinary actions, like Milly Theale's death-bed generosity to those who have betrayed her, are both good and beautiful; and these qualities are also combined in James's own writing, which speaks up for virtue in such elegant tones. Within his works, however, virtue can be gauche and unattractive, like Catherine Sloper in *Washington Square*. As with Jane Austen's Fanny Price, we are compelled to see that this is the unlovely price which pure-heartedness, in these particular social circumstances, must pay to survive.

Much the same is true of the truth, which in James can turn out to be distinctly ugly. There is in his work a rabid form of what Freud called 'epistemophilia', or a lust for knowledge. Sexual knowledge – a hunt for the primal scene or traumatic sexual secret – is often the model for this passion in James; but art is a form of knowledge as well. And since it is knowledge for its own sake – knowledge which is in a sense entirely useless – it can offer an alternative to the pressing of knowledge into the service of power. Dr Sloper of *Washington Square* combines both forms of knowledge: he is one of James's aesthetic spectators, who reaps sadistic entertainment from his daughter's plight; but he also uses his remarkable intelligence as a means of dominating her. It is significant that he is a physician, since medics are scientists, prizing knowledge for its own sake, but also putting it to practical use.

James associates intelligence with moral insight, but Sloper is an ominous example of how it can lapse into pure amoral cleverness. His intellect has come adrift from his feelings, so that while he sees the truth about Catherine's scheming lover Morris Townsend, he lacks compassion for her. Knowledge and feeling, truth and kind-heartedness, are not necessarily at one. Sloper values truth over virtue; in fact, knowledge, not least knowing that he is right, is for him a well-nigh aesthetic pleasure. But since this is also the intellectual pride of the rationalist, truth and beauty come together in Sloper in all the wrong ways. If Mrs Penniman treats Catherine's life as material for her own fervid fantasies, her father makes her the object of his cruelly clinical reason. Knowledge and intelligence are what you need in a deceptive, exploitative world, but they are also what allow you to deceive and

exploit. Who knows what, who is pretending to know and who pretending not to know, is a vital question in James, for knowledge is intimately bound up with power.

But if the truth of this world is ugly, how can knowledge be compatible with innocence? It can, perhaps, in a child like Maisie, who seems uncorrupted by the knowledge she gains; but this may be because there is so much that she *doesn't* know. Her author is a different case: there seems to be no limit to what Henry knew – indeed, Denscombe, the James-like hero of 'The Middle Years', comments that 'I know everything. One *has* to, to write decently!'. Artistic knowledge can be innocent because, as we have seen already, it is entirely useless, garnered purely for its own sake. It has no value in the market place, and is thus the very opposite of a commodity. Strether is a 'non-purchaser' who is determined to get nothing out of his Parisian experience for himself, and accordingly turns down a couple of lucrative offers of marriage. He has had his vision, as Virginia Woolf might say, and that is enough. But at the same time knowledge avoids being a commodity only because it is a kind of absence or failure. In the case of the Jamesian artist, it is the bitter fruit of not having really lived. It is, even so, a beautiful substitute for living, not least in a world where action involves injury; and James himself – not without profound regret – was prepared to make this sacrifice.

For James, as a good liberal, the cardinal crime is to use others for your own selfish ends. Yet this happens all the time, from Mrs Penniman's horrific meddling in Catherine's affairs in *Washington Square*, to Ralph Touchett's well-meaning but irresponsible setting up of Isabel as a rich heiress to be exploited. How far is it permissible for anyone to intervene in another's life, or are there times when is it irresponsible not to? Dominating, manipulating and emotionally blackmailing others is a chronic condition in James. 'I make them do what I like', remarks Maggie Verver of some fellow characters, suggesting that the ultimate freedom may be the power to constrain the freedom of others.

In the midst of this terrifying vision of human affairs, there is usually a 'mediator' or 'broker' figure – go-betweens, like Maisie or Strether, who can ironically become objects of contention themselves, as in the internecine struggle in *The Bostonians* between Olive Chancellor and Basil Ransom over the innocent Verena Tarrant. The mediator's hope is simply to 'square' the others, reconciling their discordant interests. This, however, is a wan hope in a viciously zero-sum world where the gain of one character is often enough the loss of another. The only 'squaring' in the end is the novel itself,

whose form brings these warring interests harmoniously together and lavishes equal attention on them all. If there is an 'organic' social order still in existence, it can only be the novel itself. For James, the chief issue in writing fiction was to find the vantage-point – one peculiar to every narrative – from which disparate materials converged into unity. But that is to say that the only organic order which survives is a flagrantly constructed one. Perhaps art is the last home of human unity.

Jamesian 'free spirits' like Isabel Archer aim to be the authors of their own narratives, but continually find themselves the objects of someone else's. We all have bit parts in one another's private dramas, sharing as we do in some plot which we are not even aware of. Simply by living out our own destiny, we are unavoidably shaping somebody else's; and this recognition is a kind of updated version of original sin, for which we are caught up in guilt-ridden complicity with each other even though we never chose this condition. If human existence is 'textual', each fate or figure intricately interwoven with the rest, then the American idea of the autonomous takes something of a battering. To be self-authoring, disavowing the history which went into your making, is a common American fantasy. So is the notion of an entirely undetermined choice. Strether in *The Ambassadors* refuses to play a compliant role in Mrs Newsome's narrative, and begins instead to digress from the story-line she sets him. In refusing to bring Chad back to America, he loses the plot. The paranoid governess of 'The Turn of the Screw' arrives belatedly on the scene of her pupils' lives, as we are in a sense always belated; but in typically American spirit (though she is actually English) she seeks to impose her own narrative on that history, in order to bring it under her authority and enshrine herself at its centre.

The governess writes her way into the children's lives, remoulding them for her own ends, foisting a convincing meta-narrative on everything that takes place. Like Nietzsche, James tends to believe that truth is a matter of whose power-driven interpretation finally wins out by gaining general acceptance. The governess is a servant who, with her master's indulgence, usurps her place to become a master narrator herself, rather as novelists may delegate their authority to an omniscient narrator within their work. What undermines her hermeneutical power is the narrative itself, which permits different interpretations on the reader's part.

Paranoia, in the loose sense of the word, is a condition in which everything appears oppressively meaningful, and in which all of these meanings hang together to compose a totally integrated system. The world becomes a single master-narrative, a plot (in both senses of the word) in which there is

no room for contingency. Nothing that happens is accidental; everything is instantly legible. There are secret correspondences between the most apparently diverse characters and events. Since this is in fact true, as the novel from Dickens to Joyce amply demonstrates, paranoia is a reasonable enough frame of mind. Freud thought that the nearest thing to paranoia was philosophy, which in its Casaubonish way has traditionally sought the key to all reality; but fiction would be an eligible candidate too. For fiction gathers various bits and pieces of the world into a coherent vision, and even its apparently free-wheeling details are there for a purpose. The artist, who is supersensitive to finding significance everywhere, and whose imagination reveals patterns which it sometimes secretly creates, is simply the paranoiac pushed on a stage. You can see too much as well as too little. The phrase 'seeing things' is neatly ambiguous. A hungry imagination needs material to go to work on, and will fabricate the stuff if it seems too slim a basis on which to exercise its supreme powers of observation.

For James, in fact, all truth is a kind of fiction, just as fiction discloses a kind of truth. Truth is fiction because, like a novel, it is always a selection of events from a specific viewpoint according to particular assumptions. Society itself is a kind of elaborate fiction, since it is held together by forms, conventions and shared illusions. There is no order in reality itself, which sprawls infinitely in all directions. The trick of literary art, then, is to find the viewpoint from which there appears to be such an order, even if it is one created by a rigorous process of editing, selecting and reshaping. This is sufficiently like paranoia to be disturbing. It is what the governess does in 'The Turn of the Screw', as well as being what the narrator of *The Sacred Fount*, who is probably insane, gets up to. Not to accept that there are contingencies is a form of madness.

One difference between fiction and paranoia is that fiction is aware that the world hangs together only from a specific standpoint. If the paranoiac makes an absolute out of that standpoint, the novelist is ironically conscious of other possible interpretations. In fact, James finally arrives at the point where it is simply undecidable on the textual evidence whether, say, Maggie Verver is to be commended or condemned. With this author, it is sometimes not possible to say with any certainty whether something is happening or not. The true secret may be that there is no secret at all. Knowledge for the artist is always indeterminate, even if one sometimes needs determinate knowledge in order to protect oneself from the machinations of others. The truth is of vital importance in a society thick with mutual mystfication, but you can make a fetish of it, too, like the narrators

of 'The Figure in the Carpet' and 'The Aspern Papers'. Instead of being at the service of humanity, truth then becomes implacably hostile to the human, as you consider marrying or betraying someone simply to lay your hands on it.

In the end, the most 'beautiful' act for James – the meeting-point of the ethical and the aesthetic – is that of renunciation. It is, typically, loss and negation which seize his imagination most deeply. The burning of the Aspern papers and the spoils of Poynton; Christopher Newman renouncing revenge on the Europeans who have humiliated him; Eugenia leaving America with empty hands in *The Europeans*; Isabel Archer's decision to return to a loveless marriage, perhaps in the conviction that you must stay true to the consequences of your actions: these are definitive moments of James's fiction, as are Catherine Sloper's turning her face from life; Milly Theale's turning her face to the wall; the final loss, shame and humiliation of Olive Chancellor of *The Bostonians*; or the disinterested detachment of a Strether. In common with Hardy and Conrad, James is a tragic novelist, unlike the Brontes, Dickens and George Eliot. And lurking beneath all these resignations and repudiations is the renunciation of art itself, that most tragic, triumphant of life-forms.

JOSEPH CONRAD

J oseph Conrad was both Polish and English, artist and seaman, sceptic
and idealist, anti-imperialist and a champion of the British Empire, high
modernist writer and a spinner of rattling good yarns. How can we
account for these conflicts?

Conrad was the child of traditionalist Polish landowners who rebelled
against Russian rule over their country, and were sent into exile along with
their small son. His background, then, was a mixture of conservatism and
dissent, and this was to mark his fiction deeply. If he inherited the sense of
rootedness, patriotism and tradition of the Polish gentry from which he
sprang, he also knew the experience of dissent, exile and illegality. His early
life was influenced by his parents' struggle against imperialism, but they
fought the Russian autocracy for conservative rather than revolutionary
reasons. We will find a similar ambiguity in his own political views as a
novelist. Like many an exile of the time, he found in England an enclave of
hierarchy, stability and traditionalism which provided him with a welcome
refuge from the political turbulence of the Continent. Indeed, like many of
his fellow literary migrants and refugees (Oscar Wilde, Henry James, T. S.
Eliot), he was to become in some ways more English than the English. If the
immigrant often proves to be more loyal and patriotic than the native, it is
because he or she has made a conscious option for the culture, and has good
reason to feel grateful to it.

Even so, Conrad is not quite an 'English' writer, if there is indeed such an
animal. Despite being one of the most finely evocative stylists of the literature, his use of the English language (it was, astonishingly, only his third
tongue, after Polish and French) can be distinctly non-native. He commits
grammatical errors or pens awkward phrases. But he is also untypical of an

232

English writer in his 'extremism', his cosmopolitan range, and his interest in metaphysical ideas. He has few of the suave ironies or mannered gestures of an Austen or an E. M. Forster. The writing of men like Oscar Wilde and Henry James can be seen among other things as an elaborate version of these qualities by outsiders trying hard to become insiders. On the other hand, Conrad is stoutly 'English' in his conservative affection for tradition, hierarchy, hard work, loyalty and human solidarity, all of which he found exemplified in the crews of the British Merchant Navy in which he served for many years as a sailor.

England seemed to Conrad to be a model of these 'organic' virtues, and thus to recall the Polish patriotism with which he grew up. But it also struck him as a place where individual rights were respected, as they had not been in Russian-dominated Poland. It catered, then, both for the sense of community of the patriot and the individualism of the exile. So did seafaring, which offered Conrad both an image of freedom and a model of community. And so, finally, did art itself, which springs from the fantasies of the solitary individual, yet evokes what Conrad called 'a latent feeling of fellowship with all creation'. It is thus an affirmation of hope and solidarity, as well as a reflection of one's isolated impressions. 'We exist only in so far as we hang together', remarks Marlow in *Lord Jim*. As if to prove the point, Decoud in *Nostromo* dies of solitude. His death shows up the autonomous self as a fiction.

Art is a question of inspiration; but it is also, at least for the depressive, tormented Conrad, a matter of sweated labour, as he struggled in the manner of his great mentor Gustave Flaubert to wrench a meaning from the slippery, recalcitrant stuff of language. The Protestant work ethic which Conrad champions in society at large is involved for him in the act of writing – in what he sees as the ceaseless struggle for a communication which proves ultimately impossible. The result of this writerly struggle is a readerly one too, as readers, confronted by a painstakingly sculptured work of language, find themselves unable simply to 'consume' it but are forced instead into their own labour of interpretation. Conrad's novels, for all their flamboyant, action-packed, gung-ho aspects, do not slip down easily.

Conrad was equally typical of traditionalist England in his hatred of socialism ('infernal doctrines born in the continental backslums'), his disgust with democracy ('I have no taste for democracy'), and his patronizing attitude to the common people ('For the great mass of mankind, the only saving grace that is needed is steady fidelity to what is nearest to hand and heart'). He despised the notion of equality, detested the liberal values of pity, sentiment, pacifism and humanitarianism (we shall see a similar aversion in D. H. Lawrence), and harboured a Baden-Powellish belief in the virtues of discipline, deference, fidelity, male bonding and an unthinking respect for authority and tradition. His women characters, with one or two admirable exceptions, are sketchy or embarrassing stereotypes.

In *The Nigger of the Narcissus*, for example, the seaman Donkin is a lurid caricature of a working-class agitator, sly, cowardly, blustering and indolent. James Wait, the 'nigger' of the title, is an equally whining, truculent, egoistic figure whose apparent sickness seduces the ship's crew into a treacherous pity and tenderness. The men become excessively sensitive, decadent and imaginative, qualities which jeopardise their unreflective work routine. In a sense, they become artists, and art for Conrad is dangerous because it involves a self-consciousness which is the foe of action and spontaneous loyalty. Conrad admires stolidly unimaginative types like McWhirr in *Typhoon*, the French lieutenant in *Lord Jim* or Captain Mitchell in *Nostromo*, men whose very obtuseness or insensitive egoism lend them a kind of bovine courage. They are steadfast servants of custom and authority, unlike faithless, socially subversive intellectuals whose speculations undermine the need for decisive action. Yet the imagination, described in *Lord Jim* as 'the enemy of men, the father of all terrors', is of course what Conrad himself lives by. It is also what enables him to create unimaginative figures like McWhirr and Mitchell. Such is the contradiction of a simple seafarer turned professional novelist.

In fact, if Conrad is so hostile to what Wait symbolizes, it is partly because he himself feels its seductive beguilement only too keenly. If part of him is the macho, male-bonding, chuckle-headed sea-dog, full of instinctive pieties and simple-minded certainties, the other part is the criminal, rootless individualist, ridden by guilty fantasy and corrosive doubt. It is no wonder that he is so fascinated by deceit, betrayal and double agents, both in *The Secret Agent* and *Under Western Eyes*. Lord Jim is part hearty, clean-limbed public schoolboy who uses slang like 'bally' and 'by Jove', and part loner and enigmatic fantasist. He moves in the novel from traditional English values to foreign exile, a reversal of his author's own trek.

This sense of a secret, lawless self is among other things a hangover from Conrad's Polish background, one that could never be entirely integrated with his new identity as an Englishman. It is there in the very title of his story 'The Secret Sharer', in which a respectable ship's captain feels an unaccountable sense of kinship with a murderous stowaway. It can also be found in *The Shadow Line*, as well as in the ambiguous relationship between

Marlow and Jim in *Lord Jim*, or between Jim and Brown. It emerges most starkly in the ominous affinity between Marlow and Kurtz in *Heart of Darkness*, where the former sees a submerged part of himself reflected in the unspeakable truth of the latter. In *The Secret Agent*, the police inspector and the anarchist are mirror-images of one another. There is a treacherous, underground, illicit self – a thing of darkness which one either struggles to shuck off, or which one must come to acknowledge as one's own. Lord Jim wavers between denying the guilty self which deserted a shipload of Muslims, and striving to make reparation for it.

This shadowy self in Conrad is by no means a simple-hearted English Tory. On the contrary, it is a full-blooded Continental sceptic, influenced by the thought of philosophers like Schopenhauer and Nietzsche. In what is scarcely the cheeriest of viewpoints, Conrad would seem to hold that personal identity is an illusion, truth and meaning eternally elusive, language fundamentally inadequate, human consciousness an unhappy accident, and Nature a meaningless, impenetrable chaos. History is a futile cycle of violence and savagery, progress is a chimera, civilization is a higher form of barbarism, and egoism is the underlying truth of human conduct. Motivations for action are arbitrary and irrational, and action itself a gross simplification of the unfathomable complexity of the world and the self. Solitude is the natural condition of humanity, reason is a treacherous falsification of the world, and human beings are strangers to themselves and to each other. We are not the authors of our own actions; rather, our sense of freedom is simply a delusion bred in us by Nature or History, which uses us for its own enigmatic purposes. The hero of *Lord Jim* is still strenuously trying to shape his own destiny; by the time of *Nostromo*, such an aim has become effectively out of the question.

Much of this is off-the-peg nineteenth-century irrationalism. But it is also the ideology of the exile, one whose sense of identity has been undermined early on by the burden of an imperial autocracy, and who has lived through a profound historical crisis at the heart of Europe. Conrad belongs to a European history which, as it approaches the turn of the twentieth century, is moving out of its more buoyant, affirmative phase, with its belief in the free, self-determining individual, into a darker, more downbeat civilization altogether. The capitalist system has been pitched into the prolonged economic slump which will play its part in 1914 in staging history's first global imperialist war. Indeed, the very institution of imperialism brings these two phases of history together. If it involves swashbuckling Romantic individualists like Jim, it is also a sordid narrative of greed, conflict and exploitation which seems under no individual's control. At the high-point of one's dominion, the world becomes alien and inscrutable.

In terms of literary form, this is reflected in a running battle between romance and realism. Imperialism is a form of Romantic idealism, with its flag-waving rhetoric of God and nation and its vision of a transformed earth. But it is an idealism motivated by a less than godly materialism. The ship's deck is the thin partition between the two, separating the idealized comradeship of the crew from the profitable commercial goods in the hold. You can then, as in Conrad's fiction, celebrate the hard work, loyalty and conscientiousness on deck while forgetting the material ends which all this ultimately serves.

There are other contradictions as well. Imperialism demands faith, resolute action and an unswerving belief in one's own values. But it also brings you into contact with other cultures which are different from your own, but which seem despite this lamentable misfortune to be in reasonable working order. Such encounters are then bound to raise awkward questions about the absoluteness of one's own way of life. In doing so, they threaten to subvert one's sense of supremacy at exactly the point where it is most urgently needed. Imperialism breeds a disabling cultural relativism. By Conrad's time, the liberal, humanistic values which had served the West so splendidly in its earlier, more self-assured historical phase are being called into question, by Yeats, Freud, T. S. Eliot, Ezra Pound, Martin Heidegger and D. H. Lawrence as much as by the ferociously anti-Enlightenment Pole. Reason and progress have been unmasked as a lie, truth and objectivity exposed as delusions, and on all sides there is a return to the mythical and primitive, savage gods and mystical archetypes.

How does Conrad reconcile the sea-captain in himself with the sceptic? One answer might be: by the agonized, perpetually unsuccessful act of writing, which seeks to dredge order from chaos. But Conrad also resolves these claims through his belief that though action, ideals, values and identities may be illusory, they are nevertheless *saving* illusions which we cannot simply shuck off. Values and beliefs may have no sure grounding in a random evolutionary universe; but by clinging tenaciously to our ideals, whether they are represented by the Koran or a standard of seamanlike conduct, we confer meaning and order on our inherently pointless lives. And for this purpose, any ideal will really do. What matters is not so much the content of our beliefs as the passionate intensity with which we stay faithful to them. It is an ethic which is on the turn, so to speak, from Romanticism to existentialism. You must live fictionally, hypothetically, *as if* your values had an unimpeachable basis. It is in this way that full-blown sceptics like Martin Decoud of *Nostromo* can be worsted.

Yet things are not so simple. For if the sceptic is destructive, so is the idealist. Lofty ideals can dismember bodies. *Nostromo* is littered with lethal or ineffectual idealists (or self-idealizers), from Charles Gould, Don Avellanos and Giorgio Viola to Holroyd, Dr Monygham and Nostromo himself. Conrad's own fictions constantly idealize or inflate figures like Jim, Kurtz and Nostromo even when there is no real evidence that such a move is justified – though this may be the narrator's skewed way of seeing as much as the author's. There is no satisfactory balance in *Nostromo* between the ideal and the material, just as there is no such equipoise in a work like *The Secret Agent*, torn as it is between the squalid materialism of Verloc's overblown body and the fanatical idealism of the anarchist professor.

All these in Conrad are questions of literary form, not just of content. What strikes one about his prose is how it manages to be vivid and concrete yet ambiguous and equivocal. In this mixture of the immediate and the intangible, his writing has the quality of a dream, which seems both more and less intense than waking life. Indeed, Conrad often sees human existence as a kind of dream. The typical Conradian story is a colourful tale of action and adventure, surrounded by a misty penumbra of elusive meanings. One critic aptly describes *Heart of Darkness* as 'a detective story gone modernist'.[1] If the focus is too firmly on the narrative, the tale loses its 'artistic' evocativeness; but if we delve too deeply into the surrounding mist, the solidity of the narrative might be undermined. The storyline of *Heart of Darkness* threatens constantly to dissolve into a montage of static, dream-like tableaux. Yet one has to stay faithful to the evanescent meanings which flicker round the story's margins, just as one has to keep faith with an elusive Other like Jim or Kurtz. The conflict in Conrad between 'difficult' modernist and *Boys Own* adventure writer is a formal version of the conflict between sceptical émigré and English conservative.

If Conrad's prose is visually graphic and finely sculptured, it is not at all because he has a robust faith in the powers of language. It is rather because, like many a modernist writer, he has exceedingly little. Every word and meaning, he once remarked, floats in a sea of doubts and indeterminacies. To be valid, language must stay close to one's sensations, which for Conrad are more trustworthy than the alienated intellect. But sensations are also notoriously deceptive and impressionistic. If the prose of the novels is so meticulously wrought, it is partly because their author regards language as threadbare and duplicitous. It shares in what he sees as the dismal inauthenticity of everyday social life. Language faces outwards towards the light, but at the same time gestures inwards towards an inexpressible darkness. Only by being intensively pared and chiselled can it capture the odd fleeting ghost of meaning; but even this is ultimately doomed to failure. The preface to *The Nigger of the Narcissus* famously declares that its author's aim is to make us *see*; yet this, in any literal sense, is the last thing that writing can do. All it can do is produce the effect of seeing. Marlow in *Lord Jim* is conscious of how visual impressions are falsified by the act of putting them into language.

The world for Conrad is impenetrable and opaque. It is resistant to human meaning. One of his favourite images of this recalcitrance is the sea, which diminishes human existence by its sheer shapeless immensity. Telling a story, trying to cuff this meaningless mass of materials into a purposeful shape, is in the end as futile as ploughing the ocean. If colonialism is to be criticized, it is among other things because it, too, imagines like the story-teller that it can impose order on a formless world. It tries to hammer disorderly peoples into unity, lick them into shape. The fact that this enterprise is fruitless is a compliment neither to the colonizers nor to the colonized. It suggests that the former are obtuse and the latter are inherently unruly. Something of the same ambiguity can be found in E. M. Forster's *A Passage to India*. The imperial invaders are discredited, but not in a way which particularly flatters the natives.

Narrative, then, is forever seeking to net down a truth which refuses to yield itself up. It is bound to betray the truth in the act of trying to communicate it, so that every truth has its admixture of illusion. This is one reason why Conrad employs narrators who are hardly remarkable for their brilliance of insight, like Marlow or the professor of *Under Western Eyes*, so that the partial, angled nature of every narrative perspective can be put on show. In this way, the problem of narration is incorporated into the narrative itself. In some of Conrad's novels we get narratives within narratives, reports of reports of reports. There is no longer such a thing as the plain, unnarrated truth. There are no events which are undocumented.

Discovering the truth is a matter of finding a form, recounting a story; yet in doing so one finds oneself sculpting a void, since the world itself no longer constitutes a coherent narrative. Just as history displays no built-in progress, so there is no longer any credence to be placed in the shapely unfolding of a tale. The truth is no longer narratable. You will not disclose it, as George Eliot trusted one might, by patiently unravelling the chains of cause and effect. Chronology is no longer any reliable guide to reality. Time

and space are just cultural constructs to which the world itself is utterly indifferent.

All you can hope to do, then, is come at the truth now from one angle and now from another, slicing in and out of the story, skating backwards and forwards in time. You can loop, suspend and replay your narrative until it might just yield you the ghost of a truth – a truth that is not itself historical or orderly, and which can be shown rather than stated. In fact, storytelling involves a double falsehood, since reality is itself shot through with illusion, and the act of trying to communicate this in language is equally distorting. When Marlow in *Heart of Darkness* finally hears what he persuades himself is the pure voice of truth, one which will give his journey meaning, it is merely Kurtz's cry 'The horror, the horror'. The 'final' word is empty, negative, absent. As a modern theorist might put it, there is no transcendental signifier, but it is the fruitless search for it which makes narrative possible. Any particular story-line is bound to be arbitrary, just as Marlow's voyage in *Heart of Darkness* is gratuitous and unmotivated. In any case, even if truth can be discovered, it is not clear that there is anyone out there to receive it. The Marlow of *Heart of Darkness* is quite literally delivering his tale in the dark, unable to see his audience as he squats on deck. It is a graphic image of the problems of the modernist writer and his or her dwindling, anonymous readership.

There is, in fact, a kind of absent centre in almost all of Conrad's works – some missing factor, enigma or core of silence which resists being represented. In *Heart of Darkness*, it is signalled in the very title. There is the elusive selfhood of Lord Jim and Nostromo, the dark, brooding passivity of James Wait in *The Nigger of the Narcissus*, and Heyst's non-existent treasure in *Victory*. The central event of *Lord Jim* is a jump which even Jim himself seems not to have witnessed, though it is he who performs it. *Heart of Darkness* turns on Kurtz, who is seen and heard only obliquely, and his unseen unspeakable rites; while at the centre of *Nostromo* lie the unseen silver – the invisible cause of all the political turmoil – and the Montero revolution, a crucial event which is squinted at sideways. The novel has all the scope, rich social texture and psychological subtlety of a great realist work, yet with a resounding postrealist vacancy at its heart. It is as though that realist form has been remorselessly emptied of its positive content.

The Secret Agent revolves on an explosion at Greenwich Observatory which we never actually witness, as well as on the cryptic silence of young Stevie. In *Under Western Eyes*, we are confronted with the eternal enigma of the 'Russian soul', that tediously overemphasized mystery which eludes the understanding of the provincial English narrator. Characters in Conrad are either too baffling to be known, or – like Mitchell and McWhirr – too simple. As with Dickens, there is something mysterious about things and people which appear to be no more than themselves. Like a riddle, they rebuff understanding. Jim is both too subtle, and too simple, to be intelligible. Nostromo is unknowable because he is hollow to the core, a mere assemblage of other people's opinions of him. Kurtz also has a hollowed centre, like the place he occupies in the tale.

Some things and characters in Conrad are unfathomable because they are swathed in obscurity, and some because there is nothing there to be known. Is the heart of Africa dark because we Westerners cannot penetrate it, or is it dark, so to speak, inherently? Is it meaningless in itself, or simply obscure from our standpoint? Is it the thing itself which is askew, or our way of seeing it? Is there an 'objective' chaos and horror there, or is it just a case of our blurred vision? How can something which has no meaning in the first place be said to be inscrutable?

Conrad's texts, then, work by virtue of an absence. It is silence which stirs them into eloquence, a haziness which impels them to be so specific, something unrepresentable at their heart which drives their language and narrative so energetically onward. But this unrepresentable thing at their centre is also nothing less than the human subject. For the human subject is defined by its freedom, and the world for Conrad is by and large a deterministic place, mechanical and anonymous in its operations. It has the inevitability of a narrative with none of its plot or purposiveness. In this sense, it rather resembles a modernist work of art. The world is not really designed for human consciousness, and certainly not for freedom. Men and women are not the agents of their own destinies. So how are the novels to represent moments of transformation, vital decisions and revolutionary events? The simple answer is that they do not, and cannot. In a mechanistic world, freedom must itself remain a mystery. What is most precious about us is also most indecipherable.

The unpredictable – like the cowardly Hirsch of *Nostromo* spitting in his torturer's face at the point of death – cannot really be accommodated. (In a sense, there can be no more free an action than that performed at the point of death, since you will not be around to be effected by the consequences.) The free act is just a kind of gratuitous happening without rhyme or reason, an inexplicable break in the iron chains of causality. So Hirsch's extraordinary gesture is reported to us second-hand, not viewed directly or from the inside, and the same goes for Winnie Verloc's killing of her repulsive husband in *The Secret Agent*. In a kind of cinematic jump, we see the shadow of the knife on the wall at one moment, and its blade buried in Verloc's breast at the next; but what occurs in between – the unfathomable moment of free human agency – must go unreported. We are barred access to Winnie's experience.

The same goes for the blowing up of Stevie in the novel, an event involving a hole, an erasure and an eternal silence which is itself represented in the novel only at second hand. Human freedom cannot be represented: to do so would be to reduce it to an object, which means that it would no longer be freedom at all. Freedom is the riddle at the heart of the universe. We see what leads up to the murder of Verloc, Jim's jump from the *Patna* and the nationalist revolution in *Nostromo*, just as we see what happens immediately afterwards. But something vital has been elided in between.

Jumping is an apt image of this process (there are several jumps in Conrad's fiction), since to jump is a free decision which, once taken, hands you over to the determining forces of gravity. Like all human action, but more graphically than most, it is irrevocable. You cannot decide to turn back in mid-air. A jump illuminates the gap between the self that chooses and acts, and the self that seems a mere manipulated object in the world. It is the gap between the Jim who is still on board the *Patna*, and the Jim who suddenly finds himself in the lifeboat. Into this blank space between freedom and fate, being and doing, the self as subject and the self as object, language in Conrad disappears.

We can rewrite subject and object here as spirit and body. Inert, grossly material bodies, like that of the obese Verloc in *The Secret Agent*, seem like fleshly objects, so that the fact that they are also subjects – that Verloc can (just about) speak and move – becomes something of a mystery. In the case of Jim and others, this clash between spirit and body is also a rift between the ideal and the real – between the dreams one has in the moment before acting, and the inevitable let-down of putting them into material form. We cannot be free without acting, yet we end up imprisoned in our own actions like a convict in his cell. Charles Gould of *Nostromo* will discover that – in this kind of acquisitive society at least – there is something about freedom which turns inexorably into imprisonment.

If colonialism is a false imposition of order on chaos, then one might expect Conrad to be straightforwardly opposed to it. But little in Conrad is straightforward. Narrative is also a falsifying sort of order, but it is indispensable even so. The anti-imperialist aspects of *Heart of Darkness* are evident enough in, say, Marlow's withering remarks about those who snatch land from those who have slightly flatter noses than ourselves. But there is also something disturbing about the tale's presentation of imperialism. It is not just the reach-me-down racism of its portraits of 'natives', or its apparent endorsement of British as opposed to Belgian colonization. It is also that the whole imperialist enterprise is represented as essentially *absurd*. It is a surreally pointless exercise, symbolized by a ship firing purposelessly into a river bank, a pail with a hole in it, a hollow in the ground excavated for no apparent purpose, a man weirdly garbed in motley, and a chief accountant conducting himself in the middle of the jungle as he might in an English drawing-room.

All this makes for powerful dramatic effect; but it also suggests that imperialism is simply a kind of irrational fantasy, a waking nightmare or absurdist theatre, which is far from being the case. On the contrary, nothing could be more grimly rational, at least in one rather anaemic sense of the word. There is nothing in the least futile or unreal about sailing in, massacring the inhabitants, grabbing their raw resources and sailing out again. In the period between Conrad's own visit to the Congo in 1890, and the First World War, millions of Africans were slaughtered by European imperial powers for hard-headed political and economic reasons. Imperialism is not in the least pointless.

Indeed, the much-quoted passage in *Heart of Darkness* which describes the ship firing its guns into the jungle concludes with the suggestion that there is indeed a hostile camp of 'natives' around the place, so that the assault is perhaps not quite so 'insane' after all. Conrad pulls his narrative back within the protective limits of realism just in time. He does, however, harbour the belief, typical of some right-wing thought of the time, that beneath all apparently purposeful public action lie irrational private motives; and we shall see this view writ large in *Nostromo*. As a result, imperialism is seen in *Heart of Darkness* not as a purposeful, historically intelligible system, but as a kind of nightmarish aberration.

The difference between right-wing irrationalism and capitalist imperialism is a vital one to the understanding of Conrad's political attitudes. What he dislikes about imperialism, quite apart from its greed and brutality, is that it is supposedly inspired by enlightened ideals of reason, progress, altruism, peace, prosperity, civilization and the like, ideals which he despises. As a right-wing irrationalist, Conrad believes instead in the realities of egoism, barbarism and eternal conflict, the frailty of reason and the relative unimportance of such mundane matters as prosperity. He also suspects that history, far from progressing, is actually slipping backwards into savagery. So his views give no comfort to imperialism; but neither do they lend support to its left-wing opponents.

The leading critics of imperialism of Conrad's age were political radicals who believed, not without reason, that history could be more than barbarism; that social improvement, however arduous, was possible, and had taken place in the past; and that human action was governed by more than egoism. These men and women held that a reasoned analysis of the colonialist system was vital to the fight against it; that only the privileged can afford to scoff at issues of material prosperity; and that civilization need not be in an eternal state of warfare.

It is important to see, then, that Kurtz in *Heart of Darkness* is a left-winger, or at least was when he first came to Africa, which is one reason why Conrad detests him so much. Those 'unspeakable rites' and secret abominations are among other things Conrad's revenge on social reformers. Scratch a humanitarian and you find a monster. Kurtz is an 'emissary of pity, and science, and progress, and devil knows what else', who would have made a good politician 'on the popular side', and who has a formidable capacity for populist rhetoric. In acting out the degradation of Kurtz, then, *Heart of Darkness* is not only exposing the real rapacity which lurks beneath high-sounding imperial ideals; it is also seeking to discredit the leftists who did most to challenge that predatory system.

In this way, it can win for itself the best of both political worlds, spurning the greedy middle-class commercialists and colonialists (for whom Conrad anyway feels a patrician disdain), while also rebuffing their radical opponents. Instead, it advances a more scandalous, tough-minded revelation than either camp is supposedly capable of: beneath imperialism lies the eternal barbarousness of the human condition. What is awry is not political history but the human heart. This makes the whole situation more dramatic and deep-rooted, but only at the cost of rendering it unalterable. If it is true, there seems little that can be done about the imperialist system – a message which is more welcome to its champions than to its critics. Besides, if the nihilists are right and human values are a sham, then there would seem no more reason not to exploit Africans than to do so. And if enslaving Africans is simply the effect of original sin, it may be as natural and inevitable as it is regrettable.

In the end, so *Heart of Darkness* suggests, high-flown ideals and fancy sentiments will never save us from the persistent fact of savagery. Such ideals, like human civilization itself, are only skin-deep. Civilization is merely a subtle form of barbarism; in fact, it is in some ways worse than actual barbarism, since to live it out self-consciously, as the decadent Kurtz does, is to exacerbate it. All moderns are cannibals in thin disguise. Our brutishness persists beneath the skin, as Marlow recognizes when Kurtz's supposed primitivism evokes in him an appalled affinity. Civility, in what one might call the *Lord of the Flies* syndrome, is precariously paper-thin, and we can regress from it at any moment to our bestial origins.

As Marlow's story and journey press forward, they simultaneously drift backward into a primitive past which civilization has never really abandoned. Conservative, pessimistic seafarers like Conrad and Golding are out to persuade us that there is no faith to be placed in human culture or history. With Golding, the message has a theological twist in its tail. The only issue in the end is whether we, like Kurtz, have the courage to confess that we are at heart savages as well. As well as who, though? It is surely something of a back-handed compliment to inform the inhabitants of Borneo or the Congo that we are quite as brutal and bloodthirsty as they are. Is this supposed to make them feel better?

It is hard not to suspect that the Marlow of *Heart of Darkness* is a touch deranged. His account is so coloured, hyperbolic and latently hysterical as to be only dubiously reliable. Either that, or Conrad's own writing here is remarkably garish and lurid, with nothing like the supple leanness of the prose of *Nostromo*. Perhaps one could try reading the tale like Henry James's 'The Turn of the Screw', as an apparently reliable story delivered by a deluded narrator. So much in the book seems to be relentlessly dragooned into generating an ominous 'atmosphere', in a kind of verbal overkill or visual equivalent of melodrama. Take, for example, this description of a woman's expression: 'Her face had a tragic and fierce aspect of wild sorrow and of dumb pain mingled with the fear of some struggling, half-shaped resolve'. Trying to imitate this ludicrously complicated expression, which exists almost purely at the level of language, would be a useful exercise for a drama school, if a dispiriting one.

Marlow has only to hear the innocuous names of some African villages to feel that they 'belong to some sordid farce acted in front of a sinister back-cloth', and this before anything even faintly sinister has even happened. He is grimly set on whipping up a sensational drama out of a minor incident, and has only to see some Africans wandering harmlessly around to feel a 'taint of imbecile rapacity' in the air. His steamer is not allowed simply to travel along the river bank; instead, it must toil along 'the edge of a black and incomprehensible frenzy'. An African cannot step casually into the jungle without the wilderness having taken him again to its bosom. The whole thing is contrived, heavy-handed, laboriously unreal, and very much as though Marlow is seeing what he is at all costs determined to see. If this were not a fiction, it would cry out for comparison with someone else's account of the whole affair.

The constant emphasis on the mystery and genius of Kurtz is another rather flat-footed device, since it is clear enough that this image is being generated only to be deflated. There is very little hard evidence to back up this breathless reverence, just as there is precious little to support Lord Jim's receiving as much fascinated attention as the novel lavishes on him. Kurtz is an early example of a kind of character we encounter often enough in modern fiction: one who is commended not so much for what he says or does, but for pushing himself to an extreme, staying faithful to the truth of himself, and living out his desires to the full. With Kurtz and his ilk, we have moved deep into the Romantic or existential cult of 'authenticity'. What matters, for this deeply suspect doctrine, is the sheer intensity of your commitment, not its actual content. What counts is going all the way, not so much the direction in which you are headed. Whereas others live a timorously conventional existence, these modern heroes are prepared to break through the thin crust of social life, peer defiantly into the abyss which gapes beneath it, and dance exultantly on its edge. It is, to be sure, a horrific sort of freedom; but it is admirable in its resolute self-abandonment, in contrast to the hollow men of the middle-class suburbs.

There are few more shopsoiled modernist clichés than the idea that every-day social existence is shallow and inauthentic. Only when this existence is pushed to an extreme will the truth reveal itself. Most people, sunk in false consciousness as they are, cannot bear too much reality. The only real men, so the theory goes, are the spiritual elite who may choose to do evil, but who at least in doing so are genuinely alive. For this case, with its contemptuous, alienated view of the life of ordinary men and women, you can discover ultimate reality only in some African jungle, dark ocean gulf or Room 101 of the spirit. What you say when you come face to face with horror – when (as in George Orwell's 1984) a cage of ravenous rats is strapped to your face – is bound to be the truth. The opposite case is surely far more convincing. Most people in such situations would say anything whatsoever. There is more than a dash of the Boy Scout ethic about this notion, with its belief in life as a kind of strenuous self-testing. But why should what you uncover in yourself at an extreme of despair or endurance be 'the truth'?

Something of this modernist ideology, which can find truth only in crisis and extremity, lurks in *Lord Jim*. Jim may have failed in leaping from the *Patna*, but at least he refuses to back down from the question of his own identity. He may be a Romantic fantasist, but fantasy, as Stein insists in the novel, redeems as well as destroys. It is the destructive element which will nonetheless buoy you up and save you from drowning. To be without illusions is to be safe but dull, so why not follow the dream? It is hard to say whether Jim does in fact finally redeem himself: is his final encounter with death an act of atonement, defiance, martyrdom, suicide or extravagant egoism? Yet his victory, so we are invited to believe, has been there all along, in his fidelity to an ideal of pure self-presence – some act or moment of epiphany in which he could realize himself whole and entire. The contrast is with his earlier jump, in which – as with most action for Conrad – he ends up confronting himself as a stranger. Jim's ideal may be a matter of pride and vanity, as well as an illusion for creatures like us enslaved to time and chance, but it is nonetheless noble. Better perhaps to be deluded and heroic than clear-eyed and commonplace. Anyway, just as truth is shot through with illusion, so illusion can disclose a kind of truth. What else, after all, is literary fiction?

An uncharitable way of describing Jim's progress from being the betrayer of the *Patna* to the colonialist master of Patusan is that he atones for selling out one group of non-Western people by lording it over another. He arrives in Patusan as a cross between a liberator and a social worker; but this cannot conceal the fact that he is the benevolent despot of the place (though his commercial interests are discreetly downplayed). His altruism is among other things an 'exalted egoism'. Perhaps Conrad feels that colonialism is justified when one settles in a territory rather than just dropping in to plunder its resources. It is not a view usually shared by the colonials. There is a suggestion that the former type of colonial power is the benign British model, to be approved, and the latter typical of the avaricious Belgians and others, to be condemned.

Both modes of imperialism are combined in *Nostromo*, one of the finest of all English historical novels. Charles Gould, though English, is a native of the Costaguana he economically exploits, but his American backer Holroyd is not. In its astonishing epic scope, the novel recounts the story (in typically crab-wise Conradian fashion, to be sure) of Costaguana's turbulent voyage from military dictatorship (Bento), through a conservative-democratic revolt against this regime (Riberia's Blancos), to the rise of imperialistic capitalism (Holroyd and Charles Gould). From there, it shifts to a failed nationalist

revolution against that foreign-backed power (the Monteros), and finally to the emergence of socialist forces which look to a postcapitalist future for the region. As the novel ends, the scene is set for a Marxist revolution.

Whether all this constitutes progress, however, is far from obvious. The novel's Shakespearian epigraph, 'So foul a sky clears not without a storm', suggests that turbulence is unavoidable if you are out for improvement, and many critics have claimed that the province is in better shape at the end of the novel than it was at the beginning. Yet the deliberately broken-backed narrative, full of flashbacks, deferments and multiple perspectives like *Lord Jim*, is enough in itself to question the view that there is any simple upward evolution at stake here. Indeed, Dr Monygham foresees a time when the supposedly civilizing San Tome mine will come to weigh as heavily on the backs of the common people as the 'barbarism, cruelty, and misrule' of an earlier epoch. Once more, for Conrad, it is not a simple choice between civilization and barbarism; civilization *is* a form of barbarism. The Parisian intellectual Martin Decoud harks back sardonically to the old days when the 'persistent barbarism of our native continent did not wear the black coats of politicians . . .'. It is the authentic note of *Heart of Darkness*. In hoping to break with the lawless past, you find yourself perpetuating it in a new form. All striving for a brave new future turns out to be atavistic, recycling the 'primitive' past. The capitalist San Tome mine is just a latter-day version of the slave mines of the Spanish colonial conquerors.

The silver which is meant to lay the basis for peace and prosperity is also, ironically, what tears the country apart. Even the three characters who smuggle it out of Sulaco on a lighter end up on the craft for entirely different reasons. Nostromo is there for the sake of his public image, Decoud for the sake of his beloved Antonia, and Hirsch is fleeing for his life. (There is, incidentally, no finer image of Conrad's sceptical view of human existence than that of three men who care nothing for each other steering a load of meaningless matter through an impenetrable darkness for no very good reason.) The silver which was intended as a principle of unity becomes a focus and force of division. Order is simply controlled disorder. Capitalism is an irrational system, as pointless as the cosmos itself, since it provides the material resources for human well-being only to undermine it. Material interests are an essential means for human flourishing, as Charles Gould recognizes; but for him and his colleagues they rapidly become an end in themselves, one to which human flourishing is brutally sacrificed. Gould is prepared to blow up his own mine rather than yield it to his political enemies, and is thus a kind of bandit or terrorist himself. The outlaw is the

mirror-image of the businessman. In a neat reversal of the reflection, the bandit Hernandez is hired as a soldier.

It is hardly accidental that this dourly pessimistic tale of political chaos is set in Latin America. The novel connives with the racist notion that the whole continent is simply one enormous soap opera. Conrad himself referred to *Nostromo* as a 'tragic farce'. If you want to promote the view that political life is simply a sordid, repetitive round of greed, corruption, lawlessness and squalid power-struggles, what more convenient than to set your work in a Third World continent notorious for its supposed natural anarchy? To see the place as 'ungovernable' is to give no comfort to those who try to colonize it; but it is also an insult to its native peoples. Montero's revolutionary struggle against US imperialism and its Costaguana lackeys is seen as motivated by nothing more than greed, power and ambition. There is nothing to choose between the rulers and the rebels. This, in fact, is a grotesque travesty of a good many anti-colonial movements in Latin America and elsewhere, which were driven by selfless motives as well as by self-interested ones. The vision, courage and self-sacrifice of such movements are reduced here to little more than self-aggrandisement.

For the sceptical Conrad, however, selflessness is a dubious affair. The kindliness and humanity of Mrs Gould, a Bloomsbury-like matron who seems to have strayed into the book from some novel by Woolf or Forster, is in one sense real enough; but it is also ineffectual, as well as being the kind of humanitarianism which the novel, with some justice, regards simply as the benevolent face of capitalism. There will usually be a well-intentioned liberal wing to imperial power, one which tries to mop up some of the human damage it wreaks; and this is one way of seeing the relationship between Emilia Gould and her husband. Otherwise, everyone in the novel is driven by 'irrational' or egoistic motives. Even Holroyd, the US imperial backer of the San Tome mine, treats the place as a sort of hobby, as though imperialism were no more than a private eccentricity. Charles Gould, a little like Gerald Crich in D. H. Lawrence's *Women in Love*, idealizes the mine as a spiritual principle, turning it into an idol or fetish; but this simply rationalizes greed, rivalry and the lust for power. Ideals are no more than masks for material interests. Objectivity is a convenient fiction, the human subject has no abiding core of truth, and so-called civilized notions are in the service of power and desire. *Nostromo* is a Nietzschean novel through and through.

Alternatively, ideals may be in the service of love, as in the case of Martin Decoud, though this may be just a more devious form of egoism. Decoud is actually more of an altruistic patriot than either he or the novel will allow;

but he is painted as a faithless sceptic full of abstract ideas, Parisian flippancy and dilettantish irony. This is partly because his world view is actually uncomfortably close to his author's, and thus needs to be kept at arm's length. He is one of Conrad's secret sharers. Like Conrad, Decoud views the politics of his country as a futile farce. Like Conrad, too, he sees patriotism and other ideals as cloaks for material exploitation. Yet he also rejects all belief as odiously narrow, which allows the conservative side of Conrad to write him off. In despicably Gallic style, he has faith only in his own sensations. He regards all convictions as turning finally into a form of madness, which is certainly true of Charles Gould's obsession with the mine. Even Gould himself observes that 'liberty, democracy, patriotism, government – all of them have a flavour of folly and murder'.

Yet ideals are as necessary as they are death-dealing, which is what, from the novel's viewpoint, Decoud's cynicism fails to appreciate. He does indeed have one illusory ideal: his love for Antonia; but he is aware of his own illusion, which is the next best thing to having none at all. To know one is deluded is the nearest one can come to clear-sightedness. Marooned with nothing but his own sensations in the Placido gulf, he dies, so to speak, from a taste of his own medicine. Intellectuals like Decoud are more mind than action; and since for Conrad it is action that gives us the illusion of an independent identity, Decoud finally dissolves away.

Ideals, then, are egoistic; but so too can be the hard-headed opportunism which dismisses them, like that of Sotillo or Montero, or the kind of steely disenchantment which claims to see through them. If the common people are too credulous, which makes them prey to unscrupulous political adventurers, the intelligentsia are too little so. Dr Monygham is a misanthrope who has no illusions about history or humankind; but even this is a kind of rationalization of a personal failure, since he was broken by torture. Even disenchantment can be a kind of sublimation. Anyway, despite his sceptical view of public affairs, Monygham fosters a private ideal in his devotion to Mrs Gould. Public actions and viewpoints in *Nostromo* usually conceal private, irrational motivations. Decoud is a patriot because of Antonia, while Captain Mitchell is a courageous public character only because he is too self-centred and unimaginative to conceive of a genuine threat to himself. As often in Conrad, lack of imagination gets you a long way. Popular revolution is a consequence of private ambition, and public prosperity springs from private greed. What may look like order and purpose in history is simply the sum-total of arbitrary private appetites. Those who have no ideals are as short-sighted as those who, like the veteran Italian republican Giorgio

Viola, have been left with nothing else. In Conrad's eyes, there is much to be admired in Viola's austere, old-school idealism of duty, fidelity and brotherhood; but such values could never be materially realized without being degraded. Much the same goes for the old-fashioned liberal idealism of Don Avellanos.

Nostromo himself exists purely as a public persona. He has no value in himself, only in the way he is regarded by others. He exists, as he remarks, to be spoken well of. In this, he resembles a commodity like the silver, which similarly has value only because it is thought well of. A commodity like silver accrues its worth only in what people make of it. This, indeed, is true for Conrad in general. Nature and history are meaningless in themselves, and people or objects take on value only because of the energies which men and women subjectively invest in them. The silver of the mine is in itself just inert material stuff; but in generating this whole enthralling drama, it becomes in Conrad's own words the hero of the novel. As men and women are turned into objects for others' power or profit, so objects like the mine begin to assume an oppressive life of their own.

Nostromo, then, exists as a fiction, like the novel he inhabits. Just as the novel itself exists only through language, so its protagonist lives only through his good name. His public altruism is thus in the service of private egoism. Like Kurtz, he is hollow to the core; like the silver, he comes to life only in the fantasies of others. He is entranced by a myth of himself, a self-idealizer and self-fetishist. His name can mean 'our man', suggesting that like Decoud he is the hired lackey of the ruling class of Sulaco. Decoud's job is to lend his political masters some intellectual muscle, while Nostromo's is to keep the common people in order. One who has no identity of his own, however, being the mere instrument of others, has no personal self to pledge to them. It is not surprising, then, that Nostromo should finally come to 'betray' his overlords. Everybody's man is nobody's man.

What the novel sees as Nostromo's betrayal – his stealing of the silver – is also the dawning in him of class consciousness. He comes to realize that he and his colleagues are being exploited by the capitalist class for their own selfish motives, and is moved to rebellion. He thus becomes 'our man' in a different sense, affirming political solidarity with his fellow workers. For Nostromo, this is far from an act of treachery, since so far he has had no identity of his own to be true to. On the contrary, it is he who feels that he has been sold out by his disloyal paymasters. This justified resentment, however, conveniently allows the novel to rationalize his new-found political identity as sheer pique and vanity, vices which can then be added to his

acquisitiveness. Nostromo is still a slave to the mine, but now a private rather than a public one. He has merely moved from one kind of vacancy – his reliance for personal identity on his bosses – to another kind of vacancy: his servile dependence on the silver. His new socialist identity and sense of comradeship with others must be discredited as yet more delusions.

Though Nostromo is right to see that he has been a cat's-paw, and right too to declare on his deathbed that 'the world rests on the poor', he is carefully not allowed to become a socialist hero. By the end of the novel, an increasingly Europeanized, commercialized Sulaco, having beaten off the forces of revolutionary nationalism, is buzzing with Marxists and socialists bent upon fighting foreign imperialism. In one of the several historical ironies of the novel, capitalism is now building up for its own self-interested ends the very forces which could potentially take it over. Previously divided between Blancos and Montero supporters, the workers are now promoting their own interests as a class rather than acting as the tools of others.

The novel's view of this historical twist is sufficiently indicated by the fact that it portrays the workers' leader as a bloodthirsty, hunchbacked 'monkey', which is easier than having to engage in reasoned debate with his convictions. Like Dickens, Conrad often makes his point by the disreputable technique of caricaturing those he disapproves of. These socialist militants, like the nationalists, are fighting the regime with its own material weapons, and so can be written off as no more than its alter egos. They are not idealists like Giorgio Viola – though ironically he, too, can be written off, since his revolutionary idealism is so distant from the real world as to be poignantly ineffectual. Conrad admires radical ideals only when there is no danger of their being realized. The novel, then, places left-wingers in a crafty double-bind. Like a good deal else in its pages, they are either too idealist or too materialist. It is Viola who mistakenly kills his spiritual son Nostromo – an act which symbolizes his short-sightedness, but which also suggests that the materially minded Nostromo is no true inheritor of the old man's revolutionary idealism. In a neat double effect, both characters are accordingly diminished.

The career of Nostromo can be seen as summarizing the fortunes of the country's working class. Enlisted and exploited in the industrializing of Costaguana, it continues to struggle for political interests other than its own by backing the separatist revolution of the Monterists. Emerging from this debacle into independent consciousness, it is still too bound by material interests (symbolized by the silver) to represent an authentic political alter-native to its capitalist masters, and is purged by a traditional idealist (Viola) of its own camp. Even so, the political separatism which has allowed the Occidental Province to cut adrift from the rest of the country, and thus to evolve a more advanced form of capitalism within its borders, is busy breeding the proletarian forces which might eventually seize state power. And since that for Conrad would mean lawlessness and oppression, it is hard to know whether in his eyes Costaguana has progressed at all from its early years of military dictatorship.

The ideal and the material are just as incapable of resolution in *The Secret Agent*. The novel presents us with a seedy, mechanistic, densely material world, one which cannot really accommodate freedom and idealism. Life is just an endless recycling of meaningless matter. It is against this drab, mindlessly conformist world that the mad anarchist Professor revolts. His dream is to blow a huge hole in matter, wiping the slate clean so that humanity can start again from scratch. The fact that the bomb explosion in the novel takes place at Greenwich Observatory, the marker of the prime meridian or still point of the turning world, suggests some fantastic attempt to blow up time itself. The Professor moves in some limbo between life and death, time and eternity, wired up with an explosive device and prepared to blow himself to pieces at any moment; and this signifies a terrifying kind of freedom. To live permanently with your own death is to disarm it.

Yet matter proves impossible to destroy. Bits and pieces of Stevie's body are left scattered around as tell-tale signs. And this, in a sense, is cheering news: all revolutionary schemes are futile, since the world is too dense to make a significant dent in. The very form of the novel, with its stolid thickness of social texture, makes the world it presents seem unbudgeable. The naturalistic style of the novel presents us with a slimy, foggy Dickensian London populated by grotesque, slow-moving, object-like figures, which it would take a lot more than a bomb to blow apart. In another sense, however, this is not cheering news at all. If things resist change, it is because, like Verloc, they are obscenely gross and meaningless. They resist being assigned a new value because they are strangers to value altogether.

The novel veers between portraying the anarchists as profoundly alarming figures, and suggesting that they are ludicrously ineffectual. The Professor's nihilism is in one sense a potent threat to everything traditionalist England holds dear; but in another sense he is part of the same social game as the police inspector. Without criminals, no police officers; without transgression, no upholding of norms and laws. There is no real place for freedom or agency in this mechanically determined world, and this is bad news for the anarchists; but it is not especially good news for anyone else.

Determinism seems a high price to pay for averting revolution. The world is only not changeable because it is not particularly valuable. It is too baldly factual a place to be hospitable to human value, which is one reason why Stevie's humane feelings are inarticulate. If the Professor is the mad anarchist, Stevie is the mad artist, whose broken speech gestures to a world of love and comradeship which can never be realized in material form, and whose frantically scribbled loops and whorls hint in symbolist fashion at an eternity which can never be expressed. Just to make sure that we do not take his humane values too positively, the novel makes him a degenerate mental defective. In a world where nothing can be altered, the only appropriate kind of moral value is also the most useless: pity.

In a typical piece of Conradian ambiguity, the everyday world is shabby and corrupt, but the ideals which might transform it are mad. It is a choice between a dingy but stable English normality, and a fascinating but repellent Continental nihilism. The reader is allowed nowhere else to stand. Either you do not look too closely into things, as with the spiritually myopic Winnie Verloc, or, like the Professor, you glare straight through human existence into the abyss which lies beneath it. Verloc treads a line between the two: if he is a grubby little shopkeeper, he is also caught up in the extremist politics which despatch Stevie to his death. Like the rest of us, he is a double agent; but he does not see the gulf which yawns at his feet. As with *Heart of Darkness*, it is a choice between an inauthentic society and a terrifying authenticity. It is our compromises and illusions which allow us to survive; but is this kind of life really worth having, compared with the fanatical spiritual elite who are able to stare death unflinchingly in the face?

A similar pincer movement is at work in that uninspired late offering, *Under Western Eyes*. In this novel, a melodramatic tale of the inscrutable 'Russian soul' is delivered by a conventionally minded English narrator who harks with tedious repetitiveness on the limits of his own understanding. This device helps to detach the reader from an 'extremist' struggle between Russian autocrats and anarchists, thus underlining the English values of decency and common sense. Yet at the same time the Russian events are allowed to show up the provincial restrictions of the narrator. Each perspective ironically qualifies the other; and this might seem to strike the note of 'scrupulous impartiality' which, so Conrad tells us in his preface, he has been searching for.

The novel, however, is about as impartial in its judgement as an old-style Mississippi jury. The truth is that the revolutionaries are savagely caricatured, a move which the work hopes to justify by its narrator's self-ironizing insistence that his judgement on these impenetrable foreigners is not wholly to be trusted. The unreliable narrator is thus a device behind which the novel can conceal its own full-blooded loathing of most of its Russian characters. Like *The Secret Agent*, the story vacillates between a virulent hatred of revolutionaries, and a pose of ironic detachment which would suggest a plague on all political houses. 'In this world of men', the protagonist reflects, 'nothing can be changed – neither happiness nor misery'. As in *The Secret Agent*, Conrad invokes a bleak determinism in order to deny that the revolutionaries could ever succeed. But if history is determined, then so are the motives of the revolutionaries themselves, which absolves them from being morally condemned. And this is at odds with the way they are actually treated.

A similar ambiguity informs the novel's treatment of its protagonist, Razumov. In his cruel cynicism and malicious egoism, he, too, is an unsavoury instance of the 'Russian soul'. Yet the novel treats him more sympathetically than it does the revolutionaries, not least because he is their victim. It is prepared to use his 'foreignness' to excuse him, which it is not prepared to do in the case of the anarchistic 'apes' and megalomaniac frauds who use him as their tool. This is largely because Razumov, despite his Slavic inscrutability, shares many of the narrator's political values. They are both, after all, resolutely anti-revolutionary – one in a 'spiritual' and the other in a commonsensical way.

Yet the novel also needs its English narrator in order to distance itself from the more sceptical, 'extremist' aspects of Razumov, just as it needs Razumov in order to mount a criticism of the revolutionaries from the inside. For all his 'Russian' unbalancedness, his judgement is more likely to win credence than the opinions of a bumbling, parochially minded Englishman who admits that he has little idea of what he is talking about. A critique of revolution which comes from the emotionally theatrical Razumov can hardly be accused of lacking an insight into human passions.

In the end, then, the novel can have its political cake and eat it. The 'passionate' spirit of Russia shows up the limits of English empiricism, while its violence and cynicism underlines the English virtues of tolerance and fair play. In the figure of Razumov, the novel can indulge a very un-English nihilism and despair, while at the same time dissociating itself from it under cover of its plain-minded narrator. Razumov slips beyond the narrator's befuddled comprehension, thus safely distancing foreign 'extremism' from English moderation; but for the same reason he also slips beyond the narrator's power of criticism. In this way, *Under Western Eyes* can safeguard

English decency from foreign barbarity, while drawing on foreign 'passion' and 'nobility' to satirize the timorous conventionalism of English culture. Razumov stands midway between the world of English practicality and a Slavic grandeur of soul, but he testifies to how little they can be reconciled. In the end, the contradictions through which the Englishman and émigré Conrad lived were too acute to be resolved by means of such narrative devices.

D. H. LAWRENCE

Few novelists divide their audience more drastically than D. H. Lawrence. For Lawrence's champions, who since the 1960s have been growing thinner on the ground by the year, his writing has a depth and intensity which makes almost every other author look pallid. For his detractors, these racist, proto-fascist, male-supremacist works are enough to make any civilized readers feel queasy in the pit of their stomachs. One can sometimes feel both things simultaneously; but there is rarely any middle way when it comes to reading Lawrence, just as there is rarely any middle way for Lawrence himself. The fact that his works are the subject of such ferocious contention says something significant about them. There is an absolutism about his writing which is foreign to the liberal mainstream of English culture. Despite Lawrence's undoubted 'Englishness', there is a sense in which these novels belong more to the world of Dostoevesky or Thomas Mann than they do to that of Jane Austen and E. M. Forster. Lawrence is a full-bloodedly 'metaphysical' novelist; and these, in English culture, are rare birds. He is not mannered, civilized or sociable.

In Lawrence's defence, one can appeal to such testimony as the magnificent *Sons and Lovers*, a novel published in 1913 but one whose graphic social realism and laconic modern style could well spring from the England of the 1950s or 1960s. Here, almost for the first time in English fiction, are working-class characters portrayed as living subjects rather than observed objects. They are fashioned unself-consciously from the inside, rather than patronizingly indulged or exhibited as sociological specimens. Lawrence was an extraordinarily path-breaking author, a courageous avant-gardist in an age of sedate English naturalism. There is nothing quite like *The Rainbow* or *Women in Love* anywhere in English fiction, as there are things like, say,

The Portrait of a Lady or *A Passage to India*. The entire British press united to brand this profoundly serious writer as a pornographer as soon as his death was announced, which might also win him a little credit with us liberal-minded moderns. They did so, incidentally, despite the fact that he described the last section of Joyce's *Ulysses* as 'the dirtiest, most indecent, most obscene thing ever written'. Being an Irish Catholic, Joyce is insufficiently puritanical for the English-Protestant Lawrence, not *serious* enough about sex.

On the other hand, there is nothing quite like *Kangaroo* or *The Plumed Serpent* either, a fact for which we have reason to feel profoundly grateful. The Lawrence who could create a Gertrude Morel or Ursula Brangwen, give us the vividly etched Marsh Farm of *The Rainbow*, or sustain the re-markable 'water-party' episode of *Women in Love*, could also perpetrate passages like these:

> Oh, and the beauty of the subjection of his loins, white and dimly luminous as he climbed over the side of the boat, made her want to die, to die. The beauty of his dim and luminous loins as he climbed into the boat, his back rounded and soft – ah, this was too much for her, too final a vision. She knew it, and it was fatal . . .
>
> Besides, she had a full mystic knowledge of his suave loins of darkness, dark-clad and suave . . . He sat still like an Egyptian Pharaoh, driving the car . . .
>
> It was a dark flood of electric passion she released from him, drew into herself. She had established a rich new circuit, a new current of passional electric energy, between the two of them, released from the darkest poles of the body and established in perfect circuit.
>
> (*Women in Love*)

With Lawrence at his worst, the sublime *is* the ridiculous. The woman in the final passage sounds more like an electrician than an eroticist. Law-rence's solemnity about sex is very masculine. Like many writers, however, his flaws are the flipside of his strengths. If his language can be cloying and rhapsodic, flushed with a strange, abstract intensity, this is not simply a failing. It is also because he is striving for a new kind of discourse altogether, one which will have broken with the clapped-out realism of the Victorian and Edwardian ages. And this puts him among the great avant-garde revolu-tionaries of his time. He is searching for a language which will capture the very rhythms and motions of 'being' itself, not just one which describes a birch tree or a bakery.

Such a language must cut deeper than the merely psychological. Lawrence is not really interested in feelings, which he seems to consider are the monopoly of the middle classes. His art aims to cut far below character, consciousness, personality, emotion, and all the tattered old baggage of literary realism. The novel must be a new kind of invention altogether, as strange, palpable and elemental as an Expressionist painting. This is why Lawrence pens such phrases as 'the fire went black in his veins', or 'the dark soul rose in him, his eyes glowed black and evil, he was fiendish in his thwarted soul', or 'he went out, dark and destroyed, his soul running its blood'. It is a purplish, melodramatic kind of prose which hovers between the physical and the spiritual, a style of writing in which nothing is commonplace but in which everything glows, palpitates, vibrates. His fiction X-rays things for the shimmering life within them. At various points in Lawrence's writing, different modes of being are said to be heavy or moist, dark or gleaming, pallid or glittering, tense or loose, electric or metallic, quivering, inert, lambent, closed-off, sharply separate, clenched, straining or wavering, akin to moonlight or hard fire, ashen, quick, fluid or ponderous, luminous, rat-like, unclean or abstracted. It is not the kind of thing one finds in Jeffrey Archer.

If Lawrence can sometimes be repellent and absurd, it is partly because he is so breathtakingly radical. His radicalism was political as well as spiritual – though as we shall see in a moment, it is a radicalism of the political right, not of the left. If he could write with embarrassingly breathless solemnity, he could also write (not least about Nature) with a sensuous delicacy and freshness of perception which matches the finest passages of English fiction. Lawrence had a kind of ragged, wayward Romantic genius, but he lacked classical tact and judiciousness. He did not know where to stop.

This is perhaps where we should pause to examine the well-known scandal that many of the most eminent writers of twentieth-century England held fairly obnoxious political views. Joseph Conrad, T. S. Eliot, Ezra Pound, W. B. Yeats, D. H. Lawrence, Wyndham Lewis: taken together, these authors can be convicted of racism, sexism, elitism, imperialism, homophobia and anti-Semitism. By and large, they are deeply hostile to democracy, scathing about equality, and darkly suspicious of the working-class movement. In their different ways, they believe in a 'corporate' social order to which individuals must sacrifice their freedom for the sake of a deeper identity. So what are we to say of these authors? Great art, dreadful politics? This is surely too feeble: art and politics do not inhabit different planets. It would be like claiming that the death-obsessed canvases of a painter had nothing to do with the fact that he was an accomplished serial killer.

It would be nearer the truth to venture the dangerous paradox: great art *because* of dreadful politics. All of the writers just mentioned were in various ways migrant figures, caught between different cultures and fully at home in none of them. Displaced, uprooted and insecure, they clung to the values of order, authority, hierarchy and tradition more tenaciously than some of their less unsettled colleagues. And this was a major source of their political conservatism. Yet the fact that they were more cosmopolitan than most native English writers also meant that they had at their disposal a richer span of cultural traditions. It also meant that they were personally exposed to a crisis of identity and tradition typical of their times; and all this nourished in them a more searching, ambitious art than the work of those more insulated from such disruptions. If they clung to right-wing values, they could also, precisely as outsiders, cast a more critical eye on conventional middle-class England than most of their more moderate fellow artists.

Conrad, Eliot, Pound, Yeats, Lewis and Lawrence were all right-wingers; but they were *radical* right-wingers, with little sympathy for the values of liberal, suburban, industrial-capitalist England. The anxieties which bred so much hatred in them, along with such a destabilizing desire for stability, also helped to breed an art finely sensitive to some of the key problems of their age. The major English literature of the early twentieth century sprang not from mainstream middle-class England, but from literal or metaphorical exiles (Virginia Woolf, like Lawrence, was of the latter kind). They were men and women whose visions were less parochial, as well as more fruitfully ambiguous, than those of most native English writers, and who could therefore pose some fundamental questions to that civilization as a whole. If this radicalism came largely from the political right, it was partly because of the weakness of the revolutionary left.

The most sinister example of right-wing radicalism in the modern age is fascism. Like the revolutionary left, fascism is critical of middle-class liberalism, parliamentary democracy, monarchy, individualism, the church, Enlightenment and unrestrained market forces. It is not to be confused with middle-of-the-road conservatism. Some of the most prominent names of the modern English literary canon can be loosely associated with this current. Most of them, to be sure, were not literally fascists. Lawrence rejected the movement partly because he was too much of an anarchic individualist to submit to the disciplines of a totalitarian state. He condemned Mussolini, and regarded fascism as a spurious solution to the crisis of middle-class civilization. It was really just more soulless mechanism. Nor did he relish its cult of the will. Somers, the hero of *Kangaroo*, revolts against the fascistic Kangaroo partly because Kangaroo has a political programme, which Lawrence's Romantic anarchism always finds hard to stomach.

Even so, there are aspects of Lawrence's thought – his hostility to the intellect ('Let all schools be closed at once'), his belief in so-called 'blood-consciousness', not to speak of his racism and anti-Semitism – which sail perilously close to the fascist creed. One might say that Lawrence was not a fascist rather in the sense that he was not a homosexual. He spurned both ways of life, while finding both unconsciously alluring. It is difficult, faced with right-wing modernist writings, to draw a line within it between a critique of reason which is plain irrationalist, and one which questions not reasoning as such, but the alienated, dominative forms of reason typical of the post-Enlightenment age. Fascism and feminism, for example, are both critical of orthodox Western rationality, but on quite different grounds. Lawrence at his finest represents an angry, eloquent protest against a mechanized reason which beats men and women down; at his most dangerous he invites us to discard rationality as itself a kind of alienation, and think with the blood and racial instincts instead. It was this aspect of his work which Bertrand Russell considered led straight to Auschwitz.

It is not then, *just* a case of dreadful politics – rather as with these authors it is not always a case of great art. Lawrence's racism, male chauvinism and cult of authoritarian leadership are abhorrent, as well as at times plain silly. But they sprang from a rejection of liberal, progressive middle-class values which also involved him in a critique of industrial capitalism – one quite as ferocious and unforgiving as that of the most revolutionary socialist. If we tend today to recall the male-chauvinist Lawrence, we tend to forget the Lawrence who wrote of his own civilization in terms like this:

> The industrial problem arises from the base forcing of all human energy into a competition of mere acquisition. . . . The great crime which the moneyed classes and promoters of industry committed in the palmy Victorian days was the condemning of the workers to ugliness, ugliness, ugliness: meanness and formless and ugly surroundings, ugly ideals, ugly religion, ugly hope, ugly love . . . ugly relationships between workers and employers.
>
> ('Nottingham and the Mining Country')

Lawrence was a divided writer in many senses, caught between working class and middle class, masculine and feminine, realism and non-realism,

community and individualism, the provincial and the cosmopolitan. But he was also born on a frontier between rural and industrial England, in a countryside warrened with coalmines, and could see the encroachment of the ugliness he speaks of from his own home windows as a child. Moreover, the Lawrence who came to despise democracy as the rule of the weak could also write of it like this:

> So, we know the first great purpose of Democracy: that each man shall be spontaneously himself – each man himself, each woman herself, without any question of equality or inequality entering in at all; and that no man shall try to determine the being of any other man, or of any other woman. . . . When I stand in the presence of another man, and I am my own pure self, am I aware of the presence of an equal, or of an inferior, or of a superior? I am not. When I stand with another man, who is himself, and when I am truly myself, then I am aware only of a Presence, and of the strange reality of Otherness. There is me, and there is *another being*. . . . There is no comparing or estimating.
>
> ('Democracy')

This belongs with Lawrence's anarchic individualism; but there is a wisdom about it even so. Indeed, it ranks among some of the finest commentaries on equality of our time. Marx believed that human equality was necessary; but he also thought that it was part of the way capitalist society homogenized human uniqueness, making everyone abstractly exchangeable with everyone else. Socialists are not unequivocal champions of equality, even though they struggle for it. The doctrine of equality, as Lawrence recognizes, can deny human difference or otherness quite as much as the idea of inequality can. For Lawrence, other people are not inferior or superior, but a sort of intimate strangeness which is finally unmasterable. Lydia Brangwen in *The Rainbow* is literally a foreigner to her husband Tom, which is a source of profound satisfaction to him. (For Lawrence, the fact that a man cannot understand what a woman is saying is of no great importance.) The unforgivable sin – what he called the blasphemy against the Holy Spirit – is to try to determine the being of another by force of will. This is not a belief which class-society finds particularly palatable.

Strangeness, however, was for Lawrence even more intimate than the presence of another. It was first of all a matter of one's presence to oneself. The key to Lawrence's thought – what he called in somewhat un-English manner his 'metaphysic' – is the idea that we are strangers to ourselves. This is hardly a novel insight in the era of Freud, but Lawrence's claim is not of this psychoanalytical kind. For him, the self is a law unto itself – not unto *oneself*. At the centre of each individual self is a kind of unfathomable darkness or otherness, which is what makes us what we are. What brings us into being as unique persons, in a familiar modern irony, is something – call it Life, the Infinite, the dark gods, the Holy Spirit, the unconscious – which is in itself profoundly impersonal. At the very core of the self lies that which is implacably other to it, though not hostile. If this being which is closer to us than we are to ourselves once bore the name of God, it has now been suitably secularized as what Lawrence calls the Other, the Infinite or spontaneous-creative life. When he commented that all art was religious, it was this above all that he had in mind. For Lawrence, we give utterance to what is not ourselves. When we are at our most authentic and spontaneous, we express a principle at work within us whose roots lie incomparably deeper than personality or individual identity.

In this sense, we are stewards of our selves rather than proprietors of them. Possession, Lawrence writes, is a kind of illness of the spirit. Will Brangwen in *The Rainbow* knows that 'he did not belong to himself'. Ursula Brangwen believes that 'Self was a oneness with the Infinite. To be oneself was a supreme, gleaming triumph of Infinity'. For Lawrence, as for William Blake, singularity and infinity are not opposites: on the contrary, simply to see something as it is, in all of its unique specificity, is to perceive a kind of infinity. Nothing is more singular than infinity, since there can be nothing beyond it. Our task is to be faithful transmitters of the Infinite, not to seek to create ourselves by our own actions. The self is not ours to create. It is a mysterious gift, which we should cherish and nurture as tenderly and disinterestedly as though it were the being of another. We simply have to stand by, so to speak, and watch this marvellous efflorescence known as our self flourish into life, without seeking to master or manipulate it. We cannot determine our own future. Tom Brangwen knows that it is his destiny to marry Lydia. When Mellors finds himself sexually aroused by Connie for the first time in *Lady Chatterley's Lover*, he submits to what he knows will follow as a kind of fate. At the deepest level, one has no choice in the matter.

Lawrence is not a liberal, concerned with freedom and decision. He is a kind of spiritual determinist for whom things secretly hang together in ways which resist the meddling of the human will. As he writes in his essay 'Democracy', there must be 'no pulling open the buds to see what the blossom will be. . . . We know the flower of today, but the flower of tomorrow is all beyond us'. If we wait patiently, unknowingly, on the next flourishing of the self, as Ursula Brangwen does at the end of *The Rainbow*, we experience a kind of secular equivalent of religious faith. But there is also a secular equivalent of sin, which is to deny the life in us by seeking dominion over ourselves or others.

This is a wise, deeply dangerous ethic. On the one hand, Lawrence has a wonderful sense of what the philosopher Martin Heidegger calls *Gelassenheit* – the capacity simply to let things and other people subsist in their own unique modes of being, without seeking to meddle with them. And this ethic is profoundly at odds with the capitalist or imperialist cult of the will, which Lawrence regarded as a moral obscenity. The so-called American dream – the idea that if you strain hard and long enough you can hammer yourself into whatever shape you please – would for him be the last word in blasphemy. Man's dominion over Nature, his masterful bending of the world to his overbearing will, is the calamity of modern humanism. It is the moment of our Fall into modernity – the moment in which human consciousness abstracts itself from its sensuous links with its world, and sets itself over against it. One can see the havoc this wreaks in Gerald Crich of *Women in Love*, a devotee of nation, efficiency, will-power and competition who is in the grip of 'the plausible ethics of productivity'.

Lawrence himself is not really a humanist, despite having a sense of human potential richer and deeper than many of his fellow English novelists. For him, the vital distinction is not between the human and the non-human, but between those who are sensitive transmitters of Life and those who are not. As far as that goes, a violet or a kangaroo may be more valuable than a duchess or a coalminer. Humanism involves the belief that we are agents of our own destiny, a belief which Lawrence rejects. We cannot help what we become. We can be midwives to ourselves, so to speak, assisting at the process of our own flowering into being by a reverent openness to whatever is dimly stirring within us; but we are not the sources of ourselves. We are not self-fashioners.

It is not up to us to choose whether to realize the self or not. Any impulse which springs spontaneously from the depths of the self demands its expression. How, then, do we judge which impulses are 'authentic', in the sense of stemming truly from the self, and which are not? By hearkening attentively to what our self is telling us. So if your self is murmuring seductively that you should strangle your footman, it would be a violation to suppress this impulse. For you, anyway, if not for the footman. In any case, Lawrence (or at least Birkin) holds the bizarre theory that people who get murdered ('murderees') are unconsciously asking for it. Nothing happens by accident.

Like many Romantics, Lawrence has a problem with notions of human will, agency and consciousness. At his most irrationalist, he tends to see consciousness as a kind of flaw in our make-up. It is a mechanistic categorizing and manipulating of things, which results in our being damagingly estranged from them. You can make a conscious cult of the sensuous and primitive, like Hermione in *Women in Love*; but this is just a decadent way of having life (or sex) in the head, rather than having it for real. For the drowsy infant to sunder the sensuous unity of its being by struggling into consciousness is itself a kind of Fall. Lawrence is exasperated with those who chuck babies encouragingly under the chin. He himself is more than half-inclined to leave such creatures to sleep on in their blissful Eden. In *Sons and Lovers*, he feels much the same about Mrs Morel's high-minded middle-class attempts to stir her working-class husband into a more conscious moral life.

Elsewhere in his writing, however, consciousness is seen more positively as a kind of enthralling adventure – a perpetual movement into a deeper, richer life, as Lawrence himself broke with what he sometimes saw as the creaturely sensuousness of the Nottinghamshire mining community to launch himself into a wider, freer world. He was aware that the Fall from Eden was a happy one – that it involved both gains and losses. Without it, he would not have been able to write; yet because of it, he wrote about a world which was irreparably lost. To *write* about a working-class upbringing, however sympathetically, is already to indicate that you are beyond it.

Spontaneity is an alternative to the brutal will of industrial capitalism, yet it is a peculiarly passive one. You cannot actually change this society as a whole, for to do so – to act politically – would require the very sort of will, agency and rational analysis which the society itself prizes so dearly. For Lawrence, movements like socialism and feminism are thus part and parcel of the situation they object to. They are yet more forms of mechanistic consciousness. Like capitalism, they lump unique individuals indifferently together. Indeed, this is true of thinking itself, which is one reason why Romantics like Lawrence are so wary of reason. To say 'rabbit', an inevitably general term, is on this rather curious view to violate the uniqueness of each particular rabbit. You must think with the blood and body, not with the falsely abstracting mind, a case which was championed among other places in Nazi Germany. If you want to know something vital, then (in the concluding words of *Aaron's Rod*) 'Your soul will tell you'. It is a version of the Protestant conscience or 'inner light' (Lawrence was brought up in a Methodist culture). It is not clear what you should do if your soul tells you to massacre every last child in the village.

Lawrence's individualism is a reaction against industrial capitalist society, but it is also a reflection of it. If it is a protest against uniformity and exploitation, it is also a kind of spiritual version of the unbridled individualism of the marketplace. Indeed, Lawrence is so radical an individualist that he has a problem with the whole idea of human relationship. For him, the self is not at root a relational matter. I know that I am I in distinction from the whole world, he argues in *Fantasia of the Unconscious*, and coming to relate to others is a secondary matter. The self is not born of its intercourse with the selves around it, but of the infinite. Identity is not for him a matter of difference; it is an absolute. You need the selves around you so that you can blossom into your own being; but the cornerstone of Lawrence's world is the individual self, not human relationship.

This is one of several reasons why, contrary to popular rumour, Lawrence's writing is not primarily concerned with sexuality. Others may help you to attain your selfhood; but they are not the source of it, and neither are they its goal. Finding your true selfhood in another is known as love, but Lawrence, like Birkin in *Women in Love*, does not rate this as the most precious state of being. There is a distinction between finding your fulfilment *in* another person, and – as Lawrence desires – finding it *through* them. To desire the Infinite may sound selfless enough; yet this Infinite, which dwells at the very core of one's identity, is really a word for one's own self-realization, which is rather less of an altruistic affair. Besides, if other people are vital for your own coming into being, they can also be obstacles to it. This is one reason why conflict is built into relationships in Lawrence's fiction, as it is not in, say, George Eliot or E. M. Forster. If every self is unique, yet needs other selves for its flowering into being, spiritual warfare seems unavoidable.

The power-struggles between Will and Anna Brangwen, Gertrude and Walter Morel, Paul and Miriam, or Gerald and Gudrun, illustrate this well enough. Will can bring Anna only a personal relationship, rather than providing her with a doorway to the Other. Lawrence's characters need relationship to be fulfilled, yet they are sometimes so intent on their own fulfilment that they find it hard to sustain. Otherness is a necessity for the self, but also a source of rage and resentment, as it is with Tom Brangwen when confronted with the enigmatic Lydia, or Will with the infuriatingly independent Anna. Otherness is both precious and problematic. Men and women are caught between wanting to possess and needing to let be.

Lawrence's basic attitude to human relationships, then, is an instrumental one. And this, ironically, is a spiritual version of the very 'mechanistic' capitalism he detests, for which people are only valuable for what you can get out of them. If human beings are not ends in themelves for car salesmen and company executives, neither are they in a different sense for Lawrence. Paul Morel actually has the impudence to refer to Miriam Leivers as his 'thrashing floor', meaning that she helps him to self-realization by acting as a sort of springboard for his beliefs. She was not, Paul remarks, what he reached for, but what he reached *with*. Later, when he meets Clara Dawes, it is not she whom he desires, but an impersonal otherness which she can bring him – something which 'happened because of her, but it was not her'. (It is typical of Paul's selfless sensitivity to women that when his mother's lips turn blue with heart trouble, he feels that someone is pushing a knife in *his* chest.)

The most fulfilling relationship in Lawrence's eyes is one in which each partner acts as a kind of opening on to an unfathomable otherness for the other. The personal relationship, so to speak, is triangulated by Otherness, which plays gooseberry between the two partners. Just as a mysterious otherness lies at the pith of the self, so it does at the heart of a fruitful human relationship. Birkin wants a relationship with Ursula which has passed beyond love, intimacy, emotion and all that old-fashioned humanistic baggage – a relationship beyond relationship, so to speak, one which has transcended the mess of the human into some pure, uncluttered, radically inhuman realm. In this condition, which is almost beyond the scope of language, the two partners will be together yet apart, each preserving a pure separateness of identity while polarized like stars. It is not hard to suspect that this is a fancy way of having no relationship at all.

Such a relationship is binding, fateful and eternal (Lawrence has no time for personal choice or so-called free love), at the same time as it somehow leaves you entirely free. If Lawrence is so preoccupied with sexuality, it is partly because men and women are for him fundamentally different kinds of animal, so that the risks of losing your identity in a sexual relationship are not so acute. On the other hand, the woman for the phallocentric Lawrence is forever trying to violate the man's proud singleness of being, so that relationships between them are bound to be contentious. Better, perhaps, to turn to relationships between men like that between Birkin and Gerald, which because they are supposedly not sexual (though a suppressed prologue to *Women in Love* speaks of a sexual attraction between the two), are less invasive and more cleanly polarized. A spot of naked wrestling on the hearthrug is less threatening to the self than the claustrophobic broodings of a Miriam, at least as Paul Morel experiences them in *Sons and Lovers*.

The love between a mother and her son, given the incest taboo, is also less likely to violate one's identity than an explicitly sexual liaison, which is one reason why Paul Morel renounces other women for his mother. On the other hand, mothers for Lawrence can be voraciously devouring creatures; and Paul (who ends up by killing his mother) has a largely unconscious rage and resentment against her exactly because she stands in the way of his sexual and spiritual fulfilment. He can neither possess her nor break free of her. In rejecting other women for his mother, he is also unconsciously rejecting her in them.

Lawrence has a well-nigh pathological horror of what he calls the 'horrid merging and mingling' of selves. A kind of spiritual standoffishness runs very deep in him, traceable back to his class situation as a child (he felt superior to the working class around him), as well as to his fear of being engulfed by women, not least by his possessive mother. Almost all the most admired figures in his fiction have a certain 'apartness', a proud separateness of self which is not always easy to distinguish from straightforward social snobbery. The fear of being invaded by another rouses him to murderously infantile fury. For Lawrence, you need to be apart and autonomous in your being, but not closed and self-complete, like Gudrun and Loerke in *Women in Love*.

The point of relationship, then, is to define the borders of the self, not to blur them. Ursula, who is still too emotional and interpersonal for Birkin's taste, is not entirely convinced by his theorizing, as well she might not be. It is not easy to say whether this is a brave utopian vision or a typical Lawrentian piece of misogyny. Perhaps it is just an elaborate way of trying to give Ursula the push. It seems too convenient a way for Birkin to reconcile his need for a relationship with his hankering to be left well alone. Which is to say, his desire for women with his aggression towards them.

There is something oddly ruthless about Lawrence's respect for otherness. Just as his talk of 'Life' can become more abstract and dehumanizing the more reverently he insists on it, so there is a kind of anti-humanism about the idea of otherness in his work which is close to that of the various artistic avant-gardes of his day. 'Life' is remorseless in its demands: it seizes upon a person or a thing as a means to its own self-expression, but it has a kind of Darwinian indifference to any individual in particular. It will discard one in order to move on to another, rather as Ursula in *The Rainbow* unceremoniously ditches Skrebensky, or Connie Chatterley her disabled husband. If you are unable to act as a transmitter for it, Life will merely toss you nonchalantly aside. And this is not something to be regretted.

Indeed, Birkin in *Women in Love* yearns for the day when the human race itself will pass away, and the life-force will discover some other, less disreputable medium of its expression. There is nothing absolute about humanity, just as there is nothing absolute about any specific social institution or system of belief. They are just the transient forms which Life assumes for its own impenetrable purposes. When they become ossified and inert, Life will cast them off and evolve beyond them. Things for Lawrence, including men and women, only have reality in a derivative kind of way: they are real only in so far as they give utterance to the sole absolute there is, which is Life itself. Social institutions – feminist movements, trade unions, the care of the sick, the rearing of the young – are just so much external 'mechanism', which Lawrence finds it hard to take seriously. Whether this is a revolutionary vision or a bleakly alienated one is then a question worth raising.

Life cannot be worsted. If it fails to find fulfilment in one spot, it will shift its abode to another. It is indestructible, which is to say that Lawrence's vision, unusually for a major modernist artist, is triumphalistic and anti-tragic. Just as some Victorians believed that historical progress was unstoppable, so Lawrence feels much the same about Life. To fail to affirm Life is to do dirt on it; to doubt that it will prevail is a squalid betrayal. Lawrence's novels do not end tragically but tentatively, as you wait in darkness for some inevitable rebirth or, like Paul Morel, turn your face resolutely from the dead to the quick. Those who deny life are neither tragic, evil nor genuinely challenging, since they are almost literally nothing. Like Skrebensky, Gerald Crich and Clifford Chatterley, they are just negations of being, hollow parodies of the living, empty husks sucked dry of spontaneity. There is nothing to be pitied in their failure; if you are confined to a wheelchair and sexually impotent like Clifford, that is just too bad. As for Gerald Crich, the 'creative mystery' will in the end simply dispense with him, as a sort of mutant or monster who has failed to develop properly. He is one of Life's abortions. Gerald, unusually for a Lawrentian life-denier, is placed at the very centre of the novel in which he figures, since it has other sorts of interest in him; but most of the other life-deniers in Lawrence's work can simply be shucked off like a pair of old shoes. Like the American dream, he has no time for failure. As for James Joyce, though for rather different reasons, there can be no final breakdown or absolute loss.

Lawrence wrote novels much more original and ambitious than *Sons and Lovers*, but he never achieved anything so superbly authentic, so magnificently free of false notes. Later, there were to be whole symphonies of them. His prose here manages to be at once imaginative and workaday, vivid and precise without being self-consciously crafted. There is nothing of the portentousness or phoney prophetic tone of some of the later writings. Though Lawrence himself is hardly remarkable for his humour, he can wonderfully capture in this novel the dry, sardonic repartee of the English working class.

Like all realist works, *Sons and Lovers*'s view of the world is skilfully edited. It is difficult not to feel, for example, that a less prejudiced observer than Lawrence might offer a more positive account of Walter Morel and a more negative one of his wife Gertrude, if we may be allowed for a moment to conceive of these characters as existing outside their author's mind. The novel admires Morel in some ways; but he also represents the working-class community from which his son Paul must break away, and this lowers his profile fairly drastically. As Paul himself moves to the forefront, becoming a kind of substitute husband for his emotionally unfulfilled mother, his father is shifted into the background as a dwindled, diminished figure.

This, to be sure, is in one sense plain realism. The traditional working-class father tends to take a back seat at home, which is largely a place where he recuperates from his hard labour at work. The exhausting, oppressive toil of the mine or factory is likely to make for a certain passivity, even irritability or outright violence, at home. Morel's lack of education makes it hard for him to articulate his feelings, or to relate to his children other than by his practical skills. Besides, the working-class man may come like Morel to exert a despotic authority in the household partly to compensate for his lack of power at work. If he selfishly expects the family to centre on himself, it is partly because the workplace very obviously does not. The novel tells us with a rather suspect rhetorical flourish that Morel has 'denied the god in him'; but even if this is true, it has more to do with his burdensome social conditions than with some spiritual deficiency. It is not as though Morel has been reading Lawrence's essays on spontaneous-creative life and decided that it is not for him.

The young Lawrence, brought up in a coal-mining region of the English Midlands, must surely have understood a good deal of this. But the social pressures on Walter Morel are for the most part edited out by the novel, leaving him more open to criticism than might otherwise be the case. The novel, so to speak, largely takes his wife's side against him. Because of Morel's alienation from the household, one caused in part by the division of labour between men and women, the children find emotional refuge in their mother, who is then spared some of the criticisms which the novel might otherwise justifiably direct at her. Mrs Morel is in fact a selfish, quietly domineering, ferociously possessive woman who almost ruins her son's chances of sexual and spiritual independence. Because she has social aspirations, she represents the force which pushes Paul out into the wider world; it is he who will vicariously achieve for her what she lacks. At just the same time, however, her suffocating love for her son pulls him back in, and this contradiction threatens to tear him apart. In urging him on to mature individual identity, she also forestalls it. In the end, Paul takes part in the mercy-killing of his mother, an ambiguous act of love, revenge and self-liberation. Lawrence's terror and hatred of women, later to emerge in full ugly flow, is already present in this novel, but mutedly, subliminally, in a way which protects the mother from the full infantile fury of the son.

Caught in this crippling Oedipal conflict, Paul is almost broken. Yet much of his animus against his mother is displaced on to other women – not least on to Miriam, who one senses would have an interesting story to deliver had the novel seen fit to hand her the microphone. What Paul feels as Miriam's dread of being possessed may well be a projection on to her of his own anxieties. As often, however, what a narrative tells us is somewhat at odds with what it shows. Lawrence's artistic integrity cannot help but reveal the more congenial aspects of the father, just as it cannot help alerting us to a more caustic view of the mother. In the figure of Baxter Dawes, in some ways a Walter Morel surrogate, the novel might be seen as making unconscious reparation for its denigration of Walter, as well as showing Paul himself in a fairly negative light. It is Baxter, who first enters the book as a sort of stage villain or stereotypical lout, who can finally fulfil Clara the independent feminist, not the more sophisticated, theoretically minded Paul. Clara is there partly for us to measure the degree of damage which Mrs Morel has wrought in her drifting, spiritually undermined son. The novel may look at things largely from Paul's own standpoint, conspiring in its very narrative structure with his own skewed vision; but it is also conscious enough that he is something of a prig and snob.

In this novel, Lawrence is not only writing about the working class, but literally writing himself out of it. It is predictable, then, that his sympathies lie for the most part with Gertrude Morel, who symbolizes that 'venture into consciousness'. Even so, we are made aware of something of what is lost in this gain. Paul, who speaks Standard English most of the time but can slip into the Nottinghamshire dialect in moments of tenderness, remarks that one draws one's ideas from the middle class and one's warmth and life from the working class. Lawrence himself tries to combine the two by having a number of big ideas about life. For Paul, however, there are dangers involved in extricating himself from his working-class community; and the novel's downgrading of his father may be among other things a way of diminishing the pain of this loss.

It is also a way of underestimating the size and nature of that privation. What Paul is leaving behind him in abandoning the working class is not just warmth and life, but something quite as precious. The miners who are portrayed by Lawrence as sensuous, passive, inarticulate creatures were responsible, in the year in which *Sons and Lovers* was completed, for the greatest industrial strike which Britain had ever witnessed. At the time of the book's appearance, class warfare was rife throughout the British coalfields. These were not the actions of sensuous hulks. In leaving behind the real-life Walter Morels, Lawrence was also exchanging political solidarity for a rootless individualism. This, to be sure, was not his fault; it belonged to the Faustian pact which middle-class society makes with its less socially eminent members, a few of whom are allowed to climb the social ladder. A ladder can hold one or two people only, not a whole community at the same time. The idea of advancement thus becomes inseparable from the notion of self-interest.

In one sense, it is not surprising that Lawrence should associate working men with a dumb, brooding sensuousness and women with a more aspiring, emancipated vision. This, after all, was the lesson he drew from the contrast between his proletarian father and petty-bourgeois mother. In the astonishing set-piece opening of *The Rainbow*, it is the men of the farm who turn inward to the blood-heat of the beasts, and the women who gaze expectantly outward to a broader horizon. Anna Brangwen, like Ursula after her, desires to be singular and separate, whereas her husband Will wants a sensuous merging. In another sense, however, this dichotomy is indeed surprising, since this is exactly the opposite of how Lawrence characterizes the so-called male and female principles in his 'metaphysical' writings. The male principle, in a commonplace piece of sexist stereotyping, is a matter of power, spirit, consciousness, activism, individuation; the female principle, in an account with a curiously familiar ring to it, is one of flesh, sensuality, intimacy, permanence, passivity.

This then provides Lawrence with two mutually contradictory reasons for hating women. On the one hand, they stand for the sensuous flesh which inhibits one's (male) drive to freedom and self-realization. Yet they can themselves be symbolic of that life of freedom, and so can be blamed for tearing you from the bodily instincts, the human community and your sensuous roots in Nature. Lawrence also arranges the male and female principles on an historical axis. The first age was one of Law, flesh, woman; the second, which is now drawing to a close, is one of Love, man, spirit, idealism; and the coming era will dialectically unite the two. When in doubt, one posits a dialectic. It is because Mrs Morel combines both principles that she almost destroys her son.

This raises the vexed question of the relations between Lawrence's 'metaphysic' and his fiction – or, one might say, between his theory and his practice. He is, as we have suggested, unusual among English novelists for his spiritual absolutism. Like many a modernist artist, he is an enemy of compromise, routine and half-measures, depicting the world in starkly dualistic terms. Unlike Jane Austen or Thomas Hardy, he deals in extreme states of ecstasy, dissolution, affirmation and spiritual vacancy. Yet once all this is transposed into fiction, it often emerges in modified shape.

Like Marxist critics, Lawrence believed that artists often unwittingly betrayed their own theoretical purposes. Every art-work, he thought, must contain a system of doctrine (which he called 'law'), but also a critique of it (which he called 'love'). If Lawrence is an absolutist about Life, he is a relativist about the novel form itself, which he sees as provisional, unstable and open-ended. Almost all of his novels end on an open, interrogative note. The novel for him is a perpetual flow and recoil of sympathies, a delicate balance of forces which cannot be nailed down to any dogmatic system. If you try to do that, he comments, it will simply get up and walk away with the nail. This is why he urges us to trust the tale rather than the teller. This suspicion of dogma is one heartily endorsed by the liberal, but Lawrence is not to be enlisted into these ranks. If he is an enemy of system, it is because he believes that Life is an absolute which will brook no constraint. His open-endedness, ironically, is in the name of an utter certainty.

Realist novels, by virtue of their form, have to take account of a plurality of viewpoints, as well as showing how abstractions stand up to the test of concrete experience. Like a lot of writers, Lawrence is at his least impressive when his fiction obediently reflects his ideology, rather than putting it into question. The execrable *The Plumed Serpent* may serve as an example. But to say this is not to give comfort to the philistines (who sometimes call themselves aesthetes) for whom art is one thing and ideas quite another. For someone who was both Anglo-Saxon and anti-intellectual, a not infrequent combination, Lawrence is oddly, indeed passionately, concerned with ideas. *Women in Love* is a novel which deeply distrusts the intellect, yet which at one point puts two of its characters on a train simply so that they can discuss ideas without their author having to bother to describe the world around them in the meantime. This is one of several ways in which Lawrence is an odd man out in F. R. Leavis's 'great tradition' of the English novel.

Sons and Lovers is a straightforwardly realist work, though there are one or two premonitory flashes of its author's later, more intensely 'psychical' language, not least in the scenes with Clara Dawes. With *The Rainbow*, we find ourselves cusped between that realism and a more adventurous modernist experiment. Or, to put it another way, the language of realist description, and the language of the inner life, are beginning to break apart, as Lawrence himself moves further from his childhood community into his more isolated, uprooted adult life. *The Rainbow* preserves the structure of the great nineteenth-century realist narrative, charting the history of a family over several generations; but as this narrative evolves it presses more deeply into an inward spiritual history, which gradually comes to take precedence over its social realism.

This makes for a powerfully original fiction, one of the finest in English writing. The novel has the quick, vivid realism of *Sons and Lovers*: we note Lawrence's characteristic joy in ordinary things (a tiny flower, a ship-like goose, a cell glimpsed down a microscope). But it blends these delicately delineated portraits of farmhouse and school classroom with an extraordinarily innovative language of the inner life. There are things in the novel which George Eliot would delightedly recognize, and others which would leave her deeply bemused. When this language of being (as we might call it) loses touch with the real world, it becomes rhapsodic, liturgical, full of a breathlessly abstract intensity: 'Blind and destroyed, he pressed forward, nearer, nearer, to receive the consummation of himself, be received within the darkness which should swallow him and yield him up to himself'. (This is a relatively mild example: there are far more oratorical stretches in the book, not least in the 'cathedral' scene.)

The result is a revolutionary new idiom – but one which threatens to devalue the common social world. The vision of *The Rainbow* is at once more intense and more alienated than that of early novels like *The White Peacock* and *Sons and Lovers*, and the two qualities are closely related. There is a growing rift between what *The Rainbow* calls 'the vision world and the weekday world'. Ursula Brangwen and some other characters have a haughtily superior sense that the 'external' world is brittle and unreal compared with the depth and opulence of the inner life. What we are given, in effect, is an alienated vision of an alienated world. A social order which genuinely is soulless, acquisitive, ugly and mechanistic is portrayed so externally and disdainfully, from such a lofty height, that these qualities are exacerbated by the very way they are perceived. This is Lawrence looking at an England he once knew from the inside from a long way off.

The form of the novel struggles to hold these divergent discourses of inner and outer together, and only just pulls it off. Lawrence's favoured characters are natural aristocrats, like the changeling child Paul Morel. By the time of *The Rainbow*, they have become elitists of the blood for whom (as Ursula comments) democracy is suitable only for degenerate races. The Protestant doctrine of the elect, for which only a privileged minority of those moving in the mysterious darkness of the Godhead are selected for salvation, has been translated into the outlook of a coterie of bohemian intellectuals who scorn the world around them. The more audaciously experimental Lawrence grows, the more divorced from common sympathies he becomes.

Even so, *The Rainbow* does not entirely abandon social hope; and this, given the mechanized, alienated industrial world it portrays, is a remarkably courageous keeping of faith. We are told in the book's apocalyptic final passage that the rainbow, symbol of human regeneration, is still living in the blood of the 'hard-scaled' creatures (ordinary men and women) who creep on the corrupted earth. We have seen little evidence of this in the novel, and viewing people as insects is hardly the finest compliment one could pay them; but the claim, even so, is heartening to hear. The rainbow is certainly still living in the blood of Ursula Brangwen, who has cast off the avatars of a mechanical civilization like so many sloughed skins. The militaristic, spiritually vacuous Skrebensky has been sexually annihilated, his baby will be lost, and the lesbian Winifred Inger is married off to a machine-worshipping colliery manager – a suitable punishment, in Lawrence's eyes, for such a despicably mechanistic sexual practice.

By the time of *Women in Love*, the social has become almost entirely subordinated to the symbolic. In place of a realist grand narrative, we have a kind of fragmented montage of scenes ('Totem', 'Water-Party', 'Moony', 'Rabbit' and the like) which form only a vague temporal sequence. The form of the novel itself intimates that there is no longer any hope to be placed in history, as there was in *The Rainbow*'s evolution towards a more emancipated spiritual condition. In that novel, you took what was of value from the previous generation and tried to unfold it further. The spirit of George Eliot could still be detected. In the avant-gardist *Women in Love*, history and genealogy are to be cast off in the name of some ineffable new creation. If children were vital beings in *The Rainbow*, they are negligible in *Women in Love*. Knowing where you come from – family ties, local loyalties and generational bonds – will no longer help you. History has now been frozen, arrested, spatialized, as Western civilization trembles on the brink of the apocalyptic crack-up which is the First World War. (The book's original title was *The Latter Days*.) Through this degraded, dehistoricized world, a group of drop-outs, deadbeats and spiritually disinherited artists, drift aimlessly in search of power, love, sensation or salvation. They move in a limbo or time-warp, trapped between the unusably old and the inconceivably new. It is not clear whether they are the fag-end of the past or the first glimmerings of the future.

Like *The Rainbow*, this is an extraordinarily original achievement. In its own bizarre way, *Women in Love* is a hair-raisingly revolutionary text. In order to say what he wants, Lawerence has been compelled to transgress the limits of realism for a startling new kind of fictional form. Realism of a kind lingers on, but most of the novel's major scenes provoke such a reading only to defy it. It is not in every sedate English suburb that a bridegroom chases his bride up the church path, a neurotic socialite bashes the man she loves with a paperweight, two male friends engage in nude wrestling, an inspector of schools rolls naked among primroses and manically stones the moon's reflection, and a female artist dances hypnotically before a group of cows. (Birkin, incidentally, is about as convincing an inspector of schools as Dorothea Brooke would be a barmaid.)

Women in Love is about a civilization which trembles on the brink of being dissolved, and the novel dramatizes two ways of responding to this crisis – responses which look alike but are fundamentally different. You can take the path of a Rupert Birkin and embrace dissolution in the trust that the Infinite will in time conjure some inconceivable new life from the historical wreckage. If you are prepared to engage in an act of revolutionary self-abandonment, relinquishing love, history, property, society, feeling, personality, even the idea of humanity itself, chaos and decay may finally turn out to be fertile. Or you can take the path of 'decadence' and delight in corruption and dissolution as ends in themselves, like Gudrun and Loerke. You can derive a cerebral thrill from the 'corrupt gorgeousness' of social disintegration by living it out self-consciously, like Hermione, thus destroying spontaneity in the act of celebrating it.

The choice between Birkin and this cult of decadence is one between rejecting the social conventions in some spiritually profound sense, and being 'unconventional' in the most trivial, fashionable of ways. Such modish iconoclasts, as Lawrence wrote in an essay on the novelist John Galsworthy, are 'merely social beings behaving in an anti-social manner'. It is a matter of distinguishing a creative kind of nothingness from a cynical nihilism. In the first case, death is in the service of life; in the second case, you reap a kind of spectral parody of life from a perverse joy in destruction and disintegration.

For this novel, authentic living flows only from a Birkin-like readiness to abandon a false way of life and submit to a necessary death. (For Lawrence, one expression of this life-in-death is sodomy – of the heterosexual kind, needless to say – which plunges into the dissolution of the 'excremental' only to find a renewal of creative life there. The act in his view has the additional advantage of purging uppity women of their pride and prudishness.) Gudrun, Gerald and Loerke, by contrast, along with the raffish crew of hedonists of cafe society, are in the terrifying grip of the death drive, which cajoles them into taking a kind of obscene pleasure in their own disintegration. Loerke is Jewish, probably homosexual, and an aesthete or formalist who divorces art from life. He is cynical, decadent, flippantly playful, rootlessly cosmopolitan, and from a socially inferior background (a 'sewer rat'). It would be hard to assemble a figure more thoroughly odious in the eyes of his author, unless one were to throw in genocide and paedophilia for good measure. Loerke is detestable not least because he is in some respects his creator's monstrous alter ego. As for Gerald, his dominative will is just this death drive turned outwards, an aggressive assertion of the ego beneath which he is inwardly lapsing into the putrescence of non-being.

Like most oppositions, however, this one can be partly dismantled As Gamini Salgado excellently puts it: 'Corruption and regeneration, orgiastic abandonment and liberating freedom, insane will and necessary self-discipline, proud singleness and egoistic separateness . . . are constantly losing their distinctiveness . . .'.[1] Birkin may ultimately trust to life, but he, too, is a decadent of sorts, half-in-love with death. Death is the final inhumanity, and as such is an image of the ultra-human relationship which Birkin desires with an understandably reluctant Ursula. The novel's other, more negative image of the ultra-human is the machine; yet even this has a seductiveness about it in its freedom from messy inwardness and self-indulgent emotion. The machine, like the death drive, is a kind of simulacrum of life, one which exploits living energies for its own deathly ends. It imposes a discipline which is both oppressive and energizing. There is a gleaming aesthetic purity about mechanisms such as Gerald's coal mines, which have their own perverse allure. The machine has an impersonality which Lawrence admires

– one that it shares with death, the Infinite, and the kind of 'non-human' relationship which Birkin is listlessly seeking.

The question, however, is whether what might be called the radical anti-humanism of *Women in Love* is on the side of life or death. On the one hand, Birkin's 'philosophical' anti-humanism is a critique of a diseased humanity in the name of Life. On the other hand, his world-weary misanthropy is anti-human in a rather less visionary sense: people don't matter, some of them are better off dead, humanity is a mistake, the common people are inferior creatures, the world would be better off if the human race were exterminated, and other such right-wing ecological ravings. All of this springs not from hope, but from a savagely apocalyptic despair and self-loathing at the very heart of the book. Birkin is not of course identical with his author, but something of his virulent contempt for humanity can be found in some of Lawrence's own recorded words. Rarely has a piece of fiction spoken up so clamorously for Life while betraying such revulsion for the actual thing. Birkin and Ursula may belong to a spiritual vanguard, attuned to some unrepresentable utopia on the far side of the collapse of civilization; but it is never easy to distinguish a vanguard from an elite, whose deepest wish is not to transform the common life but to extricate themselves from it. How does being a revolutionary differ from being a snob? Is Birkin sickened by *this* civilization, or by civilization as such?

A similar ambiguity can be found in the novel's treatment of Thomas Crich, Gerald's mine-owning father. The transition from Thomas's to Gerald's management of the mines is symbolic of a deeper historical shift from a liberal, paternalistic Christian humanism to a mechanical, ruthlessly impersonal order based on power and will. Or, as Lawrence puts it in his essay 'Blessed are the Powerful': 'The reign of love is passing, and the reign of power is coming again'. It is an evolution from female 'heart' to male 'soul'. The reign of love for Lawrence includes the clapped-out 'feminized' creeds of liberalism, Judaism, Christianity, democracy, socialism, pacifism, humanitarianism and women's emancipation, all of which bring out the bellicose Nietzschean Superman in him. It encompasses what he calls in *Fantasia of the Unconscious* 'beastly benevolence, and foul good-will, and stinking charity, and poisonous ideals'.

Women in Love is a novel which has the word 'love' in its title but little of it between its covers. Birkin believes the word should be banned, Gerald isn't up to it, and Gudrun prefers the sleek eroticism of power. The old humanistic order, with its pity, altruism and cult of the personal, is part of what has gone under with the global war and the crack-up of liberal civilization, and Lawrence is not sorry to see the back of it. With admirable shrewdness, the novel recognizes that old Crich's brand of humanitarianism can be simply the acceptable face of capitalism. It is the sentimentalism of the manufacturer who fires a worker only to weep over his famished child. Humanitarianism is the tearful visage which humanism turns to the world – humanism in the negative sense of the human domination of Nature. It is as impotent as humanism is all-powerful. With Gerald's inheritance of his father's role, the old order gives way to this dynamic, death-dealing cult of the masterful will. If the poor for Thomas Crich are signs of God's kingdom, they are a foul, whining bunch of parasites for his hard-headed Nietzschean son.

With extraordinary perceptiveness, *Women in Love* sees that liberal humanitarianism, the cult of the dominative will, and a kind of decadent sensationalism are all secretly facets of the same reality. The 'humane' can be no more than a mask for dominion, while decadence is a turning of the will back upon one's body and a revelling in its destructive power. What is supposed to break with all this is the ethic of Birkin. Yet it is not only that Birkin is inevitably complicit in what he rejects. It is also that he cannot articulate this rejection in definitive terms, since he could do so only in the degraded, outmoded language of the present. He is an avant-gardist, who can image the future only negatively, in gestures of radical renunciation. And these gestures bind him to the world he detests in their very disgustedness. It is a familiar modernist dilemma, from Theodor Adorno to Michel Foucault: to propose alternatives to the present is to perpetuate its deathly logic.

Unfortunately, Lawrence failed to take a hint from his own character's reticence. In novels like the unfortunately entitled *Aaron's Rod*, as well as in *Kangaroo* and *The Plumed Serpent*, he tries to resolve the deadlock by turning Gerald's cult of power, which ends up for Gerald with death in the snow, to revolutionary rather than conservative ends. Social realism, along with loving relationships between men and women, are now abandoned for a proto-fascist veneration of power, 'blood hierarchy', racial purity, male bonding, charismatic leadership, the revival of 'primitive' ritual and mythology, and the brutal subjugation of women. This is not a complete break with Lawrence's earlier thinking, not least because power for him is not a matter of the will – of what he rather tautologically calls 'mental consciousness' – but of the blood and body.

Power is male and positive, whereas the will is female and negative. Women should not oppose their petty wills to men's noble schemes, just as

they should not reap active enjoyment from sex. The so-called female principle of compassion, idealism and sexual tenderness ('slimy, creepy personal
intimacy', as Aaron Sisson calls it in *Aaron's Rod*) must yield to the male
principle of discipline, separateness and mystical impersonality. Lawrence's
fantasies of male supremacy, blood brotherhood and the mutilation of meekly
submissive women reach their revolting apogee in stories like 'The Woman
Who Rode Away'.[2] As he grows more ideologically strident, the forms of
his fiction begin to fall apart. Torn between myth, ritual, fragmentary plot,
spiritual autobiography, social documentation and shrill didacticism, these
tetchy, self-dramatizing, misanthropic fictions seem incapable of sustaining
an adequate narrative. The daring loosening-up of literary form of *Women in
Love* now threatens to lapse into sheer disintegration.

Raymond Williams writes of Lawrence's career in *Culture and Society 1780–
1950* as the tragedy of the working-class boy who did not live to come
home.[3] If this is sentimental in one sense, it is accurate enough in another.
Having left the experience of human community behind him in his mining
village, Lawrence spent the rest of his life in a series of doomed, increasingly
desperate efforts to recreate it, all the way from Mexico to Australia. His
writing was a vital part of this exploration. He was not, after all, just an
individualist, though that, by and large, is what his history forced him to
become. On the contrary, he remarked of himself that the instinct of community ran deeper in him than the sexual one, and wrote in his *Studies in
Classic American Literature* that 'Men are free when they are in a living homeland, not when they are straying and breaking away'. Birkin's idea of freedom, by contrast, is a purely negative one – a question of voiding, renouncing,
being left alone.

'Our civilization', Lawrence comments in an essay entitled 'The State of
Funk', '. . . has almost destroyed the natural flow of common sympathy
between men and men, and men and women. And it is this that I want to
restore to life'. If art had a point for him, it was because it could renew vital
sympathies which had gone dead. If sexuality mattered so much, it was
because it was one of the few places left in an alienated world where
'spontaneous-creative life' could be experienced most intensely. But that life
was relevant to a great deal more than sexuality itself.

In the end, Lawrence did come home, at least after a fashion. *Lady
Chatterley's Lover* is the fruit of that return, a novel in which Lawrence
reverts after years of self-exile to the provincial England he knew, and tries
to salvage from it something of value. Mellors, the novel's male protagonist,
is among other things an 11th-hour attempt to rehabilitate his father, thus

making reparation for his portrayal as Walter Morel. Mellors combines impersonal male power with 'female' tenderness, and working-class roughness with a dash of middle-class education. He is the last of Lawrence's natural aristocrats; but this means that he is hardly typical of the 'common people' with whom Connie Chatterley seeks to unite. Mellors has lived abroad, has acquired some education, and despises his own class, not least its 'vulgar' womenfolk. In the first draft of the novel he was even a Communist.

Connie revolts against her husband's 'nasty, sterile want of sympathy', and turns to Mellors instead. But precisely because Mellors is not really a common working man, she can do so while continuing to share several of her husband's more unpleasantly elitist attitudes. She, too, is 'absolutely afraid of the industrial masses', who are now no longer recognizable individuals like Walter Morel or Tom Brangwen but 'weird fauna of the coal-seams'. Retrieving words like 'fuck' from their obscene misuses, while an honourable enough task, is hardly likely to make much of a dent in this alienated vision. *Lady Chatterley's Lover* is a courageous performance, but not because it talks about penises and vaginas. It is courageous because despite everything – exile, fury, loneliness, despair, raging aggression – Lawrence refuses even at this belated point to deny what he sees as the inexhaustible creativity of the human spirit.

JAMES JOYCE

It is debatable whether James Joyce should really figure in this book, as he was not an English writer and did not live in Britain. Indeed, had he been asked whether he was English, he might well have replied in the words of his friend Samuel Beckett, whose response to the query was 'Au contraire'. Joyce was a citizen of an English colony, and it was, he remarked, his freedom from English social and literary convention which lay at the source of his talent. What he meant, perhaps, was that as a colonial from a country whose cultural traditions were notably fragmented, he was freed from the constraints of an established literary canon and tradition, and could therefore experiment all the more boldly. He could pick and mix his cultures and linguistic forms.

Irish history was indeed notoriously crisis-ridden and disrupted, a story of wars, rebellions, famines and emigrations with little of the cultural continuity of Britain. It was an Irishman, Edmund Burke, who preached cultural continuity to the British, aware of its lamentable absence at home. History, as Stephen Dedalus of *Ulysses* famously remarks, is a nightmare from which he is trying to awaken, and art, one might say, is his alarm clock. *Ulysses* itself was written during the catastrophe of the First World War. Nowadays, as Irish writers feel the gigantic shadow of Joyce fall across their computers, *Ulysses* itself has become the nightmare from which Ireland is trying to awaken. This sense of crisis and catastrophe is not the way the English typically regard their history.

Literary realism depends on a degree of social stability and continuity, and there was precious little of that in the turbulent history of Ireland. This is one of several ways in which colonialism and modernist experiment are closely related. To some extent, then, England relied on its colonial subjects

to write its modernist literature for it. Indeed, the English are past masters at claiming as their own those of their colonials or postcolonials who make good, from Oliver Goldsmith and Oscar Wilde to V. S. Naipaul and Salman Rushdie, and Joyce has been accordingly welcomed into the English literary pantheon. Those Irish who fail to make good are a different matter. When the Irish actor Richard Harris won an award for one of his films, the English newspapers announced: 'English actor honoured'. When he was arrested for a brawl in a bar, the English press reported: 'Irish actor arrested'.

Joyce's work stands out among the other great modernist writers in several ways. It has, to begin with, the quality of being magnificently commonplace. Not just banal, trivial and prosaic, but triumphantly, remorselessly so. Rarely has so poetic a writer had such a prosaic imagination. As we have seen, he once described himself as having a mind like a grocer, by which he presumably meant that he dealt in mundane realities, but also perhaps that he dealt with them in an orderly, row-stacking fashion. Like Beckett, Joyce has a fastidiously scholastic turn of mind, as befits one who hailed from a Roman Catholic culture and was deep in Dante and Aquinas. Both Irishmen are obsessional categorizers, combining the same few bits and pieces into ever more ingeniously pointless patterns, squeezing more and more elaborate possibilities out of a meagre set of materials. This systematizing cast of mind is far removed from the English liberal sensibility, with its delight in the muddled, diffuse and open-ended.

Indeed, what is striking about Beckett's writing is the scrupulous exactness with which it permutates uncertainties and ambiguities. His art makes a ritual out of vagueness. It prefers paucity to prodigality. Joyce was fascinated by the alphabet, a mere 26 elements from which you could generate a countless number of items. Like a structuralist, he seems to have thought that all stories, events and individuals were variations on the same few types. Everyone in *Ulysses* and *Finnegans Wake* is a recycled version of somebody else. There is a fundamental solidarity to human existence across space and time, however estranged from one another modern men and women may feel.

This is far removed from English liberal humanism, with its belief in the uniqueness of the individual life. Perhaps the true Joycean hero is less Stephen Dedalus or Leopold Bloom than language itself. The interior monologue in Joyce, which gives us privileged access to the inner life of an individual, is quite often a collection of cliches and banalities. There is no suggestion, as there is, say, in Virginia Woolf, that the inner life is necessarily more

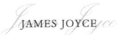

precious than the outer one. As far as uniquely portrayed characters go, *Ulysses* contains a stage Irishman (Mulligan), a stage Englishman (Haines), a stereotypical poetic poseur (Stephen), a Man of the People (Bloom) and a woman, Molly, who seems as much some Jungian Anima or Eternal Female as a particular Dublin housewife.

Despite his suspicion of mass politics, Joyce is in some ways a collectivist thinker, the product of a preurban, preindustrial nation which had only a marginal middle class and a repressively corporate church. There was thus little tradition in Ireland of liberal individualism. This is one reason why Joyce is so beguiled by myth, which in Ireland has been as plentiful as potatoes. Myth can be seen as the collective unconscious of the race, its storehouse of shared symbols and archetypes. It is preindividual, rather as the modernists are in search of a postindividualist order; and the two can consequently merge in curious ways in the work of authors like Joyce, Lawrence and T. S. Eliot.

Modernism is a high-brow affair, not usually as captivated as Joyce is by the dingy and everyday. If it takes an interest in the common people, it is more as an idealized 'folk' than as common-or-garden city-dwellers. Alternatively, as with Flaubert or T. S. Eliot, it may plunge into the gutter but signal its well-bred distaste in the act of doing so. There is a difference between genuine sympathy for everyday life, and an artistic cult of the commonplace. Some modernist writing admires 'primitive' vitality, the peasant or the South Sea islander, and has a smack of spiritualized earthiness about it; but it is not really at home with the kind of non-exotic types you run into in the supermarket.

Joyce had an almost prurient obsession with ordinariness, as *Ulysses* suggests, but he managed to combine this cult of the commonplace with a fervent sense of affinity with it. *Ulysses* is one of the very first novels in English to portray what we would now call mass culture. It is also awash with the more traditional culture of the people, from song and anecdote to jokes, pub talk, gossip, satirical invective and political wrangling. A former Provost of Trinity College, Dublin, at that time the academic home of the Anglo-Irish upper classes, remarked that the novel proved what a blunder it had been to establish a special university (University College, Dublin, which Joyce attended) 'for the aborigines of this island, for the corner-boys who spit in the Liffey'. Another panic-stricken critic compared the book to a famous Irish Republican bombing at Clerkenwell in London, seeing it as 'an attempted Clerkenwell explosion in the well-guarded, well-built, classical prison of English Literature'. It is interesting how this parallel forces the critic into a surely unintended metaphor, that of English Literature as a prison.

Virginia Woolf responded to *Ulysses* with odious snobbery, denouncing it as the work of 'a queasy undergraduate scratching his pimples'. What this overlooks is the fact that *Ulysses* is among other things a mischievous send-up of the English naturalistic novel by a colonial outsider. It is a satire of naturalism's obsession with the exact shade of lilac of the serving maid's stockings, or the precise number of dirty teaspoons in the sink. Irish literature, which numbers among its most distinguished works *Gulliver's Travels*, *Tristram Shandy*, *Castle Rackrent*, *Dracula* and *At Swim-Two-Birds*, is in general much less respectful of realism than its English counterpart. *Ulysses* trades in the humdrum stuff of ordinary life, but by handling it in such a self-conscious, scrupulously stylized language, it also manages to dissociate itself ironically from it. The form, as it were, rises above the content. Readers, while dutifully labouring their way through this distended mass of materials, are at the same time uneasily aware that there may be some con trick at work here – that the book's 'meaning', if it has such a thing, lies altogether elsewhere. High modernist form and low naturalistic content put each other satirically into question – suitably enough for a writer who moved from the provincial lower middle class to the cosmopolitan avant-garde while retaining a root in the former.

Yet the novel is also genuinely fascinated by these workaday details, and considers in its cosmically accepting way that nothing is too humble, trivial or outrageous to be fit material for art. As a writer from a small, downtrodden country, Joyce keeps faith with whatever is modest and inconspicuous, as Samuel Beckett was to do later. Like Dickens, he is a demotic, vernacular writer, at home in the cheap restaurant and on the city tram. Indeed, he is the first great urban writer of Ireland, a country in which cities are still the exception rather than the rule. By depicting lower-middle-class life in Dublin, he was among other things challenging the mythological Ireland of Yeats and his colleagues, who wrote of ancient warriors and mystic twilights rather than middle-aged cuckolds squatting glumly on the lavatory. Joyce was the man who forged a mythology instead out of a stagnant, preindustrial, priest-ridden colonial capital, and in doing so placed it permanently on the global map.

Joyce, then, is that rare creature, an avant-garde artist who is also a genuine democrat. Hardly any other modernist writer is at once so esoteric and down to earth. There is a carnivalesque quality to his writing, a gusto, humour and sense of ease with the body, which exists cheek-by-jowl with the high-modernist difficulty of his writing. *Ulysses* has been described as an 'epic of the body', and is secretly structured around various bodily organs. On the other hand, if Joyce could create the extravagantly mediocre Leopold Bloom and his ribald wife Molly, he also produced what has a claim to be the most obscure novel ever written, *Finnegans Wake*.

Many of the great modernist writers loathed some social group or other, whether women, Jews, socialists or the common people. Joyce, by contrast, stands out among these dismally benighted ranks for his tolerance and generosity of spirit. He also lacks the mandarin tone of so many of his modernist colleagues. If he is outrageously experimental, he is also deeply egalitarian. This may have something to do with hailing from a small country without as defined a class system as England, in which a communal ethic survived and the sense of all being in the same boat was strong. Unlike the Americans, the Irish are on the whole suspicious of success, and tend either to satirize or begrudge it.

There were advantages, then, to growing up in a philistine, religiously oppressive, politically contentious, economically backward colony. On the one hand, women-hating clerics and querulous Sinn Feiners helped to drive Joyce into exile, where he could find an alternative to that way of life by setting up home with art. If he felt cast out by his own country, he could pluck a virtue from that necessity, inhabiting a myriad countries of the mind instead. On the other hand, he bore with him to the Continent the wit, iconoclasm and verbal exuberance of the Dublin street. In turning that debunkery against church and state, he was pitting one aspect of Irish culture against another.

There is, in fact, an Irish context to this combination of the everyday and the esoteric. The country had a tradition of spirituality and high scholastic learning, along with an Irish-language literature of remarkable subtlety and elaborateness. But it had also been a wretchedly poor society marked by war, famine, imperial occupation and the baulking of native ambitions. It was, as Joyce tartly commented, 'an afterthought of Europe', and its inhabitants were 'the most belated race in Europe'. The country's routine social existence was for the most part dingy, stifling and monotonous. It is not for nothing that the author of *Waiting for Godot* was an Irishman. The Ireland which Joyce abandoned for Continental Europe was in some ways more like a Third World than a First World nation. Dull repetition, rather than dynamic progress, was its hallmark, as Leopold Bloom of *Ulysses* perambulates around its scruffy capital only to go to bed, get up and do the same again.

This combination of high and low, the metaphysical and the mundane, is a recurrent feature of Irish writing. Bathos – the figure in which the sublime is deflated by the ridiculous – crops up from Swift to Beckett. 'What do you mean', Lynch asks Stephen Dedalus in Joyce's *A Portrait of the Artist as a Young Man*, 'by prating about beauty and the imagination in this miserable Godforsaken island?' Dreaminess and dreariness go together: the more sterile one's actual situation, the stronger the impulse to escape into idle fantasy or utopian idealism. Yet the more absurd this idealism then appears. There is a good deal of satirical cutting down to size in Irish writing from *Gulliver's Travels* onward, a savagely aggressive humour which delights in puncturing human pretensions. *Ulysses* is among other things a satirical deflation of Homer's *Odyssey*. Irish culture is one of wit, debunkery and self-irony, unlike, say, much modern American culture, where the point is to talk yourself up, not down.

Part of the point of such wit is to give you a momentary edge over a barren existence. Wit, language and fantasy, as Joyce's fellow Dubliner Oscar Wilde insisted, are where you can momentarily transcend those sterile surroundings. Wilde thought that the body was determined but that the mind was free. When we act we are puppets, but when we speak we are poets. Words cost nothing, and can substitute themselves for kinds of action which are denied you. Another traditional Irish form of fantasizing is known as drink, which flows into the mouth as words flow out of it.

Poverty and oppression encourage you to dream, but they also deny you the chance to realize those fantasies other than in jokes, art or anecdotes. Verbal exuberance can compensate a little for the meagreness of everyday life. But if language is in this sense a mark of impotence, it can also be a sign of hope. Its very excessiveness – its detachment from the degraded present – can be seen as prefiguring a reality which has yet to come to birth. Just as the Irish Free State was proclaimed rhetorically into existence on the steps of the Dublin General Post Office in 1916, so Joyce conjures from language what he called the moral history of his nation – a history which his words help to bring into existence. In its playfulness and plurality, its rich inclusiveness and multiple identities, his work prefigures an Ireland which has yet to come into being.

All this, then, is likely to lend itself to literary modernism, which trades in fantasy and non-realist experiment. Joyce could learn very little from the great English realist novel, since his own situation was simply too different. That novel depended on a sense of continuity and evolution, on a belief in progress, balance and harmonious resolution, as well as on a society rich in 'manners'. Its characters were well-rounded, sharply individuated beings who were free to shape their own destinies. Little of this was available in Ireland – so that if Joyce were to be true to his own situation, he needed to invent a new kind of literary form. And his situation on the sidelines left him free to do so.

Modernism is the moment at which language becomes peculiarly conscious of itself, and this, too, finds a resonance on the colonial margins. Language in Ireland had always been a political and cultural minefield, as the tongue of the colonialist vied with the despised discourse of the natives. In a nation where you could move between several kinds of speech (Irish, English, Hiberno-English, Ulster Scots and so on), writers were more likely to be aware of the problematic nature of language than those who, like the English, could take their so-called mother tongue largely for granted. Language in such situations is less a transparent medium than an object of concern and contention in its own right. And this aligns it with modernism rather than with realism.

Even for writers like Wilde, Joyce and Yeats who had little or no mastery of Irish, there was still a residual sense (as was literally the case with Joseph Conrad) that the idiom in which they wrote was not quite their own. This was even truer of a playwright like J. M. Synge, who was said by some wag to write in English and Irish simultaneously. The Hiberno-English which Joyce sometimes writes enrichens Standard English by being slightly foreign to it, estranging it so that we experience the language afresh. Joyce earned his living for a while as a teacher of English to foreigners, a job which is more likely to make you conscious of the peculiarities of your native speech than being a botanist or a lap dancer.

This colonial self-consciousness about language in Joyce feeds into his modernism. For modernism is among other things a crisis of representation – a sense that the relationship between the world, and the language in which we represent it, is now deeply problematic. The more we become aware of language as a reality in itself, in all its material texture and density, the more puzzling it is to know how it 'refers' to a world beyond it. Language now seems more part of that world than a mirror of it. Besides, the more idiolects and technical jargons proliferate in modern society, the more we become conscious of the partial, provisional nature of them all. Each of them interprets the world in a particular way; but there seems no longer to be any 'meta-language' which would accommodate them all. Perhaps there is no longer any single world which all these modes of signifying share in common.

Some modernist art, then, moves from representing the world to representing our ways of representing it. A novel like *Ulysses* is an enormous repertoire of 'packaged' styles and discourses, no one of which is absolute. These styles are not ranked in any particular order, in the way that the voice of Maggie Tulliver in *The Mill on the Floss* is more authoritative than the voices of the Dodsons. Perhaps there is now no way of speaking which is closer to the world than any other – no language which the world itself would speak, as it were, if it were able to pipe up. It is as though the First World War and the events surrounding it have put paid to the idea that there is a single grand narrative in history, an authoritative 'voice-over' which will guide our efforts at interpretation.

In Ireland, in any case, there was much less of a canonical literary language than in England. What, for example, is James Joyce's style? The question is almost impossible to answer, as it is not in the case of Jane Austen or William Faulkner. *Dubliners* is less a plain style than a parody of a plain style. The language of *A Portrait of the Artist as a Young Man* ranges from baby talk to a hell-fire sermon to a brief treatise on aesthetics. *Ulysses* includes tabloid journalism, metaphysical reflection, interior monologue, catechism, mock-heroic, scientific jargon, women's magazines, pastiches of English literature, a mini-Expressionist drama, the discourse of the unconscious, and a good deal more. In what language is *Finnegans Wake* written? 'English' is probably the answer, but only just. Joyce's writing reflects a linguistically unstable situation, not just in Ireland but in a newly cosmopolitanized world in which it is less and less obvious that there is a master or a mother tongue. His writing is motley, hybrid, mongrelized, a thing of shreds and patches. Words are shot through with other words, one style is bounced off another, one language folded within a second.

Unlike many of the major modernist writers, for whom language is a slippery, untrustworthy medium, Joyce has a robust belief in the power of words to articulate more or less anything. This may be partly because there lies behind him a tradition of Irish rhetoric – of language as preaching, polemicizing or persuading. There had been a vigorous oral tradition in the country, of which there may be some late echoes in Molly Bloom's great monologue. But this faith in language may also reflect the fact that in the world of modern capitalism, the sign is indeed becoming more and more powerful. It is no accident that Leopold Bloom, the modern Odysseus, is an advertising agent. As the capitalist economy develops, it comes to run more and more on words and images.

Joyce's verbal universe is the new multilingual world of exile and migrations, newsprint and advertising, urban slang and specialized jargon. We are now in a print culture, and to remind us of the fact Joyce uses typographical devices in his work to draw attention to the fact that his books are books. They are material objects which somehow give the illusion of speech. Like his predecessor Laurence Sterne, he is fascinated by the way in which inanimate black marks on white sheets can somehow become living human meanings. *Finnegans Wake* can even be read as an act of colonial vengeance, in which, having been deprived by the English of your own native speech, you strike back by seizing their language, contaminating it with a babble of other dialects, and deploying it with such dazzling virtuosity that it falls apart in your hands. The master tongue is stripped of its privilege by a skilled verbal scavenger.

English itself is made foreign, as it had been to so many of Joyce's Irish ancestors. The strange dialect of the *Wake* is a way of not speaking English for those of the Irish who cannot speak their native tongue either. It is also a way of speaking English even more abundantly and ebulliently than the English do. The English language is supposed to be intimately wedded to English culture, as its unique medium of expression; but Joyce impudently detaches the language from the culture and converts it into an international currency. The scandal is to see English used to express distinctly 'non-English' realities. The exile belongs to no particular language, and can therefore be at home, or not at home, in any of them. Joyce is the great parodist of other people's literary forms, as a colonized nation is itself a kind of parody of an authentic nation-state. It is parasitic on the history and culture of others, inventing little by itself.

There is a sense in which Joyce, too, initiates very little, preferring to cobble together fragments of various cultures, recycling the same old elements in modified ways. He is no fan of Romantic innovation. For him, everything is manufactured out of something else. There is no original, only an endless chain of derivatives. Yet what is produced out of this non-innovation is one of the most original forms of art of modern times. The mimic becomes the modernizer – rather as Oscar Wilde created something quite new by imitating English high society drama with such ironic exactness. In a similar way, in the very year of publication of *Ulysses*, the Irish produced out of a history which had been so often a poor imitation of Britishness, an arrestingly original creation known as the Irish Free State. It was the first postcolonial nation-state of the twentieth century, and therefore, like the art of Joyce and Beckett, it had to improvise itself as it went along, lacking any well-established paradigm on which to model itself.

Joyce was never an enthusiast of Irish nationalism, though for a while he admired Sinn Fein for left-wing reasons. He was always, however, a sharp critic of British colonialism. Even towards the end of his life, when he had moved away from his early political radicalism, he agreed with an interviewer that the influence of British imperialism on his country had been 'villainous'. If he opposed nationalism in his youth it was from a socialist perspective, not a pro-colonialist one; he thought it was simply not revolutionary enough. The nationalists, for example, opposed the British state but were mostly loyal to the Catholic church, which seemed to Joyce grotesquely inconsistent. Both forms of oppressions, political and religious, had to be challenged together. Stephen Dedalus in *A Portrait of the Artist as a Young Man* is an anti-nationalist on quasi-nationalist grounds: he accuses the nationalists of having betrayed his country to the British, and for all his disdain of such ethnic politics speaks of his art as forging 'the uncreated conscience of [his] race'. This may not be the voice of Sinn Fein, but neither is it the voice of middle England.

Joyce also disliked what he saw as the nationalists' chauvinism, sexism, and cultural purism. He rejected their violence, xenophobia and religious bigotry, from his own pluralist, pacifist, cosmopolitan standpoint. One of the two leading characters of *Ulysses* is an Irish Hungarian Jew. As a disciple of Ibsen and European naturalism, he also scoffed at the Romantic dreams of Celtic visionaries like Yeats. He blamed the Irish bitterly for having colluded in their own colonization. As a pacifist, he detested the nationalists' cult of heroism, which he also saw as underlying the carnage of the First World War. Leopold Bloom, an 'unmanned' cuckold who abhors military aggression and has a pronounced feminine side to him, is a satirical deflation of that macho world. Or perhaps what is truly heroic is a tolerant acceptance of human difference and frailty, of the kind that Bloom practises.

In the end, Joyce was a rebel rather than a revolutionary. He was more Bohemian than Bolshevik. Yet despite his scorn for nationalism, he sprang from the social class in Ireland which provided the backbone of the nationalist movement: the urban lower middle class. And there is a sense in which his own 'revolution of the word', as it has been called, parallels that political revolution against the British state. If his writing satirizes nationalism, it is also part of the great explosion of creative energies which helped to give birth to it. Like many an eminent modernist, Joyce stood in contradictory relation to his own culture, nourished by it and spurning it at the same time.

He was an exile – yet no experience is more typically Irish. If Joyce was not at home in the country, neither were the great majority of his compatriots, far more of whom lived abroad than in Ireland. He debunked his own people, but this is a familiar Irish practice. He savaged the Roman Catholic church, but substituted a priesthood of art for a religious one. As Cranley remarks to the atheistic Stephen Dedalus in the *Portrait*: 'It is a curious thing . . . how your mind is supersaturated with the religion in which you say you disbelieve'. There have been many ways of being religious in Ireland, and atheism is one of the most distinguished.

Joyce rejected religious doctrines, but retained some of the systematic bent of scholastic thought. He was, he wryly observed, a scholastic in everything but the premises. To oppose the repressive puritanism of Catholic Ireland, he drew on a carnivalesque celebration of the body which was, ironically, very much part of Irish popular culture. If the nationalist rebels of the 1916 Easter Rising put Ireland on the international map, Joyce's work did so just as successfully at exactly the same moment. *A Portrait of the Artist as a Young Man* was published in that year. In the grotesque figure of the Citizen in *Ulysses*, he lampooned the bigotry and belligerence of the narrower kinds of nationalism, while being aware that some of the Citizen's criticisms of Britain were accurate and justified. He knew this because he had voiced some of those criticisms himself, in his non-fictional work. For all his ugly racism, the Citizen's language is far closer to Joyce's own scabrous wit, humour and satire than is the more pallid, polite language of Leopold Bloom. It is the meek Bloom who speaks up for capital punishment, and the ferocious Citizen who speaks against it.

Joyce, then, may not have been a revolutionary Irish nationalist, but neither was he a middle-class Anglo-Saxon liberal. Throughout his writings there is a good deal of anti-colonial polemic, which Anglo-Saxon critics generally play down. Some of them prefer to adopt him as a kind of honorary English liberal humanist with a mildly unfamiliar accent. If Joyce criticized Irish nationalism, however, it was not out of any love for British rule in Ireland, but because he thought that nationalism had failed to break deeply enough with it. Though his period as a self-declared socialist was fairly brief, he stands out among the politically unsavoury crew of European modernists, several of whom sailed close to fascism, as a democrat, populist and egalitarian. He is among the few leftist or liberal-leftist examples of such artists. *Finnegans Wake* was once praised by a French critic as a great anti-fascist novel – not because it has much to say about fascism, but because its Pentecostal mingling of tongues and mixing of national myths is the very

opposite of ethnic purity. It is the novel's form which is political, not its content.

Nationalism is a Janus-faced creed, which turns back to an idealized past in order to gather the mythological resources with which to leap forward into a politically independent future. In Joyce's own day, W. B. Yeats is a prime example of this facing-both-ways. The Ireland of the time was itself a mixture of the new and the old, as the forces of modernization flourished alongside cultural forms which were often quite traditional. The place was both European *and* a colony, both advanced and underdeveloped. Modernism often thrives in this kind of time-warp, and is as double-visaged as nationalism. If some modernist art ditches the past and looks to a utopian future, other strains of it are primitivist and archaic. Much modernism is both at once. There are many reasons for this ambivalence, but one of them concerns the return of mythology in the modern epoch. Myth can be seen as an enclosed symbolic world which endlessly repeats itself. It is a sphere in which the same fundamental items are continually shuffled into different patterns. It is also a world in which great impersonal forces – gods or Nature or one's ancestors – rigorously determine one's action and identity.

As European capitalism begins to move from its more liberal-individualist to its corporate or monopoly phase in the early twentieth century, myth – the very old – stages a strange reappearance just as we seem to be advancing into the very new. The world of a more systematic form of capitalism, in which individuals are less central than they were before, seems curiously like the ancient world of mythology. In the universe of *Ulysses* and the *Wake*, it is as though we are once again shaped by great anonymous forces, of which individual men and women are merely passive functions – only this time they are the forces of the commodity and market society rather than gods and demons. Nobody in *Ulysses* really takes any decisive action. Nobody does much work. In a volume of several hundred pages, nothing of any great moment happens. We are no longer in an old-fashioned capitalist world of individual agents strenuously making their own history. Indeed, in Ireland we never were.

Nor are we in a world of personal relationships. There are few such relationships in Joyce, of the complex, psychologically subtle kind dear to English realism. In metropolitan nations like Britain, it was possible to imagine that personal relationships were what made the world go round. In colonial ones like Ireland, the political and economic forces which shaped men and women's lives were too palpable to allow for any such delusion. In its relative lack of interest in the psychology of personal relationship, Joyce's writing is also in line with traditional Irish storytelling.

All of the characters in *Ulysses*, unknown to themselves, are controlled by a hidden logic – the logic of the Homeric myth which organizes the book. This literary device reflects the way in which we moderns seem to be shaped by a system whose logic is rarely apparent on the surface. On the surface, things in modern society seem random and fragmented, as in the desultory narrative of Bloom and Stephen's day in Dublin; but one cannot help suspecting that deeper down there are systematic forces at work. There is a secret sub-text to this surface text, one which determines it in every quarter but which is entirely invisible. As Marx commented, all the most important processes of capitalist society go on 'behind the backs' of the individuals involved. There is a plot somewhere, but it is off-stage, hard to decipher, absent from our consciousness, as Bloom is unaware of the Odysseus of whom he is a modern-day version.

This sense of a determining system was becoming true in Joyce's day of the world as a whole; but it is more acute in a colony like Ireland, where there had never been much sense of men and women as free agents who fashioned their own history. The lives of colonial peoples are always ultimately determined from elsewhere – just as what characters in Joyce are able to think or feel seems determined by the peculiar style of language available to them, which is not a matter of their choosing. So the colony can become a microcosm of modern civilization as a whole. It symbolizes a world which works by laws quite independent of specific men and women. The relations between colony and metropolis are reversed: Joyce takes a peripheral city, Dublin, and makes it the capital of the world. The politically marginal becomes spiritually central.

Like myth, the world of the commodity is, in Joycean phrase, 'never-changing everchanging'. One thinks, for example, of fashion, in which we meet with variations on the stalely familiar. Just as in myth the same items can be made to serve different functions, so any commodity can in principle be exchanged with any other. The 'content' of this society is purely contingent, as anything can stand in for anything else; but its forms seem abstract, repetitive and unchangeable. In this sense, too, the modern reverts to the mythological. Myth tells the same old stories over and over again, using symbols and situations which are interchangeable. And this is what Joyce's fiction does as well.

You can use myth to lend unity and coherence to the chaos of modern urban experience, and this is part of what is afoot in *Ulysses*. The Homeric myth creates a complex web of correspondences out of what are really random fragments. It brings together characters like Stephen, Bloom and Molly who are cut off from one another, marooned within their own monologues, and thus manufactures a kind of symbolic community to make up for the lack of an actual one. As in Dickens, men and women are superficially solitary yet linked at some deeper level.

Yet whereas in Dickens there are 'real' connections between apparently isolated characters, in Joyce we are aware that this unity is artificially imposed. It has to be, since there is no longer any logic or pattern inherent in reality itself. The Odysseus myth is artfully deployed to give shape to a day in Dublin, but we cannot help suspecting (as indeed we are intended to) that any other myth might have done the job just as well. In this sense, the double structure of the novel is an enormous joke. It says something about the arbitrariness of meaning in the modern world. And the fact that the myth is so elaborately applied to a Dublin with which it has no real connection is an ironic way of making the point. The novel is aware of its own fictionality. Its last words are not 'and yes I said yes I will Yes', but *Trieste-Zürich-Paris, 1914–1921.*

In this sense, the act of myth-making is ironic: in order to be authentic, it must draw attention to its own arbitrariness. The meaning of *Ulysses* lies as much in the comical gap between the world of Homeric epic and the degraded modern world as in their unity. The Homeric myth satirizes the modern world, but at the same time lends it value and significance. Bloom is a poor sort of Odysseus, yet perhaps, even so, he is a hero after his own humble fashion. The aloofly intellectual Stephen Dedalus is eloquent in his spurning of the common life; but since he is also something of a prig, we do not take his rejection of it at face value. Everyday life, in a typical Joycean ambiguity, is both deflated and affirmed.

Myth and the commodity are both great levellers. All things become equal, because anything can be exchanged with anything else. The world of the commodity is one hostile to hierarchy. In the modern period, places are also becoming interchangeable, as cities, nations, languages and people become more uniform, pitched together by the processes of international capitalism. If anywhere is everywhere, then Joyce can scribble away in Zürich or Trieste without ever having left Dublin. In *Finnegans Wake*, all languages, myths and cultures are equalized, so that they can be combined in ever more complex ways. A single word can act as a switchboard between half-

a-dozen different meanings. Characters can glide into each other, merge into unity and split off again. All stories are secretly one story. History goes round and round, its events at once identical and different. Leopold Bloom takes a mild interest in reincarnation. The world of the commodity is a degraded one, in which things have been drained of their intrinsic value; but just because of this, they are now free to be put to all kinds of ingenious, innovatory uses. The other side of degradation is emancipation. This is one reason why it is not easy to say whether *Ulysses* is a satire of a stagnant modern world or a celebration of it. Or, to be sure, both at the same time.

What is supposed to escape being a commodity is Joyce's fiction itself. The very difficulty of it is meant to prevent us from 'consuming' it too easily. Joyce rejected the Romantic idea of artistic inspiration, which he saw, correctly, as the philistine's version of the artist. In elevating artists to god-like status, it also denigrates them, since their achievement has nothing to do with skill. Instead, Joyce regarded writing as a form of sweated labour, as he toiled for a whole day over a couple of sentences. Writing for him was a form of production rather than a means of self-expression. It was a matter of sculpting language lovingly into shape, chiselling and polishing the stuff until he had achieved the exact nuance of meaning he required. The result of this was a form of writing far too esoteric to be easily absorbed. Instead, it turned the reader into a kind of producer as well, labouring away to decipher the text. A review in the English *Daily Express* complained that reading *Finnegans Wake* was like taking a trip through the alien territory of Soviet Russia.

With typical arrogance, Joyce announced that he intended readers of the *Wake* to spend as much time reading it as he had done writing it. Since writing the book took him about 17 years, this would not have left his readers much time for living. This would not have bothered Joyce unduly. He himself, rather like Henry James, lived for the sake of his art, and expected his readers to make no less a sacrifice. What justified experience for him was the fact that it could end up in a book. It could be salvaged from the ravages of time and laid up in the eternity of art. The artist was a kind of secular priest, transforming the bread and wine of everyday life into the imperishable stuff of the eucharist. Yet the Joyce who stretched out his body on the altar of art was also an avant-garde iconoclast who revolutionized the whole conception of the novel. *Ulysses* and *Finnegans Wake* are examples of high literature which are also subversive assaults on it – monstrous, unreadable anti-novels crammed with obscenities, chunks of popular culture and offensives against syntax and grammar, which outraged the cultural establishment of the time.

If everything returns again – and it may well be that the final words of *Finnegans Wake* lead us back to the beginning of the book – then the idea of history as perpetual progress can be unmasked for the imperial myth that it is. It is the British who think of history as a grand narrative of increasing affluence and enlightenment, and their colonial subjects who know that this is an illusion. If the English realist novel evolves in a linear way, *Ulysses* and the *Wake* simply revolve on themselves, their tails tucked into their mouths. Yet at the same time, if everything comes around again, there can be no ultimate loss or breakdown, and therefore no genuine tragedy. In this sense, too, Joyce differs from many a fellow modernist. He is a comic writer, not a tragic one – and comic not only because he is very funny, but in the deeper, Dantean sense of seeing the world as fundamentally harmonious. This, for an author who wrote the first of his great novels during one world war, and published the other on the eve of a second, is no mean achievement.

A good deal of modern writing is tragic in the sense of not feeling fundamentally at home in the world, but Joyce the perpetual wanderer seems, ironically, to feel just the opposite. Nothing in reality is alien to the human. His sense of the fundamental equality of all things means that even the most apparently vile or squalid aspects of existence are to be affirmed. Whether this includes two world wars is a question worth raising. Joyce also stands out among his fellow modernists for the sheer materialism of his imagination. Most of his modernist colleagues are devotees of the spirit, whereas Joyce is a celebrant of the world's body. Reality itself acknowledges no distinctions between high and low, sacred or profane, central or peripheral, original and copy, and neither should art. If everything is subtly interwoven with everything else, then the humblest piece of existence has its part to play in the great cosmic drama. Joyce's scepticism of the distinction between centres and sidelines, the essential and the accidental, is among other things a view from the colonies.

The drama of the cosmos has no purpose in itself. It is supremely pointless, exists entirely for its own sake, and has no relations with anything outside itself (since there *is* nothing outside itself). In this sense, the universe is a kind of stupendous work of art. The sealed structure of Joyce's own art reflects the enclosed structure of the cosmos. Any minute part of this cosmos is a microcosm of the whole, so that an unremarkable day in Dublin becomes a symbol of creation itself. And if every bit of it is somehow necessary, then the artist's task is less to judge than to accept. Perhaps Molly

Bloom breathes 'yes' rather too easily; there is not much value in an acqui-
escence which might spring from indifference. Or perhaps her 'yes' represents the all-inclusive multiplicity of the universe itself, in contrast with the
caustic judgements and quibbling discriminations of the scholastically minded
Stephen.

Joyce's vision could even be described as utopian. In *Ulysses*, the world
depicted by the novel is for the most part seedy and inert, but the language
used to portray it is dynamic and endlessly resourceful. There is an ironic
discrepancy between form and content, signifier and signified. It is as though
the content of the novel belongs to the world of the present, while the
language which portrays it anticipates the future. It prefigures a world of
freedom and plurality, sexual emancipation and shifting identities. If this is
so, then the novel is a critique of Irish nationalism as much in its form as in
its content. It marks out the limits of the Irish national revolution, which for
all its pioneering achievements gave birth to an independent nation which
was (among other, more reputable things) philistine, puritanical, patriarchal
and chauvinistic. If all this helped to drive Joyce into exile, what he wrote in
that exile sketches in its very style the kind of Ireland to which he might
have felt able to return.

Freedom for the Sinn Feiners meant freedom to affirm your national
identity, whereas freedom for Joyce meant being able to shift identities,
weave several of them into one, cross frontiers, bend meanings, mix gen-
ders, undercut fixed hierarchies and confound distinctions. The revolution,
in short, has not been revolutionary enough. It had perpetuated the past as
well as breaking with it. There is little advance in the Irish middle classes
seizing the state from Britain and using it themselves to exploit the Irish
poor. There was, in the words of Stephen Dedalus, a loveliness which had
not yet come into the world. Joyce's art pointed to what still remained to be
done – to the cultural revolution which must accompany the anti-colonial
one, as a kind of depth within it. Yet without the anti-colonial revolution, no
such cultural transformation would be remotely possible. In this, at least,
the nationalists were in the right of it.

Dubliners is a collection of short stories, a popular literary genre in Ireland.
The Irish author Sean O'Faolain, himself an accomplished writer of short
stories, thought that the novel needed the kind of 'complex social machinery'
which was lacking in the country. He saw the place as a 'thin' society, without the rich texture of 'manners', cultural traditions and elaborate institutions

on which the English novel was able to draw. In this situation, the short story is a more apt literary medium, turning as it so often does on a single figure, insight or event, recording a fleeting encounter or revelation. It is also a form well adapted to the solitary mind; and since solitude is the typical condition of the writer in a philistine society – Joyce's Stephen Dedalas may serve as an example – the short story proved an hospitable form there. The novel, by contrast, usually needs to justify its length by assembling a varied cast of characters.

Joyce called such fleeting moments of revelation 'epiphanies', a religious term which he hijacked for secular purposes. But there is a sense in which the stories in *Dubliners* turn rather on 'anti-epiphanies'. Most of them focus on some ambition not achieved, some vision or desire frustrated, some key moment which turns out to be sourly disenchanting. What promises to be an epiphany of love in 'Two Gallants' is exposed as a cheap act of cadging money. A typical situation is one of a man or woman trapped, catching a glimpse of a way out, and failing to take it. As with Henry James, the stories revolve often enough on loss and absence: the broken priest of 'The Sisters' whom we see only as a corpse; the sexual act which is just off-frame in 'An Encounter'; the non-existence of the splendid exotic bazaar in 'Araby', or the bungled possibility of love in 'A Painful Case' and 'The Dead'.

The tales of *Dubliners* are thronged not with the city's most populous group of inhabitants at the time – the tenement dwellers of its notorious Calcutta-like slums – but with members of the lower middle class from which Joyce himself sprang. We move in a drab, disenchanted world of down-at-heel clerks, ruined priests, seedy boarding houses, drunken spinsters, sad sexual perverts, socially pretentious mothers, frustrated minor poets and cold-hearted loners. They are people with enough awareness and education to aspire, but without the means to realize their aspirations. For the most part, they are not even impressive enough to be tragic. Pathos and poignancy are the emotional keynotes. Work is drudgery, politics a farce, religion either empty ritual or a form of madness, and domestic life a prison. Desire is warped and degraded. Solitude, ironically, is what is most deeply shared. Shame, guilt, rage, violence and humiliation simmer beneath the threadbare surfaces of social life. Later in Joyce's work, narrative will be thinned down in order to allow for a free play of language; here, it is more a question of stories which crank themselves off the ground only to find themselves aborted. The folk tale is sometimes seen as a repository of traditional wisdom; here, however, we have the empty forms of that story without the content.

This meagreness is captured in what Joyce himself referred to as the 'scrupulous meanness' of his prose in the book – a deliberately flattened, anaemic, economical style which captures what he saw as the 'spiritual paralysis' of his city and his country. It is a style which would be beyond the attainment of any of the work's characters, but not utterly out of their reach, as the language of *Ulysses* or the *Wake* would be. In its spare, meticulously neutral realism it reflects the shrunken world of the Irish capital. Such a style closes a gap which one often finds in Irish writing. In *Ulysses*, the drama of J. M. Synge and a number of other works, there is an clash between the sparseness of the subject-matter, and the verbal opulence with which it is treated. In *Dubliners*, language and content are more equally matched.

Yet in reflecting this shabby world so dispassionately, the style of the book also detaches itself from it. In its blank, bloodless fashion, it deliberately offers no comment on the material it presents, least of all a moralizing one. If it signals an intimacy with Dublin life, it makes no attempt to evoke our sympathies for it. It is, among other things, a style in revolt against the lush, oracular language of the Irish Literary Revival, which was in full spate at the time. Samuel Beckett's minimalist, mathematically exact prose, along with his decision to write in French, were similar rebellions against what is sometimes known in Ireland today as 'Oirishness'.

It is not entirely a world without hope. Joyce himself spoke of *Dubliners* as a necessary step in 'the spiritual liberation of my country'. Indeed, the social class which these stories portray as morally bankrupt was one which was soon to spearhead the twentieth century's first revolutionary war of independence, bringing the world's mightiest imperial power to its knees. Politics in 'Ivy Day in the Committee Room' may have declined from the heroic days of the Irish nationalist leader Charles Stewart Parnell to a bunch of down-at-heel electoral dogsbodies gossiping in a cold, unfurnished room, but the story shimmers with the wit and irony of Dublin, as does the marvellously rendered vernacular speech of 'Grace'. That story concerns an effort at spiritual conversion, but it is one which can express itself only in the language of the old order. Joyce himself, as in the word 'epiphany', reverses those priorities, hijacking the vocabulary of the old order for his own creatively blasphemous ends.

Love and escape are possible, but the will to grasp them is slack and palsied. The harassed, pathetic Maria of 'Clay' is allowed her moment of epiphany in song; indeed, several of these narratives liberate a fresh voice, hope, memory or snatch of music or poetry on the very brink of desolation.

The living may be half-dead, but there are also intimations of life in death, not least in 'The Dead'. If the snow of that story freezes and deadens, it also secretes the sources of new life. If it is dreary and dispiriting, it also serves as a negative image of community and continuity, folding living and dead alike in its embrace. It is bracingly unclear whether Gabriel, at the end of the story, is turning his face toward death or resurrection.

We know, anyhow, that the stagnant nation to which Gabriel Conroy belongs was indeed reborn, however imperfectly, two years after the volume in which he appears was published. The Irish revolution, as one writer remarked, was not an immaculate conception, but then revolutions never are. It did, however, embody a vision and energy which makes one wonder in retrospect just how realist the pages of *Dubliners* are. The work is set in the years just before the revolution, one of the most politically dynamic, culturally prodigious periods of Ireland's history. If *Dubliners* has, in its author's own words, a 'scrupulous meanness' about it, it is not only a matter of style; it is also a question of deliberately excluding this explosive vitality. We are not allowed to see working-class militancy, the thriving Gaelic language movement, the flourishing of Anglo-Irish artistic energy centred on Yeats's Abbey Theatre, the growth of a revolutionary Irish feminism, or the rapid modernization of the whole island at the time.

The book's ambiguous interweaving of life and death – a familiar enough motif in popular Irish culture – is nowhere more evident than in 'The Dead'. One can read the story, as almost all critics do, as a satire on the stiflingly conventional middle-class Dublin which Gabriel Conroy represents, in contrast to the world of living passion symbolized by his wife Gretta and her dead lover Michael Furey. Yet if the tale invites this Romantic reading, it also rebuffs it. Gabriel, who is full of guilt and self-disgust, is not necessarily to be taken at his own cripplingly low self-estimation. His speech at dinner may be florid and rather smug; he is a bookish man out of touch with the people, who needs no doubt to find his Bloom. He has an unpleasant sense of cultural superiority, but this is more a burden to him than a source of satisfaction. For all its mildly priggish, father-of-the bride tone, his speech is gracious and kindly intended, delighting the hearts of the elderly women at whom it is directed.

Gabriel may betray a lack of conviction in his encounter with the earnestly nationalistic Miss Ivors; he is certainly both wrong and self-righteous to impute humourlessness to nationalists in general. Miss Ivors is certainly not incapable of a laugh, as the story goes out of its way to show us. All the same, it is pretty pushy of her to instruct Gabriel where to go on holiday.

He himself has a cosmopolitan outlook which is closer to his author's view of the world than to hers. His marriage may be fairly moribund, but this is scarcely a sociologically unique phenomenon, and there is no particular suggestion that it is his fault. When he recalls his life with Gretta it is with joy and tenderness, and she can still move him to intense desire. An epiphany can transfigure everyday life, as Gabriel, seeing his wife on the staircase, sees the possibility of their marriage being recreated. But it can also empty the common world of meaning and value in contrast with its own sudden splendour. Perhaps this is the effect which the memory of Michael Furey has on Gretta.

Even when Gretta has dropped the bombshell of her past love for Furey, Gabriel's response to her is generous, pitying and affectionate. He is far from the fatuous clown he imagines himself to be. Furey may be full of Romantic allure, but the bald fact is that he recklessly threw away his life in a semi-suicidal gesture, which is scarcely the basis for a sustained relationship. Gretta's rekindled love for him could just as well be seen as a morbid fixation on the past, as she overlooks a living passion in the name of a dead one. Both she and her West-of-Ireland lover may exemplify the cult of nostalgia and futile self-sacrifice which Joyce detested so deeply in Irish nationalism. Perhaps Gabriel is finally duped by this false but forceful image into despairing of his own life, in which case he may be doing himself a serious injustice. The self-loathing intellectual comes to feel for himself the kind of contempt that he imagines the passionate peasant does. But Joyce was not generally given to respecting the views of peasants, passionate or otherwise.

The title *A Portrait of the Artist as a Young Man* might lead us to believe that the work is written in the first person, whereas it is in fact written in the third. It is, so to speak, an autobiography in the third person. It is thus both intimate with the consciousness of its hero, Stephen Dedalus, and studiously impersonal. Its language is too close to Stephen to pass judgements on him, while in no sense canvassing our sympathy for him. It does not bother to point out explicitly what a prig he grows up to be. Instead, it disconcerts readers by providing them with a point of identification which is hard to identify with. It is a mixture of the remote and familiar which one might feel in contemplating one's younger self. Joyce's style records ardent feelings but stays scrupulously clear of them. And because there are so many styles in the book, all the way from naturalism, sermonizing and *fin-de-siècle* 'decadence' to poetic reverie and student argot, we are made aware of language itself, in a way which prevents us from simply reading through it to the emotion or the action.

Joyce even tucks into the book a lengthy scholastic discussion of aesthetics, with nonchalant disregard for realism. It is not quite the kind of thing one is likely to stumble across in E. M. Forster. It underlines how very 'foreign' a work this is, from an English realist viewpoint. H. G. Wells found it both loathsome and alarming. Intellectuals like Stephen rarely figure as protagonists in the English novel, partly because they are associated neither with action nor with emotion. Whereas the English novel is much preoccupied with marriage, property, kinship and inheritance, the footloose Joyce is suspicious of all these institutions. Stephen refuses to fulfil his religious obligations by making his Easter duty; *Ulysses* rejects paternity as a legal fiction; children are mostly absent from the writing; and the chief marriage in Joyce's work, that of Leopold and Molly Bloom, is deeply dysfunctional.

Ulysses, like an extraordinary amount of Irish writing, is among other things about the failure of the father, who betrays and abandons his children, and the need for a spiritual surrogate, which is what Stephen is no doubt seeking in Bloom. Bloom, whose own son is dead, is searching for a spiritual son in Stephen, and the novel is thronged with imagery of paternity, filial adoption, self-fathering, origins and derivations. In English society, the family could provide a haven of emotional warmth in a predatory world; in Ireland, it was traditionally locked into that world, governed by its harsh utilitarian logic. On the Irish farm, the family was a working economic unit under the thumb of a patriarch, not something to wax sentimental about. Love and personal affection might well matter less than marriage dowries, emigration, the inheritance of property and the labour power of the young. The Irish themselves are for the most part an unsentimental people who exist largely so that other people can wax sentimental about them.

Like all small children, Stephen starts off as a prisoner of his own senses, unable to exert control over his environment. He fumbles for the relations between words, the senses, and the spirit. Roman Catholicism, a notably sensuous brand of religion, combines all three, but subjects the senses to the spirit. The hell-fire sermons in *Portrait of the Artist* press the senses into the service of the spirit, as the preacher drives home his anti-carnal point with luridly fleshly images. Politics, at least where Irish nationalism is concerned, is also a combination of the mundane and the idealistic; but Stephen finds both dimensions distasteful. Nationalism is at once too worldly, concerned with power and proprietorship, and too unworldly, full of rhetorical blather and morbid sentimentalism. The discourse of both church and politics is that of rhetoric, performance, persuasion – and this for Stephen is a 'kinetic'

language caught up in power and desire, rather than the static, transcendent language of art.

The adolescent Stephen is unable to get the relations between senses and spirit right, veering wildly between sensual debauchery and monkish asceticism. Repressing the senses is simply the flipside of indulging them. In the novel's own terms, he is either too 'kinetic' or excessively 'static'. Art, like the church, combines the senses and the spirit: Stephen is interested in words both for their meanings and their delectable sounds. But the aesthetic theory which he finally comes up with still has the balance awry. It is too bloodless, formalist a conception of art, without the earthiness of Joyce's own aesthetic. Joyce himself was much preoccupied in his youth with the naturalism of Europeans like Ibsen, which rooted art in the actual. We can see this clearly enough in *Stephen Hero*, an early version of the *Portrait*. The creator of Molly Bloom would not have been particularly impressed by the aesthetic opinions of the young Stephen Dedalus. We are indeed dealing here with the artist as a young man.

The work of art for Stephen is supremely autonomous, cut loose from all relationship to reality; and this is pretty much the state which he wishes to achieve for himself. *A Portrait of the Artist as a Work of Art* would not be a bad alternative title for the book. Like the Ireland which he refuses to serve, Stephen will progress from victim to rebel. Rather than being 'spoken' by the discourses of religion, politics and Gaelic culture, he will forge his own speech. Renouncing both the flesh represented by his mother and the law embodied by his father, Stephen becomes a Satanic nay-sayer and denier, a flouter of church and state, religion and nationalism, family and kinship, race and inheritance. He disowns biology and the body, all those unchosen bonds which tie you to your species. He wishes to fly by these nets rather than come to terms with them, and like Icarus, the son of his mythological namesake, he is thus bound to come a cropper. If you want to transcend the real world, you have to pay the price of doing so; and this, in the case of the artist, means the sweated labour of immersing yourself in the place in order to gather it into the eternity of art. You must know the world, the devil and the flesh if you wish to soar above them.

Stephen's passion for freedom involves renouncing his nation; yet ironically it also reflects Ireland's own growth towards autonomy and self-reliance. In this sense, Joyce's hero reflects the history of his nation in the very act of repudiating it. The impulse which spurs him to break with his past is not wholly distinct from the force which drives Ireland to throw off its colonial history. It is not just a question of spurning politics for art, as so many commentators on the work have claimed. The opposition itself, at least in Irish conditions, is simple-minded. In a nation like Ireland without much tradition of liberal dissent, it was the artist who could play the role of political rebel. Joyce is 'non-political' only in an absurdly narrow sense of the term 'political'. His verbal self-consciousness, hunger for personal liberty, refusal of an oppressive history, concern for sexual emancipation and 'decentring' of identities: none of this could fail to strike a political resonance in the conformist, repressive climate of the Irish colony. Verbal self-absorption may appear the very opposite of political engagement, but it is clearly nothing of the kind. A delight in language for its own sake means a rejection of it as a blunt instrument of power.

Stephen is an avant-gardist who dreams of breaking altogether with the shackling, humiliating past; but if the past is disavowed rather than actively dealt with, it will simply return. The nightmare of history is not so easily awoken from. To imagine that you have awoken when in fact you have not is simply more of the nightmare. Stephen's very disgust binds him to the world he repudiates. By the opening of *Ulysses*, young Dedalus has returned to Ireland after his flight to the Continent, no freer than he was before. His author, by contrast, is at work on a novel (starring young Dedalus) which immerses itself in the real world with more grubby relish than almost any other of its age. Stephen's exile signifies one of the tragedies of the modern age – that it seems possible to be free only by being homeless. It is becoming harder and harder to be both free and rooted, independent and affiliated.

The truth that you can be free only through your affiliations, not in spite of them, is not one which Stephen wishes to hear. He still has to learn that achieving independence is not the same as some proud Luciferian fantasy that you are self-created. Since this involves rejecting the idea that you were ever fathered, 'Oedipal' fantasy would do here just as well. It is a question of how you are to acknowledge the past without being a prisoner of it. How are you to manufacture something radically new – a new type of novel, a new kind of postcolonial state – when the materials of the past are really all you have to work with? How do you utilize the past, revering its honourable achievements, without lapsing into 'Oirish' nostalgia? Perhaps Stephen's haughty desire to be self-born is just the reverse side of that nostalgia, and so part of the problem rather than the solution.

Ulysses is Joyce's definitive attempt to resolve these problems. Two insider-outsiders – an alienated Irish artist (Stephen Dedalus) and an Irish Hungarian Jew (Leopold Bloom) – weave their aimless way around Dublin, stage one or two near-miss encounters, and finally meet up. It is not the most intricate of plots for a novel of over nine hundred pages. The meeting of the two men may be significant: a few more upbeat critics have suggested that as a result of it, Stephen goes off to write *Ulysses*, or that the Bloom's rocky marriage is mended. But this is pretty improbable. Just as the stories of *Dubliners* turn on moments of anti-climax, so this gargantuan modern epic revolves on nothing in particular. The non-event of the encounter of the two chief characters is among other things a debunking of English realism, with its yearning for closure and settlement, for tying up loose ends in some gratifying solution. This novel, by contrast, ends not with such signings and sealings, but with a monstrous outpouring of unpunctuated language from Molly Bloom's unconscious which could in principle go on for ever.

Ulysses, then, does not get anywhere, any more than its peripetetic characters do. Like God or the cosmos, it exists purely for its own sake. The inertia of colonial life, which also seems to get nowhere, is transformed into the autonomy of art. Yet not trying to get anywhere is a reputable enough way of living, so that the novel has moral relevance in its very refusal to be purposeful. Anyway, there is a sense in which the meeting of Stephen and Bloom may indeed prove momentous. The native who grows up an outsider, and the outsider who has gone native, are both different and alike enough to give something precious to each other. Stephen is still arrested in his posture of Satanic revolt, unable to come to terms with his material surroundings. He is capable only of the negative freedom of rejection, rather than the positive freedom of participating in a form of life larger than himself. But if Stephen accepts too little, Bloom arguably accepts too much. He has the meek, forebearing equipoise of spirit which Stephen lacks, along with a humaneness and liberality of mind; but he is too passively mired in material circumstance, as Stephen is too damagingly aloof from it.

Bloom is, in fact, by no means the unqualified liberal-humanist hero for which some starry-eyed critics have taken him. Joyce never allows us any easy or obvious point of identification. If this Hungarian Irishman is open to the fleshly, biological world, he is also remarkably squeamish. His hygienic, ungregarious spirit makes a telling contrast with the carnivalesque wit and rumbustious vitality of the Dubliners around him. His fussiness and solitary act of masturbation are hardly in the uproarious Rabelaisian spirit. Where others might see life and pleasure, Bloom sees a world of gross appetite and savage mutual preying. In its own way, it is as alienated a vision as Stephen's supercilious contempt for his fellows.

If Bloom is attractively feminized, a critic of macho aggression, he is also rather too acquiescent for his own good. He is, for example, something of a sexual masochist. He speaks up bravely and movingly for love, in the teeth of the spite and bigotry around him; but it is by no means certain that he is right to see love as the opposite of hatred. Freud would certainly not have thought so. Besides, love may well inspire one to hatred of oppression and injustice. His admirable humanitarianism involves a set of shallow, mildly crankish schemes for social reform, fit meat for his author's satiric debunkery.

Much the same ambiguity adheres to the figure of Molly. Is she a triumph of the feminine, or a sexist image of women? Is she brimming with earthy energy or stuffed with vapid lower-middle-class clichés? Is she restricted, repetitive and amoral, or universal, fertile and all-inclusive? Is her final 'yes' the kind of cosmic affirmation which Stephen must learn to practise, or a cynically indifferent act of assent? Molly is portrayed in a way which makes these questions well-nigh undecidable. If she is eternal Nature, she is also full of country-cuteness; if she is vital and carnivalesque, her discourse is arguably monotonous and mechanical. She is elemental, but also of her place and time, an impersonal process as much as a particular person. For all its racy idiosyncrasy, her monologue is so constructed as to prevent us from reading her as a rounded, coherent 'character'. In all this, she is a symbol of the work in which she figures, which resists any single interpretation.

Perhaps the meeting of Stephen and Bloom is significant in this sense – that unless it had already taken place in the person of Joyce himself, *Ulysses* could not have been produced. Stephen arguably has the intellectual and artistic talent to write it, but not the self-effacing exposure to the everyday; Bloom has that right enough, but (despite having 'a touch of the artist' about him) cannot rise to Stephen's fineness of consciousness. The fact that *Ulysses* exists suggests that the two figures, or rather the qualities they respectively represent, have indeed had a constructive encounter, however casual and inconclusive their actual contact in the book. It is in the process of production of the work, rather than in the finished product, that these two worlds – the one rebellious, elitist and abstruse, the other acquiescent, broad-minded and down-to-earth – converge most fruitfully.

One must neither disavow history, kinship and the material world, as the cerebral Stephen tries to do, nor flounder helplessly in them, a fate which risks overtaking Bloom. Instead, one must find a way of being original – of inaugurating something radically new – on the basis of what one receives from the past and present. One must accept the fact that all inheritances are tainted, not least those which former colonies receive from their erstwhile proprietors. If you must avoid a sickly nostalgia for the past, you must also

recognize that nobody can be entirely self-fashioning. History, like art, forges something new out of a cunning recycling of the old.

The act of writing, which depends on raw materials it then proceeds to transform, is a metaphor of this. The point is to find a way of relating to one's history which will allow you to go beyond it. For Joyce himself, one name for this relationship is exile. The quickest way to Tara (the cultural capital of ancient Ireland), as Stephen Dedalus remarks in *Ulysses*, is the road to Holyhead, port of entry to England. Once he is free of Ireland, he is also free to recreate it. The other name for this relationship is art, which unites detachment and engagement, stasis and kinesis, lowly flesh and lofty spirit. It was through his art that Joyce was finally able to reconcile two of the strongest impulses he inherited from Ireland: his delight in its popular life and language, and his rejection of its major institutions. As the well-known ballad puts it:

> What with clerics and Sinn Feiners, our Jim was in a mess
> So he upped and offed to Zürich and to Paris and Trieste,
> With love and hate for Ireland at war within his heart
> He knew what can't be done in life can still be on in art.
>
> So he settled down in Trieste town, produced a mighty tome
> It's all about two geezers, one a Jew and one ex-Rome
> And a buxom lass called Molly who's quite a little duck
> But the High Court didn't like the way she kept on saying 'Damn'.

VIRGINIA WOOLF

L ike almost any writer, Virginia Woolf was riddled with inconsistencies. She disliked the word 'feminist', but wrote one of the most
magnificent essays on women of the twentieth century, *A Room of
One's Own*. Indeed, the work has a claim to be among the finest political
statements of the modern age. Few political texts have been at once so
elegant and *engagé*, playful and polemical. Born into an upper-middle-class
Victorian family, and a member of the exclusive Bloomsbury coterie, she
could be odiously snobbish and high-handed; yet she also taught courses for
working-class men and women, opened her splendid house to women's
political meetings, and was avidly curious about the lives of the common
people. She believed in wholeness and unity, yet thought that art and politics should be kept strictly apart. She could scorn title and privilege, yet she
could revel in them too.

Woolf's writing is extraordinarily radical, courageous and innovative.
Perhaps more than any other English novelist, she forges a unique, astonishingly original style and form of her own This is partly because the business
of running the country and running women along with it had reduced men
to such a state of hopelessness that it seemed idle simply to hijack their own
conventions. Instead, one had to create, both politically and artistically, a
room of one's own. But Woolf's writing also reflects its upper-class context
in being largely ungenial in tone, occasionally precious and kid-gloved in
manner, witty and satirical but not often funny, and lacking in the kind of
warmth and earthiness which distinguishes the novel from Fielding and
Dickens to Joyce.

Woolf was a socialist of sorts, bravely enough for a woman of her genteel
background, who condemned what she called 'the instinct for possession,

the rage for acquisition'; yet she was blessed with a surplus of possessions herself. She enjoyed sending up dim-witted aristocrats, but this was partly because she was not herself an aristocrat. Like Jane Austen, she had a remarkably quick eye for status and income, as well as for the most microscopic nuances of class distinction. She could be both racist and homophobic. Like most of her class and circle she made anti-Semitic remarks, but unlike most of them she also married a down-at-heel Jewish socialist, and through him gained access to the world of active left-wing politics. She celebrates the uniquely individual life, yet sometimes indulges in the most offensive social stereotyping. If the six characters of *The Waves* share anything, it is their contempt for the common people.

If Woolf was a snob, however, she was at least a self-critical one. She was well aware of the incongruities of her situation, and was at least determined to avoid the bad faith of those radicals who indulged in a spot of slumming, or who pretended to be what they were not. She lived in an age when it was too late for Victorian paternalism and still somewhat early for socialist democracy. As far as bad faith goes, she would have agreed with E. M. Forster's Margaret Schlegel of *Howards End*, who declares that she refuses to draw her income and at the same time sneer at those who guarantee it. Woolf knew that for a woman like herself, only a source of 'independent' wealth could ensure her freedom as a writer; so that (although no wealth is in fact 'independent'), it was only by relying upon her well-heeled background that she could gain any degree of autonomy from it.

For all its inconsistencies, Woolf's position in English society was in fact a fairly common one. It was that of the dissident sons and daughters of the governing class – those who knew that class from the inside, and shared its privileges, but who formed a kind of nonconformist fraction within it. Whereas the 'official' ruling class concerns itself with rank, custom, stability, continuity, public spirit and pragmatic knowledge, these internal émigrés are more drawn to privacy, transgression, timeless intensities, sexual experiment, personal relations, subjective states of mind and 'metaphysical' broodings. Women like Woolf and male homosexuals like Forster bulk large in their ranks, as those sidelined because of their gender join forces with the 'unmanned' sons of the virile patriarchs.

These, then, are the 'free spirits', who still share many of the assumptions of their social background, but who are in revolt against its arrogance and philistinism. They are artists, bohemians, free thinkers, sexual liberationists, spiritual anarchists – and they bring to this nonconformism all the *sang froid* and self-assurance of their patrician backgrounds. The bohemian may be careless of social convention, but so also is the aristocrat. Those at the apex of society can afford to flout its rules just like those in its margins. There is an unspoken compact between the rebel and the ruler, and Bloomsbury was both at once. It is a complicity we can observe in Woolf's early novel *Night and Day*, in which Katherine Hilbery breaks free of a conventional upper-class background with her disreputable lover Ralph Denham, only to discover that the upper-class coterie to which she belongs is adaptable enough to clasp them both forgivingly to its bosom.

Such men and women also bring to their rebellion an instinctive elitism. It is just that the elite has now been transposed from the generals and merchant bankers to the aesthetes and iconoclasts. The Bloomsbury group to which Woolf belonged was a coterie which saw itself as a vanguard. Coteries and vanguards may look much alike, as small bands of like-minded men and women. But whereas the coterie or elite sees itself as inherently superior to the social masses, the vanguard sees itself simply as historically out ahead of them. Because of its privileged position in the present, the vanguard can prefigure here and now a more emancipated future; but this future, so it trusts, will in time become available for everyone. It is just that they themselves are fortunate enough to be out in front for the moment. Vanguards, whatever their defects, at least look forward eagerly to a time when they will no longer exist, which is more than one can say for elites.

In reality, however, the line between elite and vanguard is notoriously hard to draw. If the vanguard is to succeed, bringing a new world of freedom and equality into being, it must end up by undermining its own privileges; and this was not a step which most of the Bloomsbury group were prepared to take. Nor is it easy with these high-class heretics to draw a line between the genuinely radical and the fashionably outrageous – between speaking up bravely against war on the one hand and talking loudly about semen on the other.

Woolf, then, alternately denounced and defended her own social position. A true liberal must be liberal enough to call into question her own liberalism. This, no doubt, is one reason why liberals are so perpetually agonized. E. M. Forster is just such a self-critical liberal: in *Where Angels Fear to Tread*, for example, a young upper-middle-class English woman runs off with a rather roughneck Italian, to the horror of her snobbish, stiff-necked family; but the tables are mischievously turned on the broad-minded reader when the Italian indeed turns out to be an appalling brute. For the conscientious liberal, honesty demands that you recognize how much your ideals of freedom are dependent on your social privileges. You must acknowledge

the material basis of your own beliefs, rather than succumbing to some fit of bad faith and kicking away the very wealth and status which allows those beliefs to thrive. You must realize that your personal liberty is parasitic on the exploitation of anonymous millions both at home and abroad; but this is no good reason to abandon it in a surge of guilt. How would this clean-handedness benefit the anonymous millions? And what image would they then have of their own potential freedom?

One can trace this ambiguity in Woolf's writing. Take, for example, her belief that the world is a fragmented place, full of haphazard sensations and random revelations. What imposes unity on this flux of impressions is art. Art is what orders experience into significant design. 'Nothing makes a whole except when I am writing', Woolf commented. Bernard, the writer charac-ter of *The Waves*, tells us how he 'retrieved [the trees] from formlessness with words'. The world has no meaning or value in itself, but art may provisionally elicit a pattern from it – a pattern which is then likely to vanish as quickly as it has emerged. This, one might claim, is one of the great clichés of modernism. The idea that the world is fractured, but that art makes it whole, is as familiar to modernism as the phrase 'You've got to stop running' is to bad movies. It has become one of the great pieties of literary criticism. Yet it is surely questionable. For one thing, why is unity so vital? What is wrong with disunity? Isn't there something oddly formalistic about the assumption (one which Woolf, despite her avant-gardism, seems to share) that finding patterns in things is a good in itself?

Anyway, for whom exactly does experience seem like a swirl of vivid odds and ends? It might have seemed this way to Virginia Woolf, but it is unlikely that it did so to the servants who rose not long after dawn to lay her fires and polish her fenders. It is hard to imagine them swooning over sudden epiphanies, or relishing the arbitrary flickers of shadow across the well-shaved lawn. The truth, surely, is that to see the world as delectably or alarmingly in pieces is to view it from a specific standpoint. It is not likely to seem this way for those who work on production lines or in inner-city schools. It is a viewpoint which depends among other things on enjoying a large degree of leisure, having little set routine, viewing the world contem-platively, and being able to do, within reason, pretty much as one wishes. It also depends on having a conception of unity, without which the notion of a fragment is logically impossible.

Like many partial viewpoints, this one is then offered to us as a universal truth. It is rather as if someone were to sigh 'Life is meaningless', to which one might riposte 'Well, yours might be'. The truth, surely, is that the world always comes to us significantly shaped by human projects. If we think of ourselves as agents rather than spectators or consumers, we are unlikely to regard reality as sheer disorder. The world we encounter is already scored through with the enterprises and intentions of others, which lend it some rough-and-ready coherence. The fact that there is no order or unity in the world in the way that Dante might have understood it does not mean that there is no order or unity at all.

Human purposes also endow things with a sense of necessity which Woolf's fiction often lacks. As Peter Walsh reflects in *Mrs Dalloway*: 'Where should he go? No matter. Up the street, then, towards Regent's Park'. For a leisurely loiterer, one destination is pretty much as good as another. Yet a world in which all seems minor miracle and epiphany, which lacks the predictability of custom and routine, is not exactly a pleasant place to be. 'Was there no safety?' Lily Briscoe asks herself in *To the Lighthouse*. 'No learning by heart of the ways of the world? No guide, no shelter, but always miracle, and leaping from the pinnacle of a tower into the air?'

If reality were not relatively calculable and coherent, we could not act purposively at all, since the world would not stay still long enough for us to execute our intentions. And if we cannot act purposively, then we cannot be free. This is because freedom is not just, as the Bloomsburyites tended to imagine, a matter of being free *from* something – patriarchy, social convention, class privilege, militarist ideology – but of being free to realize our goals in practice. And for this we need, if not a tightly structured world, then at least one which is more than a stream of disconnected sensations. The question of art then becomes not one of imposing order on chaos, but of transforming one kind of order into another. And this is a much more complex, demanding way of seeing the matter.

In any case, the idea that the world is 'meaningless' suggests that meaning is something that the world might contain but happens not to, rather as King Arthur might be buried beneath Wigan Town Hall but probably isn't. But things do not 'have' meanings in the sense that they have shapes and colours – which is not to say that they are meaning*less* either. The fact that objects do not happen along with their meanings written on their faces does not mean that they are pointless or absurd. Life does not 'have a meaning' which with luck we might stumble across, as we know there is an answer to the question 'What is the capital of North Dakota?' even though we do not know what it is.

As an upper-class woman, Woolf was inevitably somewhat remote from the world of social and political practice; and some of her ideas of accident and design, or life and art, have more to do with this distance than may at first appear. It is a matter of putting these ideas back in their social context, not of blaming Woolf for failing to negotiate a wage increase on behalf of tram drivers in Barnsley. She herself was deeply conscious of the historical roots of ideas which seemed at first glance universal; but it is usually our own convictions which prove the most difficult to historicize.

Even so, Woolf's views on the subject of accident and design are well worth having. She may have overestimated the general incoherence of life, but in doing so she struck a devastating blow at the paranoid cult of order of the patriarchs. She also saw well enough that this masculine fetishism of order led straight to fascism. Woolf's novels, in their very form, are political deconstructions of the masculine rage for order. They are aimed implicitly against what she refers to in *Three Guineas* as 'the arts of dominating other people . . . the arts of ruling, of killing, of acquiring land and capital'. Almost no other major English novelist could match the radicalism of that statement. Woolf's novels do not need to denounce Hitler or Mussolini to be anti-fascist works: this is a form of politics present in their very texture and syntax, in the mischievous sport they have with conventional narrative forms, their affection for the provisional and imperfect, the delicacy with which they focus upon stray feelings and loose ends.

One thinks, for example, of *Orlando*, which is among other things an exuberant literary sport at the expense of the stony-faced scholars. You must not unify in a way which undermines the sheer plurality and contingency of things. Lucy Swithin of *Between the Acts* believes in her liberal-humanist way that all historical epochs are the same under the skin, but it is questionable whether her author endorses this opinion. Perhaps the unity which the pageant in the book bestows on English history is no more than a provisional fiction. Theatre, after all, is the most perishable of art forms, and that, ironically, because it is the most real. Woolf's narrative forms reveal an impulse to unity, but they must also be loose enough to accommodate different viewpoints within the whole. Clarissa Dalloway feels herself to be an assemblage of disparate parts, not at all as 'composed' as she looks. The apparent stability of the English village at the centre of *Between the Acts* belies a war-torn history. Colonial conquest and a barbarous prehistory are never far beneath the civilized surfaces of the fiction.

Those who make a fetish out of law and order are those most likely to spread mayhem and misery around them. The conservatives whom Woolf has in her satirical sights are men who nurse a quasi-pathological fear that unless boundaries and distinctions are absolute, the result will be utter anarchy. They do not see that this simply makes them inverted anarchists. A certain kind of anarchist believes that chaos always lies just an inch or two beneath the surface of any order, and so does a certain kind of conservative. It is just that the former rejoices in the fact, whereas the latter laments it. In suspecting that the tiniest breach of order will lead instantly to orgy, carnival and armed revolt, the conservative ironically betrays his lack of trust in the very rules and regulations he so righteously upholds.

The idea that art imposes order on a dishevelled world has, ironically, a patriarchal ring to it. It is discomfortingly close to the Enlightenment belief that the mind must subjugate the world to its own purposes. Lily Briscoe, the artist of *To the Lighthouse*, has to wrench her painted shapes into doing her bidding. But there is a vital distinction all the same. Woolf is not of course an Enlightenment rationalist who believes that to know is to dominate. For her, the point of art is that it can compose things into a pattern without violating their specific natures. It can draw them together without flattening them out. This is why Lily finds it so difficult to finish her painting: things resist one's designs on them, refuse to fall deferentially into place. Composition will never be final; there is no total harmony; and the great moment of revelation never quite arrives. Even Lily says that she has *had* her vision, as though the reader has somehow missed it.

Art is thus a challenge to Enlightenment rationality, not a version of it. It is a model of true knowledge, one which respects its subject-matter rather than steamrollers it. It is also a form of irony, since it knows that its patterns are provisional. It does not mistake its own fictions for the truth. The vision, Lily comments, must be perpetually remade. In *The Years*, history coalesces into a pattern only to lapse once more into the shattered and discontinuous. Art is as much failure as triumph. It is in this sense that it is most realistic.

There are times when Woolf's writing has an almost hallucinatory sense of the specificity of things. This is by no means an unmixed blessing. It is sometimes as though she feels persecuted by reality itself, by the sheer brute, gratuitous existence of things, as Septimus Smith does in *Mrs Dalloway*. A sense of the sickening precariousness of the world, a fear that it might at any moment evaporate into nothingness, goes hand in hand with a heightened relish for its shapes and textures. Life is both glitteringly profuse and terrifyingly abundant. What makes it so rich is also what makes it so frighteningly hard to find your bearings in it. Woolf's sense of a vacancy at the heart of things no doubt springs in part from her forced exclusion from the world of social action. It is by our practice that we establish the solidity of things, not least ourselves. If the world dissolves into unreality, so too does the human subject, deprived of a way of confirming its identity. The fragmenting of reality, and the splintering of the human subject, are aspects of the same process.

Woolf, rather like D. H. Lawrence, has an extraordinary receptivity to objects, a capacity to open herself to their unique modes of being without foisting grand designs upon them. And this powerfully undercuts the masculinist cult of the imperious will. Her politics, in this way as in others, are folded into her style and imagination. At the same time, such a susceptibility to impressions, if pressed too far, may lead to madness. And this sense of the autonomous existence of things co-exists in her writing with a kind of solipsism. The world is brilliantly, radiantly *there*, yet it is also somehow dependent on the mind. This is not the case for an 'objectivist' philosopher like Mr Ramsay, for whom the world is solidly present whatever our perception of it. (It is ironic, incidentally, that this stout objectivist should also be such an emotional egoist, centring the world on his own needs even as he asserts its independence of the human.) Woolf's concern with the way the mind at least half-creates the world is among other things a reaction to this creed. There is a kind of artistry involved in the very act of perception.

The mind, then, needs to open itself to the world, without allowing the magisterial male ego to get in the way of their encounter. But it is the mind, even so, which endows that world with meaning and value. It is as though nothing for Woolf is entirely real unless it has first been filtered through consciousness, seized and enriched by a solitary act of imagination. This is no doubt one reason why her work is full of audacious, strikingly inventive metaphors and similes which see Nature in human terms. In *Between the Acts*, we read of the birds 'attacking the dawn like so many choir boys attacking an iced cake'. Natural objects like cows are incorporated into the novel's pageant, as though they were somehow 'meant'. Woolf's fertility and exuberance of metaphor and similes, some of it deliberately extravagant and self-flaunting, counts among her most arresting features. Such metaphors and similes mark the precarious edge which the mind has over reality, as well as the creative looseness of relation between the two. Things in Woolf's prose are often bathed in an aura of something else, as objects flow into their surroundings or melt into other objects.

In one sense, the fact that it is the mind which lends meaning to the world is plausible enough. Events are not comic or momentous, nor are tastes acrid or odours fragrant, for anyone but ourselves. Badgers presumably do not find shipwrecks distressing, or the smell of coffee enticing. But this means that what makes the world precious – the fact that we can imbue it with value – is also what makes it precarious, since that value seems arbitrary and subjective. We ourselves are the only guardians of it. In itself, the world for Woolf is sometimes simply blank. It is as though she is only really interested in the common life when it can be wrought into aesthetic shape. The external world is thus both heightened and devalued. Otherwise, ordinary unpoetical life is quite often seen as dreary and banal, to be mentioned literally in parentheses. 'I haven't that "reality" gift', she confesses in her diary. 'I insubstantise, wilfully to some extent, distrusting reality – its cheapness'. Among other things, this is an implicit kind of class judgement. It belongs with the side of Woolf which languidly dismissed politics as a bore, even though she knew perfectly well how vital they were to women's well-being. With Woolf, the novel has come a long way from its early root in the enthralling nature of everyday life.

In a celebrated passage in her essay 'Modern Novels', Woolf writes that 'The mind, exposed to the ordinary course of life, receives upon its surface a myriad impressions – trivial, fantastic, evanescent, or engraved with the sharpness of steel. From all sides they come, an incessant shower of innumerable atoms, composing in their sum what we might venture to call life itself'. This gives the effect of a lavish diversity of experience – though in suggesting that life consists of impressions rather than realities, it also implies, somewhat less affirmatively, that we are all cut off from the real world, confined within the prison-house of our senses. The word 'composing' in the quoted passage is mildly ironic, since in Woolf it generally refers to the act of unifying, and one problem implicit in this image is how human experience can achieve any more coherence than a patch of mist.

We may note, too, that if impressions are in one sense what are most real, in the sense of being most vivid, they are also unreal, in the sense of being 'evanescent'. They thus capture Woolf's ambiguous sense of existence in general. And since all impressions, whether trifling or momentous, have in common the fact that they are impressions, they have the effect of levelling hierarchies of value. A sensation of toothache may be quite as insistent as a perception of tragedy. This is a subversive move from the standpoint of those who cling to strict hierarchies; but it is also a cause for anxiety. For one thing, tragedy *is* more momentous than toothache; for another thing, a world in which nothing is more significant than anything else is flat and barren. The problem is that impressions alone will not tell you what bits of reality are more or less significant than other bits, since they all lie on a level.

Woolf's sense of the mind as passive, bombarded by random sensations, belongs partly with the confines of gender (since women are stereotyped as passive); partly with the contemplative stance of the leisured classes, and partly with a rather disreputable vein of English philosophy. What we see when we look at an elephant is not a fuzzy patch of grey, but an elephant. A fuzzy patch of grey is, ironically, an *abstraction* from what we actually see. Yet what Woolf did was to transform these *symptoms* of her social situation into a searching *critique* of it. The passivity of the human subject becomes a protest against the dominative will of war, capitalism and imperialism. The fractured nature of the self unmasks the tightly unified male ego as a myth. The fact that all one really has is one's impressions is a guard against dogmatism, since impressions are by nature provisional. A sensuous vulnerability to the world is a scandal to those who must stamp their mark on it by force, and who see nothing but their own faces in its mirror. It also blurs the distinction between subject and object, to the dismay of those ideologues for whom mind or spirit is one thing, and matter or the body quite another.

Much the same double-edgedness can be seen in Woolf's suspicion of linear narrative, in which things are laid out strictly end to end. It is fashionable these days to associate such linearity with the dominative and exclusive, in contrast to a more 'synchronic', all-inclusive form of being. (Curiously, most of those who insist on this distinction are also opposed to binary oppositions.) This case has a good deal going for it: grand narratives which unfurl inexorably, step by deterministic step, are scarcely the most fruitful way of picturing human affairs. But the linear is by no means to be so naively discarded. To do so may just be a sign of social privilege. For one thing, there can be no effective emancipatory politics without it. Goals and strategies, ends and means, set-backs and advances, crises and recoveries, failures and achievements: these are all part of efforts at radical transformation. And they are all inescapably bound up with the unfolding of time. To see this complex process as a rigorous unfolding from *a* to *z* would indeed be destructive, but not many devotees of the linear are foolish enough to do so. George Eliot believes in the possibility of progress, but she does not see it as a simple chain of cause and effect.

Equally, not all assaults on 'linear' thinking are on the side of the political angels. The eternal cycles of mythology have often enough been used by right-wing thinkers as a way of discrediting the very idea of history. The concept of multi-dimensional time may seem more congenial than some fatalistic grand narrative, but it is by no means always so. Take, for example, the situation of so many impoverished postcolonial nations today, which find themselves squeezed between the premodern and the postmodern, oxen and wooden ploughs in the countryside and US corporate executives in the cities. What exactly is desirable about this kind of time-warping? Ought we to congratulate these societies on being so bracingly non-linear? There are those old-fashioned radicals who believe it desirable that everyone should make progress towards social justice; but there are also those who, distrusting such tedious grand narratives, might think it preferable to leave some groups behind in the political Stone Age, just for the sake of difference and plurality.

Woolf's distaste for the linear partly reflects her distance from the unavoidably cause-and-effect nature of actual political struggle. Yet at the same time it valuably garbles the grand narratives of the warmongers and empire-builders. And it suggests that a political strategy which does not include the time of the body, the psyche, Nature, perception and everyday experience, along with clock time and public history, is not likely to be worth very much. One space in which all these time-schemes can be interwoven is known as the novel. In typically modernist fashion, Woolf has a keen sense of the presentness of the past, not just of its pastness – of the ways in which the past is alive and burgeoning in us, rather as in the present we are all intricately bound up with countless anonymous lives which we never actually encounter.

This sense of the fundamental communality of human life runs deep in this apparently individualist writer. Despite her fascination with the fine-drawn individual consciousness, Woolf is intensely interested in anonymous forces, the obscure life of the masses, the determining power of circumstance, the moulding effects of inheritance and of specific places and times. These are not the usual preoccupations of liberals like herself. It is not surprising, however, that a feminist writer should have been alert to such questions. Had she been a male member of her class, Woolf might well been content with the idea of the 'free individual' who soars above historical circumstance. Her feminism, however, makes her aware in a materialist way that the lives and labour of countless unsung men and women go into the production of the Great Man or the distinguished literary work. She recognized that the individual self so ardently cherished by so-called great men was decentred by the historical forces which went into its making. And she was not slow to acknowledge the almost overwhelming force of such circumstances. The pageant in *Between the Acts* can be read as record-

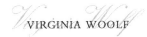

ing the steady disintegration of a collective English tradition into an errant
individualism.

On the other hand, Woolf is indeed a liberal individualist, one for whom
the self is quite frighteningly isolated. It is not that she believes in the *ego*; on
the contrary, she invents a form of writing which shifts attention from this
deceptively self-sufficient entity to that much more fluid, fragile, borderless
thing known as the *subject*. Yet though this human subject is splintered and
diffuse, it remains as marooned in its own being as Crusoe on his island. The
self is a 'wedged-shaped core of darkness . . . something invisible to others'
(*To The Lighthouse*). This belief, as Henry Fielding might have observed, has
only one defect, namely that it is not true. Our inner lives are not in principle invisible to others at all. The word 'inner' here, suggesting 'secret', is
quite misleading. Our selves are made manifest to others all the time in
language, action and the body. Indeed, unless we were intelligible to others,
we would not be intelligible to ourselves. We do not need to peer into each
other's skulls to glimpse each other's 'inner' life; we are observing it all the
time.

Selfhood is not in Woolf's eyes what we might nowadays call 'dialogical',
formed by its interactions with others. Indeed, there is relatively little dialogue in her novels even in the more familiar sense of the word. The six
monologues of *The Waves* speak into a luminous void; they do not actually
address one another. Language, in typically modernist fashion, is not a reliable mode of communication. It must be poetically charged if it is to capture
the immediacy of experience. Whenever one encounters such gorgeously
wrought language, it is worth asking whether this reflects a distrust in language in its unvarnished everyday condition. Language for Woolf is public,
whereas experience and sensation are essentially private; and a chasm looms
between the two.

This, in fact, is the other great modernist cliché to surface in her work,
and one as doubtfully valid as her views on order and chaos. Because our
sense-impressions are the touchstone of what is real, and because these
impressions are finally incommunicable, we are all at some level solitary
monads sealed off from each other. Characters at the beginning of *Mrs
Dalloway* are linked by seeing the same motor car or aeroplane, but while
this points to the interwovenness of apparently separate lives in the modern
city, it is also a kind of irony. Like the men on the lighter in *Nostromo*,
bringing together different characters in this deliberately arbitrary, external
way also shows up just how isolated from each other they actually are,

sharing the same experiences from quite different perspectives. That the *Mrs Dalloway* motor car is a mere device in this respect is underlined by the fact that it does not matter who is inside it.

Once again, it may be that Woolf is here confusing a specific historical state with a universal one. The idea that the self is doomed to solitude is largely a modern one. Virgil, Dante, Milton and Pope do not brood in Conradian fashion over the eternal isolation of human beings. It is true that the Bloomsburyites were renowned for their cultivation of human relationships, to the point of making something of a religious cult out of them. (When one finds such an intense focusing on personal relationships, it is always worth asking what kinds of experience it may be forcibly excluding.) Yet Woolf and Bloomsbury were also heirs to a tradition of robust English individualism which made just as much of a cult out of the eccentric and aberrant. The English love a 'character', meaning someone who is stubbornly, anarchically, himself. If they also love a lord, it is because lords are privileged enough to be like this too. The other side of this delight in the idiosyncratic, however, is the anxiety that each of us is ultimately alone. And this belief may have more to do with the nature of our own civilization than with the 'human condition' as a whole.

Behind the relative lack of dialogue in some of Woolf's novels lurks a very English reticence. What is communicated is often done so wordlessly, obliquely, by nuance, tone, brushstroke or gesture. It is a world in which speech is simply the tip of the iceberg of personal experience, and in which one arrives at mutual understanding as much by subliminal vibration as by candid declaration. Far less is out in the open than is concealed. This is not a puritanical culture like the United States, in which one feels the compulsive impulse to externalize the self in order to avoid the guilt of the unconfessed. In Woolf, the idea of the public does not exert such a despotic force. People in her fiction tend to haunt each other rather than relate directly. We are moving in the tacit, reserved sphere of upper-class England, in which an immense amount is going on inside characters, but is outwardly disowned or dissembled. What is important is not just what is not said, but how it is not said. It is a culture in which Mrs Ramsay fails to tell her husband that she loves him, but in which the couple can establish the fact in a luminous moment of wordless communion.

It may be that Woolf's sense of communality is not ultimately at odds with this sharply separated selfhood. Instead, the former may be something of a refuge from the latter. There is a strong impulse towards the communal and collective at work in her writing, one which occasionally presses towards a semi-mystical belief in universal love and an 'oceanic' merging of the self into some deeper dimension. It is a depth associated with death – an extreme reaction to the extremity of egoism in this social order. Personality in Woolf is not something discrete and sharply bounded, a fact which is as much a cause of anxiety as of affirmation. It may also be one reason why there can be a curiously bodiless feel about her fiction, for all its sensory intensities, since the body is the most obvious boundary of the self.

Septimus Smith, who can feel the leaves of trees through his body and hears birds talking to him, is possessed by some such 'oceanic' belief, though it does not help the case that he is mad. He also thinks that he can see into everything and know its meaning, which makes him just the kind of omniscient narrator whom Woolf disapproves of in the realist novel. (Bernard, the writer in *The Waves*, can tell snatches of story but not the 'one true story' to which they all refer. There can be, as we might say, no meta-language or grand narrative – whereas Louis in the same novel wants to 'plait into one cable' the diverse threads of the characters' history.) For Septimus, who thinks that strangers are signalling to him, there is too much meaning in the world rather than, as often in Woolf, too little. To see everything as ominously bound up with everything else is a kind of paranoia, just as to see the world as a heap of fragments is (in the loose sense of the word) a sort of schizophrenia. The self, anyway, is a network of strands and fibres which curl around the roots of other lives, so that, as with Lawrence, one is never the proprietor of one's own being. The web which for George Eliot was a metaphor of society is now an image of personal identity.

There is, then, an obscure region into which the self sends down its tentacular roots, a place far beyond language, where our lives are unconsciously intertwined. The two main characters of Mrs Dalloway, Clarissa and Septimus, feel a kind of vital contact with each other without ever meeting. The only alternative to alienation – the sharp separation of subject and object – would seem to be empathy, in which subject and object blur together. Woolf has grave doubts about this alternative, but there is something logical about it even so. Empathy of this kind overcomes the historical distinctions between individuals, so that what the private self and the collective self have in common is that they are both equally unhistorical. A good deal of modernist art leaps from the private to the eternal with nothing much in between; and Woolf sometimes links the private self to the communal one by taking a detour around actual history. Her novels tend to thin out the social and historical in order to make direct links between the personal and metaphysical.

Even so, few things are more politically and historically important than sexuality and the family, which is why Woolf, like Jane Austen, can engage with the wider world simply by recording what goes on at home. She described *Mrs Dalloway* as a criticism of the social system, just as *To the Lighthouse* can be read as a critique of the Victorian family. Clarissa Dalloway, like her author, is both insider and outsider, a woman who has become complicit with the ruling social order but who is conscious of this, and who still feels some underground springs of rebellion. When it comes to the social establishment, she is both disdainful and dependent. In fact, all the novel's 'free spirits' have compromised with the system. Clarissa, once a left-wing idealist, is now the high-society spouse of a Tory MP; the once roguish, unconventional Sally Seton has settled down to a sedate bourgeois life in Manchester; and Peter Walsh, a fairly bogus radical to begin with, has been a colonial administrator in India and is not so disaffected with the metropolitan socialite scene that he gives up attending its parties.

As for the establishment itself, the novel's satire is brilliantly acerbic. Hugh Whitbread is an outrageous snob, while Richard Dalloway is a toothless reformer. Sir William Bradshaw, the pompous, authoritarian physician who bullies, pigeon-holes and incarcerates his patients, is a man Michel Foucault would cheerfully have murdered. Lady Bradshaw is portrayed with splendid malice as dressed 'in grey and silver, balancing like a sea-lion at the edge of its tank, barking for invitations'. This violent, emotionally autistic governing class is increasingly outdated, as new social formations (not least the women's movement) are emerging, and old ones, not least the empire, declining. These people have thrust the horrors of war too hygienically out of sight, whereas Septimus has repressed them all too little. In the 'Time Passing' section of *To The Lighthouse*, we observe the gradual decay of a whole class, not just of a house or a family.

Yet criticism of the system in *Mrs Dalloway* is also deflected. Miss Kilman is a sharp critic of the heroine, but the fact that she is gripped by personal bitterness and social resentment helps to discredit her testimony. Radical critics or lower-class rebels in Woolf quite often turn out to be self-pitying, chip-on-shoulder types. Peter Walsh, back from colonial India, can bring the air of a broader world to this claustrophobic coterie, but he is also a cranky, bookish deviant from his social class, a kind of failed nomad, all of which serves to qualify his dissent. He sees Clarissa as tainted by the imperial,

public-spirited, governing-class ethos; but he has been, after all, a sexual rival to the husband who drew her into this world, and so is by no means an impartial witness. In Woolf, there is no such thing.

Clarissa, for her part, is the hostess as artist. While Woolf herself weaves the strands of her text together to create a whole, Clarissa Dalloway's own work of art is a party, which (if it goes well) brings men and women into momentary unity. Mrs Ramsay's art-work in *To the Lighthouse* is a meal, one which she does not even cook herself. Meals and parties are like works of art because they are carefully crafted compositions with an air of spontaneity, events which bring those who participate in them into a form of fellowship. But they are also like works of art because they are created for their own sake, with no particular purpose in mind. (It is true that one has to eat something, but one does not have to eat *Boeuf en Daube*, as the Ramsays do. And most people – though not all – can survive without parties).

Haute cuisine and party-giving are where the domestic and artistic, the everyday and the epiphanic, come together, if only in irony. They are the secular equivalents of the eucharist. Like the queenly Mrs Ramsay in *To The Lighthouse*, these events simply *are*. They have nothing as vulgar as a function, any more than Woolf and her friends do. The charismatic Mrs Ramsay is herself a kind of maternal artist. She is a skilled creator of harmonies, a domestic negotiator who reconciles the contentions around her by her radiant resourcefulness of being. Like a work of art, she integrates unruly elements. Like Emma Woodhouse, she also 'composes' rather too freely, plotting possible relationships for her companions.

The other thing which seems to exist just for itself, without rhyme or reason, is death; so it is fitting that the shadow of death, in the form of Septimus's suicide, should fall over Clarissa's party. Death is at once more and less real than life – more final and dramatic, yet also a kind of vacancy – and this is how Clarissa feels about parties, too. Death is central to all Woolf's fiction. In *The Voyage Out*, it is what saves the heroine from marriage. (An extreme enough remedy, one might consider, rather like cutting off someone's head to stop them squinting.) Death is the Real which lies at the core of the social order, yet which cannot be represented there. Septimus's death, for instance, is scarcely seen at all, while Mrs Ramsay's is announced in a famous, rather too calculatedly casual parenthesis. It is, in fact, an occupational hazard of maternal figures in Bloomsbury novels to die with indecent suddenness: the same happens to Forster's Mrs Wilcox and Mrs Moore. Percival, the dead hero or absent centre of *The Waves*, is not seen at all, either dead or alive. Bloomsbury novels are full of absent centres, vortices around which the action swirls and which hint at an absolute reality which can never be symbolized.

Clarissa finds something alluring as well as alarming about Septimus's death. It is a kind of defiance, which stands in judgement on the triviality of her own party. One vacancy (death) calls another (high society) into question. Death articulates the emptiness at the heart of all human experience – an emptiness most obvious in the transience of things. Ironically, the very fleetingness of life, the fact that it is a kind of ceaseless death or passing away, recalls what is permanent and imperishable. Life may pass away, but death will not. Death is also inviting because it represents a form of absoluteness and finality in a world of flux. Indeed, it may be the only absolute to survive in this sceptical, relativistic world.

The modernists in general are much taken by the idea of something stable and eternal at the heart of our experience, of which we can catch only a passing glimpse. Art is one name for such glimpses. Another, at least for James Joyce, is an 'epiphany': a fleeting revelation of the infinite. Postmodernism calls off this wistful hunt for the absolute, and contents itself instead with the unredeemed fragments of time. The tragedy of modernism, however, is that it cannot abdicate its yearning for the absolute even though it knows it to be a kind of fiction. As a kind of compromise, then, the absolute tends to make its appearance in the form of absence rather than presence – and death, being an absolute absence, can then become the sign of an absent absolute. One can easily fall in love with death, seduced by its purity and finality.

There is, anyway, something at the very core of human experience which seems abiding and immune from change, and Mrs Ramsay in *To The Lighthouse* is a symbol of this stability in her serene self-possession. So in a way is the lighthouse itself, which combines motion (the moving beam of light) with stillness. The lighthouse, incidentally, is what one might call a symbol of a symbol, rather like the Marabar caves in Forster's *A Passage to India*. It is so obviously, self-consciously a symbol that it is a kind of literary joke as well as seriously intended. Woolf herself wrote of it that 'one has to have a central line down the middle of the book to hold the design together', implying that it is as much an arbitrary, purely formal device as the Homeric myth in *Ulysses*.

Lily Briscoe feels the presence of this Real – this absolute at the heart of reality which only the absence known as death can truly signify. She feels herself drawn out of the community around her, of what we might call the symbolic order of society, into 'the presence of this formidable enemy of hers – this other thing, this truth, this reality, which suddenly laid hands on her, emerged stark at the back of appearances and demanded her attention'. The death in question here is the brute, gratuitous decease of Mrs Ramsay, which like all death (but sudden death in particular) seems to fall outside the realm of meaning, and which Lily, like the reader, has to make some sense of without turning it into some simple-minded symbol.

Mrs Ramsay's permanence of being, the apparent 'necessity' of her existence, has turned out to be a fiction; she was, after all, as contingent as everything else in this ephemeral world. But the distance which this then allows Lily to establish from her also allows her to resolve her ambivalent feelings towards this somewhat oppressively charismatic figure, and thus to complete her canvas. What has been lost in life can be recreated in death. In life, Mrs Ramsay seemed, like a symbolist poem, to 'be' rather than to 'mean'; now death has distanced her being to the point where some kind of meaning might be able to emerge from it. She can now be turned into a signifier, a process which always involves a loss of pure presence.

The absence Lily has to confront, however, is not only that of death, but of desire. In one sense, death is the opposite of desire, since it removes the loved object forever from our presence. But in doing so it signifies the ultimate impossibility of desire, the fact that it can never entirely achieve its goal. The object which would fulfil it can never be wholly accessible. Mrs Ramsay's self-completeness of being, which lends her a sense of remoteness, signifies this inaccessibility in her life, thus anticipating her death. So desire, like death, turns on an absolute absence. It also resembles death in being a kind of lack. This lack acts as the dynamic of human existence, but also prefigures the absence in which it will end. What Lily feels after Mrs Ramsay's death is a kind of pure, contentless longing, one which defeats language. It defeats language not by being too full for words, but by being too empty. Mrs Ramsay has been the object of this desire; and since she is now dead, Lily is left, so to speak, with desire itself – desire without an object, and so at its most pure and real. What will overcome it, at least for the moment, is art.

It is art – in this case, Lily's painting – which sublimates desire into stillness, making things both more and less real, framing and distancing them yet in that very act bringing them more vividly alive. Art is a play of presence and absence, since it represents what is not actually there; in this sense it is akin to death and desire, which are also ambiguous blendings of presence and absence. It also has the impersonality of them both. In fact, art occupies a space somewhere between death and desire, combining the achieved stillness of the former with the living flow of the latter.

Mrs Ramsay, though much idealized and mythologized by others, is of course by no means uncriticized by the novel. Unlike her author, she believes firmly in the traditional roles of wife and mother; she is also meddlesome, uninformed and emotionally inhibited. Like Clarissa Dalloway, she is something of a sceptic beneath her socially decorous surface, aware of just how flawed, self-seeking and despicable human beings really are. The one whose role is to be broker – the wife and mother – is also the observer best placed to have a low opinion of those she seeks to conciliate. She spends too much of herself, which, as in Henry James, can be a subtle form of power.

It is she, rather than her husband, who stands for the Law in the book; but it is that most seductive, insidious kind of authority, the law of love and the flesh. Mrs Ramsay's very beauty of being persuades you to obey her; whereas Mr Ramsay is an image of the hollowness of the patriarchal law, which for all its brutal power is no more than an imposture. Ramsay's irascible authoritarianism is just the other side of his infantile neediness. The point for Lily is to distance herself from the image of Mrs Ramsay to the point where she can freely acknowledge its influence. Her art allows her to do both, drawing the image of Mrs Ramsay closer yet also 'placing' her, and so in a way triumphing over her.

This illustrates a more general truth. Only by acknowledging the sources of our being, acknowledging our unsavoury historical heritage, can we have the power to free ourselves from them. If we are to sever ourselves from the maternal body and move beyond it, it can only be by recognizing our con-tinuing dependence on it. What the older generation gives us most valuably of all is the confidence to break with it and venture forth into independent existence. If we cannot do this, then we shall simply find ourselves reliving the past, fixated on our elders in a posture of enraged rejection. We will find ourselves caught in a fruitless cycle of fury at the parent, followed by an attempt to shield that loved figure from our own aggression in an access of remorse and reparation.

Virginia Woolf did not believe that art could spring from anger, which is why she divided off polemics like *Three Guineas* from her fiction. It is hardly true of, say, Jonathan Swift that art and anger are eternally at odds. But it is surely the case that unless you nurture a hope for reconciliation alongside your anger, then you will quickly come to forget what you are angry in the name of. You cannot protest against injustice unless you have some image of justice by which to identify it.

Lily Briscoe achieves a reconciliation of a kind, and so does Mr Ramsay, who by the end of the novel has been transformed from a comic or pathetic figure into a semi-heroic one. In finally arriving at the lighthouse, he too has his encounter with the Real, one skilfully orchestrated with Lily's; and as usual in Woolf this traumatic confrontation with death, loss and bitter reality represents a resurgence of life. It is particularly courageous of a modernist novel to end on this tentative note of regeneration, since in the modern age nothing seems more naive than hope. That the ending is also profoundly moving is even more testimony to Woolf's sure touch.

Woolf is famous for her assault in her essay 'Mr Bennett and Mrs Brown' on the realism of Arnold Bennett and his colleagues – on the kind of literary art which sticks to the external detail and fails to bring out the inner life. This, in fact, is something of a caricature of Bennett and others, who were more attuned to 'psychology' than Woolf is willing to acknowledge. It is also more a rejection of naturalism than of realism. Wolf disliked this kind of fiction partly because it was open-ended – an ironic enough view for a writer devoted to process and provisionality. Such works, she thought, pointed beyond themselves, towards the need for political action or simply, by virtue of their referential language, to an independent world. Her objection to them thus springs partly from a fetishism of unity. The work of art must be self-contained, sharply demarcated from everyday life. Yet why it should be is never really argued for. It is simply another modernist piety.

In fact, Woolf herself spoke up for realism at various times, portraying art as a matter of seeing things as they are. It is just that she thought the best way to do this was to put 'external' reality, so to speak, in brackets, so as the better to attend to the 'inner' life. (How much sense this distinction makes is a different matter.) Critics have noticed the way that she does this more or less literally in her writing: '. . . saying to herself, as she took the pad with the telephone message on it, how moments like this are buds on the tree of life, flowers of darkness they are . . .' (Mrs Dalloway). The prose repeatedly tucks away a reference to the external world in a sub-clause or parenthesis, usually in the middle of some metaphysical flight of fancy.

This is partly a way of momentarily anchoring the mind in real life, lest it soar off altogether into some ethereal realm. But it is also deliberately ironic, although not in a Joycean sense. In Joyce, these interpolated references to telephones, dining forks and the like would probably act as mischievous deflations of the flights of fancy. In Woolf, they are reminders of how arbitrary the intersections are between the mind and the world, or the private and public domains. We are in a world of tumultuous inward drama in which, externally speaking, nothing very noteworthy happens; and this trick of style calls the fact to our attention. Private and public worlds, or what Woolf called 'vision' and 'fact', collide in a way which highlights their essential apartness. Elsewhere in her writing there is an asymmetry between inner and outer lives, so that psychological states (like James Ramsay's fury with his father at not going to the lighthouse) seem excessive of their material causes, or blankly disconnected from them. Woolf believed deeply, like George Eliot, that the public and private worlds were inseparably connected, and says as much in *Three Guineas*. What else, after all, is art? It is also clear that she knew an impressive amount about property, militarism, education, social conditions, sexual politics and the like. It was not ignorance of these matters which kept them out of her fiction. It was rather that she had a conception of art which for the most part kept them at bay.

In the end, Woolf could find no way of writing which might combine the two spheres. The writer who blended them most triumphantly in her time was Marcel Proust, chronicler of the French upper classes and exquisitely subtle investigator of the psyche. Proust, moreover, has two qualities which Woolf for the most part lacks: intellectual depth and ecstatic comedy. Woolf tried to unify fact and vision in an early draft of *The Years*, but gave it up as a bad job. Hence her strict separation of politics and art, which is another name for this dichotomy. The claim that the didactic or polemical are fatal to art is another weary commonplace of literary criticism, and one which Woolf, for all her unorthodoxy in other respects, fully endorsed. But it is not one borne out by the record. Some medieval drama is didactic, but to fine effect. *Gulliver's Travels* includes some magnificent polemic. One of the most resourceful of all literary genres, from John Donne to John Henry Newman, is the sermon. Edmund Burke is both poetic and polemical. Dickens's *Bleak House* has some magnificently preachy moments. That didacticism is always the ruin of art is yet another modern cliché.

In any case, Woolf's art does not cease to be political simply because much of it is not, in the usual sense of the word, realist. The idea that you can best get at the truth of things by 'bracketing off' the external world belongs to phenomenology, a philosophical current in vogue in Woolf's day. The phenomenologists 'suspend' the everyday world in order the more closely to investigate the workings of the mind. They are interested less in the object 'in itself' than in how it presents itself to consciousness. Woolf's art is in some ways a literary version of this method; but this does not make

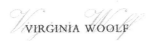

it either non-historical or non-political. Indeed, the irony of her writing is that by 'bracketing' the external world, thus risking the charge of being aloof and elitist, she can more fully explore questions of feeling, value, identity and subjectivity which are themselves thoroughly political in their implications. Few questions could be more momentous for dispossessed groups like women than those of feeling and subjectivity. As in phenomenology, what looks like a turning away from the everyday world is in fact a way of engaging with it more deeply.

The real criticism to be made of Woolf's writing is not that it is not realist, but that it is not dramatic. Though she speaks of human differences, she finds it hard to 'perform' them in her art – to flesh out characters by letting them speak and act out their idiosyncrasies for themselves. She is poor at capturing in speech or action the distinctive tone of a personality, as opposed to brilliantly describing it from a narrational viewpoint. This, no doubt, is one reason why the six monologuing characters of *The Waves* are so notoriously hard to tell apart, like the Snow White dwarfs on an overcast evening. The prose of the book is both beautiful and (in the technical sense of the word) monotonous. It can delineate differences, but it cannot *do* them. Woolf, one suspects, would have made a dreadful mimic, restricted as she is like so many of the upper-class English to the tones of her own class. Dickens, by contrast, was no doubt a superb one; he was certainly a talented actor, as indeed was James Joyce, which one imagines Woolf could never have been. Despite her belief in the protean nature of the self, her own selfhood is socially restricted. She does not see people in terms of their unique self-performances. And in one sense this is not surprising. Action and discourse are places where the private and public worlds intersect; but such convergences in Woolf are fairly rare.

Woolf was not a realist, though *The Years* is a realist historical novel, and the theme of warfare runs throughout her work from *Jacob's Room* to *Between the Acts*. What she was, rather more importantly, was a materialist. And it was her feminism which led her to be so. She used the word 'materialist' disparagingly of writers like Bennett and Wells, but by this she really meant 'naturalistic', in the sense of an art too myopically devoted to external appearances. She herself was a materialist in a more valuable sense, as is clear when she remarks in *A Room Of One's Own* that 'One cannot think well, love well, sleep well, if one has not dined well'. It is a deliberately coat-trailing comment, one which cuts against the grain of the cultural idealism (both then and now) of the social establishment. Cultural idealists do not like to hear, as Woolf suggests elsewhere in the book, that women have

succeeded as authors because of the cheapness of writing paper. They prefer to think of art as transcendent, whereas Woolf, as a feminist, is necessarily concerned with the material preconditions of cultural production. She is interested less in art as reflecting material reality, than in the material realities which make it possible. In all this, the influence of her gender pulls against the influence of her social class.

Woolf was, in short, that somewhat rare animal, a materialist modernist. She was materialist and historicist in her political thought, but rightly saw no reason why this should go hand-in-hand with a realist art. Mayakovsky, Bertolt Brecht and André Breton thought much the same. On the contrary, it was exactly because she was so conscious of the material and historical restrictions on women's lives that she wanted to create an art that could perform two functions at once. It would investigate this condition in imaginative terms, while giving it the slip in its sportive, transgressive, deconstructed forms. It would, in other words, be both ideology and utopia.

The Irish writer Flann O'Brien tells the story of the peasant family in their cabin who tried to keep the wolf from the door for fear that it would get out. Virginia Woolf certainly did that.

POSTSCRIPT:
AFTER THE *WAKE*

Modern English literature reached its zenith in the period of high modernism, now some 80 years or so behind us. Between the death of Henry James in 1916, and the death of Joseph Conrad in 1924, we witness an astonishing outbreak of literary innovation: T. S. Eliot's *Prufrock* (1917) and *The Waste Land* (1922), Joyce's *Portrait* (1916) and *Ulysses* (1922), Ezra Pound's *Hugh Selwyn Mauberley* (1920), Lawrence's *The Rainbow* (1915) and *Women in Love* (1920), W. B. Yeats's *The Wild Swans at Coole* (1919), Virginia Woolf's *Jacob's Room* (1922). Only two of these virtuosi of English literature were English.

The era of major literary achievement, in other words, was the tumultuous years around the First World War, when European civilization itself was called radically into question. For the first time, but not for the last, the clash of competing national capitalisms leads to global conflagration. Futility, despair and spiritual disintegration strike at the heart of Western culture. There is a sense of impending apocalypse and collapse. The continent is shaken by mass social and political militancy, of a kind not witnessed for well over half a century. Few of the great liberal ideals which served earlier middle-class society so finely emerge unscathed from the wreckage. After Ypres and the Somme, there is less callow talk of reason, progress and civility. The barbarism which was previously thought to lurk on the colonial margins now seemed to have infiltrated the very heart of the imperial metropolis.

The relations between all this, and the flourishing of the most adventurous fiction and poetry of the modern age, are doubtless complex. Yet there are clear affinities between the collapse of old forms and the emergence of new ones in literature and in civilization at large. If the period was one of trauma and catastrophe, it was also one of creative possibility. As a whole traditional way of life was called increasingly into discredit, there was a need to think with imaginative boldness in both literature and politics. It was out of this seismic upheaval that the major English novel of the twentieth century emerged, in an achievement not to be repeated since. Joyce's *Finnegans Wake*, published on the eve of a new global conflagration in 1939, is a lonely outpost of this extraordinary epoch. By that time, however, a less ambitiously experimental form of writing (Auden, Orwell, Isherwood) had already overtaken it, leaving the *Wake* like some exotic mammoth marooned by the ice age in an alien landscape. Realism had been reinstalled – if occasionally with a suitably modernist inflection, as in John Fowles's *The French Lieutenant's Woman*.

The Second World War was to witness no equivalent peak of fictional achievement. Nothing happens twice, partly because it has happened once already. The moulds had already been shattered by the early twentieth-century pioneers. After the Second World War, some of their literary successors did their best to pretend that everything was exactly as it had been. Philip Larkin, the unofficial Poet Laureate of the second half of the twentieth century, turned his back on Eliot, Pound and Joyce and peered back over their heads to Hardy and Edward Thomas. Many other poets did the same – some out of sheer provincialism, others because the act had proved too hard to follow. The novel resumed its parochial perspectives. The great modernist adventure began to seem more and more like an aberration, a momentary capitulation to foreign madness. A native English philistinism, which detested fancy ideas as much as it was wary of free-loving foreigners, was back in business.

For an exhilarating moment in the 1950s and 1960s, it looked as though this dank orthodoxy was about to be overthrown from below. A brash new school of social realists – Kingsley Amis, Alan Sillitoe, John Braine, John Wain and others – sounded the note of the new postwar Britain: unheroic, egalitarian, anti-Establishment, plebeian or lower-middle-class, sexually emancipated, morally adrift, upwardly mobile, socially dissenting, satirical of received pieties. Amis's *Lucky Jim* and Braine's *Room at the Top* felt the pulse of a new generation, one caught on the hop between a traditional working-class community which was on the wane, and a patrician upper class which was becoming equally outdated. It proved, however, to be something of a revolutionary damp squib. Once they had reaped their wealth and celebrity, most of these so-called Angry Young Men became dyspeptic old reactionaries. But it was not simply a question of turning their political coats. Their social protests had always been more individualist, self-centred and opportunistic than had at first appeared.

In the end, it was not from below that the literary orthodoxies were to be challenged, but from beyond. The postwar period witnessed the dismantling of the British Empire, a process which contributed to the climate of malaise and self-doubt rife throughout the nation. The sense of baulked energy and cult of anti-heroic debunkery of the Angry Young Men had much to do with this distempered mood. By the 1960s and 1970s, with the novels of V. S. Naipaul, Doris Lessing, Patrick White, Nadine Gordimer, Wilson Harris, J. M. Coetzee, Chinua Achebe, Ngugi wa Thiong'o, Salman Rushdie and their colleagues, the postimperial countries were flexing their literary muscles and, in an agreeable act of reversal, threatening to overshadow the culture of the English natives in their range, depth and technical sophistication. What helped to enervate the metropolis also helped to revitalize the peripheries.

Finnegans Wake had been the work of a colonial writer who hijacked the English language for cosmopolitan, avant-garde, alarmingly non-English ends, and in the process discovered fathomless new resources in it. Like Joyce, the writing of the new wave of postcolonial authors was less shackled by the realist conventions of the native English than were the H. G. Wellses, George Orwells and Angus Wilsons of the literature. Like Joyce, too, it displayed the linguistic virtuosity of those whose consciousness of the medium is sharpened by a sense of coming to it as a part-stranger. Not literally so in most of these cases, any more than it had been for Joyce, Eliot and Yeats; but the fertile ambiguities of the earlier generations of exiles and émigrés – where do I belong, which of several possible tongues do I speak, what power, tradition or affinity does that imply? – were now being inherited by the postcolonial novelists, whether they stayed at home, settled in England or were British-born.

The earlier émigrés handed the baton of literary distinction to a later generation of British ethnic-minority writers. At much the same time, the very idea of Britishness was beginning to unravel at the seams, as writers newly but non-parochially aware of their Scottishness, Welshness or Irishness broke beyond the confines of English middle-class suburbia. The novels of the Welsh Raymond Williams, for all their stilted, abstracted quality, are notably 'non-English' in their historical scope and political depth, just as the work of the Irish John Banville is more historically aware, philosophically alert, verbally exploratory and technically experimental than most novels which stem from London.

All this proved something of a windfall for the English novel, since the home-grown variety of the species appeared to be in deep trouble. It was as though there was something about postwar, postimperial mainstream English culture which was peculiarly inhospitable to the production of major fiction. Perhaps this is one reason why so many English novelists have set their work abroad, from Graham Greene and Lawrence Durrell to Malcolm Lowry and John Le Carré. African outposts of empire, exotic Egyptian cities, Latino cultures or the Moscow criminal underworld have all proved more stirring settings than Reigate or Bradford. In these supposedly less civilized habitations, where human life is more violent, desperate and extreme but also more frankly sensual or erotic, you can confront what you take to be the palpable truth of the human condition, without the veneer of English hypocrisy or the anodyne comforts of suburban existence. Or so the theory goes.

There is generally a hint of Conrad here, as there is in that latter-day version of *Heart of Darkness*, William Golding's *Lord of the Flies*. Robert Graves's *Goodbye to All That* escapes the parochial confines of England through war. George Orwell's Burma, Jean Rhys's Parisian *demi-monde*, Anthony Burgess's Catholic Europe and south-east Asia, J. G. Ballard's wartime Japan, J. G. Farrell's imperial Ireland or India, and Bruce Chatwin's Patagonia or Australian outback, have lent themelves to high-quality fiction more readily than Bangor or Birmingham. Alternatively, you can float your fictional world offshore, as in William Golding's or Patrick O'Brian's novels of the sea.

With some notable exceptions, English culture has been better at turning out exquisite cameos of suburban adultery than spreading itself on a more ambitious historical or metaphysical canvas. Its novelistic art has been for the most part scrupulous, modest, reticent and quietly perceptive. It had none of the noisiness, ambition and dishevelled energies of Americans like Pynchon, Bellow and Roth. The work of William Trevor, Anita Brookner or Penelope Lively is exemplary here, but the point holds for scores of others. The later writing of Martin Amis and Ian McEwan suggest an impatience with this spiritual slenderness, turning to more ambitious cultural or historical landscapes. In Amis's case, however, a brilliance of technique is qualified by a postmodern brittleness, one which makes his work seem as much a symptom of that culture as a critique of it.

As we have seen already, the English novel has not, by and large, been a novel of ideas. The cerebrations of Aldous Huxley have remained fairly untypical. William Golding is a full-bloodedly metaphysical author, but his transcendent truths are matters of experience rather than concepts. Iris Murdoch's metaphysical speculations might seem a major exception to the rule, but Murdoch was Irish, not English. Her work belongs among other things to a lineage of Anglo-Irish art, one ambiguous about realism, prodigal of ideas, rich in unconscious symbolism and shimmering with perverse fantasy. W. G. Sebald, whose art is similarly innovatory, intellectually rewarding and only partly realist, was a German émigré in England.

One problem with trying to portray English culture as a whole is its class-divided nature. It sometimes seems that there is no 'whole' to be had. The world of Evelyn Waugh and Anthony Powell is not that of Beryl Bainbridge and Margaret Drabble. The fiction of Ivy Compton-Burnett knows itself to belong to an *haut bourgeois* world which has all but vanished. The point is true in a different way of the Anglo-Irish ascendancy twilight of Elizabeth Bowen. An upper-class novel of some distinction emerged in modern Britain, of which Waugh's superbly crafted, emotionally anaesthetized satires are among the most coruscating examples. *Brideshead Revisited* is a major piece of late realism, an historic milestone in the evolution of modern English society. Anthony Powell's *Dance to the Music of Time* fashions an entire upper-class world of its own, in a kind of cut-price version of Proust.

Yet these patrician landscapes, as with the whimsical fables of P. G. Wodehouse or the Gothic scenarios of Mervyn Peake, are too socially marginal to be much more than splendid curios. Much the same can be said of the fantasy worlds of the Oxford conservative medievalists (Tolkien, C. S. Lewis), natural aristocrats who, unable to see modern democratic life as much more than a dismal decline, took refuge in their own self-enclosed mythological worlds. The notion of a 'spiritual', traditional or authentic England underlying the degradations of the modern is inherited in different style by Peter Ackroyd. This mixture of myth, magic, freakishness and social realism has recently staged a momentous come-back with J. K. Rowling's Harry Potter novels. Alternatively, you could find a self-contained world by looking to place rather than nation, as in the organic communities of Laurie Lee and John Cowper Powys, Peter Ackroyd's fascination with London, Melvyn Bragg's Cumbria, Graham Swift's *Waterland* or Ian Rankin's Edinburgh. Where surreal fantasy and social satire intersect most fruitfully is in the women's novel, not the Woosterish one. This combination, which can be found in women writers as different as Muriel Spark, Fay Weldon and Jeanette Winterson, is at its most potent in the Gothic or carnivalesque imaginings of Angela Carter, one of the finest of all postwar English fiction writers.

The great European novel of the early twentieth century – Proust, Mann, Musil – was able to weave together myth and history, psychological insight and social commentary, ethics and politics, satire and spirituality, comedy and tragedy, realist narrative and a fantasia of the unconscious. As such, it offered to bring together the various domains – aesthetics, politics, ethics, history, psychology, mythology – which modernity itself had split off into so many uncommunicating fragments. In fact, it was almost the only place where these divided domains could still be drawn together. It was the novel, above all, which resisted the division of intellectual labour typical of modernity.

What happens later, with some notable exceptions, is that each of these spheres – myth, satire, social realism, individual psychology, the symbolism of the unconscious – goes its own sweet way and finds its own fictional niche. We may look to Evelyn Waugh for social satire, Virginia Woolf for psychological *aperçus*, William Golding for metaphysical resonance and early Kingsley Amis for comedy, but Proust's great novel encompasses them all. Feminist writing, however, is less content with this division of literary labour, just as it has good political reasons to be dissatisifed with the separa- tion of ethics, politics, fantasy and individual psychology in everyday life. It does not aim to recreate the monumental syntheses of a Proust or Mann; but in its own less grandly 'totalizing' manner it draws together genres of fiction which have become damagingly divorced from each other.

The Harry Potter novels centre on a school, and so, in the American sense of the term, do the 'campus' novels of authors like David Lodge, Malcolm Bradbury and Howard Jacobson, or the threadbare plots of C. P. Snow's *Strangers and Brothers* sequence. Far from being a place for the inves- tigation of ideas, a fair slice of English fiction is devoted to finding intellec- tuals funny. This fits well with English self-irony, since writers count as intellectuals themselves. It also fits with the postwar climate of anti-heroism and satirical debunkery, since intellectuals are generally perceived as pathetic, bumblingly ineffectual souls. They are a cross-breed of clown, monk and lunatic, mocked and revered in equal measure. There is something sinister about the life of the intellect, but something silly as well. Like Tolkien, Lewis and Peake, however, the campus also allows you to set up a whole alternative universe, since it seems almost as self-contained as the sphere of mythology. As a place, it is both mundane and mildly glamorous, everyday enough for the reader to identify with its goings on yet also intriguingly unfamiliar. It belongs to the real world but is also apart from it, rather like art itself. It is an interesting enough sphere to generate human drama, but since the intrigues of academia do not really matter much in the long run, the drama can also be comically undercut.

As early as E. M. Forster, what one might call the novel of liberal humanism is acknowledging the limits of its own vision. In a typically wry irony, it is aware that its own world of personal relationships and psychological intricacies depends on a wider, harsher world of labour, empire and exploitation which it is finally unable to comprehend. All it can do is mark out the confines of its own understanding, in a negative version of the truth. A novelist like Angus Wilson inherits this recognition in the postwar world. This kind of novel, which springs from the mainstream of English middle-class society, proves too slim, self-doubting a basis to play the role which the earlier realist novel had played for the Victorians. Indeed, liberal humanism as an ideology is already rapidly souring in the later George Eliot, and in the writings of Henry James finds itself confronting its own relative impotence in the face of power, greed, evil and violence.

It remains, however, an extraordinarily powerful influence in the contemporary English novel, as it does in the English theatre. For all their manifest differences, it is the world-view which unites Ian McEwan and Fay Weldon, A. S. Byatt and Martin Amis, Julian Barnes and Rose Tremain. It is, in a word, the official ethical and political doctrine of literary London – a remarkably resilient, deep-seated consensus which has survived a whole series of historical upheavals, and which helps to determine what counts as acceptable belief or fiction today. It is an honourable world view, humane, enlightened and morally serious. Whether it is adequate to a globalized world of terrorism and transnational corporations is a different question.

There is the odd self-conscious political outsider like the working-class Scot James Kelman, or authors with a more heterodox political history like the impressive Jim Crace. But in a postsocialist, postfeminist world, in which Salman Rushdie has come to embrace aspects of American imperial power, Doris Lessing to break with her radical past, and Fay Weldon to renounce her commitment to the women's movement, the contemporary English novel is doing dismally little to disturb the reigning orthodoxies. So-called postmodernism has made significantly little difference to this situation; it has been, for the most part, liberal humanism in cooler clothing. We are still looking for a form of writing that would be equal to a world which has changed beyond recognition since James Joyce completed *Finnegans Wake*, or rather left its final sentence to circle back to its first.

NOTES

CHAPTER 1 WHAT IS A NOVEL?

1 Margaret Anne Doody, *The True Story of the Novel* (New Brunswick, NJ: Rutgers University Press, 1997).

2 For Bakhtin on the novel, see Caryl Emerson and Michael Holquist (eds), *The Dialogical Imagination: Four Essays by M. M. Bakhtin* (Austin, TX: University of Texas Press, 1981). The best general study of Bakhtin is Ken Hirschkop, *Mikhail Bakhtin: An Aesthetic for Democracy* (Oxford: Oxford University Press, 1999).

3 Eric Auerbach, *Mimesis: The Representation of Reality in Western Literature*, trans. W. R. Trask (Princeton, NJ: Princeton University Press, 1953).

4 See Charles Taylor, *The Sources of the Self* (Cambridge, MA: Harvard University Press, 1989), Part 3.

5 Ian Watt, *The Rise of the Novel: Studies in Defoe, Richardson and Fielding* (Harmondworth, UK: Penguin, 1966).

6 F. R. Leavis, *The Great Tradition: George Eliot, Henry James, Joseph Conrad* (Harmondsworth, UK: Penguin, [1948] 1983).

7 On this and other points in this commentary, see J. M. Bernstein's excellent study *The Philosophy of the Novel* (Brighton, UK: Harvester, 1984).

8 Roland Barthes, 'Lecture in Inauguration of the Chair of Literary Semiology, College de France', *Oxford Literary Review* (Autumn, 1979), p. 36.

9 Georg Lukács, *Theory of the Novel*, trans. Anna Bostock (Cambridge, MA: MIT Press, [1916] 1990).

CHAPTER 2 DANIEL DEFOE AND JONATHAN SWIFT

1 Quoted by John Richetti in his Introduction to Daniel Defoe, *Robinson Crusoe* (London: Penguin, 2001), p. xxviii.

2 Claude Rawson, in *Gulliver and the Gentle Reader: Studies in Swift and Our Time* (London: Routledge, 1973).

3 Ibid.

4 F. R. Leavis, *The Common Pursuit* (London: Chatto and Windus, 1952).

CHAPTER 3   HENRY FIELDING AND SAMUEL RICHARDSON

1 One of his great predecessors in this opinion is Niccolo Machiavelli. In rejecting the classical humanist doctrine of Cicero and others that only virtuous conduct will result in worldly success, Machiavelli is one of the chief sources of the severing of the link between virtue and power, or value and fact, which characterizes modernity.

2 Judith Wilt, 'He Could Go No Farther: A Modest Proposal About Lovelace and Clarissa', *PMLA* (1977), 92(1): 19–32.

3 Empson in 'Tom Jones,' *The Kenyon Review* (1958), 20, p. 238.

4 Ian Watt, *The Rise of the Novel: Studies in Defoe, Richardson and Fielding* (Harmondworth, UK: Penguin, 1966), p. 247.

5 Dorothy van Ghent, *The English Novel: Form and Function* (New York: Rinehart, 1961), p. 45.

CHAPTER 4   LAURENCE STERNE

1 Victor Shklovsky, 'On the Theory of Prose', in L. T. Lemon and M. J. Reis (eds.), *Russian Formalist Criticism* (Lincoln: University of Nebraska Press, 1965), p. 57.

CHAPTER 5   WALTER SCOTT AND JANE AUSTEN

1 I am much indebted in what follows to Katie Trumpener's invaluable study *Bardic Nationalism: The Romantic Novel and the British Empire* (Princeton, NJ: Princeton University Press, 1997).

2 Franco Moretti, *The Way of the World* (London: Verso, 1987).

3 Benedict Anderson, *Imagined Communities: Reflections on the Origin and Spread of Nationalism* (London: Verso Press, 1983).

4 Georg Lukács, *The Historical Novel*, trans. Hannah Mitchell and Stanley Mitchell (Lincoln: University of Nebraska Press, [1955] 1983).

5 Raymond Williams, *The Country and the City* (London: Chatto & Windus, 1973).

CHAPTER 6   THE BRONTËS

1   Raymond Williams, *The English Novel from Dickens to Lawrence* (London: Chatto and Windus, 1970), p. 60.
2   If Charlotte's novels are mildly schizoid, they are also faintly paranoid. They portray a world of spying and surveillance, sinister Jesuitical plots and nameless mysteries behind closed doors.
3   Quoted in J. Hillis Miller, *The Disappearance of God* (Cambridge, MA: Harvard University Press, 1963), p. 163.
4   Williams, *The English Novel from Dickens to Lawrence*, p. 64.

CHAPTER 7   CHARLES DICKENS

1   See Raymond Williams, *The English Novel from Dickens to Lawrence* (London: Chatto and Windus, 1970), pp. 32–3.
2   See Richard Sennett, *The Fall of Public Man* (London: Penguin, 2002), chapter 8.
3   F. R. Leavis, *The Great Tradition: George Eliot, Henry James, Joseph Conrad* (Harmondsworth, UK: Penguin, [1948] 1983).

CHAPTER 8   GEORGE ELIOT

1   Raymond Williams, *The English Novel from Dickens to Lawrence* (London: Chatto and Windus, 1970), pp. 15–18.
2   Charles Swann (ed.), *Collected Esssays of John Goode* (Keele, UK: University Press, Keele, 1995), p. 45.
3   David Carroll (ed.), *George Eliot: The Critical Heritage* (London: Routledge and Kegan Paul, 1971), p. 179.
4   Swann (ed.), *Collected Esssays of John Goode*, p. 56.
5   See Franco Moretti, *The Way of the World* (London: Verso, 1987), chapter 1.

CHAPTER 9   THOMAS HARDY

1   See Raymond Williams, *The English Novel from Dickens to Lawrence* (London: Chatto and Windus, 1970), p. 96.
2   See Penny Boumelha, *Thomas Hardy and Women* (Brighton, UK: Harvester, 1982).
3   Ibid., p. 32.
4   John Goode, *Thomas Hardy: The Offensive Truth* (Oxford: Blackwell, 1988).

5   Boumelha, *Thomas Hardy and Women*, p. 100.
6   See Bayley's Introduction to the Wessex Edition volume of *Far From The Madding Crowd* (London: Macmillan, 1974).
7   See Williams, *The English Novel from Dickens to Lawrence*, pp. 107–9.

CHAPTER 10   HENRY JAMES

1   Quoted in Henry James, *The Wings of the Dove*, ed. Peter Brooks (Oxford: Oxford University Press, 1998), p. xi.

CHAPTER 11   JOSEPH CONRAD

1   Peter Brook, *Reading for the Plot: Design and Intention in Narrative Image* (Cambridge, MA: Harvard University Press, 1992), ch. 9.

CHAPTER 12   D. H. LAWRENCE

1   Gamini Salgado, 'Taking a Nail for a Walk: On Reading *Women in Love*', in Peter Widdowson (ed.), *D. H. Lawrence* (London and New York: Longman, 1992), p. 142.
2   For a critique of Lawrence's sexism, see Kate Millett, *Sexual Politics* (London: Rupert Hart-Davis, 1969).
3   Raymond Williams, *Culture and Society 1780–1950* (Harmondsworth, UK: Penguin, 1963), p. 212.

INDEX

*Index compiled by Meg Davies (Registered
Indexer, Society of Indexers)*

Lightning Source UK Ltd.
Milton Keynes UK
UKOW06f0803060915

258119UK00001B/75/P